*The*

# RIVER READER

# *The* RIVER READER

TWELFTH EDITION

Joseph F. Trimmer
Ball State University

CENGAGE
Learning™

Australia • Brazil • Mexico • Singapore • United Kingdom • United States

CENGAGE
Learning™

The River Reader, Twelfth Edition

Joseph F. Trimmer

Product Director: Monica Eckman

Product Manager: Kate Derrick

Senior Content Developer:
Kathy Sands-Boehmer

Media Developer: Janine Tangney

Senior Managing Developer:
Cara Douglass-Graff

Associate Content Developer: Erin Bosco

Product Assistant: Mario Davila

Marketing Director: Stacey Purviance

Senior Content Project Manager:
Michael Lepera

Senior Art Director: Marissa Falco

Manufacturing Planner: Betsy Donaghey

IP Analyst: Ann Hoffman

IP Project Manager: Farah Fard

Production Service/Compositor:
SPi Global

Interior design: Diana Graham

Interior image: Shutterstock/
Miroslava Hlavacova

Cover Designer: Sarah Bishins

Cover Image: David Henderson/
OJO Images/Getty Images

© 2017, 2014, 2011 Cengage Learning

WCN: 01-100-101

For product information and technology assistance, contact us at
**Cengage Learning Customer & Sales Support,
1-800-354-9706**

For permission to use material from this text or product, submit all requests online at
**www.cengage.com/permissions.**
Further permissions questions can be emailed to **permissionrequest@cengage.com.**

Library of Congress Control Number: 2015947528

Student Edition:
ISBN: 978-1-305-63411-4

Loose-leaf Edition:
ISBN: 978-1-305-67310-6

**Cengage Learning**
20 Channel Center Street
Boston, MA 02210
USA

Cengage Learning is a leading provider of customized learning solutions with employees residing in nearly 40 different countries and sales in more than 125 countries around the world. Find your local representative at **www.cengage.com**.

Cengage Learning products are represented in Canada by Nelson Education, Ltd.

To learn more about Cengage Learning Solutions, visit **www.cengage.com.**
Purchase any of our products at your local college store or at our preferred online store **www.cengagebrain.com.**

Printed in the United States of America
Print Number: 01    Print Year: 2015

# Contents

---

## INTRODUCTION    1

---

VIRGINIA WOOLF  *Shakespeare's Sister*
(sample analysis of an essay)    6

> One of the twentieth century's most famous novelists creates a
> fantasy of seventeenth-century life to dramatize the obstacles faced
> by talented women of that time.

## CHAPTER 1

---

## NARRATION AND DESCRIPTION    33

---

MARJANE SATRAPI  *The Veil* (visual text)    39

MAYA ANGELOU:  *My Name Is Margaret*    40

> An African American writer recalls how she found a way to break the
> dominance of an arrogant white woman who refused to call her by
> her right name.

## CHAPTER 2

### PROCESS ANALYSIS   80

## CHAPTER 3

## COMPARISON AND CONTRAST     117

## CHAPTER 4

## DIVISION AND CLASSIFICATION        155

## CHAPTER 5

## DEFINITION       206

## CHAPTER 6

### CAUSE AND EFFECT    246

## CHAPTER 8

### RESOURCES FOR WRITING: FOOD: A CASEBOOK   333

# Thematic Table of Contents

## Women

## The Other

## Heroes

## Habits

*Ethical Issues*

# Preface

For almost three decades, *The River Reader* has set the standard for rhetorical readers. Its explanations of purpose, audience, and strategies have enabled a generation of students to read prose models effectively and to write their own essays successfully. Indeed, its thorough coverage and thoughtful advice about many issues and problems embedded in the reading and writing processes have established this book as one of the core texts in the college composition curriculum.

The twelfth edition of *The River Reader*, like its predecessors, presents essays by acknowledged masters of prose style, including George Orwell, Flannery O'Connor, Richard Russo, and Alice Walker, along with many other voices, such as David Sedaris, Suzanne Britt Jordan, Laurie Colwin, and Gloria Naylor. Over one-third of the selections are new to this edition. As always, introductions, readings, critical thinking questions, and writing assignments are clear, creative, and cogent.

## THE PURPOSE OF *THE RIVER READER*

The first seven chapters in this reader are arranged in a sequence familiar to most writing teachers. Beginning with narration and description, moving through the five expository patterns, and ending with persuasion and argument, these chapters group readings according to traditional writing strategies.

The readings within each chapter have been chosen to illustrate what the chapter introductions say they illustrate: there are no strange hybrids or confusing models. Within each chapter, the selections are arranged in an ascending order of complexity. The ultimate purpose of *The River Reader* is to produce good writing. For that reason, the writing assignments in this book are presented after each selection. The four assignments after each selection prompt students to analyze, practice, argue, and synthesize both the rhetorical strategies and the content of the selection.

## THE ENDURING FEATURES OF
### *THE RIVER READER*

At the core of *The River Reader* is the desire to assist students with their reading and writing by helping them see the interaction between the two processes.

- The **connection between the reading and writing process** is highlighted in the Introduction. The familiar terminology of *purpose, audience,* and *strategies* provides a framework for the Introduction and for subsequent study questions and writing assignments.
- **Guidelines for Reading an Essay** is paired with **Guidelines for Determining Your Purpose, Guidelines for Analyzing Your Audience**, and **Guidelines for Selecting Your Strategy** to enhance and advance the students' understanding of the reading/writing connection.
- An **annotated essay** by Virginia Woolf, "Shakespeare's Sister," demonstrates how one reader responds to reading by writing.
- A **student essay**, Kristie Ferguson's "The Scenic Route," is illustrated in its various stages of development. The essay, which focuses on one student's early experiences as a writer, is followed by commentary on what the student discovered about her writing.
- To demonstrate the increasing importance of visual literacy in our culture, each chapter features a **visual text**—such as a cartoon, picture, or advertisement. Each of these texts is followed by an assignment that encourages students to look more closely at the image, discuss its significance to the chapter's rhetorical strategy, and write about what they have discovered.
- An **extended Introduction** now provides more in-depth discussions of the reading and writing processes, including additional coverage of *purpose, audience,* and *strategies.*
- A **Points to Remember** list concludes each chapter introduction and provides a convenient summary of the essential tasks and techniques of each strategy.

- A **short story** concludes each chapter to provide an interesting perspective on a particular writing strategy and to give students opportunities to broaden their reading skills. *New* to this edition are Richard Russo's "Dog", Alice Adams's "Truth or Consequences" and Andre Dubus's "The Fat Girl."
- The chapter introductions to **Cause and Effect** and **Persuasion and Argument** have been substantially rewritten.
- *New!* An emphasis on critical thinking has been added after each reading.
- *New!* Selections in the **Persuasion and Argument** chapter are new to this edition and are paired to present different perspectives on the purpose of student athletics and a liberal arts education.
- *New!* **A new case study, "Food,"** presents variations on the theme of food. The eight essays and one short story, which are arranged to repeat the patterns presented in the seven rhetorical chapters, illustrate how such strategies enable a writer to investigate a theme from a variety of perspectives.
- *New!* An eight-page **color photographic essay**, "Photo Essay on Food," emphasizes the power of images to evoke ideas and insights. Each image is followed by a writing assignment that encourages students to connect what they see with what they read and plan to write.
- A **Thematic Table of Contents** is provided for teachers who wish to organize their course by themes or issues.
- This edition also includes a compact **Rhetorical Glossary** that defines the key terms used throughout the rhetorical information provided in the text.

## ONLINE RESOURCES

MindTap® English for Trimmer's *The River Reader*, 12th edition, engages your students to help them become better thinkers, communicators, and writers by blending your course materials with content that supports every aspect of the writing process.

- Interactive activities on grammar and mechanics promote application in student writing.
- Easy-to-use paper management system helps prevent plagiarism and allows for electronic submission, grading, and peer review.
- A vast database of scholarly sources with video tutorials and examples supports every step of the research process.
- Professional tutoring guides students from rough drafts to polished writing.
- Visual analytics track student progress and engagement.
- Seamless integration into your campus learning management system keeps all your course materials in one place.

MindTap lets you compose your course, your way.

## ACKNOWLEDGMENTS

I am grateful to the following reviewers of this edition: Carrie Ameling, Limestone College; Mcgan Anderson, Limestone College; Benjamin Banks, Community College of Philadelphia; Katawana Caldwell, Eastfield College; Julie Long, College of the Albemarle; John Manear, Seton-La Salle High School; Victoria Manninon, Christian Brothers Academy; Jamie Pickering, Paradise Valley High School; Bradley Waltman, University of Southern Nevada; Mitali Wong, Claflin University; and Nikka Vrieze, Rochester Community and Technical College.

A special thanks to my product manager, Kate Derrick, and my content developer, Kathy Sands-Boehmer. And, of course, my debt to all my students is ongoing.

# Introduction

People who do well in college are nearly always good readers and good writers. They have to read well to absorb and evaluate the wealth of information they encounter online and in articles and books, and they have to write well to show that they are thinking and learning. In this book, we try to help you connect your reading and writing and become skillful at both crafts, for they are complementary skills, and you can master both of them through practice.

## THE ACTIVE READING PROCESS

Although you have already discovered ways of reading that no doubt work for you, there is a big difference between being a passive reader—a reader who simply consumes, uncritically, another's writing—and an active reader—a reader who questions, challenges, and reflects on the way another writer addresses a subject and develops its interlocking topics. By practicing the following steps in the reading process, you will learn to interact effectively and critically with a text.

- *Step 1.* When you are reading a piece of writing you need to master, go over it quickly at first to get the main idea and the flavor of the piece. Just enjoy it for what you are learning. Unless you get lost or confused, don't go back to reread or stop to analyze the writer's argument.
- *Step 2.* Now slow down. If you are reading from a book or magazine you don't own, photocopy the text. If you are reading on the Internet, print the document. Go back over your paper copy, this time underlining or highlighting key points and jotting notes in the margins. You may want to develop a scheme for such annotations, such as the one illustrated in the sample annotated analysis of Virginia Woolf's essay "Shakespeare's Sister" on pages 6–9, where summaries of the main points are written in the *left* margin, and questions or objections are written in the *right* margin.
- *Step 3.* On a separate piece of paper or in a separate file, jot down your critical responses to the reading. What appeals to you about the writer's ideas? What puzzles you? What elements in the piece remind you of some of your own experiences? How does this text relate to other texts you have read? Remember there's not necessarily one "right" reaction to what you are reading. Each reader brings different experiences to reading a piece of writing. So every response will be individual, and each reader will have a slightly different perspective. The notes you take on your reading will help you if you go on to write about the piece or discuss it in class.

## READING TO BECOME A BETTER WRITER

Many people have learned to improve their performance in a sport or activity by watching a professional at work and then patterning their activity on that of the professional. In the same way, you can sharpen your reading and writing skills by paying attention to how professional writers practice their craft. This book is organized around that assumption. Thus, you will find tips about what strategies to look for as you read these authors and questions that give you insight into their writing process. Here are three things to look for:

- *What is the writer's purpose?* What does he or she want to accomplish? How does the writer communicate that purpose? For instance, in "Shakespeare's Sister," Woolf's purpose is to challenge the age-old claim that women must be, inherently, less creative than men because there have been so few famous women writers, painters, or musicians.
- *Who is the writer's audience?* What assumptions does the writer make about what the audience knows or needs to know? Woolf's immediate audience—those who first read *A Room of One's Own* (1929)—were people interested in the arts and familiar with Shakespeare's plays and poems. Certainly Woolf assumed that many of her readers were women who did not need to be convinced about the significance of her argument.
- *What are the writer's strategies?* How does the writer organize his or her information? Does he or she tell stories, give examples, analyze evidence, or assert claims? Woolf creates a narrative to dramatize her points, knowing that she will arouse sympathy for her imaginary character, Judith Shakespeare. She also uses other strategies, such as comparison and contrast and cause and effect, to advance her argument.

When you get in the habit of asking questions about a writer's purpose, audience, and strategies, you will begin to understand how writers work and begin to master some elements of their craft for your own writing.

## READING *THE RIVER READER*

Before you begin to read essays from a chapter of *The River Reader*, look over the introduction to that section to get a feel for what to expect. The introduction will explain the purpose, audience, and strategies employed in a particular writing pattern. It will also suggest how you might incorporate these strategies into your own writing. Each introduction concludes with a boxed list of Points to Remember.

Before each essay is a biographical headnote that explains the author's background and work. Following each essay is a set of questions to help you to think critically about the writer's *purpose, audience,* and *strategies.* After this set of questions are four kinds of writing assignments:

1. *Analysis:* This assignment asks you to analyze how the writer exploits the features of a particular writing pattern.
2. *Practice:* This assignment encourages you to use the strategies you have studied to write a similar kind of essay.
3. *Argument:* This assignment invites you to extend or contest the argument embedded in the essay.
4. *Synthesis:* This assignment urges you to research additional sources on the theme explored in the essay and then use them to advance your own thesis about that theme.

Each chapter concludes with a short story that evokes the writing strategy illustrated in the essays. After each story, a Comment discusses some of its main features.

Finally, at the end of the introduction each chapter, you will find a *visual text* and a series of questions and writing assignments that will enable you to see how a particular writing pattern can be represented in graphic form.

On pages 4–5 we provide you with Guidelines for Critical Thinking, and after those guidelines you will find Woolf's "Shakespeare's Sister," complete with one reader's annotations and response, a set of questions For Study and Discussion, and four assignments For Writing and Research.

## Guidelines for Critical Thinking

### I. READ THE ESSAY THROUGH CAREFULLY

a. Consider the title and what expectations it raises.
b. Note when the essay was written and where it was first published.
c. Look at the author information in the headnote, and consider what important leads that information gives you about what to expect from the essay.

d. Now go back over the essay, underlining or highlighting key ideas and jotting down any questions you have.

## II. THINK CRITICALLY ABOUT YOUR RESPONSE TO THE ESSAY

a. Note what you liked and/or disliked about the essay, and analyze why you had that reaction.
b. Decide what questions you have after reading the essay.
c. Think about the issues the essay raises for you.
d. What else have you read that suggests or refutes the issues in the essay?

## III. WRITE A BRIEF STATEMENT OF WHAT SEEMS TO BE THE AUTHOR'S PURPOSE

a. Consider how the information about the author's life and experience may account for that purpose.
b. Decide to what extent you think the author achieved his or her purpose.

## IV. AS FAR AS YOU CAN, IDENTIFY THE AUTHOR'S ORIGINAL AUDIENCE

a. Make a guess about what those readers' interests are.
b. Compare your interests and experiences to those of the readers the author had in mind when writing the essay, and decide how similar or different they are.

## V. ANALYZE THE STRATEGIES THE WRITER USES TO ENGAGE AND HOLD THE READER'S INTEREST

a. Look at the lead the author uses to engage the reader.
b. Identify the main pattern the writer uses in the essay, and consider how that pattern helps to develop his or her main idea.
c. Pick out the descriptions, events, or anecdotes that make a particular impression, and consider why they're effective.
d. Identify passages or images that you find especially powerful or that reveal that the author is using strategies from other patterns.

## VI. REFLECT ON THE ESSAY, AND TRY TO STATE ITS CONTENT AND MAIN ARGUMENT IN TWO OR THREE SENTENCES

### Virginia Woolf

Virginia Woolf (1882–1941) was born in London, England, the daughter of Victorian critic and philosopher Leslie Stephen. She educated herself in her father's magnificent library and, after his death, lived with her sister and two brothers in Bloomsbury, a district of London that later became identified with her and the group of writers and artists she entertained. In 1912, she married journalist Leonard Woolf and together they founded the Hogarth Press, which published the work of the Bloomsbury group, including Woolf's own novels. Woolf's adult life was tormented by intermittent periods of nervous depression; finally, she drowned herself in the river near her home at Rodmell. Her novels include *Mrs. Dalloway* (1925), *To the Lighthouse* (1927), and *Orlando* (1928). Woolf's essays and reviews are collected in books such as *The Common Reader* (1925). One of Woolf's most popular works is *A Room of One's Own* (1929), an extended analysis of the subject of women and creativity. In this selection, taken from that volume, Woolf creates a hypothetical argument to demonstrate the limitations encountered by women in Shakespeare's time.

### Shakespeare's Sister

States problem | It is a perennial puzzle why no woman wrote a word of that extraordinary [Elizabethan] literature when every other man, it seemed, was capable of song or sonnet. What were the conditions in which women lived, I asked myself; for fiction, imaginative work that is, is not dropped like a pebble upon | Why didn't women write?

1

Description: the ground, as science may be; fiction is like a spider's web,
Compares
science and attached ever so lightly perhaps, but still attached to life at all
fiction four corners. Often, the attachment is scarcely perceptible;
Shakespeare's plays, for instance, seem to hang there complete
by themselves. But when the web is pulled askew, hooked up
at the edge, torn in the middle, one remembers that these
webs are not spun in mid air by incorporeal creatures but
are the work of suffering human beings, and are attached to
grossly material things, like health and money and the house
we live in.

Looks for     But what I find . . . is that nothing is known about women    2
evidence     before the eighteenth century. I have no model in my mind to
turn about this way and that. Here am I asking why women did
not write poetry in the Elizabethan age, and I am not sure how   Why has
they were educated; whether they were taught to write; whether   no one
thcy had sitting-rooms to themselves; how many women had   researched
these
children before they were twenty-one; what, in short, they   questions
did from eight in the morning till eight at night. They had   before?
Cites     no money evidently; according to Professor Trevelyan, they
authority     were married whether they liked it or not before they were
out of the nursery, at fifteen or sixteen very likely. It would
have been extremely odd, even upon this showing, had one of
them suddenly written the plays of Shakespeare, I concluded,
and I thought of that old gentleman, who is dead now, but
was a bishop, I think, who declared that it was impossible for
This is over-     any woman, past, present, or to come, to have the genius of
simplified.     Shakespeare. He wrote to the papers about it. He also told a
lady who applied to him for information that cats do not as a
matter of fact go to heaven, though they have, he added, souls
of a sort. How much thinking those old gentlemen used to
save one! How the borders of ignorance shrank back at their
approach! Cats do not go to heaven. Women cannot write the
plays of Shakespeare.

Be that as it may, I could not help thinking, as I looked   3
at the works of Shakespeare on the shelf, that the bishop
was right at least in this; it would have been impossible
completely and entirely, for any woman to have written

Begins
narrative the plays of Shakespeare in the age of Shakespeare. Let me
imagine, since facts are so hard to come by, what would
Compares A.
Shakespeare have happened had Shakespeare had a wonderfully gifted
sister, called Judith, let us say. Shakespeare himself went,
very probably—his mother was an heiress—to the grammar
school, where he may have learnt Latin—Ovid, Virgil and
Horace—and the elements of grammar and logic. He was,
it is well known, a wild boy who poached rabbits, perhaps How did
he know
enough to
write plays?
shot a deer, and had, rather sooner than he should have
done, to marry a woman in the neighbourhood, who bore
him a child rather quicker than was right. That escapade
sent him to seek his fortune in London. He had, it seemed,
a taste for the theatre; he began by holding horses at the
stage door. Very soon he got work in the theatre, became
a successful actor, and lived at the hub of the universe,
meeting everybody, knowing everybody, practising his art
on the boards, exercising his wits in the streets, and even
getting access to the palace of the queen. Meanwhile his
extraordinarily gifted sister, let us suppose, remained at B. Shakespeare
sister
home. She was as adventurous, as imaginative, as agog to
see the world as he was. But she was not sent to school. She
had no chance of learning grammar and logic, let alone of Why
wasn't she
given a
chance?
reading Horace and Virgil. She picked up a book now and
then, one of her brother's perhaps, and read a few pages.
But then her parents came in and told her to mend the
stockings or mind the stew and not moon about with books
and papers. They would have spoken sharply but kindly,
for they were substantial people who knew the conditions
of life for a woman and loved their daughter—indeed,
more likely than not she was the apple of her father's eye.
Perhaps she scribbled some pages up in an apple loft on the
sly but was careful to hide them or set fire to them. Soon,
however, before she was out of her teens, she was to be
betrothed to the son of a neighboring wool- stapler. She
cried out that marriage was hateful to her, and for that she
was severely beaten by her father. Then he ceased to scold
her. He begged her instead not to hurt him, not to shame Is this why
she left?
him in this matter of her marriage. He would give her a

chain of beads or a fine petticoat, he said; and there were
tears in his eyes. How could she disobey him? How could
she break his heart? The force of her own gift alone drove
her to it. She made up a small parcel of her belongings, let
herself down by a rope one summer's night and took the
road to London. She was not seventeen. The birds that sang
in the hedge were not more musical than she was. She had
the quickest fancy, a gift like her brother's, for the tune of
words. Like him, she had a taste for the theatre. She stood at
the stage door; she wanted to act, she said. Men laughed in
her face. The manager—a fat, loose-lipped man—guffawed.
He bellowed something about poodles dancing and women
acting—no woman, he said, could possibly be an actress. He
hinted—you can imagine what. She could get no training
in her craft. Could she even seek her dinner in a tavern or
roam the streets at midnight? Yet her genius was for fiction
and lusted to feed abundantly upon the lives of men and
women and the study of their ways. At last—for she was very
young, oddly like Shakespeare the poet in her face, with the
same gray eyes and rounded brows—at last Nick Greene
the actor- manager took pity on her; she found herself with
child by that gentleman and so—who shall measure the heat
and violence of the poet's heart when caught and tangled in
a woman's body?—killed herself one winter's night and lies
buried at some cross- roads where the omnibuses now stop
outside the Elephant and Castle.

    That, more or less, is how the story would run, I think, if
a woman in Shakespeare's day had Shakespeare's genius. But
for my part, I agree with the deceased bishop, if such he was—
it is unthinkable that any woman in Shakespeare's day should
have had Shakespeare's genius. For genius like Shakespeare's
is not born among labouring, uneducated, servile people. It
was not born in England among the Saxons and the Britons.
It is not born today among the working classes. How, then,
could it have been born among women whose work began,
according to Professor Trevelyan, almost before they were out
of the nursery, who were forced to it by their parents and held
to it by all the power of law and custom?

*(marginal notes: Compares Shakespeare and sister; Why?; Moves from narrative to argument; Have laws and customs changed that much?; 4)*

## Reader's Response

Woolf paints a realistic picture. That's a shame because in her time, Shakespeare's sister would have been treated just as she was presented—as inconsequential. It makes me wonder why women weren't given the option to read and write when the head of state, Queen Elizabeth, was more capable and dynamic than most of the men of the time.

What's puzzling is why women accepted gender inequity. I know quite a few outstanding and confident women who would never have accepted that tradition.

Watching Judith's struggle to be accepted in a man's world reminds me of my own struggle to be accepted. Oftentimes, I have felt small in comparison to my world, but there always seems to be a path available to me to fit into the world. Apparently the women of a few centuries ago could not find such a path.

## For Critical Thinking

### QUESTIONS ABOUT PURPOSE

1. What is the perennial question about women and creativity that Woolf tries to answer in this essay?
2. What connection does she seek to establish between the conditions under which a person lives and what that person can accomplish?

### QUESTIONS ABOUT AUDIENCE

1. What assumptions does Woolf make about the cultural knowledge of her readers?
2. Do you think men or women would be most interested in Woolf's argument? Why?

### QUESTIONS ABOUT STRATEGIES

1. To what extent does Woolf's speculative narrative about Judith Shakespeare seem constructed from verifiable evidence?
2. What is the argument that Woolf establishes in paragraph 4? Is it convincing? Why or why not?

## For Writing and Research

1. *Analyze* the way Woolf mixes strategies—narrative, comparison and contrast, cause and effect—to construct her argument.
2. *Practice* Woolf's strategies by composing a speculative narrative about an imaginary author who reveals the experience that helped him or her to write a particular kind of book—for example, a cookbook, a children's book, or a romance novel.
3. *Argue* that in many ways today's laws and customs still discourage women from pursuing an active creative life.
4. *Synthesize* several sources that comment on how changes in laws and customs have made it possible for women to become the preeminent creative writers in our time.

## THE WRITING PROCESS

If you are like most people, you find writing hard work. But writing is also an opportunity. It allows you to express something about yourself, to explore and explain ideas, and to assess the claims of other people. At times the tasks may seem overwhelming, but the rewards make the hard work worthwhile. By working through the four stages of the writing process, you will develop the confidence you need to become an effective writer.

- *Stage 1: Planning.* Planning enables you to find and formulate information in writing. When you begin a writing project, you need to make a list to explore a variety of subjects, to experiment with alternative ways to think about a subject, and to construct a rough outline to see how to develop your information.
- *Stage 2: Drafting.* Drafting enables you to organize and develop a sustained piece of writing. Once planning has helped you to identify several subjects and to gather information on those subjects from different perspectives, you need to select one subject, organize your information into meaningful clusters, and then discover links that connect those clusters.
- *Stage 3: Revising.* Revising enables you to reexamine and reevaluate the choices that have created a piece of writing.

After you have completed a preliminary draft, you need to stand back from your text and decide whether to embark on *global revision*—a complete recreation of the world of your writing—or begin *local revision*—a concentrated effort to perfect the smaller elements of your writing.

- *Stage 4: Editing.* Editing enables you to correct spelling, mechanics, and usage. After you have revised your text, you should proofread it carefully to make sure you have not inadvertently misspelled words, mangled sentences, or created typographical errors.

## WRITING WITHIN THE PROCESS

The division of the writing process into four stages is deceptive because it suggests that *planning, drafting, revising,* and *editing* proceed in a linear sequence. According to this logic, you would have to complete all the activities in one stage before you could move on to the next. But writing is a complex mental activity that usually unfolds as a more flexible and recursive sequence of tasks. You may have to repeat the activities in one stage several times before you are ready to move on to the next, or you may have to loop back to an earlier stage before you can move forward again.

Experienced writers seem to perform within the process in different ways. Some spend an enormous amount of time planning every detail before they write; others prefer to dispense with planning and discover their direction in drafting or revising. The American humorist James Thurber once acknowledged that he and one of his collaborators worked quite differently when writing a play:

> Eliot Nugent . . . is a careful constructor. When we were working on *The Male Animal* together, he was constantly concerned with plotting the play. He could plot the thing from back to front—what was going to happen here, what sort of situation

would end the first-act curtain and so forth. I can't work that way. Nugent would say, "Well, Thurber, we've got our problem, we've got all these people in the living room. Now what are we going to do with them?" I'd say that I didn't know and couldn't tell him until I'd sat down at my typewriter and found out. I don't believe the writer should know too much where he's going.

(James Thurber, *Writers at Work:*
*The Paris Review Interviews*)

Even experienced writers with established routines for producing a particular kind of work admit that each project inevitably presents new problems. Woolf planned, drafted, and revised some of her novels with great speed, but she was bewildered by her inability to repeat the process with other novels:

. . . blundering on at *The Waves.* I write two pages of arrant nonsense, after straining; I write variations of every sentence; compromises; bad shots; possibilities; till my writing book is like a lunatic's dream. Then I trust to inspiration on re-reading; and pencil them into some sense. Still I am not satisfied . . . I press to my centre. I don't care if it all is scratched out . . . and then, if nothing comes of it—anyhow I have examined the possibilities.

(Virginia Woolf, "Boxing Day 1929,"
*A Writer's Diary*)

Writers often discover a whole set of new problems when they are asked to write in a different context. Those writers who feel comfortable telling stories about their personal experience, for example, may encounter unexpected twists and turns in their writing process when they are asked to describe the lives of other people, explain a historical event, or analyze the arguments in an intellectual controversy. Each context requires them to make adjustments in the way they typically uncover, assess, and assert information. Calvin Trillin, an especially versatile writer, admits that he changes his writing process dramatically when he shifts from writing investigative reports to writing humorous essays or weekly columns.

> In my reporting pieces, I worry a lot about structure. Everything is there—in interviews, clippings, documents—but I don't know how to get it all in. I think that's why I do what we call around the house the vomit-out. I just start writing—to see how much I've got, how it might unfold, and what I've got to do to get through to the end. In my columns and humor pieces, I usually don't know the end or even the middle. I might start with a joke, but I don't know where it's going, so I fiddle along, polishing each paragraph, hoping something will tell me what to write next. (Personal interview)

This range of responses suggests that what appears to be a simple four-stage procedure may at times be a disorderly, contradictory process. But experienced writers know that disorder and contradiction are inevitable—although temporary—disturbances in the composition of most pieces of writing. Confusion occurs when you know too little about your writing project; contradiction occurs when you think too little about what you know. The secret to moving through such temporary impasses is to keep your eye on the constants in every writing situation.

## MAKING DECISIONS IN THE WRITING PROCESS

As you write, you discover that you are constantly making decisions. Some of these decisions are complex, as when you are trying to shape ideas. Others are simple, as when you are trying to select words. But each decision, large or small, affects every other decision you make so that you are constantly adjusting and readjusting your writing to make sure it is consistent, coherent, and clear. You can test the effectiveness of your decisions by measuring them against this dictum: in every writing situation, a writer is trying to communicate a *purpose* to an *audience* by manipulating *strategies.*

Initially, think of these three elements as *prompts,* ways to consider what you want to write and how you want to write about it. Later, as you move through planning and drafting to revising and editing, think of them as *touchstones,* ways to assess what you set out to accomplish. But mainly think of them as *guidelines,* ways to control every decision you make throughout the writing process, from formulating ideas to reformatting sentences.

## DETERMINING YOUR PURPOSE

Writers write most effectively when they write with a purpose. Inexperienced writers occasionally have difficulty writing with a purpose because they see many purposes: to complete the assignment, to earn a grade, to publish their writing. These "purposes" lie *outside* the writing situation, but they certainly influence the way you think about your purpose. If you want a good grade, you will define your purpose in terms of your teacher's writing assignment. If you want to publish your essay, you will define your purpose in terms of a given publisher's statement about its editorial policies.

When *purpose* is considered an element *inside* the writing situation, the term has a specific meaning: *purpose is the overall design that governs what writers do in their writing.* Writers who have determined their purpose know what kind of information they need, how they want to organize and develop it, and why they think it's important. In effect, purpose directs and controls all the decisions writers make. It is both the *what* and the *how* of that process—that is, the specific subject the writer selects *and* the strategies the writer uses to communicate the subject most effectively.

*Forming a Working Purpose: The Hypothesis*

A *hypothesis* is a provisional conjecture that serves as a guide to an investigation. Forming a hypothesis is a major step in determining your purpose. Sometimes you come to your writing certain of your hypothesis: you know from the outset what you want to prove and how you need to prove it. More often, you need to consider various possibilities. To convey something meaningful in your writing, something that bears your own mark, you need to keep an open mind and explore your options fully. Eventually, however, you must choose one hypothesis that you think most accurately says what you want to say about your subject and how you want to say it.

How do you know which hypothesis to choose? There is no easy answer to this question. The answer ultimately emerges from your temperament, experiences, and interests and also from the requirements of the context—whether you are writing for yourself or as an assignment. Sometimes, you can make the choice intuitively as you proceed. In thinking about your subject and audience, you see at once the perspective you want to adopt and how it will direct your writing. At other times, you may find it helpful to write out various hypotheses and then consider their relative effectiveness. Which will be the most interesting to write about? Which expresses your way of looking at things? With which can you make the strongest case or most compelling assertions?

*Testing Your Hypothesis: The Discovery Draft*

After you have chosen your hypothesis, you need to determine whether this preliminary statement of purpose provides the direction and control you need to produce an effective piece of writing. You can test your hypothesis by writing a first, or *discovery*, draft. Sometimes your discovery draft demonstrates that your hypothesis works. More often, however, as you continue the writing process, you discover new information or unforeseen complications that cause you to modify your original hypothesis. In other cases, you discover you simply cannot prove what your hypothesis suggested you might be able to prove.

Whatever you discover about your hypothesis, you must proceed in writing. If your discovery draft reveals that your hypothesis represents what you want to prove and needs only slight modification, then change your perspective somewhat or find additional information so that you can modify it. If, on the other hand, your discovery draft demonstrates that your hypothesis lacks conviction or that you do not have (and suspect you cannot get) the information you need to make your case, then choose another hypothesis that reflects your intentions more accurately.

### Purpose and Thesis

Whether you proceed with your original hypothesis, modify it, or choose another, you must eventually arrive at a final decision about your purpose. You make that decision during revision, when you know what you want to do and how you want to do it. Once you have established your purpose, you can make or refine other decisions—about your organization, examples, and style. One way to express your purpose is to state your thesis. A *thesis* is a sentence that usually appears in the first paragraph of your essay and states the main idea you are going to develop. Although the thesis is often called a purpose statement, thesis and purpose are not precisely the same thing. Your purpose is both contained in and larger than your thesis: it consists of all the strategies you will use to demonstrate your thesis in a sustained and successful piece of writing.

Your thesis makes a *restricted*, *unified*, and *precise* assertion about your subject—an assertion that can be developed in the amount of space you have, that treats only one idea, and that is open to only one interpretation.

In many ways, the difference between a hypothesis (a working purpose) and a thesis (a final assertion) explains why you can speculate about your purpose *before* you write but can specify your purpose only *after* you have written. This connection between your writing process and your writing purpose requires you to pause frequently to consult the criteria set forth in the following guidelines.

## Guidelines for Determining Your Purpose

### I. WHAT ARE THE REQUIREMENTS OF YOUR WRITING PROJECT?

a. If you are writing to fulfill an assignment, do you understand the assignment?
b. If you are writing on your own, do you have definite expectations of what you want to accomplish?

### II. AS YOU PROCEED IN THIS PROJECT, WHAT DO YOU NEED TO KNOW?

a. Do you have a good understanding of your subject, or do you need more information?
b. Have you considered the possible audiences who might read your writing?

### III. WHAT HYPOTHESIS CAN YOU USE AS A WORKING PURPOSE?

a. How many different hypotheses can you formulate about your subject?
b. Which of them seems to direct and control your information in the most effective manner?

### IV. WHAT PURPOSE HAVE YOU DISCOVERED FOR THIS WRITING PROJECT?

a. Has your purpose changed as you have learned more about your subject and audience?
b. Have you discovered, by working with a hypothesis or hypotheses, what you want to do in your writing?

### V. WHAT IS YOUR THESIS?

a. How can you state your main idea in a thesis sentence?
b. Does your thesis limit the scope of your writing to what you can demonstrate in the available space?
c. Does it focus your writing on one specific assertion?
d. Does it make an exact statement about what your writing intends to do?

## ANALYZING YOUR AUDIENCE

Most inexperienced writers assume that their audience is their writing teacher. But writing teachers, like writing assignments, often vary in what they teach, what they assume, and what they expect. Such variation has often prompted inexperienced writers to define their writing tasks as "trying to figure out what the teacher wants." This definition is naïve and smart at the same time. Superficially, it suggests that the sole purpose of any writing assignment is to satisfy another person's whims. On a deeper level, it suggests that when writers analyze the knowledge, assumptions, and expectations of their readers, they develop a clearer perception of their purpose and strategies. To make this analysis truly effective, though, writers must remember that they are writing for multiple audiences, not for a single person.

The most immediate audience is *you*. You write not only to convey your ideas to others but also to clarify them for yourself. To think of yourself as an audience, however, you must stop thinking like a writer and begin thinking like a reader. This change in perspective offers advantages, for you are the reader you know best. You are also a fairly representative reader because you share broad concerns and interests with other people. If you feel your writing is clear, lively, and informed, other readers will probably feel that way, too. If you sense that your text is confused or incomplete, the rest of your audience is likely to be disappointed, too.

The main drawback to considering yourself as audience is your inclination to deceive yourself. You want every sentence and paragraph to be perfect, but you know how much time and energy you invested in composing them, and that effort may blur your judgment. You may accept bad writing from yourself even though you wouldn't accept it from someone else. For that reason, you need a second audience. These readers—usually, friends, classmates, and teachers—are your most attentive audience. They help you choose your subject, coach you through various stages of the writing process, and counsel you about how to improve your sentences and paragraphs. As you write, you must certainly anticipate detailed advice from these readers. But you must remember that writing teachers and even peers are essentially collaborators and thus not your ultimate audience. They know what you have considered, cut, and corrected. The more they help you, the more eager they are to commend your writing as it approaches their standards of acceptability.

Your most significant audience consists of readers who neither know how much time and energy you invested in your writing nor care about the many choices you considered and rejected. These readers want writing that tells them something interesting or important, and they are put off by writing that is tedious or trivial. It is this wider audience that you (and your collaborators) must consider as you work through the writing process.

At times this audience may seem like a nebulous creature, and you may wonder how you can direct your writing to it if you do not know any of its distinguishing features. In those cases, it may be helpful to imagine a single significant reader—an attentive, sensible, reasonably informed person who will give you a sympathetic reading as long as you do not waste his or her time. Imagine an important person whom you respect and whose respect you want. This reader—specifically imagined, though often termed the "general reader," the "universal reader," or the "common reader"—is essentially a fiction but a helpful fiction. Your writing will benefit from the objectivity and sincerity with which you address this reader.

Many times, however, especially as you learn more about your subject, you discover a real-world audience for your writing. More precisely, as you consider your subject in a specific context, you may identify a number of audiences, in which case you will ultimately have to choose among them. Suppose, for example, you want to write about your evolution as a writer—an essay such as the student essay on pages 26–32. After some deliberation, you see that you have three possible audiences: (1) those who love to talk about their development as writers, (2) those who refuse even to discuss an activity they despise, and (3) those who have not thought too much about how writers work.

Now that you have identified these three audiences, analyze the distinctive features of each group. What do they know? What do they think they know? What do they need to know? The more you know about each group, the more you will be able to direct your writing to their assumptions and expectations. If you have spent a lot of time discussing the challenges of writing, you will have little difficulty analyzing the devotees and detesters of the composing process. You have heard the devotees explain how they have discovered strategies for becoming successful writers. Similarly, you have heard the detesters complain that their failures have convinced them that they never want to think about writing again.

At first you may have difficulty with the third group because these readers have not developed any preconceptions about learning how to write. In some ways, readers in the third group are like the "general reader"—thoughtful, discerning people who are willing to read about the writing process if you can convince them that the subject is worth their attention.

Although this sort of audience analysis helps you to visualize a group of readers, it does not help you decide which group is most suitable for your essay. If you target one group, you may fall into the trap of allowing its preferences to determine the direction of your writing. If you try to accommodate all three groups, you may waiver indecisively among them so that your writing never finds any direction. Your decision about audience, like your decision about purpose, has to be made in the context of the complete writing situation. For that reason, look at the guidelines for analyzing your audience.

## Guidelines for Analyzing Your Audience

### I. WHO ARE THE READERS WHO WILL BE MOST INTERESTED IN YOUR WRITING?

a. What are their probable age, gender, education, economic status, and social position?

b. What values, assumptions, and prejudices characterize their general attitude toward life?

## II. WHAT DO YOUR READERS KNOW OR THINK THEY KNOW ABOUT YOUR SUBJECT?

a. What is the probable source of their knowledge—direct experience, observation, reading, rumor?
b. Will your readers react positively or negatively toward your subject?

## III. WHY WILL YOUR READERS READ YOUR WRITING?

a. If they know a great deal about your subject, what will they expect to learn from reading your writing?
b. If they know only a few things about your subject, what will they expect to be told about it?
c. Will they expect to be entertained, informed, or persuaded?

## IV. HOW CAN YOU INTEREST YOUR READERS IN YOUR SUBJECT?

a. If they are hostile toward it, how can you convince them to give your writing a fair reading?
b. If they are sympathetic, how can you fulfill and enhance their expectations?
c. If they are neutral, how can you catch and hold their attention?

## V. HOW CAN YOU HELP YOUR READERS READ YOUR WRITING?

a. What kind of organizational pattern will help them see its purpose?
b. What kind of strategies and transitional markers will they need to follow this pattern?
c. What (and how many) examples will they need to understand your general statements?

## SELECTING YOUR STRATEGY

As you work your way through the writing process, you will uncover various patterns for developing your ideas. In *planning*, these patterns often emerge as answers to the basic questions you might ask about any body of information: *What is it? How does it work? Why does it matter?* These questions are like the different lenses you attach to your camera: each lens gives you a different picture of your subject.

Suppose you want to write an essay on the subject of women and science. You might begin by asking why so few women are ranked among the world's great scientists. You might continue asking questions. What historical forces have discouraged women from becoming scientists? How do women scientists define problems, analyze evidence, and formulate conclusions; and do they go about these processes differently than men do? If women scientists look at the world differently than men do, does this difference have an effect on the established notions of inquiry? As you can see, each question not only shifts your perspective on your subject but also suggests a different method for developing your information about it.

If planning gives you the opportunity to envision your subject from a variety of perspectives, then *drafting* encourages you to develop the pattern (or patterns) that appear to you most effective for demonstrating your purpose. In some writing projects, a pattern may seem to emerge naturally from your planning. If you decide to write about your observation of a game of lacrosse, your choice seems obvious: to tell what happened. In attempting this, however, you may need to answer other questions about this unfamiliar sport: What do the field and equipment look like? What rules govern the way the game is played? How is it similar to or different from other sports? Developing this new information may complicate your original purpose.

You can solve this problem most effectively during *revision.* As you look over your draft, you will need to make two decisions. First, you must decide whether individual segments or patterns of information develop or distort your purpose. The history of lacrosse—its creation by Iroquois Indians, its discovery by French explorers, and its development by Canadians—is an interesting body of information; but it may need to be reshaped, relocated, or even eliminated to preserve your original purpose—to tell what happened. Second, you must decide whether your original design, a design that often mirrors the process by which you uncovered your information, is still the best method for presenting your information to your audience. Instead of telling "what happened," you may decide that you can best express your ideas by choosing a more formal structure—comparing lacrosse to games with which your readers are more familiar, such as soccer or hockey.

Whatever you decide, you need to understand the purpose, audience, and strategies of each pattern if you are going to use it successfully to develop a paragraph, a section of your essay, or your whole essay. For that reason, *The River Reader* is organized to demonstrate the most common patterns and questions encountered in the writing process:

> Narration and Description: What happened? What did it look like?
> Process Analysis: How do you do it?
> Comparison and Contrast: How is it similar or different?
> Division and Classification: What kind of subdivisions does it contain?
> Definition: How would you characterize it?
> Cause and Effect: Why did it happen? What happened next?
> Persuasion and Argument: How can you prove it?

The introductions to the chapters that feature each of these patterns of development explain its purpose, audience, and strategies. The essays in each chapter are arranged in an ascending order of complexity and are followed by questions that call your attention to how the writer has asserted his or her purpose, addressed his or her audience, and used the various techniques of each strategy to develop his or her essay. If you study these essays and answer these questions, you will see how you can adapt these common writing patterns to your writing.

By analyzing these strategies in action, you will also learn two important lessons. First, you will understand what you are expected to write when you encounter words such as *describe, compare,* and *define* in a writing assignment. Second, you will discover that you do not have to limit yourself to a single pattern for an entire piece of writing. Writers may structure their essay around one dominant strategy but use other strategies to enrich or advance their purpose.

The following guidelines will help you in selecting an appropriate strategy.

## *Guidelines for Selecting Your Strategy*

### I. WHAT STRATEGY DOES YOUR WRITING ASSIGNMENT REQUIRE?

a. What words—such as *define* or *defend*—are embedded in your writing assignment?
b. What assumptions and expectations do these words evoke?

### II. WHAT STRATEGY EMERGES AS YOU PLAN YOUR ESSAY?

a. What questions naturally occur to you as you study a particular subject?
b. What patterns of development do these questions suggest?

### III. WHAT OTHER STRATEGIES EMERGE AS YOU DRAFT YOUR ESSAY?

a. What new questions emerge as you draft your writing?
b. What kind of information do you need to answer these questions?

### IV. HOW CAN YOU REVISE YOUR ESSAY TO INCLUDE THIS NEW INFORMATION?

a. Does this new information distort or develop your purpose?
b. Will it require you to impose a new strategy on your information to clarify your purpose to your readers?

### V. HOW CAN YOU MIX STRATEGIES TO ENRICH YOUR ESSAY?

a. How does mixing strategies supplement your purpose?
b. How might such mixing confuse your readers?

## STUDENT ESSAY

*Student Writer in Progress*

*Kristie Ferguson, "The Scenic Route"*

The following material illustrates how one student, Kristie Ferguson, responded to a writing assignment by working her way through the writing process.

*Writing Assignment:* Read Woolf's "Shakespeare's Sister." Then compose a narrative that describes the experiences that contributed to (or prevented) your development as a writer.

*Planning (Journal Entry)*

I am not sure I ever <u>developed</u> as a writer. My teachers all seemed to want different things.

> Never made Mrs. Scott's bulletin board
> Mrs. Pageant and those dumb squirrels
> Logan and that contest

I could never figure out what they wanted. I suppose they wanted to teach me. But I always felt lost.

*Possible Hypothesis:* I should probably describe what I didn't learn. How my confusion prevented me from becoming a good writer. But then how do you explain that contest?

*Drafting (Discovery Draft)*

### What's Wrong with This Picture?

On one of those days that convinces you certain things don't belong together, like sunshine and first grade or hot flashes in Alaska, another writing period was about to begin. At the grand old age of six, I was certain that I would never learn to write. After all I had never made the list. In the corner of our room, Mrs. Scott kept a bulletin board commending those in the class who had neat handwriting and no spelling errors. I was cursed on both counts. My handwriting looked like hieroglyphics, and my spelling always made people ask, "What's wrong with this picture."

That day Mrs. Scott surprised us. "Class, I'm cutting writing period in half so that you can go to the auditorium to see a movie." Freedom! Relief! I started to clap my hands. But wait! Something was wrong with this picture. "I am going to ask you to write a brief theme," Mrs. Scott continued. "When you are done you can go to the auditorium." I knew there must be a catch. Still, it was only a brief theme and afterward there was a movie. I grabbed my Number 2 and thumbed through my notebook looking for a clean page. "One more thing," she announced. "You must spell all words neatly and correctly. No erasers or dictionaries. I may ask for do-over's." No eraser? No dictionary? Why not cut off both my arms?

How was I ever going to make it to the auditorium? I started slowly, reminding myself to make each letter and word carefully. When I finished, I went to Mrs. Scott's desk. "Too sloppy. Misspelled words." I retreated to my desk for another try. This time she smiled. "Misspelled word. Do it over." I slumped back to my desk. The next time I looked up the room was empty. Desperate, I narrowed the culprit to one of those "ie" words. I rubbed out the letters, reprinted them, and placed a dot more or less between them. I handed my paper to Mrs. Scott. "You erased," she hissed. She was such a treasure. "No ma'am." She eyed the paper and me again, and then, finally, let me go. At last—the movie.

Collapsing near my best friend Karla, I arrived in time to watch the end of a promotion film for dental hygiene. Teeth! All that for teeth!

*Revision (Revision Agenda)*

1. *What is my purpose?*
   Tell a story about my early failures as a writer. Most of my grade school teachers emphasized handwriting and spelling and I was terrible at both.

2. *Who is my audience?*
   Everyone who has gone to school. They have all had a
   Mrs. Scott. Most remember that in school good writing
   meant good handwriting and no mistakes.

3. *What strategies do I use?*
   I focused on my attempt to complete one writing assignment so I could go to a movie. I slowed the pace down
   and described the details of my writing process. I also
   used dialog to dramatize Mrs. Scott.

4. *What revisions do I want to make in my next draft?*
   a. Include other writing experiences—fourth grade,
      high school.
   b. Rework introduction—state thesis—to explain why I
      am telling these stories.

*New Hypothesis:* I like the story because it tells how I tricked
Mrs. Scott—and then myself. All that work for teeth. But I
take too long getting there. Is learning how to write simply
learning a trick? Maybe it's more like taking a trip.

*Second Draft*

# The Scenic Route

As a writer, I always seem to take the scenic route. I don't plan
it that way. My teachers provide detailed maps pointing me
down the most direct road, but somehow I miss a turn or make
a wrong turn and there I am—standing at some unmarked
crossroads, head pounding, stomach churning, hopelessly lost.
On such occasions, I used to curse my teachers, my maps, and
myself. But recently, I have come to expect, even enjoy, in a
perverse way, the confusion and panic of being lost. Left to
my own devices, I have learned to discover my own way to my
destination. And afterward, I have a story to tell.

    I did not learn this all at once. In the beginning, I was
confused about where I was going. One day in first grade,
Mrs. Scott told us that if we wrote a brief theme we could go

to a movie. I grabbed my Number 2 and listened for directions. "No erasers. No dictionaries. I may ask for do-over's." Lost! I was the worst speller in the class. My first draft was "Too sloppy. Do it over." My second, "Misspelled word. Do it over." Now I was really lost. One misspelled word. They all looked right—and then they all looked wrong. Blind luck led me to one of those "ie" words. I rubbed out the letters, reprinted them, and placed the dot between them. "Kristie, you erased," she hissed. "No ma'am." She eyed my paper and then me again, and with a sigh waved me toward the auditorium. Collapsing next to my best friend, Karla, I arrived in time to watch a film about dental hygiene. Teeth! All that for teeth!

My next problem was trying to figure out why I was going. Mrs. Pageant, my fifth-grade teacher, was the source of my confusion. Seemingly unaware of my errors, she wrote enthusiastic notes on all my essays, suggesting on one, "Kristie, you're so creative. Why don't you write a book?" Why indeed? Why should the first-grade dummy begin such a perilous journey? "You should, Kristie. You really should. You could even write a fantasy book like the one we read today." Luckily fantasy was my forte. I used to make up stories about the family of squirrels in my backyard. And so I wrote *Squirrel Family Starts a Grocery Store*, in which, after the hoopla on page one, the squirrels run out of food on page three and close their store on page four.

As she read my book to the class, Mrs. Pageant could hardly contain herself. "What a delightful story, Kristie. You must write another immediately." My head pounded. My stomach churned. I had stumbled onto one story, but why keep going? Because Mrs. Pageant "just loved" those dumb squirrels. So there was *Squirrel Family Starts a Bank*, in which the squirrels run out of money, and *Squirrel Family Starts a Newspaper*, in which they run out of stories. By then I was looking for the nearest off-ramp. I couldn't think of another squirrel story, and Karla told me that if she had to listen to one more, she would throw up.

When I got to the eleventh grade, I knew for the first time where I was going and why. The poster on Mr. Logan's bulletin board announced a writing contest: "Threats to the Free Enterprise System." Sponsored by the Blair County Board of Realtors. First prize $200. Now my problem was how to get there. Mr. Logan took us to the school library and mapped out the first half of his strategy. Look up sources in the database. Take notes. Organize notes into an outline for first draft. It seemed like a sensible plan, but, as usual, I got lost at the first turn. I pulled a few books off the shelf, but it was pointless. I couldn't find anything on free enterprise or anybody who was threatening it.

As the deadline for the first draft approached, I was so desperate I asked my parents for directions. "Ask some local business people what they think." Not bad for parents. I borrowed my father's tape recorder and made the rounds—the grocery store, the pizza parlor, the newspaper. Most of the people seemed a lot like me—lost. They talked a lot, but they didn't focus on the question. Maybe I was asking the wrong question. I listened to the tape a couple of times and picked out some common themes. Then I rewrote my questions: "How do taxes, government regulation and foreign competition threaten your business?" The next time around people seemed to know what they were talking about. I organized their answers under my three categories, wrote out my draft, and made the deadline.

In class, Mr. Logan announced the second half of his strategy. Read draft. Listen to student and teacher responses. Revise draft. Mail essay. Karla went first. She quoted every book in the school library. Looking down at my paper, I saw myself stranded again. After a few more papers I felt better. All the papers sounded alike. I knew my quotes would be different—the guy at the pizza parlor, the newspaper editor. "You didn't do any research," Karla complained. "I bet you didn't read one article." A chorus of "yes's" came from the guys in the back row. Mr. Logan didn't say anything for a while. Then, smiling, he looked at Karla. "What is research?" Now Karla looked lost. The guys looked in their notebooks. Silence. Finally, the bell. What's the answer? What am I supposed to do? Mr. Logan never said. I thought about what

I had done, considered my options, and, with a sigh, mailed my essay.

A few weeks later, I was standing not at some unmarked crossroads but in the center of town—behind the lectern in front of a room full of people. A man from the Blair County Board of Realtors handed me a trophy and an envelope and asked me to tell how I wrote the paper. I started to panic and then smiled. "Well . . . ." I caught Mr. Logan's eye. "I asked a lot of people what they thought. At first they didn't know what I was talking about. Neither did I. Then I fixed my question and they helped me figure out what to say." I looked at Mr. Logan again. He just smiled. I looked at my trophy and wondered what to say next. Finally, I said "Well . . . I guess I did research."

*Revision (Revision Agenda)*

1. *What is my purpose?*
   Describe how I learned to trust my own judgment about writing.
2. *Who is my audience?*
   Again, anyone who has gone to school. Everybody has had to write silly stories and research papers. I'll bet they all tried to write something for some dumb contest. I suppose another audience might be those guys at the Blair County Board of Realtors.
3. *What strategies do I use?*
   I use brief narratives that I try to connect with my title— "The Scenic Route." I keep Karla in each episode as a kind of commentator. I also use dialog to dramatize Mrs. Scott, Mrs. Pageant, and Mr. Logan. I try to slow the pace down at important moments—like when I read my research paper for the first time or when I was accepting my trophy.
4. *What revisions do I want to make in my next draft?*
   Rework introduction so I can get right to my thesis—"trust your own judgment." Do Mrs. Scott and Mrs. Pageant fit the thesis? If I cut them, I'll lose my funniest stuff. If I use them, I'll have to figure out a new way.

This draft seems more organized, but I force my material into the structure—*where* I was going, *why* I was going, *how* I got there. Maybe the scenic route metaphor gets in the way.

Work more with contest. It's the one story that makes my point.

Figure out "what's wrong with this picture?" This essay seems to be getting better and worse at the same time.

*Comment.* This essay takes readers on a tour of Kristie's development as a writer and highlights three memorable experiences along the way. Although the narrative focuses on her personal experiences, it conjures up memories for many fledgling writers: first, the autocratic teacher from first grade who demands perfection and loves to punish mistakes; then the sweetie-pie teacher from fifth grade who gushes and lavishes praise on stuff the writer knows is junk; finally, the practical and organized eleventh-grade teacher who outlines a writing process and guides the students through it for a real-world audience.

# CHAPTER 1

# Narration and Description

The writer who *narrates* tells a story to make a point. The writer who *describes* evokes the senses to create a picture. Although you can use either strategy by itself, you will probably discover that they work best in combination if you want to write a detailed account of some memorable experience—your first trip alone, a last-minute political victory, a picnic in some special place. When you want to explain what happened, you will need to tell the story in some kind of chronological order, putting the most important events—I took the wrong turn, she made the right speech, we picked the perfect spot—in the most prominent position. When you want to give the texture of the experience, you will need to select words and images that help your readers see, hear, and feel what happened— the road snaked to a dead end, the crowd thundered into applause, the sunshine softened our scowls. When you show and tell in this way, you can help your readers see the meaning of the experience you want to convey.

## PURPOSE

You can use narration and description for three purposes. Most simply, you can use them to introduce or illustrate a complicated subject. You might begin an analysis of the energy crisis, for example, by telling a personal anecdote that dramatizes wastefulness. Or you might conclude an argument for gun control by giving a graphic description of a shooting incident. In each case, you are using a few sentences or a detailed description to support some other strategy, such as causal analysis or argument.

Writers use narration and description most often not as isolated examples but as their primary method when they are analyzing an issue or theme. For example, you might spend a whole essay telling how you came to a new awareness of patriotism because of your experience in a foreign country. Even though your personal experience would be the center of the essay, your narrative purpose (what happened) and your descriptive purpose (what it felt like) might be linked to other purposes. You might want to *explain* what caused your new awareness (why it happened) or to *argue* that everyone needs such awareness (why everyone should reach the same conclusion you did).

The writers who use narration and description most often are those who write auto-biography, history, and fiction. If you choose to write in any of these forms, your purpose will be not so much to introduce an example or tell about an experience to throw light on your subject. You may explain why events happened as they did or argue that such events should never happen again, but you may choose to suggest your ideas subtly through telling a story or giving a description rather than stating them as direct assertions. Your primary purpose is to report the actions and describe the feelings of people entangled in the complex web of circumstance.

### Audience

As you think about writing an essay using narration and description, consider how much you will need to tell your readers and how much you will need to show them. If you are writing from personal experience, few readers will know the story before you tell it. They may know similar stories or have had similar experiences, but they do not know your story. Because you can tell your story in so many different ways—adding or deleting material to fit the occasion—you need to decide how much information your readers will need. Do they need to know every detail of your story, only brief summaries of certain parts, or some mixture of detail and summary?

To decide what details you should provide, you need to think about how much your readers know and what they are going to expect. If your subject is unusual (a trip to see an erupting volcano), your readers will need a lot of information, much of it technical, to understand the novel experience you are going to describe. They not only will expect an efficient, matter-of-fact description of volcanoes but also want you to give them some sense of how it feels to see one erupting. If your subject is familiar to most people (your experience with lawn sprinklers), your readers will need few technical details to understand your subject. But they will expect you to give them new images and insights that create a fresh vision of your subject—for example, portraying lawn sprinklers as the languid pulse of summer.

## STRATEGIES

The writers in this section demonstrate that you need to use certain strategies to write a successful narrative and descriptive essay. For openers, you must recognize that an experience and an essay about that experience are not the same thing. When you have any experience, no matter how long it lasts, your memory of that experience is going to be disorganized and poorly defined, but the essay you write about that experience must have a purpose and be sharply focused. When you want to transform your experience into an essay, start by locating the central **conflict**. It may be (1) between the writer and himself or herself, as when George Orwell finds himself in a quandary about whether to shoot the elephant; (2) between the writer and others, as when Maya Angelou responds to Mrs. Cullinan and her friends; or (3) between the writer and the environment, as when David Sedaris tries to determine his sexual identity in a culture that belittles homosexuality.

Once you have identified the conflict, arrange the action so that your readers know how the conflict started, how it developed, and how it was resolved. This coherent sequence of events is called a **plot**. Sometimes you may want to create a plot that sticks to a simple chronological pattern. In "My Name Is Margaret," Maya Angelou begins her account of events at the beginning and describes them as they occur. At other times you may want to start your essay in the middle or even near the end of the events you are describing. In "Dog" Richard Russo begins his narrative by telling his readers how his parents would tell the story. The authors choose a pattern according to their purpose. Angelou wants to describe the evolution of events leading up to the broken china; Russo wants to illustrate how different people interpret the same experience.

When you figure out what the beginning, middle, and end of your plot should be, you can establish how each event in those sections should be paced. **Pace** is the speed at which the writer recounts events. Sometimes, you can narrate events quickly by omitting details, compressing time, and summarizing experience. For example, Sedaris summarizes several scenes that reveal how his teachers present a stereotype. At other times, you may want to pace events more slowly and carefully because they are vital to your purpose. You will need to include every detail, expand on time, and present the situation as a fully realized scene rather than in summary form. Sedaris creates such a scene when he describes Jason's discovery of his note.

You can make your scenes and summaries effective by your careful **selection of details**. Just adding more details doesn't satisfy this requirement. You must select those special details that satisfy the needs of your readers and further your purpose in the essay. For example, sometimes you will need to give *objective* or *technical* details to help your reader understand your subject. Orwell provides this kind of detail when he defines imperialism. At other times, you will want to give *subjective* or *impressionistic* details to appeal to your readers' senses. Sedaris provides this kind of detail when he describes how homosexuals are represented in popular culture. Finally, you may want to present your details so they form a *figurative image* or create a *dominant impression*. Angelou uses both strategies: the first when she describes the casserole; the second when she describes how Mrs. Cullinan reacts to its destruction. To identify the conflict, organize the plot, vary the pace, and select details for your essay, you need to determine your **point of view**: the person and position of the narrator (*point*) and the attitude toward the experience being presented (*view*). You choose your *person* by deciding whether you want to tell your story as "I" saw it (as Angelou does in her story about her confrontation with Mrs. Cullinan) or as "he" or "she" saw it (as Russo does when he describes his parents' attitude toward the dog). You choose your *position* by deciding how close you want to be to the action in time and space. You may be involved in the action or view it from the position of an observer, or you may tell about the events as they are happening or many years after they have taken place. For example, Orwell, the young police officer, is the chief actor in his narrative, but Orwell, the author, still wonders, years after the event, why he shot the elephant. You create your attitude—how you view the events you intend to present and interpret—by the person and position you choose for writing your essay. The attitudes of the narrators in the following essays might be characterized as angry (Angelou), perplexed (Sedaris), and ambivalent (Orwell).

## NARRATION AND DESCRIPTION

### Points to Remember

1. Focus your narrative on the "story" in your story—that is, focus on the conflict that defines the plot.
2. Vary the pace of your narrative so that you can summarize some events quickly and render others as fully realized scenes.
3. Supply evocative details to help your readers experience the dramatic development of your narrative.
4. Establish a consistent point of view so that your readers know how you have positioned yourself in your story.
5. Represent the events in your narrative so that your story makes its point.

*In this excerpt from her graphic novel* Persepolis: The Story of a Childhood *(2003), Marjane Satrapi recounts the reaction of young schoolgirls to the law requiring them to wear "the veil." Some argue that the veil debases and even erases female identity. Others argue that it provides women with safety and secret power. How do the characters in Satrapi's narrative feel about this regulation? Write a narrative describing your own reactions to some obligatory dress code.*

Maya Angelou (1928–2014) was born in St. Louis, Missouri and spent her early years in California and Arkansas. A woman of varied accomplishments, she was a novelist, poet, playwright, stage and screen performer, composer, and singer. She is perhaps best known for her autobiographical novels: *I Know Why the Caged Bird Sings* (1970), *Gather Together in My Name* (1974), *Oh Pray My Wings Are Gonna Fit Me Well* (1975), *Singin' and Swingin' and Gettin' Merry Like Christmas* (1976), *The Heart of a Woman* (1981), *All God's Children Need Traveling Shoes* (1986), *Wouldn't Take Nothing for My Journey Now* (1993), *A Brave and Startling Truth* (1995), *A Song Flung Up to Heaven* (2002), and *Letter to My Daughter* (2008). Angelou's poetry is equally well respected and is published in her *Complete Collected Poems* (1994). President Obama presented Angelou with the Presidential Medal of Freedom in 2011. In the following selection from *I Know Why the Caged Bird Sings*, Angelou recounts how she maintained her identity in a world of prejudice.

RECENTLY A WHITE woman from Texas, who would 1 quickly describe herself as a liberal, asked me about my hometown. When I told her that in Stamps my grandmother had owned the only Negro general merchandise store since the turn of the century, she exclaimed, "Why, you were a debutante." Ridiculous and even ludicrous. But Negro girls in small Southern towns, whether poverty-stricken or just munching along on a few of life's necessities, were given as extensive and irrelevant preparations for adulthood as rich white girls shown in magazines. Admittedly, the training was not the same. While white girls learned to waltz and sit gracefully with a tea cup balanced on their knees, we were lagging behind, learning the mid-Victorian values with very little money to indulge them. (Come and see Edna Lomax spending the money she made picking cotton on five balls of ecru tatting thread. Her fingers are bound to snag the work and she'll have to repeat the stitches time and time again. But she knows that when she buys the thread.)

---

*During my tenth year, a white woman's kitchen became my finishing school.*

---

We were required to embroider and I had trunkfuls of colorful dishtowels, pillowcases, runners, and handkerchiefs to my credit. I mastered the art of crocheting and tatting, and there was a lifetime's supply of dainty doilies that would never be used in sacheted dresser drawers. It went without saying that all girls could iron and wash, but the finer touches around the home, like setting a table with real silver, baking roasts and cooking vegetables without meat, had to be learned elsewhere. Usually at the source of those habits. During my tenth year, a white woman's kitchen became my finishing school. 2

Mrs. Viola Cullinan was a plump woman who lived in a three-bedroom house somewhere behind the post office. She was singularly unattractive until she smiled, and then the lines around her eyes and mouth which made her look perpetually dirty disappeared, and her face looked like the mask of an impish elf. She usually rested her smile until late afternoon when her women friends dropped in and Miss Glory, the cook, served them cold drinks on the closed-in porch. 3

The exactness of her house was inhuman. This glass went here and only here. That cup had its place and it was an act of impudent rebellion to place it anywhere else. At twelve o'clock, 4 the table was set. At 12:15 Mrs. Cullinan sat down to dinner (whether her husband had arrived or not). At 12:16 Miss Glory brought out the food.

It took me a week to learn the difference between a salad    5 plate, a bread plate, and a dessert plate.

Mrs. Cullinan kept up the tradition of her wealthy parents.    6 She was from Virginia. Miss Glory, who was a descendant of slaves that had worked for the Cullinans, told me her history. She had married beneath her (according to Miss Glory). Her husband's family hadn't had their money very long and what they had "didn't 'mount to much."

As ugly as she was, I thought privately, she was lucky to    7 get a husband above or beneath her station. But Miss Glory wouldn't let me say a thing against her mistress. She was very patient with me, however, over the housework. She explained the dishware, silverware, and servants' bells. The large round bowl in which soup was served wasn't a soup bowl, it was a tureen. There were goblets, sherbet glasses, ice-cream glasses, wine glasses, green glass coffee cups with matching saucers, and water glasses. I had a glass to drink from, and it sat with Miss Glory's on a separate shelf from the others. Soup spoons, gravy boat, butter knives, salad forks, and carving platter were additions to my vocabulary and in fact almost represented a new language. I was fascinated with the novelty, with the fluttering Mrs. Cullinan and her Alice-in-Wonderland house.

Her husband remains, in my memory, undefined. I lumped    8 him with all the other white men that I had ever seen and tried not to see.

On our way home one evening, Miss Glory told me that    9 Mrs. Cullinan couldn't have children. She said that she was too delicate-boned. It was hard to imagine bones at all under those layers of fat. Miss Glory went on to say that the doctor had taken out all her lady organs. I reasoned that a pig's organs included the lungs, heart and liver, so if Mrs. Cullinan was walking around without those essentials, it explained why she drank alcohol out of unmarked bottles. She was keeping herself embalmed.

When I spoke to Bailey about it, he agreed that I was right,  10
but he also informed me that Mr. Cullinan had two daughters
by a colored lady and that I knew them very well. He added
that the girls were the spitting image of their father. I was
unable to remember what he looked like, although I had just
left him a few hours before, but I thought of the Coleman
girls. They were very light skinned and certainly didn't
look very much like their mother (no one ever mentioned
Mr. Coleman).

My pity for Mrs. Cullinan preceded me the next morning  11
like the Cheshire cat's smile. Those girls, who could have
been her daughters, were beautiful. They didn't have to
straighten their hair. Even when they were caught in the rain,
their braids still hung down straight like tamed snakes. Their
mouths were pouty little cupid's bows. Mrs. Cullinan didn't
know what she missed. Or maybe she did. Poor Mrs. Cullinan.

For weeks after, I arrived early, left late and tried very hard  12
to make up for her barrenness. If she had had her own children, she wouldn't have had to ask me to run a thousand
errands from her back door to the back door of her friends.
Poor old Mrs. Cullinan.

Then one evening Miss Glory told me to serve the ladies  13
on the porch. After I set the tray down and turned toward
the kitchen, one of the women asked, "What's your name,
girl?" It was the speckled-faced one. Mrs. Cullinan said, "She
doesn't talk much. Her name's Margaret."

"Is she dumb?"  14

"No. As I understand it, she can talk when she wants to but  15
she's usually quiet as a little mouse. Aren't you, Margaret?"

I smiled at her. Poor thing. No organs and couldn't even  16
pronounce my name correctly.

"She's a sweet little thing, though."  17

"Well, that may be, but the name's too long. I'd never  18
bother myself. I'd call her Mary if I was you."

I fumed into the kitchen. That horrible woman would  19
never have the chance to call me Mary because if I was starving I'd never work for her. I decided I wouldn't pee on her
if her heart was on fire. Giggles drifted in off the porch and

into Miss Glory's pots. I wondered what they could be laughing about.

Whitefolks were so strange. Could they be talking about 20 me? Everybody knew that they stuck together better than the Negroes did. It was possible that Mrs. Cullinan had friends in St. Louis who heard about a girl from Stamps being in court and wrote to tell her. Maybe she knew about Mr. Freeman.

My lunch was in my mouth a second time and I went out- 21 side and relieved myself on the bed of four-o'clocks. Miss Glory thought I might be coming down with something and told me to go on home, that Momma would give me some herb tea, and she'd explain to her mistress.

I realized how foolish I was being before I reached the 22 pond. Of course Mrs. Cullinan didn't know. Otherwise she wouldn't have given me two nice dresses that Momma cut down, and she certainly wouldn't have called me a "sweet little thing." My stomach felt fine, and I didn't mention anything to Momma.

That evening I decided to write a poem on being white, fat, 23 old, and without children. It was going to be a tragic ballad. I would have to watch her carefully to capture the essence of her loneliness and pain.

The very next day, she called me by the wrong name. 24 Miss Glory and I were washing up the lunch dishes when Mrs. Cullinan came to the doorway. "Mary?"

Miss Glory asked, "Who?" 25

Mrs. Cullinan, sagging a little, knew and I knew. "I want 26 Mary to go down to Mrs. Randall's and take her some soup. She's not been feeling well for a few days."

Miss Glory's face was a wonder to see. "You mean 27 Margaret, ma'am. Her name's Margaret."

"That's too long. She's Mary from now on. Heat that soup 28 from last night and put it in the china tureen and, Mary, I want you to carry it carefully."

Every person I knew had a hellish horror of being "called 29 out of his name." It was a dangerous practice to call a Negro anything that could be loosely construed as insulting because of the centuries of their having been called niggers, jigs, dinges, blackbirds, crows, boots, and spooks.

Miss Glory had a fleeting second of feeling sorry for me.  30
Then as she handed me the hot tureen she said, "Don't mind,
don't pay that no mind. Sticks and stones may break your
bones, but words . . . You know, I been working for her for
twenty years."

She held the back door open for me. "Twenty years. I  31
wasn't much older than you. My name used to be Hallelujah.
That's what Ma named me, but my mistress give me 'Glory,'
and it stuck. I likes it better too."

I was in the little path that ran behind the houses when  32
Miss Glory shouted, "It's shorter too."

For a few seconds, it was a tossup over whether I would  33
laugh (imagine being named Hallelujah) or cry (imagine letting some white woman rename you for her convenience).
My anger saved me from either outburst. I had to quit the
job, but the problem was going to be how to do it. Momma
wouldn't allow me to quit for just any reason.

"She's a peach. That woman is a real peach." Mrs. Randall's  34
maid was talking as she took the soup from me, and
I wondered what her name used to be and what she answered
to now.

For a week I looked into Mrs. Cullinan's face as she called  35
me Mary. She ignored my coming late and leaving early. Miss
Glory was a little annoyed because I had begun to leave egg
yolk on the dishes and wasn't putting much heart in polishing the silver. I hoped that she would complain to our boss,
but she didn't.

Then Bailey solved my dilemma. He had me describe the  36
contents of the cupboard and the particular plates she liked
best. Her favorite piece was a casserole shaped like a fish and
the green glass coffee cups. I kept his instructions in mind, so
on the next day when Miss Glory was hanging out clothes and
I had again been told to serve the old biddies on the porch,
I dropped the empty serving tray. When I heard Mrs. Cullinan
scream, "Mary!" I picked up the casserole and two of the
green glass cups in readiness. As she rounded the kitchen
door, I let them fall on the tiled floor.

I could never absolutely describe to Bailey what happened  37
next, because each time I got to the part where she fell on the

floor and screwed up her ugly face to cry, we burst out laughing. She actually wobbled around on the floor and picked up shards of the cups and cried, "Oh, Momma. Oh, dear Gawd. It's Momma's china from Virginia. Oh, Momma, I sorry."

Miss Glory came running in from the yard and the women    38
from the porch crowded around. Miss Glory was almost as broken up as her mistress. "You mean to say she broke our Virginia dishes? What we gone do?"

Mrs. Cullinan cried louder, "That clumsy nigger. Clumsy    39
little black nigger."

Old speckled-face leaned down and asked, "Who did it,    40
Viola? Was it Mary? Who did it?"

Everything was happening so fast I can't remember    41
whether her action preceded her words, but I know that Mrs. Cullinan said, "Her name's Margaret, goddamn it, her name's Margaret." And she threw a wedge of the broken plate at me. It could have been the hysteria which put her aim off, but the flying crockery caught Miss Glory right over the ear and she started screaming.

I left the front door wide open so all the neighbors could    42
hear.

Mrs. Cullinan was right about one thing. My name wasn't    43
Mary.


## For Critical Thinking

### QUESTIONS ABOUT PURPOSE

1. In what sense does Mrs. Cullinan's kitchen serve as Angelou's "finishing school"? What is she supposed to learn there? What does she learn?
2. How does Angelou's description of Mrs. Cullinan's house as *exact* and *inhuman* support her purpose in recounting the events that take place there?

## QUESTIONS ABOUT AUDIENCE

1. How does Angelou's comment about the liberal woman from Texas identify the immediate audience for her essay?
2. What assumptions does Angelou make about her other readers when she comments on the laughter of the white women on the porch?

## QUESTIONS ABOUT STRATEGIES

1. How does Angelou use the three discussions of her name to organize her narrative? How does she pace the third discussion to provide an effective resolution for her essay?
2. How does Angelou's intention to write a poem about Mrs. Cullinan establish her initial attitude toward her employer? What changes her attitude toward Mrs. Cullinan's "loneliness and pain"?

# For Writing and Research

1. *Analyze* the strategies Angelou uses to reveal her changing attitude toward Mrs. Cullinan.
2. *Practice* by enacting an experience in which someone mispronounces or forgets your name.
3. *Argue* Glory's versus Bailey's position about the destruction of the fish-shaped casserole.
4. *Synthesize* the advice given to girls in popular magazines. Then use this evidence to argue that such advice is an irrelevant preparation for adulthood.

# David Sedaris: *I Like Guys*

David Sedaris was born in New York State, raised in Raleigh, North Carolina, and educated at Kent State University and the School of the Art Institute of Chicago. He has presented his humorous autobiographical essays on National Public Radio in *This American Life*. His essay collections include *Barrel Fever* (1994), *Naked* (1997), *Dress Your Family in Corduroy and Denim* (2009), and *Let's Explore Diabetes with Owls* (2013). In 2001, he won the James Thurber Prize for American Humor and was named "Humorist of the Year" by *Time* magazine. In "I Like Guys," excerpted from *Naked*, Sedaris recounts his growing self-awareness of his own sexuality when he was a teenager.

S HORTLY BEFORE I GRADUATED from eighth grade, it was    1
announced that, come fall, our county school system would adopt a policy of racial integration by way of forced busing. My Spanish teacher broke the news in a way she hoped might lead us to a greater understanding of her beauty and generosity.

"I remember the time I was at the state fair, standing in line    2
for a Sno-Kone," she said, fingering the kiss curls that framed her squat, compact face. "And a little colored girl ran up and tugged at my skirt, asking if she could touch my hair. 'Just once,' she said. 'Just one time for good luck.'

"Now, I don't know about the rest of you, but my hair    3
means a lot to me." The members of my class nodded to signify that their hair meant a lot to them as well. They inched forward in their seats, eager to know where this story might be going. Perhaps the little Negro girl was holding a concealed razor blade. Maybe she was one of the troublemakers out for a fresh white scalp.

I sat marveling at their naïveté. Like all her previous anec-  4
dotes, this woman's story was headed straight up her ass.

"I checked to make sure she didn't have any candy on her  5
hands, and then I bent down and let this little colored girl
touch my hair." The teacher's eyes assumed the dewy, faraway
look she reserved for such Hallmark moments. "Then this
little fudge-colored girl put her hand on my cheek and said,
'Oh,' she said, 'I wish I could be white and pretty like you.'"
She paused, positioning herself on the edge of the desk as
though she were posing for a portrait the federal government
might use on a stamp commemorating gallantry. "The thing
to remember," she said, "is that more than anything in this
world, those colored people wish they were white."

---

*Fearful of drawing attention to myself,*
*I hooted and squawked along with the rest*
*of the class, all the while thinking, That's me*
*he's talking about.*

---

I wasn't buying it. This was the same teacher who when  6
announcing her pregnancy said, "I just pray that my first-born
is a boy. I'll have a boy and then maybe later I'll have a girl,
because when you do it the other way round, there's a good
chance the boy will turn out to be funny."

"'Funny' as in having no arms and legs?" I asked.  7

"That," the teacher said, "is far from funny. That is tragic,  8
and you, sir, should have your lips sewn shut for saying such
a cruel and ugly thing. When I say 'funny,' I mean funny as
in. . ." She relaxed her wrist, allowing her hand to dangle and
flop. "I mean 'funny' as in *that* kind of funny." She minced
across the room, but it failed to illustrate her point, as this was
more or less her natural walk, a series of gamboling little steps,
her back held straight, giving the impression she was balanc-
ing something of value atop her empty head. My seventh-
period math teacher did a much better version. Snatching a
purse off the back of a student's chair, he would prance about

the room, batting his eyes and blowing kisses at the boys seated in the front row. "So fairy nice to meet you," he'd say.

Fearful of drawing any attention to myself, I hooted and  9 squawked along with the rest of the class, all the while thinking, *That's me he's talking about.* If I was going to make fun of people, I had to expect a little something in return, that seemed only fair. Still, though, it bothered me that they'd found such an easy way to get a laugh. As entertainers, these teachers were nothing, zero. They could barely impersonate themselves. "Look at you!" my second-period gym teacher would shout, his sneakers squealing against the basketball court. "You're a group of ladies, a pack of tap-dancing queers."

The other boys shrugged their shoulders or smiled down  10 at their shoes. They reacted as if they had been called Buddhists or vampires; sure, it was an insult, but no one would ever mistake them for the real thing. Had they ever chanted in the privacy of their backyard temple or slept in a coffin, they would have felt the sting of recognition and shared my fear of discovery.

I had never done anything with another guy and literally  11 prayed that I never would. As much as I fantasized about it, I understood that there could be nothing worse than making it official. You'd seen them on television from time to time, the homosexuals, maybe on one of the afternoon talk shows. No one ever came out and called them a queer, but you could just tell by their voices as they flattered the host and proclaimed great respect for their fellow guests. These were the celebrities never asked about their home life, the comedians running scarves beneath their toupees or framing their puffy faces with their open palms in an effort to eliminate the circles beneath their eyes. "The poor man's face lift," my mother called it. Regardless of their natty attire, these men appeared sweaty and desperate, willing to play the fool in exchange for the studio applause they seemed to mistake for love and acceptance. I saw something of myself in their mock weary delivery, in the way they crossed their legs and laughed at their own jokes. I pictured their homes: the finicky placement of their throw rugs and sectional sofas, the magazines carefully fanned just so upon the coffee tables with no wives or children to disturb their order. I imagined the pornography hidden in their closets and envisioned them powerless and sobbing as the police led them away in shackles, past the teenage boy who stood bathed in the light of the television news camera and shouted, "That's him! He's the one who touched my hair!"

It was my hope to win a contest, cash in the prizes, and use   12
the money to visit a psychiatrist who might cure me of having homosexual thoughts. Electroshock, brain surgery, hypnotism—I was willing to try anything. Under a doctor's supervision, I would buckle down and really change, I swore I would.

My parents knew a couple whose son had killed a Presby-   13
terian minister while driving drunk. They had friends whose eldest daughter had sprinkled a Bundt cake with Comet, and knew of a child who, high on spray paint, had set fire to the family's cocker spaniel. Yet, they spoke of no one whose son was a homosexual. The odds struck me as bizarre, but the message was the same: this was clearly the worst thing that could happen to a person. The day-to-day anxiety was bad enough without my instructors taking their feeble little potshots. If my math teacher were able to subtract the alcohol from his diet, he'd still be on the football field where he belonged; and my Spanish teacher's credentials were based on nothing more than a long weekend in Tijuana, as far as I could tell. I quit taking their tests and completing their homework assignments, accepting Fs rather than delivering the grades I thought might promote their reputations as good teachers. It was a strategy that hurt only me, but I thought it cunning. We each had our self-defeating schemes, all the boys I had come to identify as homosexuals. Except for a few transfer students, I had known most of them since the third grade. We'd spent years gathered together in cinder-block offices as one speech therapist after another tried to cure us of our lisps. Had there been a walking specialist, we probably would have met there, too. These were the same boys who carried poorly forged notes to gym class and were the first to raise their hands when the English teacher asked for a volunteer to read aloud from *The Yearling* or *Lord of the Flies*.

We had long ago identified one another and understood that because of everything we had in common, we could never be friends. To socialize would have drawn too much attention to ourselves. We were members of a secret society founded on self-loathing. When a teacher or classmate made fun of a real homosexual, I made certain my laugh was louder than anyone else's. When a club member's clothing was thrown into the locker-room toilet, I was always the first to cheer. When it was my clothing, I watched as the faces of my fellows broke into recognizable expressions of relief. *Faggots*, I thought. *This should have been you.*

Several of my teachers, when discussing the upcoming school integration, would scratch at the damp stains beneath their arms, pulling back their lips to reveal every bit of tooth and gum. They made monkey noises, a manic succession of ohhs and ahhs meant to suggest that soon our school would be no different than a jungle. Had a genuine ape been seated in the room, I guessed he might have identified their calls as a cry of panic. Anything that caused them suffering brought me joy, but I doubted they would talk this way come fall. From everything I'd seen on television, the Negros would never stand for such foolishness. As a people, they seemed to stick together. They knew how to fight, and I hoped that once they arrived, the battle might come down to the gladiators, leaving the rest of us alone.          14

At the end of the school year, my sister Lisa and I were excused from our volunteer jobs and sent to Greece to attend a month-long summer camp advertised as "the Crown Jewel of the Ionian Sea." The camp was reserved exclusively for Greek Americans and featured instruction in such topics as folk singing and something called "religious prayer and flag." I despised the idea of summer camp but longed to boast that I had been to Europe. "It changes people!" our neighbor had said. Following a visit to Saint-Tropez, she had marked her garden with a series of tissue-sized international flags. A once discreet and modest woman, she now paraded about her yard wearing nothing but clogs and a flame-stitched bikini. "Europe is the best thing that can happen to a person, especially if you like wine!"          15

I saw Europe as an opportunity to re invent myself. I might   16
still look and speak the same way, but having walked those
cobblestoned streets, I would be identified as Continental.
"He has a passport," my classmates would whisper. "Quick,
let's run before he judges us!"

I told myself that I would find a girlfriend in Greece. She   17
would be a French tourist wandering the beach with a loaf of
bread beneath her arm. Lisette would prove that I wasn't a
homosexual, but a man with refined tastes. I saw us holding
hands against the silhouette of the Acropolis, the girl begging
me to take her accordion as a memento of our love. "Silly
you," I would say, brushing the tears from her eyes, "just give
me the beret, that will be enough to hold you in my heart
until the end of time."

In case no one believed me, I would have my sister as a wit   18
ness. Lisa and I weren't getting along very well, but I hoped
that the warm Mediterranean waters might melt the icicle
she seemed to have mistaken for a rectal thermometer. Faced
with a country of strangers, she would have no choice but to
appreciate my company.

Our father accompanied us to New York, where we met   19
our fellow campers for the charter flight to Athens. There
were hundreds of them, each one confident and celebratory.
They tossed their complimentary Aegean Airlines tote bags
across the room, shouting and jostling one another. This
would be the way I'd act once we'd finally returned from
camp, but not one moment before. Were it an all-girl's camp,
I would have been able to work up some enthusiasm. Had
they sent me alone to pry leeches off the backs of bloodthirsty Pygmies, I might have gone bravely—but spending a
month in a dormitory full of boys, that was asking too much.
I'd tried to put it out of my mind but faced with their bois-
terous presence, I found myself growing progressively more
hysterical. My nervous tics shifted into their highest gear, and
a small crowd gathered to watch what they believed to be an
exotic folk dance. If my sister was anxious about our trip, she
certainly didn't show it. Prying my fingers off her wrist, she
crossed the room and introduced herself to a girl who stood

picking salvageable butts out of the standing ashtray. This was a tough-looking Queens native named Stefani Heartattackus or Testicockules. I recall only that her last name had granted her a lifelong supply of resentment. Stefani wore mirrored aviator sunglasses and carried an oversized comb in the back pocket of her hiphugger jeans. Of all the girls in the room, she seemed the least likely candidate for my sister's friendship. They sat beside each other on the plane, and by the time we disembarked in Athens, Lisa was speaking in a very bad Queens accent. During the long flight, while I sat cowering beside a boy named Seamen, my sister had undergone a complete physical and cultural transformation. Her shoulder-length hair was now parted on the side, covering the left half of her face as if to conceal a nasty scar. She cursed and spat, scowling out the window of the chartered bus as if she'd come to Greece with the sole intention of kicking its dusty ass. "What a shithole," she yelled. "Jeez, if I'd knowed it was gonna be dis hot, I woulda stayed home wit my headdin da oven, right, girls!"

It shamed me to hear my sister struggle so hard with an    20
accent that did nothing but demean her, yet I silently congratulated her on the attempt. I approached her once we reached the camp, a cluster of whitewashed buildings hugging the desolate coast, far from any neighboring village.

"Listen, asshole," she said, "as far as this place is concerned,    21
I don't know you and you sure as shit don't know me, you got that?" She spoke as if she were auditioning for a touring company of *West Side Story*, one hand on her hip and the other fingering her pocket comb as if it were a switchblade.

"Hey, Carolina!" one of her new friends called.    22

"A righta ready," she brayed. "I'm comin', I'm comin'."    23

That was the last time we spoke before returning home.    24
Lisa had adjusted with remarkable ease, but something deep in my stomach suggested I wouldn't thrive nearly as well. Camp lasted a month, during which time I never once had a bowel movement. I was used to having a semiprivate bathroom and could not bring myself to occupy one of the men's room stalls, fearful that someone might recognize my shoes

or, even worse, not see my shoes at all and walk in on me. Sitting down three times a day for a heavy Greek meal became an exercise akin to packing a musket. I told myself I'd sneak off during one of our field trips, but those toilets were nothing more than a hole in the floor, a hole I could have filled with no problem whatsoever. I considered using the Ionian Sea, but for some unexplained reason, we were not allowed to swim in those waters. The camp had an Olympic-size pool that was fed from the sea and soon grew murky with stray bits of jellyfish that had been pulverized by the pump. The tiny tentacles raised welts on campers' skin, so shortly after arriving, it was announced that we could photograph both the pool *and* the ocean but could swim in neither. The Greeks had invented democracy, built the Acropolis, and then called it a day. Our swimming period was converted into "contemplation hour" for the girls and an extended soccer practice for the boys.

"I really think I'd be better off contemplating," I told the  25
coach, massaging my distended stomach. "I've got a personal problem that's sort of weighing me down."

Because we were first and foremost Americans, the camp  26
was basically an extension of junior high school except that here everyone had an excess of moles or a single eyebrow. The attractive sports-minded boys ran the show, currying favor from the staff and ruining our weekly outdoor movie with their inane heckling. From time to time, the rented tour buses would carry us to view one of the country's many splendors, and we would raid the gift shops, stealing anything that wasn't chained to the shelf or locked in a guarded case. These were cheap, plated puzzle rings and pintsize vases, little pompommed shoes, and coffee mugs reading SPARTA IS FOR A LOVER. My shoplifting experience was the only thing that gave me an edge over the popular boys. "Hold it like this," I'd whisper. "Then swivel around and slip the statue of Diana down the back of your shorts, covering it with your T-shirt. Remember to back out the door while leaving and never forget to wave good-bye."

There was one boy at camp I felt I might get along with,  27
a Detroit native named Jason who slept on the bunk beneath

mine. Jason tended to look away when talking to the other boys, shifting his eyes as though he were studying the weather conditions. Like me, he used his free time to curl into a fetal position, staring at the bedside calendar upon which he'd x-ed out all the days he had endured so far. We were finishing our 7:15 to 7:45 wash-and-rinse segment one morning when our dormitory counselor arrived for inspection shouting, "What are you, a bunch of goddamned faggots who can't make your beds?"

I giggled out loud at his stupidity. If anyone knew how to make a bed, it was a faggot. It was the others he needed to worry about. I saw Jason laughing, too, and soon we took to mocking this counselor, referring to each other first as "faggots" and then as "stinking faggots." We were "lazy faggots" and "sunburned faggots" before we eventually became "faggoty faggots." We couldn't protest the word, as that would have meant acknowledging the truth of it. The most we could do was embrace it as a joke. Embodying the term in all its clichéd glory, we minced and pranced about the room for each other's entertainment when the others weren't looking. I found myself easily outperforming my teachers, who had failed to capture the proper spirit of loopy bravado inherent in the role. *Faggot*, as a word, was always delivered in a harsh, unforgiving tone befitting those weak or stupid enough to act upon their impulses. We used it as a joke, an accusation, and finally as a dare. Late at night I'd feel my bunk buck and sway, knowing that Jason was either masturbating or beating eggs for an omelette. *Is it me he's thinking about?* I'd follow his lead and wake the next morning to find our entire iron-frame unit had wandered a good eighteen inches away from the wall. Our love had the power to move bunks.

Having no willpower, we depended on circumstances to keep us apart. *This cannot happen* was accompanied by the sound of bedsprings whining, *Oh, but maybe just this once.* There came an afternoon when, running late for flag worship, we found ourselves alone in the dormitory. What started off as name-calling escalated into a series of mock angry slaps. We wrestled each other onto one of the lower bunks, both of us longing to be pinned. "You kids think you invented sex," my

28

29

mother was fond of saying. But hadn't we? With no instruction manual or federally enforced training period, didn't we all come away feeling we'd discovered something unspeakably modern? What produced in others a feeling of exhilaration left Jason and me with a mortifying sense of guilt. We fled the room as if, in our fumblings, we had uncapped some virus we still might escape if we ran fast enough. Had one of the counselors not caught me scaling the fence, I felt certain I could have made it back to Raleigh by morning, skittering across the surface of the ocean like one of those lizards often featured on television wildlife programs.

When discovered making out with one of the Greek bus drivers, a sixteen-year-old camper was forced to stand beside the flagpole dressed in long pants and thick sweaters. We watched her cook in the hot sun until, fully roasted, she crumpled to the pavement and passed out.  30

"That," the chief counselor said, "is what happens to people who play around."  31

"We couldn't protest the word, as that would have meant acknowledging the truth of it."  32

If this was the punishment for a boy and a girl, I felt certain the penalty for two boys somehow involved barbed wire, a team of donkeys, and the nearest volcano. Nothing, however, could match the cruelty and humiliation Jason and I soon practiced upon each other. He started a rumor that I had stolen an athletic supporter from another camper and secretly wore it over my mouth like a surgical mask. I retaliated, claiming he had expressed a desire to become a dancer. "That's nothing," he said to the assembled crowd, "take a look at what I found on David's bed!" He reached into the pocket of his tennis shorts and withdrew a sheet of notebook paper upon which were written the words I LIKE GUYS. Presented as an indictment, the document was both pathetic and comic. Would I supposedly have written the note to remind myself of that fact, lest I forget? Had I intended to wear it taped to my back, advertising my preference the next time our rented buses carried us off to yet another swinging sexual playground?  33

I LIKE GUYS. He held the paper above his head, turning    34
a slow circle so that everyone might get a chance to see. I
supposed he had originally intended to plant the paper on my
bunk for one of the counselors to find. Presenting it himself
had foiled the note's intended effect. Rather than beating me
with sticks and heavy shoes, the other boys simply groaned
and looked away, wondering why he'd picked the thing up
and carried it around in his pants pocket. He might as well
have hoisted a glistening turd, shouting, "Look what he did!"
Touching such a foul document made him suspect and guilty
by association. In attempting to discredit each other, we
wound up alienating ourselves even further.

   *Jason* even his name seemed affected. During meals I stud-    35
ied him from across the room. Here I was, sweating onto
my plate, my stomach knotted and cramped, when *he* was
the one full of shit. Clearly he had tricked me, cast a spell or
slipped something into my food. I watched as he befriended
a girl named Theodora and held her hand during a screening
of *A Lovely Way to Die*, one of the cave paintings the head
counselor offered as a weekly movie.

   She wasn't a bad person, Theodora. Someday, the doctors    36
might find a way to transplant a calf's brain into a human
skull and then she'd be just as lively and intelligent as he was.
I tried to find a girlfriend of my own, but my one possible
candidate was sent back home when she tumbled down the
steps of the Parthenon, causing serious damage to her leg
brace.

   Jason looked convincing enough in the company of his    37
girlfriend. They scrambled about the various ruins, snapping
each other's pictures while I hung back fuming, watching
them nuzzle and coo. My jealousy stemmed from the belief
that he had been cured. One fistful of my flesh and he had
lost all symptoms of the disease.

   Camp ended and I flew home with my legs crossed, drop-    38
ping my bag of stolen souvenirs and racing to the bathroom,
where I spent the next several days sitting on the toilet and
studying my face in a hand mirror. *I like guys.* The words had
settled themselves into my features. I was a professional now,
and it showed.

I returned to my volunteer job at the mental hospital, car- 39
rying harsh Greek cigarettes as an incentive to some of the
more difficult patients.

"Faggot!" a woman shouted, stooping to protect her col- 40
lection of pinecones. "Get your faggoty hands away from my
radio transmitters."

"Don't mind Mary Elizabeth," the orderly said. "She's crazy." 41

Maybe not, I thought, holding a pinecone up against my 42
ear. She's gotten the faggot part right, so maybe she was onto
something.

The moment we boarded our return flight from Kennedy 43
to Raleigh, Lisa re arranged her hair, dropped her accent, and
turned to me saying, "Well, I thought that was very nice, how
about you?" Over the course of five minutes, she had eliminated all traces of her reckless European self. Why couldn't
I do the same?

In late August, my class schedule arrived along with the 44
news that I would not be bused. There had been violence in
other towns and counties, trouble as far away as Boston; but
in Raleigh the transition was peaceful. Not only students but
also many of the teachers had been shifted from one school to
another. My new science teacher was a black man very adept
at swishing his way across the room, mocking everyone from
Albert Einstein to the dweebish host of a popular children's
television program. Black and white, the teachers offered their
ridicule as though it were an olive branch. "Here," they said,
"this is something we each have in common, proof that we're
all brothers under the skin."

## For Critical Thinking

### QUESTIONS ABOUT PURPOSE

1. How does Sedaris's introduction of his narrative against the
   backdrop of his school's forced desegregation help clarify his
   purpose?
2. How does the older Sedaris (the narrator) view the education
   of the younger Sedaris (the character)?

---
### QUESTIONS ABOUT AUDIENCE
---

1. How does Sedaris assume his readers will respond to his presentation of his teacher's "performances"?
2. How does his hopes for his trip to Europe help establish a connection with his audience?

---
### QUESTIONS ABOUT STRATEGY
---

1. How does Sedaris's characterization of the secret society explain his "fear of discovery"?
2. How does he use his sister and Jason to illustrate the possibility of changing one's identity?

## For Writing and Research

1. *Analyze* the way Sedaris presents his teachers' "performances" in school.
2. *Practice* by describing your attempt to conceal some aspect of your identity while you were in school.
3. *Argue* that homosexuality is determined by genetics or life style.
4. *Synthesize* current public opinion research toward homosexuals in various social roles (e.g., teacher, husband/wife, parent, and military officer).

## George Orwell: *Shooting an Elephant*

George Orwell, the pen name for Eric Blair (1903–1950), was born in Motihari, Bengal, where his father was employed with the Bengal civil service. He was brought to England at an early age for schooling (Eton), but rather than completing his education, he served with the Indian imperial police in Burma (1922–1927). Later he returned to Europe and worked at various jobs (described in *Down and Out in Paris and London*, 1933) before fighting on the Republican side in the Spanish Civil War. (See *Homage to Catalonia*, 1938.) Orwell's attitudes toward war and government are reflected in his most famous books: *Animal Farm* (1945), *1984* (1949), and *Shooting an Elephant and Other Essays* (1950). In the title essay from the last volume, Orwell reports a "tiny incident" that gave him deeper insight into his own fears and "the real motives for which despotic governments act."

I N MOULMEIN, in lower Burma, I was hated by large 1 numbers of people—the only time in my life that I have been important enough for this to happen to me. I was subdivisional police officer of the town, and in an aimless, petty kind of way anti-European feeling was very bitter. No one had the guts to raise a riot, but if a European woman went through the bazaars alone somebody would probably spit betel juice over her dress. As a police officer I was an obvious target and was baited whenever it seemed safe to do so. When a nimble Burman tripped me up on the football field and the referee (another Burman) looked the other way, the crowd yelled with hideous laughter. This happened more than once. In the end the sneering yellow faces of young men that met

me everywhere, the insults hooted after me when I was at a
safe distance, got badly on my nerves. The young Buddhist
priests were the worst of all. There were several thousands of
them in the town and none of them seemed to have anything
to do except stand on street corners and jeer at Europeans.

---

*As soon as I saw the elephant I knew with*
*perfect certainty that I ought not to shoot him.*

---

All this was perplexing and upsetting. For at that time I had    2
already made up my mind that imperialism was an evil thing
and the sooner I chucked up my job and got out of it the
better. Theoretically—and secretly, of course—I was all for
the Burmese and all against their oppressors, the British. As
for the job I was doing, I hated it more bitterly than I can
perhaps make clear. In a job like that you see the dirty work
of Empire at close quarters. The wretched prisoners huddling
in the stinking cages of the lock-ups, the gray, cowed faces of
the long-term convicts, the scarred buttocks of the men who
had been flogged with bamboos—all these oppressed me with
an intolerable sense of guilt. But I could get nothing into perspective. I was young and ill educated and I had had to think
out my problems in the utter silence that is imposed on every
Englishman in the East. I did not even know that the British
Empire is dying, still less did I know that it is a great deal better than the younger empires that are going to supplant it. All
I knew was that I was stuck between my hatred of the empire
I served and my rage against the evil-spirited little beasts who
tried to make my job impossible. With one part of my mind
I thought of the British Raj as an unbreakable tyranny, as
something clamped down, in *saecula saeculorum*, upon the
will of prostrate peoples; with another part I thought that
the greatest joy in the world would be to drive a bayonet into
a Buddhist priest's guts. Feelings like these are the normal

by-products of imperialism; ask any Anglo-Indian official, if you can catch him off duty.

One day something happened which in a roundabout way 3 was enlightening. It was a tiny incident in itself; but it gave me a better glimpse than I had had before of the real nature of imperialism—the real motives for which despotic governments act. Early one morning the sub-inspector at a police station the other end of town rang me up on the 'phone and said that an elephant was ravaging the bazaar. Would I please come and do something about it? I did not know what I could do, but I wanted to see what was happening and I got on to a pony and started out. I took my rifle, an old .44 Winchester and much too small to kill an elephant, but I thought the noise might be useful *in terrorem*. Various Burmans stopped me on the way and told me about the elephant's doings. It was not, of course, a wild elephant, but a tame one which had gone "must." It had been chained up, as tame elephants always are when their attack of "must" is due, but on the previous night it had broken its chain and escaped. Its mahout, the only person who could manage it when it was in that state, had set out in pursuit, but had taken the wrong direction and was now twelve hours' journey away, and in the morning the elephant had suddenly reappeared in the town. The Burmese population had no weapons and were quite helpless against it. It had already destroyed somebody's bamboo hut, killed a cow, and raided some fruitstalls and devoured the stock; also it had met the municipal rubbish van and, when the driver jumped out and took to his heels, had turned the van over and inflicted violences upon it.

The Burmese sub-inspector and some Indian constables 4 were waiting for me in the quarter where the elephant had been seen. It was a very poor quarter, a labyrinth of squalid bamboo huts, thatched with palm-leaf, winding all over a steep hillside. I remember that it was a cloudy, stuffy morning at the beginning of the rains. We began questioning the people as to where the elephant had gone and, as usual, failed to get any definite information. That is invariably the case in the East; a story always sounds clear enough at a distance, but the nearer you get to the scene of events the vaguer it becomes. Some of the people said that the elephant had gone in one direction, some said that he had gone in another, some professed not even to have heard of any elephant. I had almost made up my mind that the whole story was a pack of lies, when we heard yells a little distance away. There was a loud, scandalized cry of "Go away, child! Go away this instant!" and an old woman with a switch in her hand came round the corner of a hut, violently shooing away a crowd of naked children. Some more women followed, clicking their tongues and exclaiming; evidently there was something that the children ought not to have seen. I rounded the hut and saw a man's dead body sprawling in the mud. He was an Indian, a black Dravidian coolie, almost naked, and he could not have been dead many minutes. The people said that the elephant had come suddenly upon him round the corner of the hut, caught him with its trunk, put its foot on his back, and ground him into the earth. This was the rainy season and the ground was soft, and his face had scored a trench a foot deep and a couple of yards long. He was lying on his belly with arms crucified and head sharply twisted to one side. His face was coated with mud, the eyes wide open, the teeth bared, and grinning with an expression of unendurable agony. (Never tell me, by the way, that the dead look peaceful. Most of the corpses I have seen looked devilish.) The friction of the great beast's foot had stripped the skin from his back as neatly as one skins a rabbit. As soon as I saw the dead man I sent an orderly to a friend's house nearby to borrow an elephant rifle. I had already sent back the pony, not wanting it to go mad with fright and throw me if it smelt the elephant.

The orderly came back in a few minutes with a rifle and     5 five cartridges, and meanwhile some Burmans had arrived and told us that the elephant was in the paddy fields below, only a few hundred yards away. As I started forward practically the whole population of the quarter flocked out of the houses and followed me. They had seen the rifle and were all shouting excitedly that I was going to shoot the elephant. They had not shown much interest in the elephant when he was merely ravaging their homes, but it was different now that he was going to be shot. It was a bit of fun to them, and it would be to an English crowd; besides they wanted the meat. It made me vaguely uneasy. I had no intention of shooting the elephant—I had merely sent for the rifle to defend myself if necessary—and it is always unnerving to have a crowd following you. I marched down the hill, looking and feeling a fool, with the rifle over my shoulder and an ever-growing army of people jostling at my heels. At the bottom, when you got away from the huts, there was a metalled road and beyond that a miry waste of paddy fields a thousand yards across, not yet ploughed but soggy from the first rains and dotted with coarse grass. The elephant was standing eight yards from the road, his left side toward us. He took not the slightest notice of the crowd's approach. He was tearing up bunches of grass, beating them against his knees to clean them, and stuffing them into his mouth.

I had halted on the road. As soon as I saw the elephant 6 I knew with perfect certainty that I ought not to shoot him. It is a serious matter to shoot a working elephant—it is comparable to destroying a huge and costly piece of machinery—and obviously one ought not to do it if it can possibly be avoided. And at that distance, peacefully eating, the elephant looked no more dangerous than a cow. I thought then and I think now that his attack of "must" was already passing off; in which case he would merely wander harmlessly about until the mahout came back and caught him. Moreover, I did not in the least want to shoot him. I decided that I would watch him for a little while to make sure that he did not turn savage again and then go home.

But at that moment I glanced round at the crowd that 7 had followed me. It was an immense crowd, two thousand at the least and growing every minute. It blocked the road for a long distance on either side. I looked at the sea of yellow faces above the garish clothes—faces all happy and excited over this bit of fun, all certain that the elephant was going to be shot. They were watching me as they would watch a conjurer about to perform a trick. They did not like me, but with the magical rifle in my hands I was momentarily worth watching. And suddenly I realized that I should have to shoot the elephant after all. The people expected it of me and I had got to do it; I could feel their two thousand wills pressing me forward, irresistibly. And it was at this moment, as I stood there with the rifle in my hands, that I first grasped the hollowness, the futility of the white man's dominion in the East. Here was I, the white man with his gun, standing in front of the unarmed native crowd—seemingly the leading actor of the piece; but in reality, I was only an absurd puppet pushed to and fro by the will of those yellow faces behind. I perceived in this moment that when the white man turns tyrant it is his own freedom that he destroys. He becomes a sort of hollow, posing dummy, the conventionalized figure of a sahib. For it is the condition of his rule that he shall spend his life in trying to impress the "natives," and so in every crisis he has got to do what the "natives" expect of him. He wears a mask, and his face grows to fit it. I had got to shoot the elephant. I had committed myself to doing it when I sent for the rifle. A sahib has got to act like a sahib; he has got to appear resolute, to know his own mind and do definite things. To come all that way, rifle in hand, with two thousand people marching at my heels, and then to trail feebly away, having done nothing—no, that was impossible. The crowd would laugh at me. And my whole life, every white man's life in the East, was one long struggle not to be laughed at.

But I did not want to shoot the elephant. I watched him 8 beating his bunch of grass against his knees with that preoccupied grandmotherly air that elephants have. It seemed to me that it would be murder to shoot him. At that age I was not squeamish about killing animals, but I had never shot an elephant and never wanted to. (Somehow it always seems worse to kill a *large* animal.) Besides, there was the beast's owner to be considered. Alive, the elephant was worth at least a hundred pounds; dead, he would only be worth the value of his tusks, five pounds, possibly. But I had got to act quickly. I turned to some experienced-looking Burmans who had been there when we arrived and asked them how the elephant had been behaving. They all said the same thing: he took no notice of you if you left him alone, but he might charge if you went too close to him.

It was perfectly clear to me what I ought to do. I ought 9 to walk up to within, say, twenty-five yards of the elephant and test his behavior. If he charged, I could shoot; if he took no notice of me, it would be safe to leave him until the mahout came back. But also I knew that I was going to do no such thing. I was a poor shot with a rifle and the ground was soft mud into which one would sink at every step. If the elephant charged and I missed him, I should have about as much chance as a toad under a steam-roller. But even then I was not thinking particularly of my own skin, only of the watchful yellow faces behind. For at that moment, with the crowd watching me, I was not afraid in the ordinary sense, as I would have been if I had been alone. A white man mustn't be frightened in front of "natives"; and so, in general, he isn't frightened. The sole thought in my mind was that if anything went wrong those two thousand Burmans would see me pursued, caught, trampled on, and reduced to a grinning corpse like that Indian up the hill. And if that happened it was quite probable that some of them would laugh. That would never do. There was only one alternative. I shoved the cartridges into the magazine and lay down on the road to get a better aim.

The crowd grew very still, and a deep, low, happy sigh, as 10 of people who see the theater curtain go up at last, breathed from innumerable throats. They were going to have their bit of fun after all. The rifle was a beautiful German thing with cross-hair sights. I did not then know that in shooting an elephant one would shoot to cut an imaginary bar running from earhole to earhole. I ought, therefore, as the elephant was sideways on, to have aimed straight at his earhole; actually I aimed several inches in front of this, thinking the brain would be further forward.

When I pulled the trigger I did not hear the bang or feel the 11 kick—one never does when a shot goes home—but I heard the devilish roar of glee that went up from the crowd. In that instant, in too short a time, one would have thought, even for the bullet to get there, a mysterious, terrible change had come over the elephant. He neither stirred, nor fell, but every line of his body had altered. He looked suddenly stricken, shrunken, immensely old, as though the frightful impact of the bullet had paralyzed him without knocking him down. At last, after what seemed a long time—it might have been five seconds, I dare say—he sagged flabbily to his knees. His mouth slobbered. An enormous senility seemed to have settled upon him. One could have imagined him thousands of years old. I fired again into the same spot. At the second shot he did not collapse but climbed with desperate slowness to his feet and stood weakly upright, with legs sagging and head drooping. I fired a third time. That was the shot that did for him. You could see the agony of it jolt his whole body and knock the last remnant of strength from his legs. But in falling he seemed for a moment to rise, for as his hind legs collapsed beneath him he seemed to tower upward like a huge rock toppling, his trunk reaching skyward like a tree. He trumpeted, for the first and only time. And then down he came, his belly toward me, with a crash that seemed to shake the ground even where I lay.

I got up. The Burmans were already racing past me across the mud. It was obvious that the elephant would never rise again, but he was not dead. He was breathing very rhythmically with long rattling gasps, his great mound of a side painfully rising and falling. His mouth was wide open—I could see far down into caverns of pale pink throat. I waited a long time for him to die, but his breathing did not weaken. Finally, I fired my two remaining shots into the spot where I thought his heart must be. The thick blood welled out of him like red velvet, but still he did not die. His body did not even jerk when the shots hit him, the tortured breathing continued without a pause. He was dying, very slowly and in great agony, but in some world remote from me where not even a bullet could damage him further. I felt that I had got to put an end to that dreadful noise. It seemed dreadful to see the great beast lying there, powerless to move and yet powerless

12

to die, and not even to be able to finish him. I sent back for my small rifle and poured shot after shot into his heart and down his throat. They seemed to make no impression. The tortured gasps continued as steadily as the ticking of a clock.

In the end, I could not stand it any longer and went away.   13 I heard later that it took him half an hour to die. Burmans were bringing dash and baskets even before I left, and I was told that they had stripped his body almost to the bones by the afternoon.

Afterward, of course, there were endless discussions about   14 the shooting of the elephant. The owner was furious, but he was only an Indian and could do nothing. Besides, legally I had done the right thing, for a mad elephant has to be killed, like a mad dog, if its owner fails to control it. Among the Europeans opinion was divided. The older men said I was right, the younger men said it was a damn shame to shoot an elephant for killing a coolie, because an elephant was worth more than any damn Coringhee coolie. And afterward I was very glad that the coolie had been killed; it put me legally in the right and it gave me a sufficient pretext for shooting the elephant. I often wondered whether any of the others grasped that I had done it solely to avoid looking a fool.

## For Critical Thinking

### QUESTIONS ABOUT PURPOSE

1. What thesis about "the real nature of imperialism" does Orwell prove by narrating this "tiny incident"?
2. What are the reasons Orwell considers when he tries to decide whether to shoot the elephant?

### QUESTIONS ABOUT AUDIENCE

1. How does Orwell present himself to his audience in paragraphs 6 through 9?
2. Which of the three positions stated in the final paragraph does Orwell expect his readers to agree with?

## QUESTIONS ABOUT STRATEGIES

1. Although Orwell begins narrating the incident in paragraph 3, he does not describe the elephant until the end of paragraph 5. What details does he use to intensify the dramatic conflict?
2. How does Orwell pace the shooting of the elephant in paragraphs 11 and 12?

## For Writing and Research

1. *Analyze* how Orwell's description of the elephant's slow death affects his point of view toward what he has done.
2. *Practice* by narrating an incident in which you committed an act to avoid looking like a fool.
3. *Argue* that Orwell's plight is similar to the plight of the young American soldiers who are serving in Afghanistan.
4. *Synthesize:* Research the words *imperialism* and *despotism.* Then construct an essay in which you explain how the recent actions of a foreign or domestic government could be perceived as *imperialistic* or *despotic.*

# Richard Russo: *Dog*

Richard Russo was born in 1949 in Jamestown, New York, and educated at the University of Arizona. He has worked as an actor, a screen writer, and a producer. He has taught creative writing at Southern Illinois University, Colby College, and South Connecticut State University. He used this teaching experience as the resource for his academic novel, *Straight Man* (1997). But he is best known for his novels such as *Mohawk* (1996) and *Bridge of Sighs* (2007) that depict life in the declining towns of America. He won the Pulitzer Prize for *Empire Falls* (2001), which together with *Nobody's Fool*, has been adapted for the screen. "Dog" first appeared in the *New Yorker* in 1996 and then was used as the prologue to *Straight Man*. In this story, Russo illustrated how he and his parents have a different attitude toward stories that are entertaining and exasperating.

---

*They're nice to have. A dog.*
—*F. SCOTT FITZGERALD, The Great Gatsby*

---

TRUTH BE TOLD, I'm not an easy man. I can be an entertaining one, though it's been my experience that most people don't want to be entertained. They want to be comforted. And, of course, my idea of entertaining might not be yours. I'm in complete agreement with all those people who say, regarding movies, "I just want to be entertained." 1

71

This populist position is much derided by my academic colleagues as simpleminded and unsophisticated, evidence of
questionable analytical, and critical acuity. But I agree with
the premise, and I too just want to be entertained. That I am
almost never entertained by what entertains *other* people
who just want to be entertained doesn't make us philosophi-
cally incompatible. It just means we shouldn't go to movies
together.

The kind of man I am, according to those who know me        2
best, is exasperating. According to my parents, I was an exasperating child as well. They divorced when I was in junior
high school, and they agree on little except that I was an
impossible child. The story they tell of young William Henry
Devereaux, Jr., and his first dog is eerily similar in its facts, its
conclusions, even the style of its telling, no matter which of
them is telling it. Here's the story they tell.

I was nine, and the house we were living in, which belonged       3
to the university, was my fourth. My parents were academic
nomads, my father, then and now, an academic opportunist,
always in the vanguard of whatever was trendy and chic
in literary criticism. This was the fifties, and for him, New
Criticism was already old. In early middle age, he was already
a full professor with several published books, all of them
"hot," the subject of intense debate at English department
cocktail parties. The academic position he favored was the
"distinguished visiting professor" variety, usually created for
him, duration of visit a year or two at most, perhaps because
it's hard to remain distinguished among people who know
you. Usually his teaching responsibilities were light, a course
or two a year. Otherwise, he was expected to read and think
and write and publish and acknowledge in the preface of his
next book the generosity of the institution that provided him
the academic good life. My mother, also an English professor,
was hired as part of the package deal, to teach a full load and
thereby help balance the books.

The houses we lived in were elegant, old, high-ceilinged,       4
drafty, either on or close to campus. They had hardwood

floors and smoky fireplaces with fires in them only when my father held court, which he did either on Friday afternoons, our large rooms filling up with obsequious junior faculty and nervous grad students, or Saturday evenings, when my mother gave dinner parties for the chair of the department, or the dean, or a visiting poet. In all situations I was the only child, and I must have been a lonely one, because what I wanted more than anything in the world was a dog.

Predictably, my parents did not. Probably the terms of liv-  5 ing in these university houses were specific regarding pets. By the time I was nine I'd been lobbying hard for a dog for a year or two. My father and mother were hoping I would outgrow this longing, given enough time. I could see this hope in their eyes and it steeled my resolve, intensified my desire. What did I want for Christmas? A dog. What did I want for my birthday? A dog. What did I want on my ham sandwich? A dog. It was a deeply satisfying look of pure exasperation they shared at such moments, and if I couldn't have a dog, this was the next best thing.

Life continued in this fashion until finally my mother made  6 a mistake, a doozy of a blunder born of emotional exhaustion and despair. She, far more than my father, would have preferred a happy child. One spring day after I'd been badgering her pretty relentlessly she sat me down and said, "You know, a dog is something you earn." My father heard this, got up, and left the room, grim acknowledgment that my mother had just conceded the war. Her idea was to make the dog conditional. The conditions to be imposed would be numerous and severe, and I would be incapable of fulfilling them, so when I didn't get the dog it'd be my own fault. This was her logic, and the fact that she thought such a plan might work illustrates that some people should never be parents and that she was one of them.

I immediately put into practice a plan of my own to wear  7 my mother down. Unlike hers, my plan was simple and flawless. Mornings I woke up talking about dogs and nights I fell asleep talking about them. When my mother and father changed the subject, I changed it back. "Speaking of dogs," I would say, a forkful of my mother's roast poised at my lips, and I'd be off again. Maybe no one *had* been speaking of dogs, but never mind, we were speaking of them now. At the library I checked out a half dozen books on dogs every two weeks and left them lying open around the house. I pointed out dogs we passed on the street, dogs on television, dogs in the magazines my mother subscribed to. I discussed the relative merits of various breeds at every meal. My father seldom listened to anything I said, but I began to see signs that the underpinnings of my mother's personality were beginning to corrode in the salt water of my tidal persistence, and when I judged that she was nigh to complete collapse, I took every penny of the allowance money I'd been saving and spent it on a dazzling, bejeweled dog collar and leash set at the overpriced pet store around the corner.

During this period when we were constantly "speaking of  8 dogs," I was not a model boy. I was supposed to be "earning a dog," and I was constantly checking with my mother to see how I was doing, just how much of a dog I'd earned, but I doubt my behavior had changed a jot. I wasn't really a bad boy. Just a noisy, busy, constantly needy boy. Mr. In and Out, my mother called me, because I was in and out of rooms, in and out of doors, and in and out of the refrigerator. "Henry," my mother would plead with me. "Light somewhere." One of the things I often needed was information, and I constantly interrupted my mother's reading and paper grading to get it. My father, partly to avoid having to answer my questions, spent most of his time in his book-lined office on campus, joining my mother and me only at mealtimes, so that we could speak of dogs as a family. Then he was gone again, blissfully unaware, I thought at the time, that my mother continued to glare homicidally, for long minutes after his departure, at the chair he'd so recently occupied. But he claimed to be close to finishing the book he was working on, and this was a powerful excuse to offer a woman with as much abstract respect for books and learning as my mother possessed.

Gradually, she came to understand that she was fighting a  9
battle she couldn't win and that she was fighting it alone. I
now know that this was part of a larger cluster of bitter marital
realizations, but at the time I sniffed nothing in the air but
victory. In late August, during what people refer to as "the
dog days," when she made one last, weak condition, final
evidence that I had earned a dog, I relented and truly tried
to reform my behavior. It was literally the least I could do.

What my mother wanted of me was to stop slamming  10
the screen door. The house we were living in, it must be
said, was an acoustic marvel akin to the Whispering Gallery
in St. Paul's, where muted voices travel across a great open
space and arrive, clear and intact, at the other side of the great
dome. In our house the screen door swung shut on a tight
spring, the straight wooden edge of the door encountering
the doorframe like a gunshot played through a guitar ampli-
fier set on stun, the crack transmitting perfectly, with equal
force and clarity, to every room in the house, upstairs and
down. That summer I was in and out that door dozens of
times a day, and my mother said it was like living in a shooting
gallery. It made her wish the door wasn't shooting blanks. If
I could just remember not to slam the door, then she'd see
about a dog. Soon.

I did better, remembering about half the time not to let the  11
door slam. When I forgot, I came back in to apologize, sometimes forgetting then too. Still, that I was trying, together
with the fact that I carried the expensive dog collar and leash
with me everywhere I went, apparently moved my mother,
because at the end of that first week of diminished door
slamming, my father went somewhere on Saturday morning,
refusing to reveal where, and so of course I knew. "What
*kind?*" I pleaded with my mother when he was gone. But she
claimed not to know. "Your father's doing this," she said, and
I thought I saw a trace of misgiving in her expression.

When he returned, I saw why. He'd put it in the backseat,  12
and when my father pulled the car in and parked along the
side of the house, I saw from the kitchen window its chin rest-
ing on the back of the rear seat. I think it saw me too, but if

so it did not react. Neither did it seem to notice that the car had stopped, that my father had gotten out and was holding the front seat forward. He had to reach in, take the dog by the collar, and pull.

As the animal unfolded its long legs and stepped tenta- 13 tively, arthritically, out of the car, I saw that I had been both betrayed and outsmarted. In all the time we had been "speaking of dogs," what I'd been seeing in my mind's eye was puppies. Collie puppies, beagle puppies, Lab puppies, shepherd puppies, but none of that had been inked anywhere, I now realized. If not a puppy, a young dog. A rascal, full of spirit and possibility, a dog with new tricks to learn. *This* dog was barely ambulatory. It stood, head down, as if ashamed at something done long ago in its puppydom, and I thought I detected a shiver run through its frame when my father closed the car door behind it.

The animal was, I suppose, what might have been called a 14 handsome dog. A purebred, rust-colored Irish setter, meticulously groomed, wonderfully mannered, the kind of dog you could safely bring into a house owned by the university, the sort of dog that wouldn't really violate the no pets clause, the kind of dog, I saw clearly, you'd get if you really didn't want a dog or to be bothered with a dog. It'd belonged, I later learned, to a professor emeritus of the university who'd been put into a nursing home earlier in the week, leaving the animal an orphan. It was like a painting of a dog, or a dog you'd hire to pose for a portrait, a dog you could be sure wouldn't move.

Both my father and the animal came into the kitchen reluc- 15 tantly, my father closing the screen door behind them with great care. I like to think that on the way home he'd suffered a misgiving, though I could tell that it was his intention to play the hand out boldly. My mother, who'd taken in my devastation at a glance, studied me for a moment and then my father.

"What?" he said. 16

My mother just shook her head. 17

My father looked at me, then back at her. A violent shiver 18 palsied the dog's limbs. The animal seemed to want to lie down on the cool linoleum but to have forgotten how. It offered a deep sigh that seemed to speak for all of us.

"He's a good dog," my father said, rather pointedly, to my   19
mother. "A little high-strung, but that's the way with pure-bred setters. They're all nervous."

This was not the sort of thing my father knew. Clearly he   20
was repeating the explanation he'd just been given when he picked up the dog.

"What's his name?" my mother said, apparently for some-   21
thing to say.

My father had neglected to ask. He checked the dog's col-   22
lar for clues.

"Lord," my mother said. "Lord, lord."                        23

"It's not like we can't name him ourselves," my father said,   24
irritated now. "I think it's something we can manage, don't you?"

"You could name him after a passé school of literary criti-   25
cism," my mother suggested.

"It's a she," I said, because it was.                         26

It seemed to cheer my father, at least a little, that I'd   27
allowed myself to be drawn into the conversation. "What do you say, Henry?" he wanted to know. "What'll we name him?"

This second faulty pronoun reference was too much for   28
me. "I want to go out and play now," I said, and I bolted for the screen door before an objection could be registered. It slammed behind me, hard, its gunshot report even louder than usual. As I cleared the steps in a single leap, I thought I heard a thud back in the kitchen, a dull, muffled echo of the door, and then I heard my father say, "What the hell?" I went back up the steps, cautiously now, meaning to apologize for the door. Through the screen I could see my mother and father standing together in the middle of the kitchen, look-ing down at the dog, which seemed to be napping. My father nudged a haunch with the toe of his cordovan loafer.

He dug the grave in the backyard with a shovel borrowed   29
from a neighbor. My father had soft hands and they blistered easily. I offered to help, but he just looked at me. When he was standing, midthigh, in the hole he'd dug, he shook his

head one last time in disbelief. "Dead," he said. "Before we
could even name him."

I knew better than to correct the pronoun again, so I just     30
stood there thinking about what he'd said while he climbed
out of the hole and went over to the back porch to collect the
dog where it lay under an old sheet. I could tell by the careful way he tucked that sheet under the animal that he didn't
want to touch anything dead, even newly dead. He lowered
the dog into the hole by means of the sheet, but he had to
drop it the last foot or so. When the animal thudded on the
earth and lay still, my father looked over at me and shook his
head. Then he picked up the shovel and leaned on it before
he started filling in the hole. He seemed to be waiting for me
to say something, so I said, "Red."

My father's eyes narrowed, as if I'd spoken in a foreign      31
tongue. "What?" he said.

"We'll name her Red," I explained.                            32

In the years after he left us, my father became even more     33
famous. He is sometimes credited, if credit is the word, with
being the Father of American Literary Theory. In addition
to his many books of scholarship, he's also written a literary memoir that was short listed for a major award and that
offers insight into the personalities of several major literary
figures of the twentieth century, now deceased. His photograph often graces the pages of the literary reviews. He went
through a phase where he wore crewneck sweaters and gold
chains beneath his tweed coat, but now he's mostly photo-
graphed in an oxford button-down shirt, tie, and jacket, in
his book-lined office at the university. But to me, his son,
William Henry Devereaux, Sr., is most real standing in his
ruined cordovan loafers, leaning on the handle of a borrowed
shovel, examining his dirty, blistered hands, and receiving my
suggestion of what to name a dead dog. I suspect that dig-
ging our dog's grave was one of relatively few experiences of
his life (excepting carnal ones) that did not originate on the
printed page. And when I suggested we name the dead dog
Red, he looked at me as if I myself had just stepped from the
pages of a book he'd started to read years ago and then put

down when something else caught his interest. "What?" he said, letting go of the shovel, so that its handle hit the earth between my feet. "What?"

It's not an easy time for any parent, this moment when the realization dawns that you've given birth to something that will never see things the way you do, despite the fact that it is your living legacy, that it bears your name. 34

## COMMENT ON "DOG"

"Dog" is an excellent example of how different people see the same story. The narrator admits he is "not an easy man." But he also admits that he "can be an entertaining one, though it has been my experience that most people don't want to be entertained." Although the story he tells about his childhood desire to own a dog could be perceived as entertaining, it could also be perceived—at least from his parents' point of view—as exasperating.

# CHAPTER 2

# Process Analysis

A **process** is an operation that moves through a series of steps to bring about a desired result. You can call almost any procedure a process, whether it is getting out of bed in the morning or completing a transaction on the stock exchange. A useful way to identify a particular kind of process is by its principal function. A process can be *natural* (the birth of a baby), *mechanical* (starting a car engine), *physical* (dancing), or *mental* (reading).

**Analysis** is an operation that divides something into its parts in order to understand the whole more clearly. For example, poetry readers analyze the lines of a poem to find meaning. Doctors analyze a patient's symptoms to prescribe treatment. Politicians analyze the opinions of individual voters and groups of voters to plan campaigns.

If you want to write a process-analysis essay, you need to go through three steps: (1) divide the process you are going to explain into its individual steps; (2) show the movement of the process, step by step, from beginning to end; and (3) explain how each step works, how it relates to other steps in the sequence, and how it brings about the desired result.

## PURPOSE

Usually you will write a process analysis to accomplish two purposes: *to give directions* and *to provide information*. Sometimes you might find it difficult to separate the two purposes. After all, when you give directions about how to do something (hit a baseball), you also have to provide information on how the whole process works (rules of the game—strike zone, walks, hits, base running, outs, scoring). But usually you can separate the two because you're trying to accomplish different goals. When you give directions, you want to help your readers do something (change a tire). When you give information, you want to satisfy your readers' curiosity about some process they'd like to know about but are unlikely to perform (pilot a space shuttle).

You might also write a process analysis to demonstrate that (1) a task that looks difficult is really easy or (2) a task that looks easy is really quite complex. For instance, you might want to show that selecting a specific tool can simplify a complex process (using a microwave oven to cook a six-course dinner). You might also want to show why it's important to have a prearranged plan to make a process seem simple (explaining the preparations for an informal television interview).

## AUDIENCE

When you write a process-analysis essay, you must think carefully about who your audience will be. First, you need to decide whether you're writing *to* an audience (giving directions) or writing *for* an audience (providing information). If you are writing *to* an audience, you can address directly readers who are already interested in your subject: "If you want to plant a successful garden, you must follow these seven steps." If you are writing *for* an audience, you can write from a more detached point of view, but you have to find a way to catch the interest of more casual readers: "Although many Americans say they are concerned about nuclear power, few understand how a nuclear power plant works."

Second, you have to determine how wide the knowledge gap is between you and your readers. Writing about a process suggests you are something of an expert in that area. If you can be sure your readers are also experts, you can make certain assumptions as you write your analysis. For instance, if you're outlining courtroom procedure to a group of fellow law students, you can assume you don't have to define the special meaning of the word *brief.*

On the other hand, if you feel sure your intended audience knows almost nothing about a process (or has only general knowledge), you can take nothing for granted. If you are explaining how to operate a Fitbit to readers who have never used one, you will have to define special terms and explain all procedures. If you assume your readers are experts when they are not, you will confuse or annoy them. If you assume they need to be told everything when they don't, you will bore or antagonize them. And, finally, remember that to analyze a process effectively, you must either research it carefully or have firsthand knowledge of its operation. It's risky to try to explain something you don't really understand.

## STRATEGIES

The best way to write a process analysis is to organize your essay according to five parts:

> Overview
> Special terms
> Sequence of steps
> Examples
> Results

The first two parts help your readers understand the process, the next two show the process in action, and the last one evaluates the worth of the completed process.

Begin your analysis with an *overview* of the whole process. To make such an overview, you take these four steps:

1. Define the objective of the process.
2. Identify (and number) the steps in the sequence.
3. Group some small steps into larger units.
4. Call attention to the most important steps or units.

For example, P. J. O'Rourke begins by explaining the purpose of the process he is about to explain. Scott Adams explains that his recommendations for a "real" education are intended for B-level students.

Each process has its own *special terms* to describe tools, tasks, and methods, and you will have to define those terms for your readers. You can define them at the beginning so your readers will understand the terms when you use them, but often you do better to define them as you use them. Your readers may have trouble remembering specialized language out of context, so it's often practical to define your terms throughout the course of the essay, pausing to explain their special meaning or use the first time you introduce them. Scott Adams follows this strategy by defining "entrepreneurship."

When you write a process-analysis essay, you must present the *sequence of steps* clearly and carefully. As you do so, give the reason for each step and, where appropriate, provide these reminders:

1. *Do not omit any steps.* A sequence is a sequence because all steps depend on one another. Adams explains that an entrepreneur would benefit from classes in finance and management.
2. *Do not reverse steps.* A sequence is a sequence because each step must be performed according to a necessary and logical pattern. O'Rourke advises that you should not start driving in an underdeveloped country before you know what side of the road you are supposed to drive on.
3. *Suspend certain steps.* Occasionally, a whole series of steps must be suspended and another process completed before the sequence can resume. O'Rourke suggests that a whole sequence of steps can be avoided if you suspend the sequence and give everybody "big wads of money."

4. *Do not overlook steps within steps.* Each sequence is likely to have a series of smaller steps buried within each step. Lars Eighner reminds his readers that if they start eating something before they have inspected it, they are likely to discover moldy bread or sour milk after they have put it in their mouths.

5. *Avoid certain steps.* It is often tempting to insert steps that are not recommended but that appear "logical." Although Adams understands why it might seem logical for the "brainy group" to take chemistry, calculus, and classic literature, he suggests that B students take something useful instead.

You may want to use several kinds of *examples* to explain the steps in a sequence.

1. *Pictures.* You can use graphs, charts, and diagrams to illustrate the operation of the process.

2. *Anecdotes.* Because you're claiming some level of expertise by writing a process analysis, you can clarify your explanation by using examples from your own experience. O'Rourke uses this method—for comic effect—when he describes roadblocks and animals in the right of way.

3. *Variants.* You can mention alternative steps to show that the process may not be as rigid or simplistic as it often appears. When Adams and his friends could not use the gym for their informal soccer games because the space was reserved for organized groups, they formed an organized soccer club.

4. *Comparisons.* You can use comparisons to help your readers see that a complex process is similar to a process they already know. O'Rourke uses this strategy when he compares Third World and American driving habits.

Although you focus on the movement of the process when you write a process-analysis essay, you should also try to evaluate the *results* of that process. You can move to this last part by asking two questions: How do you know it's done? How do you know it's good? Sometimes the answer is simple: The car starts; the meal turns out well. At other times, the answer is not so clear: Racial situations are not always easy to understand; eating food from a dumpster may cause dysentery.

---

## PROCESS ANALYSIS

### Points to Remember

1. Arrange the steps in your process in an orderly sequence.
2. Identify and explain the purpose of each of the steps in the process.
3. Describe the special tools, terms, and tasks needed to complete the process.
4. Provide warnings, where appropriate, about the consequences of omitting, reversing, or overlooking certain steps.
5. Supply illustrations and personal anecdotes to help clarify aspects of the process.

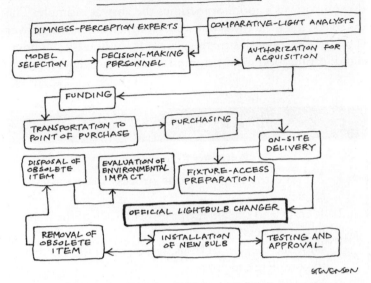

In this comic drawing, James Stevenson offers yet another variation of the old joke "How many [fill in the blank] does it take to change a light bulb?" Trace the various steps in this overwrought flowchart. Has Stevenson missed a step or placed steps out of sequence? Construct your own flowchart for a simple process such as making an ATM transaction or hitting a golf ball. Then write an analysis of your chart demonstrating why this simple process contains hidden steps or must be explained in a larger context.

## Lars Eighner:
### My Daily Dives in the Dumpster

Lars Eighner was born in 1948 in Corpus Christi, Texas, and attended the University of Texas at Austin. He held a series of jobs, including work as an attendant at the state mental hospital in Austin, before he became homeless. For five years he drifted between Austin and Hollywood, living on the streets and in abandoned buildings. Then he began to contribute essays to the *Threepenny Review*; these writings are collected in his memoir, *Travels with Lizabeth* (1993). His other writing includes a collection of short stories, *Bayou Boy and Other Stories* (1993), and a novel, *Pawn to Queen Four* (1995). In "My Daily Dives in the Dumpster," reprinted from *The Threepenny Review* (Fall 1988), Eighner analyzes the "predictable series of stages that a person goes through in learning to scavenge."

I BEGAN DUMPSTER diving about a year before I became homeless.

I prefer the term "scavenging" and use the word "scrounging" when I mean to be obscure. I have heard people, evidently meaning to be polite, use the word "foraging," but I prefer to reserve that word for gathering nuts and berries and such which I do also, according to the season and opportunity.

I like the frankness of the word "scavenging." I live from the refuse of others. I am a scavenger. I think it a sound and honorable niche, although if I could I would naturally prefer to live the comfortable consumer life, perhaps—and only perhaps—as a slightly less wasteful consumer owing to what I have learned as a scavenger.

Except for jeans, all my clothes come from Dumpsters. 4
Boom boxes, candles, bedding, toilet paper, medicine, books,
a typewriter, a virgin male love doll, change sometimes
amounting to many dollars: All came from Dumpsters. And,
yes, I eat from Dumpsters too.

There are a predictable series of stages that a person goes 5
through in learning to scavenge. At first the new scavenger is
filled with disgust and self-loathing. He is ashamed of being
seen and may lurk around trying to duck behind things, or
he may try to dive at night. (In fact, this is unnecessary, since
most people instinctively look away from scavengers.)

*Scavenging, more than most other pursuits,*
*tends to yield returns in some proportion to*
*the effort and the intelligence brought to bear.*

Every grain of rice seems to be a maggot. Everything seems 6
to stink. The scavenger can wipe the egg yolk off the found
can, but he cannot erase the stigma of eating garbage from
his mind.

This stage passes with experience. The scavenger finds a 7
pair of running shoes that fit and look and smell brand-new.
He finds a pocket calculator in perfect working order. He
finds pristine ice cream, still frozen, more than he can eat or
keep. He begins to understand: People do throw away perfectly good stuff, a lot of perfectly good stuff.

At this stage he may become lost and never recover. All the 8
Dumpster divers I have known come to the point of trying to
acquire everything they touch. Why not take it, they reason, it
is all free. This is, of course, hopeless, and most divers come to
realize that they must restrict themselves to items of relatively
immediate utility.

The finding of objects is becoming something of an urban 9
art. Even respectable, employed people will sometimes find

something tempting sticking out of a Dumpster or standing beside one. Quite a number of people, not all of them of the bohemian type, are willing to brag that they found this or that piece in the trash.

But eating from Dumpsters is the thing that separates the 10 dilettanti from the professionals. Eating safely involves three principles: using the senses and common sense to evaluate the condition of the found materials; knowing the Dumpsters of a given area and checking them regularly; and seeking always to answer the question, Why was this discarded?

Perhaps everyone who has a kitchen and a regular sup- 11 ply of groceries has, at one time or another, eaten half a sandwich before discovering mold on the bread, or has gotten a mouthful of milk before realizing the milk had turned. Nothing of the sort is likely to happen to a Dumpster diver because he is constantly reminded that most food is discarded for a reason.

Yet perfectly good food can be found in Dumpsters. 12 Canned goods, for example, turn up fairly often in the Dumpsters I frequent. All except the most phobic people would be willing to eat from a can even if it came from a Dumpster. I have few qualms about dry foods such as crackers, cookies, cereal, chips and pasta if they are free of visible contaminants and still dry and crisp. Raw fruits and vegetables with intact skins seem perfectly safe to me, excluding, of course, the obviously rotten. Many are discarded for minor imperfections that can be pared away. Chocolate is often discarded only because it has become discolored as the cocoa butter de-emulsified.

I began scavenging by pulling pizzas out of the Dump- 13 ster behind a pizza delivery shop. In general, prepared food requires caution, but in this case I knew what time the shop closed and went to the Dumpster as soon as the last of the help left.

Because the workers at these places are usually inexperi- 14 enced, pizzas are often made with the wrong topping, baked incorrectly, or refused on delivery for being cold. The products to be discarded are boxed up because inventory is kept by counting boxes: A boxed pizza can be written off; an unboxed pizza does not exist. So I had a steady supply of fresh, sometimes warm pizza.

The area I frequent is inhabited by many affluent college 15 students. I am not here by chance; the Dumpsters are very rich. Students throw out many good things, including food, particularly at the end of the semester and before and after breaks. I find it advantageous to keep an eye on the academic calendar.

A typical discard is a half jar of peanut butter—though 16 non-organic peanut butter does not require refrigeration and is unlikely to spoil in any reasonable time. Occasionally I find a cheese with a spot of mold, which, of course, I just pare off, and because it is obvious why the cheese was discarded, I treat it with less suspicion than an apparently perfect cheese found in similar circumstances. One of my favorite finds is yogurt—often discarded, still sealed, when the expiration date has passed—because it will keep for several days, even in warm weather.

I avoid ethnic foods I am unfamiliar with. If I do not know 17 what it is supposed to look or smell like when it is good, I cannot be certain I will be able to tell if it is bad.

No matter how careful I am I still get dysentery at least 18 once a month, oftener in warm weather. I do not want to paint too romantic a picture. Dumpster diving has serious drawbacks as a way of life.

Though I have a proprietary feeling about my Dumpsters, 19 I don't mind my direct competitors, other scavengers, as much as I hate the soda-can scroungers.

I have tried scrounging aluminum cans with an able- 20 bodied companion, and afoot we could make no more than a few dollars a day. I can extract the necessities of life from the Dumpsters directly with far less effort than would be required to accumulate the equivalent value in aluminum. Can scroungers, then, are people who *must* have small amounts of cash—mostly drug addicts and winos.

I do not begrudge them the cans, but can scroungers tend 21 to tear up the Dumpsters, littering the area and mixing the contents. There are precious few courtesies among scavengers, but it is a common practice to set aside surplus items: pairs of shoes, clothing, canned goods, and such. A true scavenger hates to see good stuff go to waste, and what he cannot use he leaves in good condition in plain sight. Can scroungers lay waste to everything in their path and will stir one of a pair of good shoes to the bottom of a Dumpster to be lost or ruined in the muck. They become so specialized that they can see only cans and earn my contempt by passing up change, canned goods, and readily hockable items.

Can scroungers will even go through individual garbage cans, something I have never seen a scavenger do. Going through individual garbage cans without spreading litter is almost impossible, and litter is likely to reduce the public's tolerance of scavenging. But my strongest reservation about going through individual garbage cans is that this seems to me a very personal kind of invasion, one to which I would object if I were a homeowner.   22

Though Dumpsters seem somehow less personal than garbage cans, they still contain bank statements, bills, correspondence, pill bottles, and other sensitive information. I avoid trying to draw conclusions about the people who dump in the Dumpsters I frequent. I think it would be unethical to do so, although I know many people will find the idea of scavenger ethics too funny for words.   23

Occasionally a find tells a story. I once found a small paper bag containing some unused condoms, several partial tubes of flavored sexual lubricant, a partially used compact of birth control pills, and the torn pieces of a picture of a young man. Clearly, the woman was through with him and planning to give up sex altogether.   24

Dumpster things are often sad—abandoned teddy bears, shredded wedding albums, despaired-of sales kits. I find diaries and journals. College students also discard their papers; I am horrified to discover the kind of paper that now merits an A in an undergraduate course.   25

Dumpster diving is outdoor work, often surprisingly pleasant. It is not entirely predictable; things of interest turn up   26 every day, and some days there are finds of great value. I am always very pleased when I can turn up exactly the thing I most wanted to find. Yet in spite of the element of chance, scavenging, more than most other pursuits, tends to yield returns in some proportion to the effort and intelligence brought to bear.

I think of scavenging as a modern form of self-reliance.  27
After ten years of government service, where everything is geared to the lowest common denominator, I find work that rewards initiative and effort refreshing. Certainly I would be happy to have a sinecure again, but I am not heartbroken to be without one.

I find from the experience of scavenging two rather deep  28
lessons. The first is to take what I can use and let the rest go. I have come to think that there is no value in the abstract. A thing I cannot use or make useful, perhaps by trading, has no value, however fine or rare it may be. (I mean useful in the broad sense—some art, for example, I would think valuable.)

The second lesson is the transience of material being. I do  29
not suppose that ideas are immortal, but certainly they are longer-lived than material objects.

The things I find in Dumpsters, the love letters and rag  30
dolls of so many lives, remind me of this lesson. Many times in my travels I have lost everything but the clothes on my back. Now I hardly pick up a thing without envisioning the time I will cast it away. This, I think, is a healthy state of mind. Almost everything I have now has already been cast out at least once, proving that what I own is valueless to someone.

I find that my desire to grab for the gaudy bauble has been  31
largely sated. I think this is an attitude I share with the very wealthy—we both know there is plenty more where whatever we have came from. Between us are the rat-race millions who have confounded their selves with the objects they grasp and who nightly scavenge the cable channels looking for they know not what.

I am sorry for them.                                    32

## For Critical Thinking

### QUESTIONS ABOUT PURPOSE

1. Why does Eighner prefer the term *scavenging* to *scrounging* or *foraging* to characterize the process he analyzes?
2. In what ways does he demonstrate that Dumpster diving is a "sound and honorable niche"?

### QUESTIONS ABOUT AUDIENCE

1. How does Eighner anticipate his audience's reaction to his subject by presenting the "predictable stages that a person goes through in learning to scavenge"?
2. How do his "scavenger ethics" enhance his standing with his readers?

### QUESTIONS ABOUT STRATEGIES

1. How does Eighner use the example of pizza to illustrate the three principles of eating from a Dumpster?
2. How does his analysis of the process of "soda-can scrounging" help distinguish that process from the process of "scavenging"?

## For Writing and Research

1. *Analyze* how Eighner uses anecdotes to illustrate the various steps in learning to scavenge.
2. *Practice* by listing the steps by which your readers can become conscientious consumers.
3. *Argue* that Eighner's attitudes toward consumption and waste are similar to those of the wealthy.
4. *Synthesize:* Research the current solutions to homelessness. Then construct an argument for the most effective solution to the problem.

Scott Adams was born in Windham, New York, and educated at Hartwick College and the University of California at Berkeley. For more than fifteen years, Adams worked in various jobs—such as bank teller, computer programmer, financial analyst, and product manager—for Crocker National Bank and Pacific Bell. He was not happy with any of these jobs, but he was able to use his disgruntlement as the source for his popular comic strip, *Dilbert*. He has also written numerous books based on the *Dilbert Principle*—the theory that the "most ineffective workers are systematically moved to the place where they can do the least harm: management." In "How to Get a Real Education," first published in the *Wall Street Journal*, Adams uses his stories to analyze what an education in entrepreneurship should include.

I UNDERSTAND WHY the top students in America study phys-  1
ics, chemistry, calculus and classic literature. The kids in this brainy group are the future professors, scientists, thinkers and engineers who will propel civilization forward. But why do we make B students sit through these same classes? That's like trying to train your cat to do your taxes—a waste of time and money. Wouldn't it make more sense to teach B students something useful, like entrepreneurship?

I speak from experience because I majored in entrepreneur-  2
ship at Hartwick College in Oneonta, N.Y. Technically, my major was economics. But the unsung advantage of attending a small college is that you can mold your experience any way you want.

There was a small business on our campus called The   3
Coffee House. It served beer and snacks, and featured live
entertainment. It was managed by students, and it was a
money-losing mess, subsidized by the college. I thought I
could make a difference, so I applied for an opening as the
so-called Minister of Finance. I landed the job, thanks to
my impressive interviewing skills, my can-do attitude and
the fact that everyone else in the solar system had more
interesting plans.

The drinking age in those days was 18, and the entire com-   4
pensation package for the managers of The Coffee House
was free beer. That goes a long way toward explaining why
the accounting system consisted of seven students trying to
remember where all the money went. I thought we could
do better. So I proposed to my accounting professor that
for three course credits I would build and operate a proper
accounting system for the business. And so I did. It was a
great experience. Meanwhile, some of my peers were taking
courses in art history so they'd be prepared to remember what
art looked like just in case anyone asked.

One day the managers of The Coffee House had a meeting   5
to discuss two topics. First, our Minister of Employment was
recommending that we fire a bartender, who happened to be
one of my best friends. Second, we needed to choose a leader
for our group. On the first question, there was a general consensus that my friend lacked both the will and the potential
to master the bartending arts. I reluctantly voted with the
majority to fire him.

But when it came to discussing who should be our new   6
leader, I pointed out that my friend—the soon-to-be-fired
bartender—was tall, good-looking and so gifted at b.s. that
he'd be the perfect leader. By the end of the meeting I had
persuaded the group to fire the worst bartender that any of
us had ever seen . . . and ask him if he would consider being
our leader. My friend nailed the interview and became our
Commissioner. He went on to do a terrific job. That was the
year I learned everything I know about management.

At about the same time, this same friend, along with my    7
roommate and me, hatched a plan to become the student
managers of our dormitory and to get paid to do it. The
idea involved replacing all of the professional staff, including the resident assistant, security guard and even the cleaning crew, with students who would be paid to do the work.
We imagined forming a dorm government to manage elec-
tions for various jobs, set out penalties for misbehavior and
generally take care of business. And we imagined that the
three of us, being the visionaries for this scheme, would
run the show.

We pitched our entrepreneurial idea to the dean and his    8
staff. To our surprise, the dean said that if we could get a
majority of next year's dorm residents to agree to our scheme,
the college would back it.

It was a high hurdle, but a loophole made it easier to clear.    9
We only needed a majority of students who said they *planned*
to live in the dorm next year. And we had plenty of friends
who were happy to plan just about anything so long as they
could later change their minds. That's the year I learned
that if there's a loophole, someone's going to drive a truck
through it, and the people in the truck will get paid better
than the people under it.

The dean required that our first order of business in the fall    10
would be creating a dorm constitution and getting it ratified.
That sounded like a nightmare to organize. To save time, I
wrote the constitution over the summer and didn't mention it
when classes resumed. We held a constitutional convention to
collect everyone's input, and I listened to two hours of diverse
opinions. At the end of the meeting I volunteered to take on
the daunting task of crafting a document that reflected all of
the varied and sometimes conflicting opinions that had been
aired. I waited a week, made copies of the document that I
had written over the summer, presented it to the dorm as
their own ideas and watched it get approved in a landslide
vote. That was the year I learned everything I know about
getting buy-in.

For the next two years my friends and I each had a private  11
room at no cost, a base salary and the experience of managing the dorm. On some nights I also got paid to do overnight
security, while also getting paid to clean the laundry room. At
the end of my security shift I would go to The Coffee House
and balance the books.

---

*Why do we make B students sit through the
same classes as their brainy peers? That's like
trying to train your cat to do your taxes—a
waste of time and money. Wouldn't it make
sense to teach something useful instead?*

---

My college days were full of entrepreneurial stories of this  12
sort. When my friends and I couldn't get the gym to give us
space for our informal games of indoor soccer, we considered
our options. The gym's rule was that only organized groups
could reserve time. A few days later we took another run at
it, but this time we were an organized soccer club, and I was
the president. My executive duties included filling out a form
to register the club and remembering to bring the ball.

By the time I graduated, I had mastered the strange art of  13
transforming nothing into something. Every good thing that
has happened to me as an adult can be traced back to that
training. Several years later, I finished my MBA at Berkeley's
Haas School of Business. That was the fine-tuning I needed
to see the world through an entrepreneur's eyes.

If you're having a hard time imagining what an education  14
in entrepreneurship should include, allow me to prime the
pump with some lessons I've learned along the way.

**Combine Skills.** The first thing you should learn in a  15
course on entrepreneurship is how to make yourself valuable.
It's unlikely that any average student can develop a world-class

skill in one particular area. But it's easy to learn how to do several different things fairly well. I succeeded as a cartoonist with negligible art talent, some basic writing skills, an ordinary sense of humor and a bit of experience in the business world. The "Dilbert" comic is a combination of all four skills. The world has plenty of better artists, smarter writers, funnier humorists and more experienced business people. The rare part is that each of those modest skills is collected in one person. That's how value is created.

**Fail Forward.** If you're taking risks, and you probably 16 should, you can find yourself failing 90 percent of the time. The trick is to get paid while you're doing the failing and to use the experience to gain skills that will be useful later. I failed at my first career in banking. I failed at my second career with the phone company. But you'd be surprised at how many of the skills I learned in those careers can be applied to almost any field, including cartooning. Students should be taught that failure is a process, not an obstacle.

**Find the Action.** In my senior year of college I asked my 17 adviser how I should pursue my goal of being a banker. He told me to figure out where the most innovation in banking was happening and to move there. And so I did. Banking didn't work out for me, but the advice still holds: Move to where the action is. Distance is your enemy.

**Attract Luck.** You can't manage luck directly, but you 18 can manage your career in a way that makes it easier for luck to find you. To succeed, first you must *do* something. And if that doesn't work, which can be 90 percent of the time, do something else. Luck finds the doers. Readers of the *Journal* will find this point obvious. It's not obvious to a teenager.

**Conquer Fear.** I took classes in public speaking in college 19 and a few more during my corporate days. That training was marginally useful for learning how to mask nervousness in public. Then I took the Dale Carnegie course. It was life-changing. The Dale Carnegie method ignores speaking technique entirely and trains you instead to enjoy the experience of speaking to a crowd. Once you become relaxed in front of people, technique comes automatically.

Over the years, I've given speeches to hundreds of audiences and enjoyed every minute on stage. But this isn't a plug for Dale Carnegie. The point is that people can be trained to replace fear and shyness with enthusiasm. Every entrepreneur can use that skill.

**Write Simply.** I took a two-day class in business writing 20 that taught me how to write direct sentences and to avoid extra words. Simplicity makes ideas powerful. Want examples? Read anything by Steve Jobs or Warren Buffett.

**Learn Persuasion.** Students of entrepreneurship should 21 learn the art of persuasion in all its forms, including psychology, sales, marketing, negotiating, statistics, and even design. Usually those skills are sprinkled across several disciplines. For entrepreneurs, it makes sense to teach them as a package.

That's my starter list for the sort of classes that would serve 22 B students well. The list is not meant to be complete. Obviously an entrepreneur would benefit from classes in finance, management, and more.

Remember, children are our future, and the majority of 23 them are B students. If that doesn't scare you, it probably should.

## For Critical Thinking

### QUESTIONS ABOUT PURPOSE

1. How does Adams demonstrate that entrepreneurship is the best education for B students?
2. Why is it important that he explain how to transform "nothing into something"?

### QUESTIONS ABOUT AUDIENCE

1. How does Adams establish his expertise as an entrepreneur?
2. How does his characterization of "the brainy group" help identify his readers?

---

### QUESTIONS ABOUT STRATEGY

---

1. How does Adams use his college stories to illustrate that combining skills can create value?
2. How does his essay follow his own advice about writing?

## For Writing and Research

1. *Analyze* how Adams arranges the sequence of his college stories.
2. *Practice* by analyzing what you have learned from a real-world experience.
3. *Argue* that courses in a liberal arts education are or are not valuable for a career.
4. *Synthesize:* Interview the advisors in your major and in your college career center. Then use the information to analyze the steps that will give you the best preparation for your intended career.

# P. J. O'Rourke:
## Third World Driving Hints and Tips

Patrick Jake O'Rourke was born in 1947 in Toledo, Ohio, and was educated at Miami University and Johns Hopkins University. He began his writing career working for underground newspapers such as *Harry* in Baltimore before landing jobs as a feature editor and freelance writer for the *New York Herald*, executive editor for *National Lampoon*, and correspondent for *Rolling Stone* and *Atlantic Monthly*. His humorous style is showcased in *The 1964 High School Yearbook Parody* (1974), *Modern Manners: An Etiquette Book for Rude People* (1983), *The Bachelor's Home Companion: A Practical Guide to Keeping House Like a Pig* (1987), and *Holidays in Hell* (1988). O'Rourke's humor always has a political edge, evident in books such as *Republican Party Reptile: Essays and Outrages* (1987), *Give War a Chance: Eyewitness Accounts of Mankind's Struggle Against Tyranny, Injustice and Alcohol-Free Beer* (1992), *The CEO of the Sofa* (2001), *Peace Kills: America's Fun New Imperialism* (2004), *Driving Like Crazy* (2009), and *Don't Vote—It Just Encourages the Bastards* (2010). In "Third World Driving Hints and Tips," reprinted from *Holidays in Hell*, O'Rourke analyzes the rules of the road for driving in a different country.

DURING THE PAST couple of years I've had to do my share 1 of driving in the Third World—in Mexico, Lebanon, the Philippines, Cyprus, El Salvador, Africa, and Italy. (Italy is not technically part of the Third World, but no one has told the Italians.) I don't pretend to be an expert, but I have been

making notes. Maybe these notes will be useful to readers
who are planning to do something really stupid with their
Hertz #1 Club cards.


## ROAD HAZARDS

What would be a road hazard anywhere else, in the Third   2
World is probably the road. There are two techniques for coping with this. One is to drive very fast so your wheels "get on
top" of the ruts and your car sails over the ditches and gullies.
Predictably, this will result in disaster. The other technique is
to drive very slowly. This will also result in disaster. No matter
how slowly you drive into a ten-foot hole, you're still going to
get hurt. You'll find the locals themselves can't make up their
minds. Either they drive at 2 m.p.h.—which they do every
time there's absolutely no way to get around them. Or else
they drive at 100 m.p.h.—which they do coming right at you
when you finally get a chance to pass the guy going 2 m.p.h.

---

*Never look where you're going—you'll only
scare yourself.*

---

## BASIC INFORMATION

It's important to have your facts straight before you begin   3
piloting a car around an underdeveloped country. For
instance, which side of the road do they drive on? This is easy.
They drive on your side. That is, you can depend on it, any
oncoming traffic will be on your side of the road. Also, how
do you translate kilometres into miles? Most people don't
know this, but one kilometre = ten miles, exactly. True, a
kilometre is only 62 per cent of a mile, but if something is
one hundred kilometres away, read that as one thousand miles

because the roads are 620 percent worse than anything you've ever seen. And when you see a 50-k.p.h. speed limit, you might as well figure that means 500 *m.p.h.* because nobody cares. The Third World does not have Broderick Crawford and the Highway Patrol. Outside the cities, it doesn't have many police at all. Law enforcement is in the hands of the army. And soldiers, if they feel like it, will shoot you no matter what speed you're going.

## TRAFFIC SIGNS AND SIGNALS

Most developing nations use international traffic symbols. 4 Americans may find themselves perplexed by road signs that look like Boy Scout merit badges and by such things as an iguana silhouette with a red diagonal bar across it. Don't worry, the natives don't know what they mean, either. The natives do, however, have an elaborate set of signals used to convey information to the traffic around them. For example, if you're trying to pass someone and he blinks his left turn signal, it means go ahead. Either that or it means a large truck is coming around the bend, and you'll get killed if you try. You'll find out in a moment.

Signalling is further complicated by festive decorations 5 found on many vehicles. It can be hard to tell a hazard flasher from a string of Christmas-tree lights wrapped around the bumper, and brake lights can easily be confused with the dozen red Jesus statuettes and the ten stuffed animals with blinking eyes on the package shelf.

## DANGEROUS CURVES

Dangerous curves are marked, at least in Christian lands, 6 by white wooden crosses positioned to make the curves even more dangerous. These crosses are memorials to people who've died in traffic accidents, and they give a rough statistical indication of how much trouble you're likely to have at that spot in the road. Thus, when you come through a curve in a full-power slide and are suddenly confronted with a veritable forest of crucifixes, you know you're dead.

## LEARNING TO DRIVE LIKE A NATIVE

It's important to understand that in the Third World most 7 driving is done with the horn, or "Egyptian Brake Pedal," as it is known. There is a precise and complicated etiquette of horn use. Honk your horn only under the following circumstances:

1. When anything blocks the road.
2. When anything doesn't.
3. When anything might.
4. At red lights.
5. At green lights.
6. At all other times.

## ROAD-BLOCKS

One thing you can count on in Third World countries is trou- 8 ble. There's always some uprising, coup or Marxist insurrection going on, and this means military road-blocks. There are two kinds of military road-block, the kind where you slow down so they can look you over, and the kind where you come to a full stop so they can steal your luggage. The important thing is that you must *never* stop at the slow-down kind of road-block. If you stop, they'll think you're a terrorist about to attack them, and they'll shoot you. And you must *always* stop at the full-stop kind of road-block. If you just slow down, they'll think you're a terrorist about to attack them, and they'll shoot you. How do you tell the difference between the two kinds of road-block? Here's the fun part: you can't!

(The terrorists, of course, have road-blocks of their own. 9 They always make you stop. Sometimes with land mines.)

## ANIMALS IN THE RIGHT OF WAY

As a rule of thumb, you should slow down for donkeys, speed [10] up for goats and stop for cows. Donkeys will get out of your way eventually, and so will pedestrians. But never actually stop for either of them or they'll take advantage, especially the pedestrians. If you stop in the middle of a crowd of Third World pedestrians, you'll be there buying Chiclets and bogus antiquities for days.

Drive like hell through the goats. It's almost impossible to hit [11] a goat. On the other hand, it's almost impossible *not* to hit a cow. Cows are immune to horn-honking, shouting, swats with sticks and taps on the hind quarters with the bumper. The only thing you can do to make a cow move is swerve to avoid it, which will make the cow move in front of you with lightning speed.

Actually, the most dangerous animals are the chickens. In [12] the United States, when you see a ball roll into the street, you hit your brakes because you know the next thing you'll see is a kid chasing it. In the Third World, it's not balls the kids are chasing, but chickens. Are they practising punt returns with a leghorn? Dribbling it? Playing stick-hen? I don't know. But Third Worlders are remarkably fond of their chickens and, also, their children (population problems not withstanding). If you hit one or both, they may survive. But you will not.

## ACCIDENTS

Never look where you're going—you'll only scare yourself. [13] Nonetheless, try to avoid collisions. There are bound to be more people in that bus, truck or even on that moped than there are in your car. At best you'll be screamed deaf. And if the police do happen to be around, standard procedure is to throw everyone in jail regardless of fault. This is done to forestall blood feuds, which are a popular hobby in many of these places. Remember the American consul is very busy fretting about that Marxist insurrection, and it may be months before he comes to visit.

If you do have an accident, the only thing to do is go on [14] the offensive. Throw big wads of American money at everyone, and hope for the best.

SAFETY TIPS

One nice thing about the Third World, you don't have to   15
fasten your safety belt. (Or stop smoking. Or cut down on
saturated fats.) It takes a lot off your mind when average life
expectancy is forty-five minutes.

## For Critical Thinking

### QUESTIONS ABOUT PURPOSE

1. How do O'Rourke's travels establish his credentials to provide
   advice to drivers?
2. At what point in the essay do you realize that his purpose is to
   entertain rather than inform?

### QUESTIONS ABOUT AUDIENCE

1. How does O'Rourke identify his readers when he refers to
   "Hertz #1 Club cards" and "big wads of American money"?
2. How might the "natives" referred to in this essay respond to his
   characterization of their driving habits?

### QUESTIONS ABOUT STRATEGIES

1. How does O'Rourke's analysis of the "Egyptian Brake Pedal"
   reveal that his hints are not really meant to inform?
2. How does his discussion of "animals in the right of way" and
   children complicate his analysis?

## For Writing and Research

1. *Analyze* how O'Rourke arranges the sequence of his "driving
   hints and tips."
2. *Practice* by analyzing the process by which you learned to drive.
3. *Argue* that O'Rourke's use of the words *Third World* and *underdeveloped* suggests an attitude of smug cultural superiority.
4. *Synthesize:* Interview driving instructors and police officers in
   your hometown. Then use this information to analyze the driving habits they have encountered.

Elizabeth Winthrop was born in 1948 in Washington, D.C., and educated at Sarah Lawrence College. She worked for Harper and Row editing Harper Junior Books before she began her own career as author of books for children. She has written more than 30 such books, including *Bunk Beds* (1972), *Potbellied Possums* (1977), *In My Mother's House* (1988), *The Battle for the Castle* (1993), and *As the Crow Flies* (1998). Her latest novel is *Counting on Grace* (2006) that focuses on the problem of child labor in the early years of the twentieth century. Winthrop has twice won the PEN Syndicated Fiction Contest, once in 1985 with her story "Bad News" and again in 1990 with "The Golden Darters." In the latter story, reprinted from *American Short Fiction*, a young girl betrays her father by using their creation for the wrong purpose.

I WAS TWELVE years old when my father started tying flies. 1
It was an odd habit for a man who had just undergone a serious operation on his upper back, but, as he remarked to my mother one night, at least it gave him a world over which he had some control.

The family grew used to seeing him hunched down close to 2
his tying vise, hackle pliers in one hand, thread bobbin in the other. We began to bandy about strange phrases—foxy quills, bodkins, peacock hurl. Father's corner of the living room was off limits to the maid with the voracious and destructive vacuum cleaner. Who knew what precious bit of calf's tail or rabbit fur would be sucked away never to be seen again?

Because of my father's illness, we had gone up to our sum-  3
mer cottage on the lake in New Hampshire a month early.
None of my gang of friends ever came till the end of July, so in
the beginning of that summer I hung around home watching
my father as he fussed with the flies. I was the only child he
allowed to stand near him while he worked. "Your brothers
bounce," he muttered one day as he clamped the vise onto
the curve of a model-perfect hook. "You can stay and watch
if you don't bounce."

So I took great care not to bounce or lean or even breathe  4
too noisily on him while he performed his delicate maneuvers,
holding back hackle with one hand as he pulled off the final
flourish of a whip finish with the other. I had never been so
close to my father for so long before, and while he studied his
tiny creations, I studied him. I stared at the large pores of his
skin, the sleek black hair brushed straight back from the soft
dip of his temples, the jaw muscles tightening and slackening.
Something in my father seemed always to be ticking. He did
not take well to sickness and enforced confinement.

When he leaned over his work, his shirt collar slipped down  5
to reveal the recent scar, a jagged trail of disrupted tissue. The
tender pink skin gradually paled and then toughened during
those weeks when he took his prescribed afternoon nap, lying
on his stomach on our little patch of front lawn. Our house
was one of the closest to the lake and it seemed to embarrass
my mother to have him stretch himself out on the grass for
all the swimmers and boaters to see.

"At least sleep on the porch," she would say. "That's why  6
we set the hammock up there."

"Why shouldn't a man sleep on his own front lawn if he so  7
chooses?" he would reply. "I have to mow the bloody thing.
I might as well put it to some use."

And my mother would shrug and give up.                    8

At the table when he was absorbed, he lost all sense of any-  9
thing but the magnified insect under the light. Often when
he pushed his chair back and announced the completion of
his latest project to the family, there would be a bit of down
or a tuft of dubbing stuck to the edge of his lip. I did not

tell him about it but stared, fascinated, wondering how long it would take to blow away. Sometimes it never did, and I imagine he discovered the fluff in the bathroom mirror when he went upstairs to bed. Or maybe my mother plucked it off with one of those proprietary gestures of hers that irritated my brothers so much.

In the beginning, Father wasn't very good at the fly-tying. 10 He was a large, thick-boned man with sweeping gestures, a robust laugh, and a sudden terrifying temper. If he had not loved fishing so much, I doubt he would have persevered with the fussy business of the flies. After all, the job required tools normally associated with woman's work. Thread and bobbins, soft slippery feathers, a magnifying glass, and an instruction manual that read like a cookbook. It said things like, "Cut off a bunch of yellowtail. Hold the tip end with the left hand and stroke out the short hairs."

But Father must have had a goal in mind. You tie flies 11 because one day, in the not-too-distant future, you will attach them to a tippet, wade into a stream, and lure a rainbow trout out of his quiet pool.

There was something endearing, almost childish, about 12 his stubborn nightly ritual at the corner table. His head bent under the standing lamp, his fingers trembling slightly, he would whisper encouragement to himself, talk his way through some particularly delicate operation. Once or twice I caught my mother gazing silently across my brothers' heads at him. When our eyes met, she would turn away and busy herself in the kitchen.

Finally, one night, after weeks of allowing me to watch, he 13 told me to take his seat. "Why, Father?"

"Because it's time for you to try one." 14

"That's all right. I like to watch." 15

"Nonsense, Emily. You'll do just fine." 16

He had stood up. The chair was waiting. Across the room, 17 my mother put down her knitting. Even the boys, embroiled in a noisy game of double solitaire, stopped their wrangling for a moment. They were all waiting to see what I would do. It was my fear of failing him that made me hesitate. I knew that my father put his trust in results, not in the learning process.

"Sit down, Emily."                                                    18

I obeyed, my heart pounding. I was a cautious, secretive  19
child, and I could not bear to have people watch me doing
things. My piano lesson was the hardest hour in the week.
The teacher would sit with a resigned look on her face while
my fingers groped across the keys, muddling through a sonata
that I had played perfectly just an hour before. The difference
was that then nobody had been watching.

"—so we'll start you off with a big hook." He had been  20
talking for some time. How much had I missed already?

"Ready?" he asked.                                                   21

I nodded.                                                            22

"All right then, clamp this hook into the vise. You'll be  23
making the golden darter, a streamer. A big flashy fly, the kind
that imitates a small fish as it moves underwater."

Across the room, my brothers had returned to their game,  24
but their voices were subdued. I imagined they wanted to hear
what was happening to me. My mother had left the room.

"Tilt the magnifying glass so you have a good view of the  25
hook. Right. Now tie on with the bobbin thread."

It took me three tries to line the thread up properly on the  26
hook, each silken line nesting next to its neighbor. "We're
going to do it right, Emily, no matter how long it takes."

"It's hard," I said quietly.                                         27

Slowly I grew used to the tiny tools, to the oddly enlarged  28
view of my fingers through the magnifying glass. They looked
as if they didn't belong to me anymore. The feeling in their
tips was too small for their large, clumsy movements. Despite
my father's repeated warnings, I nicked the floss once against
the barbed hook. Luckily it did not give way.

"It's Emily's bedtime," my mother called from the kitchen.  29

"Hush, she's tying in the throat. Don't bother us now."  30

I could feel his breath on my neck. The mallard barbules  31
were stubborn, curling into the hook in the wrong direction.
Behind me, I sensed my father's fingers twisting in imitation
of my own.

"You've almost got it," he whispered, his lips barely mov-  32
ing. "That's right. Keep the thread slack until you're all the
way around."

I must have tightened it too quickly. I lost control of the  33
feathers in my left hand, the clumsier one. First the gold mylar
came unwound and then the yellow floss.

"Damn it all, now look what you've done," he roared, and  34
for a second I wondered whether he was talking to me. He
sounded as if he were talking to a grown-up. He sounded
the way he had just the night before when an antique tea cup
had slipped through my mother's soapy fingers and shattered
against the hard surface of the sink. I sat back slowly, rest-
ing my aching spine against the chair for the first time since
we'd begun.

"Leave it for now, Gerald," my mother said tentatively  35
from the kitchen. Out of the corner of my eye, I could see
her sponging the kitchen counter with small, defiant sweeps
of her hand. "She can try again tomorrow."

"What happened?" called a brother. They both started  36
across the room toward us but stopped at a look from my
father.

"We'll start again," he said, his voice once more under  37
control. "Best way to learn. Get back on the horse."

With a flick of his hand, he loosened the vise, removed my  38
hook, and threw it into the wastepaper basket.

"From the beginning?" I whispered.  39

"Of course," he replied. "There's no way to rescue a mess  40
like that."

My mess had taken almost an hour to create.  41

"Gerald," my mother said again. "Don't you think—"  42

"How can we possibly work with all these interruptions?"  43
he thundered. I flinched as if he had hit me. "Go on upstairs,
all of you. Emily and I will be up when we're done. Go on,
for God's sake. Stop staring at us."

At a signal from my mother, the boys backed slowly away  44
and crept up to their room. She followed them. I felt all alone,
as trapped under my father's piercing gaze as the hook in the
grip of its vise.

We started again. This time my fingers were trembling so  45
much that I ruined three badger hackle feathers, stripping off
the useless webbing at the tip. My father did not lose his temper again. His voice dropped to an even, controlled mono-
tone that scared me more than his shouting. After an hour of
painstaking labor, we reached the same point with the stubborn mallard feathers curling into the hook. Once, twice, I
repinched them under the throat, but each time they slipped
away from me. Without a word, my father stood up and leaned
over me. With his cheek pressed against my hair, he reached
both hands around and took my fingers in his. I longed to
surrender the tools to him and slide away off the chair, but we
were so close to the end. He captured the curling stem with
the thread and trapped it in place with three quick wraps.

"Take your hands away carefully," he said. "I'll do the whip  46
finish. We don't want to risk losing it now."

I did as I was told, sat motionless with his arms around me,  47
my head tilted slightly to the side so he could have the clear
view through the magnifying glass. He cemented the head,
wiped the excess glue from the eye with a waste feather, and
hung my golden darter on the tackle box handle to dry. When
at last he pulled away, I breathlessly slid my body back against
the chair. I was still conscious of the havoc my clumsy hands
or an unexpected sneeze could wreak on the table, which was
cluttered with feathers and bits of fur.

"Now, that's the fly you tied, Emily. Isn't it beautiful?"  48
I nodded. "Yes, Father."  49
"Tomorrow, we'll do another one. An olive grouse. Smaller  50
hook but much less complicated body. Look. I'll show you
in the book."

As I waited to be released from the chair, I didn't think  51
he meant it. He was just trying to apologize for having lost
his temper, I told myself, just trying to pretend that our time
together had been wonderful. But the next morning when I
came down, late for breakfast, he was waiting for me with the
materials for the olive grouse already assembled. He was ready
to start in again, to take charge of my clumsy fingers with his
voice and talk them through the steps.

That first time was the worst, but I never felt comfortable 52
at the fly-tying table with Father's breath tickling the hair on
my neck. I completed the olive grouse, another golden darter
to match the first, two muddler minnows, and some others. I
don't remember all the names anymore.

Once I hid upstairs, pretending to be immersed in my sum- 53
mer reading books, but he came looking for me.

"Emily," he called. "Come on down. Today we'll start the 54
lead-winged coachman. I've got everything set up for you."

I lay very still and did not answer. 55

"Gerald," I heard my mother say. "Leave the child alone. 56
You're driving her crazy with those flies."

"Nonsense," he said, and started up the dark, wooden 57
stairs, one heavy step at a time.

I put my book down and rolled slowly off the bed so that 58
by the time he reached the door of my room, I was on my
feet, ready to be led back downstairs to the table.

Although we never spoke about it, my mother became 59
oddly insistent that I join her on trips to the library or the
general store.

"Are you going out again, Emily?" my father would call 60
after me. "I was hoping we'd get some work done on this
minnow."

"I'll be back soon, Father," I'd say. "I promise." 61

"Be sure you do," he said. 62

And for a while I did. 63

Then at the end of July, my old crowd of friends from 64
across the lake began to gather and I slipped away to join
them early in the morning before my father got up.

The girls were a gang. When we were all younger, we'd 65
held bicycle relay races on the ring road and played down at
the lakeside together under the watchful eyes of our mothers.
Every July, we threw ourselves joyfully back into each other's
lives. That summer we talked about boys and smoked illicit
cigarettes in Randy Kidd's basement and held leg-shaving
parties in her bedroom behind a safely locked door. Randy
was the ringleader. She was the one who suggested we pierce
our ears.

"My parents would die," I said. "They told me I'm not   66
allowed to pierce my ears until I'm seventeen."

"Your hair's so long, they won't even notice," Randy said.   67
"My sister will do it for us. She pierces all her friends' ears at
college."

In the end, only one girl pulled out. The rest of us sat in   68
a row with the obligatory ice cubes held to our ears, waiting
for the painful stab of the sterilized needle.

Randy was right. At first my parents didn't notice. Even   69
when my ears became infected, I didn't tell them. All alone in
my room, I went through the painful procedure of twisting
the gold studs and swabbing the recent wounds with alcohol.
Then on the night of the club dance, when I had changed
my clothes three times and played with my hair in front of
the mirror for hours, I came across the small plastic box with
dividers in my top bureau drawer. My father had given it to
me so that I could keep my flies in separate compartments,
untangled from one another. I poked my finger in and slid
one of the golden darters up along its plastic wall. When
I held it up, the mylar thread sparkled in the light like a
jewel. I took out the other darter, hammered down the barbs
of the two hooks, and slipped them into the raw holes in
my earlobes.

Someone's mother drove us all to the dance, and Randy   70
and I pushed through the side door into the ladies' room. I
put my hair up in a ponytail so the feathered flies could twist
and dangle above my shoulders. I liked the way they made
me look—free and different and dangerous, even. And they
made Randy notice.

"I've never seen earrings like that," Randy said. "Where   71
did you get them?"

"I made them with my father. They're flies. You know, for   72
fishing."

"They're great. Can you make me some?"   73

I hesitated. "I have some others at home I can give you,"   74
I said at last. "They're in a box in my bureau."

"Can you give them to me tomorrow?" she asked.   75

"Sure," I said with a smile. Randy had never noticed any- 76
thing I'd worn before. I went out to the dance floor, swinging
my ponytail in time to the music.

My mother noticed the earrings as soon as I got home. 77

"What has gotten into you, Emily? You know you were 78
forbidden to pierce your ears until you were in college. This
is appalling."

I didn't answer. My father was sitting in his chair behind 79
the fly-tying table. His back was better by that time, but he
still spent most of his waking hours in that chair. It was as if
he didn't like to be too far away from his flies, as if something
might blow away if he weren't keeping watch.

I saw him look up when my mother started in with me. His 80
hands drifted ever so slowly down to the surface of the table
as I came across the room toward him. I leaned over so that
he could see my earrings better in the light.

"Everybody loved them, Father. Randy says she wants a 81
pair, too. I'm going to give her the muddler minnows."

"I can't believe you did this, Emily," my mother said in a 82
loud, nervous voice. "It makes you look so cheap."

"They don't make me look cheap, do they, Father?" I 83
swung my head so he could see how they bounced, and my
hip accidentally brushed the table. A bit of rabbit fur floated
up from its pile and hung in the air for a moment before it
settled down on top of the foxy quills.

"For God's sake, Gerald, speak to her," my mother said 84
from her corner.

He stared at me for a long moment as if he didn't know 85
who I was anymore, as if I were a trusted associate who had
committed some treacherous and unspeakable act. "That is
not the purpose for which the flies were intended," he said.

"Oh, I know that," I said quickly. "But they look good this 86
way, don't they?"

He stood up and considered me in silence for a long time 87
across the top of the table lamp.

"No, they don't," he finally said. "They're hanging upside 88
down."

Then he turned off the light and I couldn't see his face  89
anymore.

## COMMENT ON "THE GOLDEN DARTERS"

"The Golden Darters" questions the purpose of learning a
particular process. Emily's father decides to tie fishing flies
to help him recuperate from back surgery. Although he is
clumsy at first, he masters the tools, the procedure, and the
artistry of tying. He has a goal in mind—to "attach [the flies]
to a tippet, wade into a stream, and lure a rainbow trout out
of his quiet pool." Emily's father decides to teach her what
he has learned, even though his presence makes her nervous
and her mistakes complicate the work process. Emily eventually escapes his obsession and joins her girlfriends to learn
other procedures—smoking, leg shaving, ear piercing. The
last procedure enables Emily to experiment—to wear two
yellow darters as earrings to the club dance. Although she
dazzles her friends, she disappoints her father, who sees her
experiment as a betrayal.

# CHAPTER 3

# *Comparison and Contrast*

Technically speaking, when you **compare** two or more things, you're looking for similarities; when you **contrast** them, you're looking for differences. In practice, of course, the operations are opposite sides of the same coin, and one implies the other. When you look for what's similar, you will also notice what is different. You can compare things at all levels, from the trivial (plaid shoelaces and plain ones) to the really serious (the differences between a career in medicine and one in advertising). Often when you compare things at a serious level, you do so to make a choice. That's why it's helpful to know how to organize your thinking so that you can analyze similarities and differences in a systematic, useful way that brings out significant differences. It's particularly helpful to have such a system when you are going to write a comparison-and-contrast essay.

## PURPOSE

You can take two approaches to writing comparison-and-contrast essays; each has a different purpose. You can make a *strict* comparison, exploring the relationship between things in the same class, or you can do a *fanciful* comparison, looking at the relationship among things from different classes.

When you write a *strict* comparison, you compare only things that are truly alike—actors with actors, musicians with musicians, but *not* actors with musicians. You're trying to find similar information about both your subjects. For instance, what are the characteristics of actors; are they movie or stage actors? How are jazz musicians and classical musicians alike, even if their music is quite different? In a strict comparison, you probably also want to show how two things in the same class are different in important ways. Often when you focus your comparison on differences, you do so to make a judgment and, finally, a choice. That's one of the main reasons people make comparisons, whether they're shopping or writing.

When you write a *fanciful* comparison, you try to set up an imaginative, illuminating comparison between two things that don't seem at all alike, and you do it for a definite reason: to help explain and clarify a complex idea. For instance, the human heart is often compared to a pump—a fanciful and useful comparison that enables one to envision the heart at work. You can use similar fanciful comparisons to help your readers see new dimensions to events. For instance, you can compare the astronauts landing on the moon to Columbus discovering the New World, or you can compare the increased drug use among young people to an epidemic spreading through part of our culture.

You may find it difficult to construct an entire essay around a fanciful comparison—such attempts tax the most creative energy and can quickly break down. Probably you can use this method of comparison most effectively as a device for enlivening your writing and highlighting dramatic similarities. When you're drawing fanciful comparisons, you're not very likely to be comparing to make judgments or recommend choices. Instead, your purpose in writing a fanciful comparison is to catch your readers' attention and show new connections between unlike things.

## AUDIENCE

As you plan a comparison-and-contrast essay, think ahead about what your readers already know and what they're going to expect. First, ask yourself what they know about the items or ideas you're going to compare. Do they know a good deal about both—for instance, two popular television programs? Do they know very little about either item—for instance, Buddhism and Shintoism? Or do they know quite a bit about one but little about the other—for instance, football and rugby?

If you're confident that your readers know a lot about both items (television programs), you can spend a little time pointing out similarities and concentrate on your reasons for making the comparison. When readers know little about either (Eastern religions), you'll have to define each, using concepts they are familiar with, before you can point out important contrasts. If readers know only one item in a pair (football and rugby), then use the known to explain the unknown. Emphasize what is familiar to them about football, and explain how rugby is like it but also how it is different.

As you think about what your readers need, remember that they want your essay to be fairly balanced, not 90 percent about Buddhism and 10 percent about Shintoism, or two paragraphs about football and nine or ten about rugby. When your focus seems so unevenly divided, you appear to be using one element in the comparison only as a springboard to talk about the other. Such an imbalance can disappoint your readers, who expect to learn about both.

## STRATEGIES

You can use two basic strategies for organizing a comparison-and-contrast essay. The first is the *divided*, or *subject-by-subject*, pattern. The second is the *alternating*, or *point-by-point*, pattern.

When you use the *divided* pattern, you present all your information on one topic before you bring in information on the other topic. Mark Twain uses this method in "Two Views of the River." First he gives an apprentice's poetic view, emphasizing the beauty of the river; then he gives the pilot's practical view, emphasizing the technical problems the river poses.

When you use the *alternating* pattern, you work your way through the comparison point by point, giving information first on one aspect of the topic, then on the other. If Twain had used an alternating pattern, he would have given the apprentice's poetic view of a particular feature of the river, then the pilot's pragmatic view of that same feature. He would have followed that pattern throughout, commenting on each feature—the wind, the surface of the river, the sunset, the color of the water—by alternating between the apprentice's and the pilot's points of view.

Although both methods are useful, you'll find that each has benefits and drawbacks. The divided pattern lets you present each part of your essay as a satisfying whole. It works especially well in short essays, such as Twain's, where you're presenting only two facets of a topic and your reader can easily keep track of the points you want to make. Its drawback is that sometimes you slip into writing what seems like two separate essays. When you're writing a long comparison essay about a complex topic, you may have trouble organizing your material clearly enough to keep your readers on track.

The alternating pattern works well when you want to show the two subjects you're comparing side by side, emphasizing the points you're comparing. You'll find it particularly good for longer essays, such as Bruce Catton's "Grant and Lee: A Study in Contrasts," when you show many complex points of comparison and need to help your readers see how those points match up. The drawback of the alternating pattern is that you may reduce your analysis to an exercise. If you use it for making only a few points of comparison in a short essay on a simple topic, your essay sounds choppy and disconnected, like a simple list.

Often you can make the best of both worlds by *combining strategies*. For example, you can start out using a divided pattern to give an overall, unified view of the topics you're going to compare. Then you can shift to an alternating pattern to show how many points of comparison you've found between your subjects. Bruce Catton uses a version of this strategy in "Grant and Lee: A Study in Contrasts" when he presents biographical sketches of Lee and then Grant before he combines his analysis of both men. Howard Moody uses a version of this strategy in "Sacred Rite or Civil Right?" when he presents the amazing diversity of religious views on marriage before he presents an alternating analysis between a religious and a secular definition of marriage.

When you want to write a good comparison-and-contrast analysis, keep three guidelines in mind: (1) *balance parts,* (2) *include reminders, and* (3) *supply reasons.* Look, for example, at how Twain reminds his readers what the visible charms of the river mean to the riverboat pilot, and how Howard Moody places his comparison in the midst of a national debate on the nature of marriage. Catton uses a similar strategy when he contrasts the lives of Robert E. Lee and Ulysses S. Grant.

## COMPARISON AND CONTRAST

### Points to Remember

1. Decide whether you want the pattern of your comparison to focus on complete units (*divided*) or specific features (*alternating*).
2. Consider the possibility of combining the two patterns.
3. Determine which subject should be placed in the first position and why.
4. Arrange the points of your comparison in a logical, balanced, and dramatic sequence.
5. Make sure you introduce and clarify the reasons for making your comparison.

SuperStock/Getty Images

*Raising the American flag on Iwa Jima.*

*Joseph Rosenthal (1911–2006) took this iconic picture of U.S. soldiers raising the American flag on Mount Suribaci on February 23, 1945, during one of the fiercest battles (February 19 to March 25, 1945) in the War of the Pacific in World War II.*

Peter Turnley/Corbis News/Corbis

*Peter Turnley (1955–) captured this picture of rescue workers raising the American flag at Ground Zero on September 20, 2001, after the terrorist attack on the World Trade Center on 9/11.*

*Select two photographs taken of the same historic event. Then explain why your pictures are worth a thousand words or why it takes a thousand words to explain them.*

Mark Twain (the pen name of Samuel Clemens, 1835–1910) was born in Florida, Missouri, and grew up in the river town of Hannibal, Missouri, where he watched the comings and goings of the steamboats he would eventually pilot. Twain spent his young adult life working as a printer, a pilot on the Mississippi, and a frontier journalist. After the Civil War, he began a career as a humorist and storyteller, writing such classics as *The Adventures of Tom Sawyer* (1876), *Life on the Mississippi* (1883), *The Adventures of Huckleberry Finn* (1884), and *A Connecticut Yankee in King Arthur's Court* (1889). His place in American writing was best characterized by editor William Dean Howells, who called Twain the "Lincoln of our literature." In "Two Views of the River," taken from *Life on the Mississippi*, Twain compares the way he saw the river as an innocent apprentice to the way he saw it as an experienced pilot.

NOW WHEN I had mastered the language of this water, 1 and had come to know every trifling feature that bordered the great river as familiarly as I knew the letters of the alphabet, I had made a valuable acquisition. But I had lost something, too. I had lost something which could never be restored to me while I lived. All the grace, the beauty, the poetry, had gone out of the majestic river! I still keep in mind a certain wonderful sunset which I witnessed when steamboating was new to me. A broad expanse of the river was turned to blood; in the middle distance the red hue brightened into gold, through which a solitary log came floating black and conspicuous; in one place a long, slanting mark lay sparkling upon the water; in another the surface was broken by boiling, tumbling rings that were as many-tinted as an opal; where the ruddy flush was faintest, was a smooth spot that was covered with graceful circles and radiating lines, ever so delicately traced; the shore on our left was densely wooded, and the somber shadow that fell from this forest was broken in one place by a long, ruffled trail that shone like silver; and high above the forest wall a clean-stemmed dead tree waved a single leafy bough that glowed like a flame in the unobstructed splendor that was flowing from the sun. There were graceful curves, reflected images, woody heights, soft distances; and over the whole scene, far and near, the dissolving lights drifted steadily, enriching it every passing moment with new marvels of coloring.

---

*When I mastered the language of this water,*
*. . . I had made a valuable acquisition.*
*But I had lost something too.*

---

     I stood like one bewitched. I drank it in, in a speechless    2
rapture. The world was new to me, and I had never seen anything like this at home. But as I have said, a day came when I began to cease from noting the glories and the charms which the moon and the sun and the twilight wrought upon the river's face; another day came when I ceased altogether to note them. Then, if that sunset scene had been repeated, I should have looked upon it without rapture, and should have commented upon it, inwardly, after this fashion: "This sun means that we are going to have wind tomorrow; that floating log means that the river is rising, small thanks to it; that slanting mark on the water refers to a bluff reef which is going to kill somebody's steamboat one of these nights, if it keeps on stretching out like that; those tumbling 'boils' show a dissolving bar and a changing channel there; the lines

and circles in the slick water over yonder are a warning that that troublesome place is shoaling up dangerously; that silver streak in the shadow of the forest is the 'break' from a new snag, and he has located himself in the very best place he could have found to fish for steamboats; that tall dead tree, with a single living branch, is not going to last long, and then how is a body ever going to get through this blind place at night without the friendly old landmark?"

No, the romance and beauty were all gone from the river.   3 All the value any feature of it had for me now was the amount of usefulness it could furnish toward compassing the safe piloting of a steamboat. Since those days, I have pitied doctors from my heart. What does the lovely flush in a beauty's cheek mean to a doctor but a "break" that ripples above some deadly disease? Are not all her visible charms sown thick with what are to him the signs and symbols of hidden decay? Does he ever see her beauty at all, or doesn't he simply view her professionally, and comment upon her unwholesome condition all to himself? And doesn't he sometimes wonder whether he has gained most or lost most by learning his trade?

## For Critical Thinking

### QUESTIONS ABOUT PURPOSE

1. What does Twain think he has gained and lost by learning the river?
2. What does Twain accomplish by *dividing* the two views of the river rather than *alternating* them beneath several headings?

### QUESTIONS ABOUT AUDIENCE

1. Which attitude—poetic or pragmatic—does Twain anticipate his readers have toward the river? Explain your answer.
2. How does he expect his readers to answer the questions he raises in paragraph 3?

## QUESTIONS ABOUT STRATEGIES

1. What sequence does Twain use to arrange the points of his comparison?
2. Where does Twain use transitional phrases and sentences to match up the parts of his comparison?

## *For Writing and Research*

1. **Analyze** the strategies Twain uses to compare and contrast his two views of the river.
2. **Practice** by describing your reactions to a special place in your childhood and then comparing the way you respond to it now.
3. **Argue** that learning too much about the technical details of a process—such as painting or singing—destroys one's ability to appreciate its beauty.
4. **Synthesize** your knowledge of Twain's life and writing. Then use this evidence to argue that creative achievement depends on the willingness to take risks.

Howard Moody was born in 1921 in Dallas, Texas, and was educated at the University of California and Yale Divinity School. He served as the chaplain at The Ohio State University before becoming the senior minister at the Judson Memorial Church in New York City, where he devoted much of his time to working with the inhabitants of Greenwich Village. A book written about his time at this church is entitled *A Voice in the Village: A Journey of a Pastor and a People* (2009). He was also active in many social causes, especially the abortion rights movement. Together with Arlene Carmen, he wrote two books on abortion rights and prostitution. His essays are collected in *The God-Man of Galilee: Studies in Christian Living* (1983). In "Sacred Rite or Civil Right?" Moody examines the various definitions of marriage.

I F MEMBERS OF the church that I served for more than three 1
decades were told I would be writing an article in defense of marriage they wouldn't believe it. My reputation was that when people came to me for counsel about getting married I tried to talk them out of it. More about that later.

We are now in the midst of a national debate on the nature 2
of marriage, and it promises to be as emotional and polemical as the issues of abortion and homosexuality have been over the past century. What all these debates have in common is that they involved both the laws of the state and the theology of the church. The purpose of this writing is to suggest that the gay-marriage debate is less about the legitimacy of the loving relationship of a same-sex couple than about the relationship of church and state and how they define marriage.

In Western civilization, the faith and beliefs of Christendom  3
played a major role in shaping the laws regarding social
relations and moral behavior. Having been nurtured in the
Christian faith from childhood and having served a lifetime
as an ordained Baptist minister, I feel obligated first to
address the religious controversy concerning the nature of
marriage. If we look at the history of religious institutions
regarding marriage we will find not much unanimity but
amazing diversity—it is really a mixed bag. Those who base
their position on "tradition" or "what the Bible says" will find
anything but clarity. It depends on which "tradition" in what
age reading from whose holy scriptures.

*In order to fully understand the conflict that
has arisen in this debate over the nature of
marriage, it is important to understand the
difference between the religious definition
of marriage and the state's secular and
civil definition.*

In the early tradition of the Jewish people, there were mul-  4
tiple wives and not all of them equal. Remember the story of
Abraham's wives, Sara and Hagar. Sara couldn't get pregnant,
so Hagar presented Abraham with a son. When Sara got angry
with Hagar, she forced Abraham to send Hagar and her son
Ishmael into the wilderness. In case Christians feel superior
about their "tradition" of marriage, I would remind them
that their scriptural basis is not as clear about marriage as we
might hope. We have Saint Paul's conflicting and condescending words about the institution: "It's better not to marry."
Karl Barth called this passage the Magna Carta of the single
person. (Maybe we should have taken Saint Paul's advice
more seriously. It might have prevented an earlier generation

of parents from harassing, cajoling and prodding our young until they were married.) In certain religious branches, the church doesn't recognize the licensed legality of marriage but requires that persons meet certain religious qualifications before the marriage is recognized by the church. For members of the Roman Catholic Church, a "legal divorce" and the right to remarry may not be recognized unless the first marriage has been declared null and void by a decree of the church. It is clear that there is no single religious view of marriage and that history has witnessed some monumental changes in the way "husband and wife" are seen in the relationship of marriage.

In my faith-based understanding, if freedom of choice 5 means anything to individuals (male or female), it means they have several options. They can be single and celibate without being thought of as strange or psychologically unbalanced. They can be single and sexually active without being labeled loose or immoral. Women can be single with child without being thought of as unfit or inadequate. If these choices had been real options, the divorce rate may never have reached nearly 50 percent.

The other, equally significant choice for people to make 6 is that of lifetime commitment to each other and to seal that desire in the vows of a wedding ceremony. That understanding of marriage came out of my community of faith. In my years of ministry I ran a tight ship in regard to the performance of weddings. It wasn't because I didn't believe in marriage (I've been married for sixty years and have two wonderful offspring) but rather my unease about the way marriage was used to force people to marry so they wouldn't be "living in sin."

The failure of the institution can be seen in divorce statis- 7 tics. I wanted people to know how challenging the promise of those vows was and not to feel this was something they had to do. My first question in premarital counseling was, "Why do you want to get married and spoil a beautiful friendship?" That question often elicited a thoughtful and emotional answer. Though I was miserly in the number of weddings I performed, I always made exceptions when there were couples who had difficulty finding clergy who would officiate. Their difficulty was because they weren't of the same religion, or they had made marital mistakes, or what they couldn't believe. Most of them were "ecclesiastical outlaws," barred from certain sacraments in the church of their choice.

The church I served had a number of gay and lesbian couples who had been together for many years, but none of them had asked for public weddings or blessings on their relationship. (There was one commitment ceremony for a gay couple at the end of my tenure.) It was as though they didn't need a piece of paper or a ritual to symbolize their lifelong commitment. They knew if they wanted a religious ceremony, their ministers would officiate and our religious community would joyfully witness.

It was my hope that since the institution of marriage had been used to exclude and demean members of the homosexual community, our church, which was open and affirming, would create with gays and lesbians a new kind of ceremony. It would be an occasion that symbolized, between two people of the same gender, a covenant of intimacy of two people to journey together, breaking new ground in human relationships—an alternative to marriage as we have known it.

However, I can understand why homosexuals want "to be married" in the old fashioned "heterosexual way." After all, most gays and lesbians were born of married parents, raised in a family of siblings; many were nourished in churches and synagogues, taught about a living God before Whom all Her creatures were equally loved. Why wouldn't they conceive their loving relationships in terms of marriage and family and desire that they be confirmed and understood as such? It follows that if these gays and lesbians see their relationship as faith-based, they would want a religious ceremony that seals their intentions to become lifelong partners, lovers and friends, that they would want to be "married."

Even though most religious denominations deny this ceremony to homosexual couples, more and more clergy are, silently and publicly, officiating at religious rituals in which gays and lesbians declare their vows before God and a faith community. One Catholic priest who defied his church's ban said: "We can bless a dog, we can bless a boat, but we can't say a prayer over two people who love each other. You don't have to call it marriage, you can call it a deep and abiding friendship, but you can bless it."

We have the right to engage in "religious disobedience" to the regulations of the judicatory that granted us the privilege to officiate at wedding ceremonies, and suffer the consequences. However, when it comes to civil law, it is my contention that the church and its clergy are on much shakier ground in defying the law.  12

In order to fully understand the conflict that has arisen in this debate over the nature of marriage, it is important to understand the difference between the religious definition of marriage and the state's secular and civil definition. The government's interest is in a legal definition of marriage—a social and voluntary contract between a man and woman in order to protect money, property and children. Marriage is a civil union without benefit of clergy or religious definition. The state is not interested in why two people are "tying the knot," whether it's to gain money, secure a dynasty or raise children. It may be hard for those of us who have a religious or romantic view of marriage to realize that loveless marriages are not that rare. Before the Pill, pregnancy was a frequent motive for getting married. The state doesn't care what the commitment of two people is, whether it's for life or as long as both of you love, whether it's sexually monogamous or an open marriage. There is nothing spiritual, mystical or romantic about the state's license to marry—it's a legal contract.  13

Thus, George W. Bush is right when he says that "marriage is a sacred institution" when speaking as a Christian, as a member of his Methodist church. But as President of the United States and leader of all Americans, believers and unbelievers, he is wrong. What will surface in this debate as litigation and court decisions multiply is the history of the conflict between the church and the state in defining the nature of  14 marriage. That history will become significant as we move toward a decision on who may be married.

After Christianity became the state religion of the Roman    15 Empire in AD 325, the church maintained absolute control over the regulation of marriage for some 1,000 years. Beginning in the sixteenth century, English kings (especially Henry VIII, who found the inability to get rid of a wife extremely oppressive) and other monarchs in Europe began to wrest control from the church over marital regulations. Ever since, kings, presidents and rulers of all kinds have seen how important the control of marriage is to the regulation of social order. In this nation, the government has always been in charge of marriage.

That is why it was not a San Francisco mayor licensing    16 same-sex couples that really threatened the President's religious understanding of marriage but rather the Supreme Judicial Court of Massachusetts; declaring marriage between same-sex couples a constitutional right, that demanded a call for constitutional amendment. I didn't understand how important that was until I read an op-ed piece in the *Boston Globe* by Peter Gomes, professor of Christian morals and the minister of Memorial Church at Harvard University, that reminds us of a seminal piece of our history:

> The Dutch made civil marriage the law of the land in 1590, and the first marriage in New England, that of Edward Winslow to the widow Susannah White, was performed on May 12, 1621, in Plymouth by Governor William Bradford, in exercise of his office as magistrate.

There would be no clergyman in Plymouth until the arrival    17 of the Rev. Ralph Smith in 1629, but even then marriage would continue to be a civil affair, as these first Puritans opposed the English custom of clerical marriage as unscriptural. Not until 1692, when Plymouth Colony was merged into that of Massachusetts Bay, were the Clergy authorized by the new province to solemnize marriages. To this day in the Commonwealth the clergy, including those of the archdiocese, solemnize marriage legally as agents of the

Commonwealth and by its civil authority. Chapter 207 of the General Laws of Massachusetts tells us who may perform such ceremonies.

Now even though it is the civil authority of the state that defines the rights and responsibilities of marriage and therefore who can be married, the state is no more infallible than the church in its judgments. It wasn't until the mid-twentieth century that the Supreme Court declared anti-miscegenation laws unconstitutional. Even after that decision, many mainline churches, where I started my ministry, unofficially discouraged interracial marriages, and many of my colleagues were forbidden to perform such weddings.

The civil law view of marriage has as much historical diversity as the church's own experience because, in part, the church continued to influence the civil law. Although it was the Bible that made "the husband the head of his wife," it was common law that "turned the married pair legally into one person— the husband," as Nancy Cott documents in her book *Public Vows: A History of Marriage and the Nation* (an indispensable resource for anyone seeking to understand the changing nature of marriage in the nation's history). She suggests that "the legal doctrine of marital unity was called coverture . . . [which] meant that the wife could not use legal avenues such as suits or contracts, own assets, or execute legal documents without her husband's collaboration." This view of the wife would not hold water in any court in the land today.

As a matter of fact, even in the religious understanding of President Bush and his followers, allowing same-sex couples the right to marry seems a logical conclusion. If marriage is "the most fundamental institution of civilization" and a major contributor to the social order in our society, why would anyone want to shut out homosexuals from the "glorious attributes" of this "sacred institution"? Obviously, the only reason one can discern is that the opponents believe that gay and lesbian people are not worthy of the benefits and spiritual blessings of "marriage."

At the heart of the controversy raging over same-sex marriage is the religious and constitutional principle of the

18

19

20

21

separation of church and state. All of us can probably agree that there was never a solid wall of separation, riddled as it is with breaches. The evidence of that is seen in the ambiguity of tax-free religious institutions, "in God we trust" printed on our money and "under God" in the Pledge of Allegiance to our country. All of us clergy, who are granted permission by the state to officiate at legal marriage ceremonies, have already compromised the "solid wall" by signing the license issued by the state. I would like to believe that my authority to perform religious ceremonies does not come from the state but derives from the vows of ordination and my commitment to God. I refuse to repeat the words, "by the authority invested in me by the State of New York, I pronounce you husband and wife," but by signing the license, I've become the state's "handmaiden."

It seems fitting therefore that we religious folk should now   22
seek to sharpen the difference between ecclesiastical law and civil law as we beseech the state to clarify who can be married by civil law. Further evidence that the issue of church and state is part of the gay-marriage controversy is that two Unitarian ministers have been arrested for solemnizing unions between same-sex couples when no state licenses were involved. Ecclesiastical law may punish those clergy who disobey marital regulations, but the state has no right to invade church practices and criminalize clergy under civil law. There should have been a noisy outcry from all churches, synagogues and mosques at the government's outrageous contravention of the sacred principle of the "free exercise of religion."

I come from a long line of Protestants who believe in   23
"a free church in a free state." In the issue before this nation, the civil law is the determinant of the regulation of marriage, regardless of our religious views, and the Supreme Court will finally decide what the principle of equality means in our Constitution in the third century of our life together as a people. It is likely that the Commonwealth of Massachusetts will probably lead the nation on this matter, as the State of New York led to the Supreme Court decision to allow women reproductive freedom.

So what is marriage? It depends on whom you ask, in what    24
era, in what culture. Like all words or institutions, human
definitions, whether religious or secular, change with time and
history. When our beloved Constitution was written, blacks,
Native Americans and, to some extent, women were quasi-
human beings with no rights or privileges, but today they are
recognized as persons with full citizenship rights. The definition of marriage has been changing over the centuries in this
nation, and it will change yet again as homosexuals are seen
as ordinary human beings.

In time, and I believe that time is now, we Americans will    25
see that all the fears foisted on us by religious zealots were
not real. Heterosexual marriage will still flourish with its statistical failures. The only difference will be that some homosexual couples will join them and probably account for about
the same number of failed relationships. And we will discover
that it did not matter whether the couples were joined in a
religious ceremony or a secular and civil occasion for the statement of their intentions.

## For Critical Thinking

### QUESTIONS ABOUT PURPOSE

1. How does Moody define the purpose of this essay?
2. How does this purpose relate to his attitude toward the debate
   about gay marriage?

### QUESTIONS ABOUT AUDIENCE

1. How does Moody's profession as a minister establish his authority for his readers?
2. How do you think his readers will respond to his "faith-based
   understanding" of freedom of choice?

---

### QUESTIONS ABOUT STRATEGIES

---

1. How does Moody illustrate that there is "no single religious view of marriage"?
2. How does he illustrate that "in this nation, the government has always been in charge of marriage"?

## For Writing and Research

1. *Analyze* how Moody presents his problems as counseling and officiating minister.
2. *Practice* by describing the changing definitions of *romance* you have applied to your various relationships.
3. *Argue* that the divorce rate is/is not proof that marriage is the eroding cornerstone of our culture.
4. *Synthesize:* Read the definitions of marriage in the Koran; then write an essay assessing whether the Christian or Islamic definition of marriage has the most beneficial impact on culture.

## Bruce Catton: *Grant and Lee: A Study in Contrasts*

Bruce Catton (1899–1978) was born in Petosky, Michigan, and attended Oberlin College. After a career as a reporter for newspapers in Boston and Cleveland, he served as a director of information for various government agencies in Washington, D.C., before accepting the position of editor of *American Heritage* magazine. His fourth book, *A Stillness at Appomattox* (1953), earned him the Pulitzer Prize, the National Book Award, and the unofficial title of America's most popular historian of the Civil War. In addition to his many books on that subject—such as *Mr. Lincoln's Army* (1951), *The Coming Fury* (1961), *and Grant Takes Command* (1964)—Catton wrote a memorable account of his own boyhood in Michigan, *Waiting for the Morning Train: An American Boyhood* (1974). "Grant and Lee: A Study in Contrasts" first appeared in *The American Story* (1956), a collection of essays by eminent historians, and has been cited often as one of the classic examples of the comparison-and-contrast essay. In his analysis, Catton considers both the differences in background and similarities in character in these two great Civil War generals.

WHEN ULYSSES S. GRANT and Robert E. Lee met in the parlor of a modest house at Appomattox Court House, Virginia, on April 9, 1865, to work out the terms for the surrender of Lee's Army of Northern Virginia, a great chapter in American life came to a close, and a great new chapter began.

These men were bringing the Civil War to its virtual fin-    2
ish. To be sure, other armies had yet to surrender, and for a
few days the fugitive Confederate government would struggle
desperately and vainly, trying to find some way to go on living now that its chief support was gone. But in effect it was
all over when Grant and Lee signed the papers. And the little
room where they wrote out the terms was the scene of one of
the poignant, dramatic contrasts in American history.

---

*They were two strong men, these oddly
different generals, and they represented the
strengths of two conflicting currents that,
through them, had come into final collision.*

---

Back of Robert E. Lee was the notion that the old aristo-    3
cratic concept might somehow survive and be dominant in
American life.

Lee was tidewater Virginia, and in his background were    4
family, culture, and tradition . . . the age of chivalry trans-
planted to a New World which was making its own legends
and its own myths. He embodied a way of life that had come
down through the age of knighthood and the English country
squire. America was a land that was beginning all over again,
dedicated to nothing much more complicated than the rather
hazy belief that all men had equal rights, and should have an
equal chance in the world. In such a land Lee stood for the
feeling that it was somehow of advantage to human society
to have a pronounced inequality in the social structure. There
should be a leisure class, backed by ownership of land; in turn,
society itself should be keyed to the land as the chief source
of wealth and influence. It would bring forth (according to
this ideal) a class of men with a strong sense of obligation
to the community; men who lived not to gain advantage for
themselves, but to meet the solemn obligations which had

been laid on them by the very fact that they were privileged. From them the country would get its leadership; to them it could look for the higher values—of thought, of conduct, of personal deportment—to give it strength and virtue.

Lee embodied the noblest elements of this aristocratic   5 ideal. Through him, the landed nobility justified itself. For four years, the Southern states had fought a desperate war to uphold the ideals for which Lee stood. In the end, it almost seemed as if the Confederacy fought for Lee; as if he himself was the Confederacy . . . the best thing that the way of life for which the Confederacy stood could ever have to offer. He had passed into legend before Appomattox. Thousands of tired, underfed, poorly clothed Confederate soldiers, long since past the simple enthusiasm of the early days of the struggle, somehow considered Lee the symbol of everything for which they had been willing to die. But they could not quite put this feeling into words. If the Lost Cause, sanctified by so much heroism and so many deaths, had a living justification, its justification was General Lee.

Grant, the son of a tanner on the Western frontier, was   6 everything Lee was not. He had come up the hard way, and embodied nothing in particular except the eternal toughness and sinewy fiber of the men who grew up beyond the mountains. He was one of a body of men who owed reverence and obeisance to no one, who were self-reliant to a fault, who cared hardly anything for the past but who had a sharp eye for the future.

These frontier men were the precise opposites of the   7 tidewater aristocrats. Back of them, in the great surge that had taken people over the Alleghenies and into the opening Western country, there was a deep, implicit dissatisfaction with a past that had settled into grooves. They stood for democracy, not from any reasoned conclusion about the proper ordering of human society, but simply because they had grown up in the middle of democracy and knew how it worked. Their society might have privileges, but they would be privileges each man had won for himself. Forms and patterns meant nothing. No man was born to anything, except perhaps to a chance to show how far he could rise. Life was competition.

Yet along with this feeling had come a deep sense of belong-  8
ing to a national community. The Westerner who developed
a farm, opened a shop or set up in business as a trader, could
hope to prosper only as his own community prospered—and
his community ran from the Atlantic to the Pacific and from
Canada down to Mexico. If the land was settled, with towns
and highways and accessible markets, he could better himself.
He saw his fate in terms of the nation's own destiny. As its
horizons expanded, so did his. He had, in other words, an
acute dollars-and-cents stake in the continued growth and
development of his country.

And that, perhaps, is where the contrast between Grant and  9
Lee becomes most striking. The Virginia aristocrat, inevitably,
saw himself in relation to his own region. He lived in a static
society which could endure almost anything except change.
Instinctively, his first loyalty would go to the locality in which
that society existed. He would fight to the limit of endurance
to defend it, because in defending it he was defending everything that gave his own life its deepest meaning.

The Westerner, on the other hand, would fight with an  10
equal tenacity for the broader concept of society. He fought
so because everything he lived by was tied to growth, expansion, and a constantly widening horizon. What he lived by
would survive or fall with the nation itself. He could not possibly stand by unmoved in the face of an attempt to destroy
the Union. He would combat it with everything he had,
because he could only see it as an effort to cut the ground
out from under his feet.

So Grant and Lee were in complete contrast, representing  11
two diametrically opposed elements in American life. Grant
was the modern man emerging; beyond him, ready to come
on the stage, was the great age of steel and machinery, of
crowded cities and a restless, burgeoning vitality. Lee might
have ridden down from the old age of chivalry, lance in hand,
silken banner fluttering over his head. Each man was the perfect champion of his cause, drawing both his strengths and
his weaknesses from the people he led.

Yet it was not all contrast, after all. Different as they were—  12
in background, in personality, in underlying aspiration—these

two great soldiers had much in common. Under everything else, they were marvelous fighters. Furthermore, their fighting qualities were really very much alike.

Each man had, to begin with, the great virtue of utter   13
tenacity and fidelity. Grant fought his way down the Mississippi Valley in spite of acute personal discouragement and profound military handicaps. Lee hung on in the trenches at Petersburg after hope itself had died. In each man there was an indomitable quality . . . the born fighter's refusal to give us as long as he can still remain on his feet and lift his two fists.

Daring and resourcefulness they had, too; the ability to   14
think faster and move faster than the enemy. These were the qualities which gave Lee the dazzling campaigns of Second Manassas and Chancellorsville and won Vicksburg for Grant.

Lastly, and perhaps greatest of all, there was the ability, at   15
the end, to turn quickly from war to peace once the fighting was over. Out of the way these two men behaved at Appomattox came the possibility of a peace of reconciliation. It was a possibility not wholly realized, in the years to come, but which did, in the end, help the two sections to become one nation again . . . after a war whose bitterness might have seemed to make such a reunion wholly impossible. No part of either man's life became him more than the part he played in their brief meeting in the McLean house at Appomattox. Their behavior there put all succeeding generations of Americans in their debt. Two great Americans, Grant and Lee— very different, yet under everything very much alike. Their encounter at Appomattox was one of the great moments of American history.

## For Critical Thinking

### QUESTIONS ABOUT PURPOSE

1. Catton's title identifies his essay as a strict comparison of two men—opposing military generals in the same war. What is his primary purpose in comparing them—to compare their biographies, their values, their military abilities, or their causes?

2. Catton's subtitle suggests that his purpose is to study contrasts. Does his analysis suggest that one man was superior to the other? Explain your answer.

## QUESTIONS ABOUT AUDIENCE

1. How much knowledge does Catton assume his readers have about the Civil War? Do they need to know the specific details of the battles of Second Manassas, Chancellorville, and Vicksburg to understand this essay? Explain your answer.
2. Although Catton's title is "Grant and Lee," he presents Lee first and Grant second. Why? Does he assume his readers know more about Lee, are more fascinated by Lee, or prefer to read about the loser first and the winner second?

## QUESTIONS ABOUT STRATEGIES

1. How does Catton arrange the points of his contrast? To what extent does he provide equal treatment of each point?
2. One strategy Catton uses to characterize his two subjects is to compare their values to the values of people in other times and places. If Lee embodies the values of chivalry, knighthood, and aristocracy, what values does Grant embody?

## For Writing and Research

1. *Analyze* the strategies Catton uses to illustrate how Grant was a good winner and Lee was a good loser.
2. *Practice* by comparing two people who share many experiences and characteristics. Consider such points as dress, behavior, education, work, and style as you try to contrast the values each character embodies.
3. *Argue* that in the final analysis military leaders show more similarities than differences.
4. *Synthesize* the research on Grant's and Lee's attitudes toward slavery. Then use this evidence to explain their position on what most historians consider the major cause of the Civil War.

Alice Walker was born in 1944 in Eatonton, Georgia, and attended Spellman College and Sarah Lawrence College. She then became active in the civil rights movement, helping to register voters in Georgia, teaching in the Head Start program in Mississippi, and working on the staff of the New York City welfare department. In subsequent years, she began her own writing career while teaching at Wellesley College, the University of California at Berkeley, and Brandeis University. Her writing reveals her interest in the themes of sexism and racism, themes she embodies in her widely acclaimed novels: *The Third Life of Grange Copeland* (1970), *Meridian* (1976), *The Color Purple* (1982), *Possessing the Secret of Joy* (1992), *Now Is the Time to Open Your Heart* (2005), and *Devil's My Enemy* (2008). Her stories, collected in *In Love and Trouble: Stories of Black Women* (1973) and *You Can't Keep a Good Woman Down* (1981), and essays found in *Living by the Word* (1988), *The Same River Twice* (1996), and *Overcoming Speechlessness* (2010), examine the complex experiences of black women. "Everyday Use" reprinted from *In Love and Trouble*, focuses on a reunion that reveals two contrasting attitudes toward the meaning of family heritage.

I WILL WAIT for her in the yard that Maggie and I made    1
so clean and wavy yesterday afternoon. A yard like this is more comfortable than most people know. It is not just a yard. It is like an extended living room. When the hard clay

is swept clean as a floor and the fine sand around the edges lined with tiny, irregular grooves anyone can come and sit and look up into the elm tree and wait for the breezes that never come inside the house.

Maggie will be nervous until after her sister goes: she will stand hopelessly in corners homely and ashamed of the burn scars down her arms and legs, eyeing her sister with a mixture of envy and awe. She thinks her sister has held life always in the palm of one hand, that "no" is a word the world never learned to say to her.

You've no doubt seen those TV shows where the child who has "made it" is confronted, as a surprise, by her own mother and father, tottering in weakly from backstage. (A pleasant surprise, of course: What would they do if parent and child came on the show only to curse out and insult each other?) On TV mother and child embrace and smile into each other's faces. Sometimes the mother and father weep, the child wraps them in her arms and leans across the table to tell how she would not have made it without their help. I have seen these programs.

Sometimes I dream a dream in which Dee and I are suddenly brought together on a TV program of this sort. Out of a dark and soft-seated limousine I am ushered into a bright room filled with many people. There I meet a smiling, gray, sporty man like Johnny Carson who shakes my hand and tells me what a fine girl I have. Then we are on the stage and Dee is embracing me with tears in her eyes. She pins on my dress a large orchid, even though she has told me once that she thinks orchids are tacky flowers.

In real life I am a large, big-boned woman with rough, man-working hands. In the winter I wear flannel nightgowns to bed and overalls during the day. I can kill and clean a hog as mercilessly as a man. My fat keeps me hot in zero weather. I can work all day, breaking ice to get water for washing. I can eat pork liver cooked over the open fire minutes after it comes steaming from the hog. One winter I knocked a bull calf straight in the brain between the eyes with a sledge hammer and had the meat hung up to chill before nightfall. But of course all this does not show on television. I am the way my daughter would want me to be: a hundred pounds lighter, my skin like an uncooked barley pancake. My hair glistens in the hot bright lights. Johnny Carson has much to do to keep up with my quick and witty tongue.

But that is a mistake. I know even before I wake up. Who    6 ever knew a Johnson with a quick tongue? Who can even imagine me looking a strange white man in the eye? It seems to me I have talked to them always with one foot raised in flight, with my head turned in whichever way is farthest from them. Dee, though. She would always look anyone in the eye. Hesitation was no part of her nature.

"How do I look, Mama?" Maggie says, showing just    7 enough of her thin body enveloped in pink skirt and red blouse for me to know she's there, almost hidden by the door.

"Come out into the yard," I say.    8

Have you ever seen a lame animal, perhaps a dog run over    9 by some careless person rich enough to own a car, sidle up to someone who is ignorant enough to be kind to him? That is the way my Maggie walks. She has been like this, chin on chest, eyes on ground, feet in shuffle, ever since the fire that burned the other house to the ground.

Dee is lighter than Maggie, with nicer hair and a fuller    10 figure. She's a woman now, though sometimes I forget. How long ago was it that the other house burned? Ten, twelve years? Sometimes I can still hear the flames and feel Maggie's arm sticking to me, her hair smoking and her dress falling off her in little black papery flakes. Her eyes seemed stretched open, blazed open by the flames reflected in them. And Dee. I see her standing off under the sweet gum tree she used to dig gum out of; a look of concentration on her face as she watched the last dingy gray board of the house fall in toward the red-hot brick chimney. Why don't you do a dance around the ashes? I'd wanted to ask her. She had hated the house that much.

I used to think she hated Maggie, too. But that was    11 before we raised the money, the church and me, to send her to Augusta to school. She used to read to us without pity;

forcing words, lies, other folks' habits, whole lives upon us two, sitting trapped and ignorant underneath her voice. She washed us in a river of make-believe, burned us with a lot of knowledge we didn't necessarily need to know. Pressed us to her with the serious way she read, to shove us away at just the moment, like dimwits, we seemed about to understand.

Dee wanted nice things. A yellow organdy dress to wear    12 to her graduation from high school; black pumps to match a green suit she'd made from an old suit somebody gave me. She was determined to stare down any disaster in her efforts. Her eyelids would not flicker for minutes at a time. Often I fought off the temptation to shake her. At sixteen she had a style of her own: and knew what style was.

I never had an education myself. After second grade the    13 school was closed down. Don't ask me why: in 1927 colored asked fewer questions than they do now. Sometimes Maggie reads to me. She stumbles along good-naturedly but can't see well. She knows she is not bright. Like good looks and money, quickness passed her by. She will marry John Thomas (who has mossy teeth in an earnest face) and then I'll be free to sit here and I guess just sing church songs to myself. Although I never was a good singer. Never could carry a tune. I was always better at a man's job. I used to love to milk till I was hoofed in the side in '49. Cows are soothing and slow and don't bother you, unless you try to milk them the wrong way.

I have deliberately turned my back on the house. It is three    14 rooms, just like the one that burned, except the roof is tin; they don't make shingle roofs any more. There are no real windows, just some holes cut in the sides, like the portholes in a ship, but not round and not square, with rawhide holding the shutters up on the outside. This house is in a pasture, too, like the other one. No doubt when Dee sees it she will want to tear it down. She wrote me once that no matter where we "choose" to live, she will manage to come see us. But she will never bring her friends. Maggie and I thought about this and Maggie asked me, "Mama, when did Dee ever *have* any friends?"

She had a few. Furtive boys in pink shirts hanging about    15 on washday after school. Nervous girls who never laughed.

Impressed with her they worshiped the well-turned phrase, the cute shape, the scalding humor that erupted like bubbles in lye. She read to them.

When she was courting Jimmy T she didn't have much     16
time to pay to us, but turned all her faultfinding power on him. He *flew* to marry a cheap gal from a family of ignorant flashy people. She hardly had time to recompose herself.

When she comes I will meet—but there they are!     17

Maggie attempts to make a dash for the house, in her shuf-     18
fling way, but I stay her with my hand. "Come back here," I say. And she stops and tries to dig a well in the sand with her toe.

It is hard to see them clearly through the strong sun. But     19
even the first glimpse of leg out of the car tells me it is Dee. Her feet were always neat-looking, as if God himself had shaped them with a certain style. From the other side of the car comes a short, stocky man. Hair is all over his head a foot long and hanging from his chin like a kinky mule tail. I hear Maggie suck in her breath. "Uhnnnh," is what it sounds like. Like when you see the wriggling end of a snake just in front of your foot on the road. "Uhnnnh."

Dee next. A dress down to the ground, in this hot weather.     20
A dress so loud it hurts my eyes. There are yellows and oranges enough to throw back the light of the sun. I feel my whole face warming from the heat waves it throws out. Earrings, too, gold and hanging down to her shoulders. Bracelets dangling and making noises when she moves her arm up to shake the folds of the dress out of her armpits. The dress is loose and flows, and as she walks closer, I like it. I hear Maggie go "Uhnnnh" again. It is her sister's hair. It stands straight up like the wool on a sheep. It is black as night and around the edges are two long pigtails that rope about like small lizards disappearing behind her ears.

"Wa-su-zo-Tean-o!" she says, coming on in that gliding     21
way the dress makes her move. The short stocky fellow with the hair to his navel is all grinning and he follows up with "Asalamalakim, my mother and sister!" He moves to hug Maggie but she falls back, right up against the back of my

chair. I feel her trembling there and when I look up I see the perspiration falling off her chin.

"Don't get up," says Dee. Since I am stout it takes some- 22 thing of a push. You can see me trying to move a second or two before I make it. She turns, showing white heels through her sandals, and goes back to the car. Out she peeks next with a Polaroid. She stoops down quickly and lines up picture after picture of me sitting there in front of the house with Maggie cowering behind me. She never takes a shot without making sure the house is included. When a cow comes nibbling around the edge of the yard she snaps it and me and Maggie *and* the house. Then she puts the Polaroid in the back seat of the car, and comes up and kisses me on the forehead.

Meanwhile Asalamalakim is going through the motions 23 with Maggie's hand. Maggie's hand is limp as a fish, and probably as cold, despite the sweat, and she keeps trying to pull it back. It looks like Asalamalakim wants to shake hands but wants to do it fancy. Or maybe he don't know how people shake hands. Anyhow, he soon gives up on Maggie.

"Well," I say. "Dee." 24

"No, Mama," she says. "Not 'Dee,' Wangero Leewanika 25 Kemanjo!"

"What happened to 'Dee'?" I wanted to know. 26

"She's dead," Wangero said. "I couldn't bear it any longer 27 being named after the people who oppress me."

"You know as well as me you was named after your aunt 28 Dicie," I said. Dicie is my sister. She named Dee. We called her "Big Dee" after Dee was born.

"But who was *she* named after?" asked Wangero. 29

"I guess after Grandma Dee," I said. 30

"And who was she named after?" asked Wangero. 31

"Her mother," I said, and saw Wangero getting tired. 32 "That's about as far back as I can trace it," I said. Though, in fact, I probably could have carried it back beyond the Civil War through the branches.

"Well," said Asalamalakim, "there you are." 33 •

"Uhnnnh," I heard Maggie say. 34

"There I was not," I said, "before 'Dicie' cropped up in   35
our family, so why should I try to trace it that far back?"

He just stood there grinning, looking down on me like   36
somebody inspecting a Model A car. Every once in a while he
and Wangero sent eye signals over my head.

"How do you pronounce this name?" I asked.   37

"You don't have to call me by it if you don't want to," said   38
Wangero.

"Why shouldn't I?" I asked. "If that's what you want us to   39
call you, we'll call you."

"I know it might sound awkward at first," said Wangero.   40

"I'll get used to it," I said. "Ream it out again."   41

Well, soon we got the name out of the way. Asalamalakim   42
had a name twice as long and three times as hard. After I
tripped over it two or three times he told me to just call him
Hakim-a-barber. I wanted to ask him was he a barber, but I
didn't really think he was, so I didn't ask.

"You must belong to those beef-cattle peoples down the   43
road," I said. They said "Asalamalakim" when they met you,
too, but they didn't shake hands. Always too busy: feeding the
cattle, fixing the fences, putting up salt-lick shelters, throwing
down hay. When the white folks poisoned some of the herd
the men stayed up all night with rifles in their hands, I walked
a mile and half just to see the sight.

Hakim-a-barber said, "I accept some of their doctrines,   44
but farming and raising cattle is not my style." (They didn't
tell me, and I didn't ask, whether Wangero [Dee] had really
gone and married him.)

We sat down to eat and right away he said he didn't eat   45
collards and pork was unclean. Wangero, though, went on
through the chitlins and corn bread, the greens and everything else. She talked a blue streak over the sweet potatoes.
Everything delighted her. Even the fact that we still used
the benches her daddy made for the table when we couldn't
afford to buy chairs.

"Oh, Mama!" she cried. Then turned to Hakim-a-barber.   46
"I never knew how lovely these benches are. You can feel
the rump prints," she said, running her hands underneath

her and along the bench. Then she gave a sigh and her hand closed over Grandma Dee's butter dish. "That's it!" she said. "I knew there was something I wanted to ask you if I could have." She jumped up from the table and went over in the corner where the churn stood, the milk in its clabber by now. She looked at the churn and looked at it.

"This churn top is what I need," she said. "Didn't Uncle Buddy whittle it out of a tree you all used to have?" 47

"Yes," I said. 48

"Uh huh," she said happily. "And I want the dasher, too." 49

"Uncle Buddy whittle that, too?" asked the barber. 50

Dee (Wangero) looked up at me. 51

"Aunt Dee's first husband whittled the dash," said Maggie 52 so low you almost couldn't hear her. "His name was Henry, but they called him Stash."

"Maggie's brain is like an elephant's," Wangero said, laugh- 53 ing. "I can use the churn top as a centerpiece for the alcove table," she said, sliding a plate over the churn, "and I'll think of something artistic to do with the dasher."

When she finished wrapping the dasher the handle stuck 54 out. I took it for a moment in my hands. You didn't even have to look close to see where hands pushing the dasher up and down to make butter had left a kind of sink in the wood. In fact, there were a lot of small sinks; you could see where thumbs and fingers had sunk into the wood. It was beautiful light yellow wood, from a tree that grew in the yard where Big Dee and Stash had lived.

After dinner Dee (Wangero) went to the trunk at the foot of 55 my bed and started rifling through it. Maggie hung back in the kitchen over the dishpan. Out came Wangero with two quilts. They had been pieced by Grandma Dee and then Big Dee and me had hung them on the quilt frames on the front porch and quilted them. One was in the Lone Star pattern. The other was Walk Around the Mountain. In both of them were scraps of dresses Grandma Dee had worn fifty and more years ago. Bits and pieces of Grandpa Jarrell's Paisley shirts. And one teeny faded blue piece, about the size of a penny matchbox, that was from Great Grandpa Ezra's uniform that he wore in the Civil War.

"Mama," Wangero said sweet as a bird. "Can I have these   56
old quilts?"

I heard something fall in the kitchen, and a minute later   57
the kitchen door slammed.

"Why don't you take one or two of the others?" I asked.   58
"These old things was just done by me and Big Dee from
some tops your grandma pieced before she died."

"No," said Wangero. "I don't want those. They are stitched   59
around the borders by machine."

"That'll make them last better," I said.   60

"That's not the point," said Wangero. "These are all pieces   61
of dresses Grandma used to wear. She did all this stitching
by hand. Imagine!" She held the quilts securely in her arms,
stroking them.

"Some of the pieces, like those lavender ones, come from   62
old clothes her mother handed down to her," I said, moving up to touch the quilts. Dee (Wangero) moved back just
enough so that I couldn't reach the quilts. They already
belonged to her.

"Imagine!" she breathed again, clutching them closely to   63
her bosom.

"The truth is," I said, "I promised to give them quilts to   64
Maggie, for when she marries John Thomas."

She gasped like a bee had stung her.   65

"Maggie can't appreciate these quilts!" she said. "She'd   66
probably be backward enough to put them to everyday use."

"I reckon she would," I said. "God knows I been saving   67
'em for long enough with nobody using 'em. I hope she will!"
I didn't want to bring up how I had offered Dee (Wangero)
a quilt when she went away to college. Then she had told me
they were old fashioned, out of style.

"But they're *priceless!*" she was saying now, furiously; for   68
she has a temper. "Maggie would put them on the bed and
in five years they'd be in rags. Less than that!"

"She can always make some more," I said. "Maggie knows   69
how to quilt."

Dee (Wangero) looked at me with hatred. "You just will   70
not understand. The point is these quilts, *these* quilts!"

"Well," I said, stumped. "What would *you* do with them?"    71

"Hang them," she said. As if that was the only thing you    72
*could* do with quilts.

Maggie by now was standing in the door. I could almost    73
hear the sound her feet made as they scraped over each other.

"She can have them, Mama," she said, like somebody used    74
to never winning anything, or having anything reserved for
her. "I can 'member Grandma Dee without the quilts."

I looked at her hard. She had filled her bottom lip with    75
checkerberry snuff and it gave her face a kind of dopey,
hangdog look. It was Grandma Dee and Big Dee who
taught her how to quilt herself. She stood there with her
scarred hands hidden in the folds of her skirt. She looked
at her sister with something like fear but she wasn't mad at
her. This was Maggie's portion. This was the way she knew
God to work.

When I looked at her like that something hit me in the    76
top of my head and ran down to the soles of my feet. Just
like when I'm in church and the spirit of God touches me
and I get happy and shout. I did something I never had done
before: hugged Maggie to me, then dragged her on into the
room, snatched the quilts out of Miss Wangero's hands and
dumped them into Maggie's lap. Maggie just sat there on my
bed with her mouth open.

"Take one or two of the others," I said to Dee.    77

But she turned without a word and went out to    78
Hakim-a-barber.

"You just don't understand," she said, as Maggie and I    79
came out to the car.

"What don't I understand?" I wanted to know.    80

"Your heritage," she said. And then she turned to Maggie,    81
kissed her and said, "You ought to try to make something of
yourself, too, Maggie. It's really a new day for us. But from
the way you and Mama still live you'd never know it."

She put on some sunglasses that hid everything above the    82
tip of her nose and her chin.

Maggie smiled; maybe at the sunglasses. But a real smile,    83
not scared. After we watched the car dust settle I asked

Maggie to bring me a dip of snuff. And then the two of us sat there just enjoying, until it was time to go in the house and go to bed.

## COMMENT ON "EVERYDAY USE"

Walker's "Everyday Use" describes a difference between a mother's and her visiting daughter's understandings of the word *heritage*. For Mama and her daughter Maggie, heritage is a matter of everyday living, of "everyday use." For Mama's other daughter, Dee (Wangero), however, heritage is a matter of style, a fashionable obsession with one's roots. These comparisons are revealed first in Walker's description of the physical appearance of the characters. Mama is fat and manly, and Maggie bears the scars from a fire. By contrast, Dee (Wangero) is beautiful and striking in her brightly colored African dress, earrings, sunglasses, and Afro hairstyle. Next, Walker compares the characters' skills. Mama can butcher a hog or break ice to get water, and Maggie is able to make beautiful quilts. Dee (Wangero), on the other hand, thinks of herself as outside this domestic world, educated by books to understand the cultural significance of her heritage. The problem posed by the debate over family possessions is whether heritage is an object to be preserved, like a priceless painting, or a process to be learned, like the creation of a quilt.

# CHAPTER 4

# Division and Classification

**Division** and **classification** are mental processes that often work together. When you *divide*, you separate something (a college and a city) into sections (departments and neighborhoods). When you *classify*, you place examples of something (restaurants, jobs) into categories or classes (restaurants: moderately expensive, expensive, very expensive; jobs: unskilled, semiskilled, and skilled).

When you divide, you move downward from a concept to the subunits of that concept. When you classify, you move upward from specific examples to classes or categories that share a common characteristic. For example, you could *divide* a television news program into subunits such as news, features, editorials, sports, and weather. And you could *classify* some element of that program—such as the editorial commentator on the six o'clock news—according to his or her style, knowledge, and trustworthiness. You can use either division or classification singly, depending on your purpose, but most of the time you will probably use them together when you are writing a classification essay. First you might identify the subunits of a college sports program—football, basketball, hockey, volleyball, and tennis; then you could classify them according to their budgets—most money budgeted for football, the least budgeted for volleyball.

## PURPOSE

When you write a classification essay, your chief purpose is to *explain*. You might want to explain an established method for organizing information, such as the Library of Congress system, or a new plan for arranging data, such as the Internal Revenue Service's latest schedule for itemizing tax deductions. On one level, your purpose in such an essay is simply to show how the system works. At a deeper level, your purpose is to define, analyze, and justify the organizing principle that underlies the system.

You can also write a classification essay to *entertain* or *persuade*. If you classify to entertain, you have an opportunity to be clever and witty. If you classify to persuade, you have a chance to be cogent and forceful. If you want to entertain, you might concoct an elaborate scheme for classifying fools, pointing out the distinguishing features of each category and giving particularly striking examples of each type. But if you want to persuade, you could explain how some new or controversial plan, such as the metric system or congressional redistricting, is organized, pointing out how the schemes use new principles to identify and organize information. Again, although you may give your readers a great deal of information in such an essay, your main purpose is to persuade them that the new plan is better than the old one.

## AUDIENCE

As with any writing assignment, when you write a classification essay, you need to think carefully about what your readers already know and what they need to learn from your writing. If you're writing on a new topic (social patterns in a primitive society) or if you're explaining a specialized system of classification (the botanist's procedure for identifying plants), your readers need precise definitions and plenty of illustrations for each subcategory. If your readers already know about your subject and the system it uses for classification (the movies' G, PG, PG-13, R, and NC-17 rating codes), then you don't need to give them an extensive demonstration. In that kind of writing situation, you might want to sketch the system briefly to refresh your readers' memories but then move on, using examples of specific movies to analyze whether the system really works.

You also need to think about how your readers might use the classification system that you explain in your essay. If you're classifying rock musicians, your readers are probably going to regard the system you create as something self-enclosed—interesting and amusing, perhaps something to quibble about, but not something they're likely to use in their everyday lives. In contrast, if you write an essay classifying digital video equipment, your readers may want to use your system when they shop. For the first audience, you can use an informal approach to classification, dividing your subject into interesting subcategories and illustrating them with vivid examples. For the other audience, you need to be careful and strict in your approach, making sure you divide your topic into all its possible classes and illustrating each class with concrete examples.

## STRATEGIES

When you write a classification essay, your basic strategy for organization should be to *divide your subject* into major categories that exhibit a common trait, then subdivide those categories into smaller units. Next, *arrange your categories* into a sequence that shows a logical or a dramatic progression. Finally, *define each of your categories*. Show how each category is different from the others; then discuss its most vivid examples.

To make this strategy succeed, you must be sure that your classification system is *consistent, complete, emphatic,* and *significant.* Here is a method for achieving this goal. First, when you divide your subject into categories, *apply the same principle of selection to each class.* You may find this hard to do if you're trying to explain a system that someone else has already established but that is actually inconsistent. You have undoubtedly discovered that record stores use overlapping and inconsistent categories. CDs by Norah Jones, for example, may be found in sections labeled *jazz, pop,* and *female vocal.* You can avoid such tangles if you create and control your own classification system.

For instance, Judith Viorst classifies four types of lies, David Cole classifies five myths about immigration, and James H. Austin classifies four kinds of chance.

After you have divided your subject into separate and consistent categories, *make sure your division is complete.* The simplest kind of division separates a subject into two categories: A and Not-A (for example, conformists and nonconformists). This kind of division, however, is rarely encouraged. It allows you to tell your readers about category A (conformists), but you won't tell them much about category Not-A (nonconformists). For this reason, you should try to exhaust your subject by finding at least three separate categories and by acknowledging any examples that don't fit into the system. When authors write a formal classification essay, such as Cole's "Five Myths About Immigration," they try to be definitive—to include everything significant. Even when writers are writing less formal classification essays, such as Viorst's "The Truth About Lying," they try to set up a reasonably complete system.

Once you have completed your process of division, *arrange your categories and examples in an emphatic order.* Austin arranges his classification of chance from blind luck to personal sensibility. The authors in this chapter reveal the principal purpose underlying their classification schemes: to show variety in similarity, challenge the arbitrariness of an established system, and point out how concepts change.

Finally, you need to *show the significance of your system of classification.* The strength of the classification process is that you can use it to analyze a subject in any number of ways. Its weakness is that you can use it to subdivide a subject into all kinds of trivial or pointless categories. You can classify people by their educational backgrounds, their work experience, or their significant achievements. You can also classify them by their shoe size, the kind of socks they wear, or their tastes in ice cream. Notice that David Cole begins his essay with a discussion of the Know-Nothing movement before he classifies the current myths that that "distort public debate and government policy relating to immigrants."

---

## DIVISION AND CLASSIFICATION

### Points to Remember

1. Determine whether you want to (a) explain an existing system of classification or (b) create your own system.
2. Divide your subject into smaller categories by applying the same principle of selection to each category.
3. Make sure that your division is complete by establishing separate and consistent types of categories.
4. Arrange your categories (and the examples you use to illustrate each category) in a logical and emphatic sequence.
5. Demonstrate the significance of your system by calling your readers' attention to its significance.

*Types of Guitar Music.*

*This image is a vector illustration of how the guitar can be used to play different styles of music. Write an essay in which you illustrate how popular musicians use their guitar to play different subcategories of one of these musical styles.*

# Judith Viorst: *The Truth About Lying*

Judith Viorst was born in 1931 in Newark, New Jersey, and educated at Rutgers University and Washington Psychoanalytic Institute. She began her career by writing a science book about NASA's space program, *Projects: Space* (1962). Viorst then turned to poetry, *The Village Square* (1965), and eventually children's literature, *Sunday Morning* (1968). In her distinguished career as a poet, fiction writer, and children's author, she has blended her wry humor with critical analysis. Her more recent books include *Super-Completely and Totally the Messiest* (2000), *Suddenly Sixty and Other Shocks of Later Life* (2000), and *I'm Too Young to Be Seventy* (2005). She received the Foremother Award for lifetime achievements from the National Research Center for Women & Families in 2011. In "The Truth About Lying," reprinted from *Redbook*, Viorst classifies lying in terms of "a series of moral puzzles."

I 'VE BEEN WANTING to write on a subject that intrigues and 1 challenges me: the subject of lying. I've found it very difficult to do. Everyone I've talked to has a quite intense and personal but often rather intolerant point of view about what we can—and can never *never*—tell lies about. I've finally reached the conclusion that I can't present any ultimate conclusions, for too many people would promptly disagree. Instead, I'd like to present a series of moral puzzles, all concerned with lying. I'll tell you what I think about them. Do you agree?

## SOCIAL LIES

Most of the people I've talked with say that they find social    2
lying acceptable and necessary. They think it's the civilized
way for folks to behave. Without these little white lies, they
say, our relationships would be short and brutish and nasty.
It's arrogant, they say, to insist on being so incorruptible and
so brave that you cause other people unnecessary embarrassment or pain by compulsively assailing them with your hon-
esty. I basically agree. What about you?

   Will you say to people, when it simply isn't true, "I like    3
your new hairdo," "You're looking much better," "It's so nice
to see you," "I had a wonderful time"?

---

*Everyone I've talked to has a quite intense
and personal but often rather intolerant
view about what we can—and can never
never—tell lies about.*

---

   Will you praise hideous presents and homely kids?    4
   Will you decline invitations with "We're busy that night—    5
so sorry we can't come," when the truth is you'd rather stay
home than dine with the So-and-sos?

   And even though, as I do, you may prefer the polite evasion    6
of "You really cooked up a storm" instead of "The soup"—
which tastes like warmed-over coffee—"is wonderful," will
you, if you must, proclaim it wonderful?

   There's one man I know who absolutely refuses to tell    7
social lies. "I can't play that game," he says; "I'm simply not
made that way." And his answer to the argument that saying nice things to someone doesn't cost anything is, "Yes, it
does—it destroys your credibility." Now, he won't, unsolic-
ited, offer his views on the painting you just bought, but you
don't ask his frank opinion unless you want *frank*, and his

silence at those moments when the rest of us liars are muttering, "Isn't it lovely?" is, for the most part, eloquent enough. My friend does not indulge in what he calls "flattery, false praise and mellifluous comments." When others tell fibs he will not go along. He says that social lying is lying, that little white lies are still lies. And he feels that telling lies is morally wrong. What about you?

## PEACE-KEEPING LIES

Many people tell peace-keeping lies; lies designed to avoid    8
irritation or argument; lies designed to shelter the liar from possible blame or pain; lies (or so it is rationalized) designed to keep trouble at bay without hurting anyone.

I tell these lies at times, and yet I always feel they're wrong.    9
I understand why we tell them, but still they feel wrong. And whenever I lie so that someone won't disapprove of me or think less of me or holler at me, I feel I'm a bit of a coward, I feel I'm dodging responsibility, I feel . . . guilty. What about you?

Do you, when you're late for a date because you overslept,    10
say that you're late because you got caught in a traffic jam?

Do you, when you forget to call a friend, say that you called    11
several times but the line was busy?

Do you, when you didn't remember that it was your    12
father's birthday, say that his present must be delayed in the mail?

And when you're planning a weekend in New York City    13
and you're not in the mood to visit your mother, who lives there, do you conceal—with a lie, if you must—the fact that you'll be in New York? Or do you have the courage—or is it the cruelty?—to say, "I'll be in New York, but sorry—I don't plan on seeing you"?

(Dave and his wife Elaine have two quite different points    14
of view on this very subject. He calls her a coward. She says she's being wise. He says she must assert her right to visit New York sometimes and not see her mother. To which she

always patiently replies: "Why should we have useless fights? My mother's too old to change. We get along much better when I lie to her.")

Finally, do you keep the peace by telling your husband lies   15
on the subject of money? Do you reduce what you really paid for your shoes? And in general do you find yourself ready, willing and able to lie to him when you make absurd mistakes or lose or break things?

"I used to have a romantic idea that part of intimacy was   16
confessing every dumb thing that you did to your husband. But after a couple of years of that," says Laura, "have I changed my mind!"

And having changed her mind, she finds herself telling   17
peace-keeping lies. And yes, I tell them too. What about you?


## PROTECTIVE LIES

Protective lies are lies folks tell—often quite serious lies—   18
because they're convinced that the truth would be too damaging. They lie because they feel there are certain human values that supersede the wrong of having lied. They lie, not for personal gain, but because they believe it's for the good of the person they're lying to. They lie to those they love, to those who trust them most of all, on the grounds that breaking this trust is justified.

They may lie to their children on money or marital matters.   19

They may lie to the dying about the state of their health.   20

They may lie about adultery, and not—so they insist—to   21
save their own hide, but to save the heart and the pride of the men they are married to.

They may lie to their closest friend because the truth about   22
her talents or son or psyche would be—or so they insist—utterly devastating.

I sometimes tell such lies, but I'm aware that it's quite   23
presumptuous to claim I know what's best for others to know. That's called playing God. That's called manipulation and

control. And we never can be sure, once we start to juggle lies, just where they'll land, exactly where they'll roll.

And furthermore, we may find ourselves lying in order to back up the lies that are backing up the lie we initially told. 24

And furthermore—let's be honest—if conditions were reversed, we certainly wouldn't want anyone lying to us. 25

Yet, having said all that, I still believe that there are times when protective lies must nonetheless be told. What about you? 26

If your Dad had a very bad heart and you had to tell him some bad family news, which would you choose: to tell him the truth or lie? 27

If your former husband failed to send his monthly child-support check and in other ways behaved like a total rat, would you allow your children—who believed he was simply wonderful—to continue to believe that he was wonderful? 28

If your dearly beloved brother selected a wife whom you deeply disliked, would you reveal your feelings or would you fake it? 29

And if you were asked, after making love, "And how was that for you?" would you reply, if it wasn't too good, "Not too good"? 30

Now, some would call a sex lie unimportant, little more than social lying, a simple act of courtesy that makes all human intercourse run smoothly. And some would say all sex lies are bad news and unacceptably protective. Because, says Ruth, "a man with an ego that fragile doesn't need your lies—he needs a psychiatrist." Still others feel that sex lies are indeed protective lies, more serious than simple social lying, and yet at times they tell them on the grounds that when it comes to matters sexual, everybody's ego is somewhat fragile. 31

"If most of the time things go well in sex," says Sue, "I think you're allowed to dissemble when they don't. I can't believe it's good to say, 'Last night was four stars, darling, but tonight's performance rates only a half.'" 32

I'm inclined to agree with Sue. What about you? 33

## TRUST-KEEPING LIES

Another group of lies are trust-keeping lies, lies that involve       34
triangulation, with *A* (that's you) telling lies to *B* on behalf
of *C* (whose trust you'd promised to keep). Most people con-
cede that once you've agreed not to betray a friend's confidence, you can't betray it, even if you must lie. But I've talked
with people who don't want you telling them anything that
they might be called on to lie about.

"I don't tell lies for myself," says Fran, "and I don't want       35
to have to tell them for other people." Which means, she
agrees, that if her best friend is having an affair, she absolutely
doesn't want to know about it.

"Are you saying," her best friend asks, "that if I went       36
off with a lover and I asked you to tell my husband I'd
been with you, that you wouldn't lie for me, that you'd
betray me?"

Fran is very pained but very adamant. "I wouldn't want to       37
betray you, so . . . don't ask me."

Fran's best friend is shocked. What about you?       38

Do you believe you can have close friends if you're not       39
prepared to receive their deepest secrets?

Do you believe you must always lie for your friends?       40

Do you believe, if your friend tells a secret that turns out       41
to be quite immoral or illegal, that once you've promised to
keep it, you must keep it?

And what if your friend were your boss—if you were per-       42
haps one of the President's men—would you betray or lie for
him over, say, Watergate?

As you can see, these issues get terribly sticky.       43

It's my belief that once we've promised to keep a trust,       44
we must tell lies to keep it. I also believe that we can't tell
Watergate lies. And if these two statements strike you as quite
contradictory, you're right—they're quite contradictory. But
for now they're the best I can do. What about you?

Some say that truth will out and thus you might as well tell       45
the truth. Some say you can't regain the trust that lies lose.
Some say that even though the truth may never be revealed,

our lies pervert and damage our relationships. Some say . . . well, here's what some of them have to say.

"I'm a coward," says Grace, "about telling close people important, difficult truths. I find that I'm unable to carry it off. And so if something is bothering me, it keeps building up inside till I end up just not seeing them anymore." 46

"I lie to my husband on sexual things, but I'm furious," says Joyce, "that he's too insensitive to know I'm lying." 47

" I suffer most from the misconception that children can't take the truth," says Emily. "But I'm starting to see that what's harder and more damaging for them is being told lies, is *not* being told the truth." 48

"I'm afraid," says Joan, "that we often wind up feeling a bit of contempt for the people we lie to." 49

And then there are those who have no talent for lying. 50

"Over the years, I tried to lie," a friend of mine explained, "but I always got found out and I always got punished. I guess I gave myself away because I feel guilty about any kind of lying. It looks as if I'm stuck with telling the truth." 51

For those of us, however, who are good at telling lies, for those of us who lie and don't get caught, the question of whether or not to lie can be a hard and serious moral problem. I liked the remark of a friend of mine who said, "I'm willing to lie. But just as a last resort—the truth's always better." 52

"Because," he explained, "though others may completely accept the lie I'm telling, I don't." 53

I tend to feel that way too. 54

What about you? 55

## *For Critical Thinking*

---

### QUESTIONS ABOUT PURPOSE

---

1. How does Viorst's confession that she finds the subject of lying intriguing, challenging, and difficult establish the purpose of her essay?
2. How does her inability to "present any ultimate conclusions" explain the design of her essay?

## QUESTIONS ABOUT AUDIENCE

1. What assumptions does Viorst make about her readers' interest in and familiarity with her subject?
2. How does she use the pronoun *you* to establish a connection with her readers?

## QUESTIONS ABOUT STRATEGIES

1. Into what main categories does Viorst divide the subject of lying? Can you think of other categories she might have included?
2. What inconsistencies does she admit she has created in some of her categories?

## For Writing and Research

1. *Analyze* how Viorst classifies the people who tell lies and the people who are lied to.
2. *Practice* by classifying the situations in which it is acceptable and appropriate to lie.
3. *Argue* that telling one lie requires telling many additional lies.
4. *Synthesize:* Research the definitions of *integrity*. Then use this information to support Viorst's suggestions about the relationship between telling the truth and maintaining trust.

David Cole was born in 1958 and educated at Yale University. He has worked as an attorney for the Center for Constitutional Rights, taught at Georgetown Law School, and served as legal correspondent for *The Nation* and legal commentator on *All Things Considered* on National Public Radio. His books include *No Equal Justice: Race and Class in the American Criminal Justice System* (1999), *Enemy Aliens: Double Standards and Constitutional Freedoms in the War on Terrorism* (2003), and (with Jules Lobel) *Less Safe, Less Free: Why America Is Losing the War on Terror* (2007) and *The Torture Memoes: Rationalizing the Unthinkable* (2009). In "Five Myths About Immigration," reprinted from *The Nation*, Cole classifies the myths that "distort public debate and government policy relating to immigrants."

F OR A BRIEF PERIOD in the mid-nineteenth century, a new political movement captured the passions of the American public. Fittingly labeled the "Know-Nothings," their unifying theme was nativism. They liked to call themselves "Native Americans," although they had no sympathy for people we call Native Americans today. And they pinned every problem in American society on immigrants. As one Know-Nothing wrote in 1856: "Four-fifths of the beggary and three-fifths of the crime spring from our foreign population; more than half the public charities, more than half the prisons and almshouses, more than half the police and the cost of administering criminal justice are for foreigners."

At the time, the greatest influx of immigrants was from Ireland, where the potato famine had struck, and Germany, which was in political and economic turmoil. Anti-alien and anti-Catholic sentiments were the order of the day, especially in New York and Massachusetts, which received the brunt of the wave of immigrants, many of whom were dirt-poor and uneducated. Politicians were quick to exploit the sentiment: There's nothing like a scapegoat to forge an alliance.

I am especially sensitive to this history: My forebears were    3
among those dirt-poor Irish Catholics who arrived in the 1860s. Fortunately for them, and me, the Know-Nothing movement fizzled within fifteen years. But its pilot light kept burning and is turned up whenever the American public begins to feel vulnerable and in need of an enemy.

> *[P]assion, misinformation and shortsighted fear often substitute for reason, fairness and human dignity in today's immigration debates.*

Although they go by different names today, the Know-    4
Nothings have returned. As in the 1850s, the movement is strongest where immigrants are most concentrated: California and Florida. The objects of prejudice are of course no longer Irish Catholics and Germans; 140 years later, "they" have become "us." The new "they"—because it seems "we" must always have a "they"—are Latin Americans (most recently, Cubans), Haitians, and Arab-Americans, among others.

But just as in the 1850s, passion, misinformation and    5
shortsighted fear often substitute for reason, fairness, and human dignity in today's immigration debates. In the interest of advancing beyond know-nothingism, let's look at five current myths that distort public debate and government policy relating to immigrants.

*America is being overrun with immigrants.* In one sense,    6
of course, this is true, but in that sense it has been true since

Christopher Columbus arrived. Except for the real Native Americans, we are a nation of immigrants.

It is not true, however, that the first-generation immigrant 7 share of our population is growing. As of 1990, foreign-born people made up only 8 percent of the population, as compared with a figure of about 15 percent from 1870 to 1920. Between 70 and 80 percent of those who immigrate every year are refugees or immediate relatives of U.S. citizens.

Much of the anti-immigrant fervor is directed against the 8 undocumented, but they make up only 13 percent of all immigrants residing in the United States, and only 1 percent of the American population. Contrary to popular belief, most such aliens do not cross the border illegally but enter legally and remain after their student or visitor visa expires. Thus, building a wall at the border, no matter how high, will not solve the problem.

*Immigrants take jobs from U.S. citizens.* There is virtually no 9 evidence to support this view, probably the most widespread misunderstanding about immigrants. As documented by a 1994 A.C.L.U. Immigrants' Rights Project report, numerous studies have found that immigrants actually *create* more jobs than they fill. The jobs immigrants take are of course easier to see, but immigrants are often highly productive, run their own businesses, and employ both immigrants and citizens. One study found that Mexican immigration to Los Angeles County between 1970 and 1980 was responsible for 78,000 new jobs. Governor Mario Cuomo reports that immigrants own more than 40,000 companies in New York, which provide thousands of jobs and $3.5 billion to the state's economy every year.

*Immigrants are a drain on society's resources.* This claim fuels 10 many of the recent efforts to cut off government benefits to immigrants. However, most studies have found that immigrants are a net benefit to the economy because, as a 1994 Urban Institute report concludes, "immigrants generate significantly more in taxes paid than they cost in services received." The Council of Economic Advisers similarly found in 1986 that "immigrants have a favorable effect on the overall standard of living."

Anti-immigrant advocates often cite studies purportedly    11
showing the contrary, but these generally focus only on taxes
and services at the local or state level. What they fail to explain
is that because most taxes go to the federal government, such
studies would also show a net loss when applied to U.S. citizens. At most, such figures suggest that some redistribution of
federal and state monies may be appropriate; they say nothing
unique about the costs of immigrants.

Some subgroups of immigrants plainly impose a net cost    12
in the short run, principally those who have most recently
arrived and have not yet "made it." California, for example,
bears substantial costs for its disproportionately large undocumented population, largely because it has on average the
poorest and least educated immigrants. But that has been
true of every wave of immigrants that has ever reached our
shores; it was as true of the Irish in the 1850s, for example, as
it is of Salvadorans today. From a long-term perspective, the
economic advantages of immigration are undeniable.

Some have suggested that we might save money and dimin-    13
ish incentives to immigrate illegally if we denied undocumented
aliens public services. In fact, undocumented immigrants are
already ineligible for most social programs, with the exception of education for schoolchildren, which is constitutionally
required, and benefits directly related to health and safety,
such as emergency medical care and nutritional assistance to
poor women, infants, and children. To deny such basic care
to people in need, apart from being inhumanly callous, would
probably cost us more in the long run by exacerbating health
problems that we would eventually have to address.

*Aliens refuse to assimilate and are depriving us of our cul-*    14
*tural and political unity.* This claim has been made about
every new group of immigrants to arrive on U.S. shores.
Supreme Court Justice Stephen Field wrote in 1884 that the
Chinese "have remained among us a separate people, retaining their original peculiarities of dress, manners, habits, and
modes of living, which are as marked as their complexion and
language." Five years later, he upheld the racially based exclu-
sion of Chinese immigrants. Similar claims have been made

over different periods of our history about Catholics, Jews, Italians, Eastern Europeans, and Latin Americans.

In most instances, such claims are simply not true; "American culture" has been created, defined, and revised by persons who for the most part are descended from immigrants once seen as anti-assimilationist. Descendants of the Irish Catholics, for example, a group once decried as separatist and alien, have become Presidents, senators, and representatives (and all of these in one family, in the case of the Kennedys). Our society exerts tremendous pressure to conform, and cultural separatism rarely survives a generation. But more important, even if this claim were true, is this a legitimate rationale for limiting immigration in a society built on the values of pluralism and tolerance? 15

*Noncitizen immigrants are not entitled to constitutional rights.* Our government has long declined to treat immigrants as full human beings, and nowhere is that more clear than in the realm of constitutional rights. Although the Constitution literally extends the fundamental protections in the Bill of Rights to all people, limiting to citizens only the right to vote and run for federal office, the federal government acts as if this were not the case. 16

In 1893, the executive branch successfully defended a statute that required Chinese laborers to establish their prior residence here by the testimony of "at least one credible white witness." The Supreme Court ruled that this law was constitutional because it was reasonable for Congress to presume that non-white witnesses could not be trusted. 17

The federal government is not much more enlightened today. In a pending case I'm handling in the Court of Appeals for the Ninth Circuit, the Clinton Administration has argued that permanent resident aliens lawfully living here should be extended no more First Amendment rights than aliens applying for first-time admission from abroad—that is, none. Under this view, students at a public university who are citizens may express themselves freely, but students who are not citizens can be deported for saying exactly what their classmates are constitutionally entitled to say. 18

Growing up, I was always taught that we will be judged by    19
how we treat others. If we are collectively judged by how we
have treated immigrants—those who would appear today to
be "other" but will in a generation be "us"—we are not in
very good shape.

## For Critical Thinking

### QUESTIONS ABOUT PURPOSE

1. Why does Cole begin his essay with a discussion of the "Know-Nothing" political movement?
2. Why does he describe his categories as *myths* rather than errors or mistakes?

### QUESTIONS ABOUT AUDIENCE

1. How does Cole use his own family history to establish a connection with his readers?
2. How does he address his readers who may favor the anti-immigrant position?

### QUESTIONS ABOUT STRATEGIES

1. What kind of evidence does Cole use to dispute each of the five myths?
2. How does he use his last paragraph to bring his analysis to an appropriate conclusion?

## For Writing and Research

1. *Analyze* the evidence Cole uses to assert the long-term economic advantages of immigration.
2. *Practice* by classifying several *myths* about a specific group of immigrants in your community.
3. *Argue* that there is some justification for the assertion that immigrants resist—or at least have great difficulty—assimilating into American culture.
4. *Synthesize:* Research the immigration history of your family. Then use this information to help explain why certain generations of your family seemed to support or refute one of Cole's myths.

# James H. Austin: *Four Kinds of Chance*

James H. Austin was born in 1925 in Cleveland, Ohio, and educated at Brown University and Harvard University Medical School. After an internship at Boston City Hospital and a residency at the Neurological Institute of New York, Austin established a private practice in neurology, first in Portland, Oregon, and then in Denver, Colorado. He currently serves as professor and head of the Department of Neurology at the University of Colorado Medical School. His major publication, *Chase, Chance, and Creativity: The Lucky Art of Novelty* (1978), addresses the issue of how "chance and creativity interact in biomedical research." His recent books include *Zen and the Brain: Toward an Understanding of Meditation and Consciousness* (1999), *Zen-Brain Reflections: Reviewing Recent Developments in Meditation and States of Consciousness* (2006), and *Meditating Selflessly: Practical Neural Zen* (2011). In this essay, published originally in *Saturday Review* (November 2, 1972), Austin distinguishes four kinds of chance by the way humans react to their environment.

WHAT IS CHANCE? Dictionaries define it as something fortuitous that happens unpredictably without discernible human intention. Chance is unintentional and capricious, but we needn't conclude that chance is immune from human intervention. Indeed, chance plays several distinct roles when humans react creatively with one another and with their environment. 1

We can readily distinguish four varieties of chance if we consider that they each involve a different kind of motor activity and a special kind of sensory receptivity. The varieties of 2 chance also involve distinctive personality traits and differ in the way one particular individual influences them.

Chance I is the pure blind luck that comes with no effort 3 on your part. If, for example, you are sitting at a bridge table of four, it's "in the cards" for you to receive a hand of all 13 spades, but it will come up only once in every 6.3 trillion deals. You will ultimately draw this lucky hand—with no intervention on your part—but it does involve a longer wait than most of us have time for.

Chance II evokes the kind of luck Charles Kettering had 4 in mind when he said: "Keep on going and the chances are you will stumble on something, perhaps when you are least expecting it. I have never heard of anyone stumbling on something sitting down."

---

*The term serendipity describes the facility for encountering unexpected good luck, as the result of accident, general exploratory behavior, or sagacity.*

---

In the sense referred to here, Chance II is not passive, 5 but springs from an energetic, generalized motor activity. A certain basal level of action "stirs up the pot," brings in random ideas that will collide and stick together in fresh combinations, lets chance operate. When someone, *anyone*, does swing into motion and keeps on going, he will increase the number of collisions between events. When a few events are linked together, they can then be exploited to have a fortuitous outcome, but many others, of course, cannot. Kettering was right. Press on. Something will turn up. We may term this the Kettering Principle.

In the two previous examples, a unique role of the indi- 6 vidual person was either lacking or minimal. Accordingly, as we move on to Chance III, we see blind luck, but in camouflage.

Chance presents the clue, the opportunity exists, but it would be missed except by that one person uniquely equipped to observe it, visualize it conceptually, and fully grasp its significance. Chance III involves a special receptivity and discernment unique to the recipient. Louis Pasteur characterized it for all time when he said: "Chance favors only the prepared mind."

Pasteur himself had it in full measure. But the classic example of his principle occurred in 1928, when Alexander Fleming's mind instantly fused at least five elements into a conceptually unified nexus. His mental sequences went something like this: (1) I see that a mold has fallen by accident into my culture dish; (2) the staphylococcal colonies residing near it failed to grow; (3) the mold must have secreted something that killed the bacteria; (4) I recall a similar experience once before; (5) if I could separate this new "something" from the mold, it could be used to kill staphylococci that cause human infections.

Actually, Fleming's mind was exceptionally well prepared for the penicillin mold. Six years earlier, while he was suffering from a cold, his own nasal drippings had found their way into a culture dish, for reasons not made entirely clear. He noted that nearby bacteria were killed and astutely followed up the lead. His observations led him to discover a bactericidal enzyme present in nasal mucus and tears, called lysozyme. Lysozyme proved too weak to be of medical use, but imagine how receptive Fleming's mind was to the penicillin mold when it later happened on the scene!

One word evokes the quality of the operations involved in the first three kinds of chance. It is *serendipity*. The term describes the facility for encountering unexpected good luck, as the result of accident (Chance I), general exploratory behavior (Chance II), or sagacity (Chance III). The word itself was coined by the Englishman-of-letters Horace Walpole, in 1754. He used it with reference to the legendary tales of the Three Princes of Serendip (Ceylon), who quite unexpectedly encountered many instances of good fortune on their travels. In today's parlance, we have usually watered down *serendipity* to mean the good luck that comes solely by accident. We think of it as a result, not an ability. We have tended to lose sight of the element of sagacity, by which term Walpole wished to emphasize that some distinctive personal receptivity is involved.

There remains a fourth element in good luck, an uninten-      10
tional but subtle personal prompting of it. The English Prime Minister Benjamin Disraeli summed up the principle underlying Chance IV when he noted that "we make our fortunes and we call them fate." Disraeli, a politician of considerable practical experience, appreciated that we each shape our own destiny, at least to some degree. One might restate the principle as follows: *Chance favors the individualized action.*

In Chance IV, the kind of luck is peculiar to one person,      11
and like a personal hobby, it takes on a distinctive individual flavor. This form of chance is one-man-made, and it is as personal as a signature. . . . Chance IV has an elusive, almost miragelike, quality. Like a mirage, it is difficult to get a firm grip on, for it tends to recede as we pursue it and advance as we step back. But we still accept a mirage when we see it, because we vaguely understand the basis for the phenomenon. A strongly heated layer of air, less dense than usual, lies next to the earth, and it bends the light rays as they pass through. The resulting image may be magnified as if by a telescopic lens in the atmosphere, and real objects, ordinarily hidden far out of sight over the horizon, are brought forward and revealed to the eye. What happens in a mirage then, and in this form of chance, not only appears farfetched but indeed is farfetched.

About a century ago, a striking example of Chance IV took      12
place in the Spanish cave of Altamira.* There, one day in 1879, Don Marcelino de Sautuola was engaged in his hobby of archaeology, searching Altamira for bones and stones. With him was his daughter, Maria, who had asked him if she could come along to the cave that day. The indulgent father had said she could. Naturally enough, he first looked where he had always found heavy objects before, on the *floor* of the cave.

---

* The cave had first been discovered some years before by an enterprising hunting dog in search of game. Curiously, in 1932, the French cave of Lascaux was discovered by still another dog.

But Maria, unhampered by any such preconceptions, looked not only at the floor but also all around the cave with the open-eyed wonder of a child! She looked up, exclaimed, and then he looked up, to see incredible works of art on the cave ceiling! The magnificent colored bison and other animals they saw at Altamira, painted more than 15,000 years ago, might lead one to call it "the Sistine Chapel of Prehistory." Passionately pursuing his interest in archaeology, de Sautuola, to his surprise, discovered man's first paintings. In quest of science, he happened upon Art.

Yes, a dog did "discover" the cave, and the initial receptivity was his daughter's, but the pivotal reason for the cave paintings' discovery hinged on a long sequence of prior events originating in de Sautuola himself. For when we dig into the background of this amateur excavator, we find he was an exceptional person. Few Spaniards were out probing into caves 100 years ago. The fact that he—not someone else—decided to dig that day in the cave of Altamira was the culmination of his passionate interest in his hobby. Here was a rare man whose avocation had been to educate himself from scratch, as it were, in the science of archaeology and cave exploration. This was no simple passive recognizer of blind luck when it came his way, but a man whose unique interests served as an active creative thrust—someone whose own actions and personality would focus the events that led circuitously but inexorably to the discovery of man's first paintings. 13

Then, too, there is a more subtle matter. How do you give full weight to the personal interests that imbue your child with your own curiosity, that inspire her to ask to join you in your own musty hobby, and that then lead you to agree to her request at the critical moment? For many reasons, at Altamira, more than the special receptivity of Chance III was required—this was a different domain, that of the personality and its actions. 14

A century ago no one had the remotest idea our caveman ancestors were highly creative artists. Weren't their talents rather minor and limited to crude flint chippings? But the paintings at Altamira, like a mirage, would quickly magnify 15 this diminutive view, bring up into full focus a distant, hidden era of man's prehistory, reveal sentient minds and well-developed aesthetic sensibilities to which men of any age might aspire. And like a mirage, the events at Altamira grew out of de Sautuola's heated personal quest and out of the invisible forces of chance we know exist yet cannot touch. Accordingly, one may introduce the term *altamirage* to identify the quality underlying Chance IV. Let us define it as the facility for encountering unexpected good luck as the result of highly individualized action. *Altamirage* goes well beyond the boundaries of serendipity in its emphasis on the role of personal action in chance.

Chance IV is favored by distinctive, if not eccentric, hob-          16
bies, personal life-styles, and modes of behavior peculiar to one individual, usually invested with some passion. The farther apart these personal activities are from the area under investigation, the more novel and unexpected will be the creative product of the encounter.

## For Critical Thinking

### QUESTIONS ABOUT PURPOSE

1. What elements of human behavior and attitude does Austin demonstrate by dividing chance into four varieties?
2. What relationship does Austin discover between the words *luck*, *serendipity*, *sagacity*, and *altamirage*?

### QUESTIONS ABOUT AUDIENCE

1. What assumptions does Austin make about his readers when he offers them *the best example* rather than several examples to illustrate each category?
2. How does Austin's attitude toward his audience change during the essay? For example, why does he speak directly to his readers when he explains Chance I but address them more formally in his discussion of other categories?

---
## QUESTIONS ABOUT STRATEGIES
---

1. How does Austin arrange his four categories? Why doesn't he give equal treatment to each category?
2. How does Austin use transitions and summaries to clarify the differences between the major categories? In particular, see paragraphs 6 and 9.

## *For Writing and Research*

1. *Analyze:* the "best" examples Austin uses to illustrate his four kinds of chance.
2. *Practice:* by classifying types of bad luck.
3. *Argue:* in favor of baseball owner Branch Rickey's assertion that "luck is the residue of design."
4. *Synthesize:* the research on those who make a career of gambling—for example, professional poker players. Then use this evidence to argue that skill does or does not contribute to this success.

Flannery O'Connor (1925–1964) was born in Savannah, Georgia, and was educated at the Women's College of Georgia and the University of Iowa. She returned to her mother's farm near Milledgeville, Georgia, when she discovered that she had contracted lupus erythematosus, the systemic disease that had killed her father and of which she herself was to die. For the last fourteen years of her life, she lived a quiet, productive life on the farm—raising peacocks, painting, and writing the extraordinary stories and novels that won her worldwide acclaim. Her novels, *Wise Blood* (1952), which was adapted for film in 1979, and *The Violent Bear It Away* (1960), deal with fanatical preachers. Her thirty-one carefully crafted stories, combining grotesque comedy and violent tragedy, appear in *A Good Man Is Hard to Find* (1955), *Everything That Rises Must Converge* (1965), and *The Complete Stories* (1971), which won the National Book Award. "Revelation," reprinted from *The Complete Stories,* dramatizes the ironic discoveries a woman makes about how different classes of people fit into the order of things.

THE DOCTOR'S WAITING room, which was very small, was     1
almost full when the Turpins entered and Mrs. Turpin, who was very large, made it look even smaller by her presence. She stood looming at the head of the magazine table set in the center of it, a living demonstration that the room was inadequate and ridiculous. Her little bright black eyes took in all the patients as she sized up the seating situation. There was one vacant chair and a place on the sofa occupied by a blond

child in a dirty blue romper who should have been told to move over and make room for the lady. He was five or six, but Mrs. Turpin saw at once that no one was going to tell him to move over. He was slumped down in the seat, his arms idle at his sides and his eyes idle in his head; his nose ran unchecked.

Mrs. Turpin put a firm hand on Claud's shoulder and said  2
in a voice that included anyone who wanted to listen, "Claud, you sit in that chair there," and gave him a push down into the vacant one. Claud was florid and bald and sturdy, somewhat shorter than Mrs. Turpin, but he sat down as if he were accustomed to doing what she told him to.

Mrs. Turpin remained standing. The only man in the room  3
besides Claud was a lean stringy old fellow with a rusty hand spread out on each knee, whose eyes were closed as if he were asleep or dead or pretending to be so as not to get up and offer her his seat. Her gaze settled agreeably on a well-dressed gray-haired lady whose eyes met hers and whose expression said: if that child belonged to me, he would have some manners and move over—there's plenty of room there for you and him too.

Claud looked up with a sigh and made as if to rise.  4

"Sit down," Mrs. Turpin said. "You know you're not sup-  5
posed to stand on that leg. He has an ulcer on his leg," she explained.

Claud lifted his foot onto the magazine table and rolled his  6
trouser leg up to reveal a purple swelling on a plump marble-white calf.

"My!" the pleasant lady said. "How did you do that?"  7

"A cow kicked him," Mrs. Turpin said.  8

"Goodness!" said the lady.  9

Claud rolled his trouser leg down.  10

"Maybe the little boy would move over," the lady sug-  11
gested, but the child did not stir.

"Somebody will be leaving in a minute," Mrs. Turpin said.  12
She could not understand why a doctor—with as much money as they made charging five dollars a day to just stick their head in the hospital door and look at you—couldn't afford a decent-sized waiting room. This one was hardly bigger than a

garage. The table was cluttered with limp-looking magazines and at one end of it there was a big green glass ash tray full of cigarette butts and cotton wads with little blood spots on them. If she had had anything to do with the running of the place, that would have been emptied every so often. There were no chairs against the wall at the head of the room. It had a rectangular-shaped panel in it that permitted a view of the office where the nurse came and went and the secretary listened to the radio. A plastic fern in a gold pot sat in the opening and trailed its fronds down almost to the floor. The radio was softly playing gospel music.

Just then the inner door opened and a nurse with the high- 13 est stack of yellow hair Mrs. Turpin had ever seen put her face in the crack and called for the next patient. The woman sitting beside Claud grasped the two arms of her chair and hoisted herself up; she pulled her dress free from her legs and lumbered through the door where the nurse had disappeared.

Mrs. Turpin eased into the vacant chair, which held her 14 tight as a corset. "I wish I could reduce," she said, and rolled her eyes and gave a comic sigh.

"Oh, *you* aren't fat," the stylish lady said. 15

"Ooooo I am too," Mrs. Turpin said. "Claud he eats all 16 he wants to and never weighs over one hundred and seventy-five pounds, but me I just look at something good to eat and I gain some weight," and her stomach and shoulders shook with laughter. "You can eat all you want to, can't you, Claud?" she asked, turning to him.

Claud only grinned. 17

"Well, as long as you have such a good disposition," the 18 stylish lady said, "I don't think it makes a bit of difference what size you are. You just can't beat a good disposition."

Next to her was a fat girl of eighteen or nineteen, scowling 19 into a thick blue book which Mrs. Turpin saw was entitled *Human Development*. The girl raised her head and directed her scowl at Mrs. Turpin as if she did not like her looks. She appeared annoyed that anyone should speak while she tried to read. The poor girl's face was blue with acne and Mrs. Turpin thought how pitiful it was to have a face like that at that age.

She gave the girl a friendly smile but the girl only scowled the harder. Mrs. Turpin herself was fat but she had always had good skin, and, though she was forty-seven years old, there was not a wrinkle in her face except around her eyes from laughing too much.

Next to the ugly girl was the child, still in exactly the same position, and next to him was a thin leathery old woman in a cotton print dress. She and Claud had three sacks of chicken feed in their pump house that was in the same print. She had seen from the first that the child belonged with the old woman. She could tell by the way they sat—kind of vacant and white-trashy, as if they would sit there until Doomsday if nobody called and told them to get up. And at right angles but next to the well-dressed pleasant lady was a lank-faced woman who was certainly the child's mother. She had on a yellow sweat shirt and wine-colored slacks, both gritty-looking, and the rims of her lips were stained with snuff. Her dirty yellow hair was tied behind with a little piece of red paper ribbon. Worse than niggers any day, Mrs. Turpin thought.

The gospel hymn playing was, "When I looked up and He looked down," and Mrs. Turpin, who knew it, supplied the last line mentally, "And wona these days I know I'll wear a crown."

Without appearing to, Mrs. Turpin always noticed people's feet. The well-dressed lady had on red and gray suede shoes to match her dress. Mrs. Turpin had on her good black patent leather pumps. The ugly girl had on Girl Scout shoes and heavy socks. The old woman had on tennis shoes and the white-trashy mother had on what appeared to be bedroom slippers, black straw with gold braid threaded through them— exactly what you would have expected her to have on.

Sometimes at night when she couldn't go to sleep, Mrs. Turpin would occupy herself with the question of who she would have chosen to be if she couldn't have been herself. If Jesus had said to her before he made her, "There's only two places available for you. You can either be a nigger or white-trash," what would she have said? "Please, Jesus, please," she would have said, "just let me wait until there's another place available," and he would have said, "No, you have to go right now and I have only those two places so make up your mind." She would have wiggled and squirmed and begged and pleaded but it would have been no use and finally she would have said, "All right, make me a nigger then—but that don't mean a trashy one." And he would have made her a neat clean respectable Negro woman, herself but black.

Next to the child's mother was a red-headed young-       24
ish woman, reading one of the magazines and working a piece of chewing gum, hell for leather, as Claud would say. Mrs. Turpin could not see the woman's feet. She was not white-trash, just common. Sometimes Mrs. Turpin occupied herself at night naming the classes of people. On the bottom of the heap were most colored people, not the kind she would have been if she had been one, but most of them; then next to them—not above, just away from—were the white-trash; then above them were the home- owners, and above them the home-and-land-owners, to which she and Claud belonged. Above she and Claud were people with a lot of money and much bigger houses and much more land. But here the complexity of it would begin to bear in on her, for some of the people with a lot of money were common and ought to be below she and Claud and some of the people who had good blood had lost their money and had to rent and then there were colored people who owned their homes and land as well. There was a colored dentist in town who had two red Lincolns and a swimming pool and a farm with registered white-face cattle on it. Usually by the time she had fallen asleep all the classes of people were moiling and roiling around in her head, and she would dream they were all crammed in together in a box car, being ridden off to be put in a gas oven.

"That's a beautiful clock," she said and nodded to her right.       25
It was a big wall clock, the face encased in a brass sunburst.

"Yes, it's very pretty," the stylish lady said agreeably. "And       26
right on the dot too," she added, glancing at her watch.

The ugly girl beside her cast an eye upward at the clock,       27
smirked, then looked directly at Mrs. Turpin and smirked again. Then she returned her eyes to her book. She was

obviously the lady's daughter because, although they didn't look anything alike as to disposition, they both had the same shape of face and the same blue eyes. On the lady they sparkled pleasantly but in the girl's seared face they appeared alternately to smolder and to blaze.

What if Jesus had said, "All right, you can be white-trash   28
or a nigger or ugly"!

Mrs. Turpin felt an awful pity for the girl, though she   29
thought it was one thing to be ugly and another to act ugly.

The woman with the snuff-stained lips turned around in   30
her chair and looked up at the clock. Then she turned back and appeared to look a little to the side of Mrs. Turpin. There was a cast in one of her eyes. "You want to know wher you can get you one of themther clocks?" she asked in a loud voice.

"No, I already have a nice clock," Mrs. Turpin said. Once   31
somebody like her got a leg in the conversation, she would be all over it.

"You can get you one with green stamps," the woman said.   32
"That's most likely wher he got hisn. Save you up enough, you can get you most anythang. I got me some joo'ry."

Ought to have got you a wash rag and some soap,   33
Mrs. Turpin thought.

"I get contour sheets with mine," the pleasant lady said.   34

The daughter slammed her book shut. She looked straight   35
in front of her, directly through Mrs. Turpin and on through the yellow curtain and the plate glass window which made the wall behind her. The girl's eyes seemed lit all of a sudden with a peculiar light, an unnatural light like night road signs give. Mrs. Turpin turned her head to see if there was anything going on outside that she should see, but she could not see anything. Figures passing cast only a pale shadow through the curtain. There was no reason the girl should single her out for her ugly looks.

"Miss Finley," the nurse said, cracking the door. The gum-   36
chewing woman got up and passed in front of her and Claud and went into the office. She had on red high-heeled shoes.

Directly across the table, the ugly girl's eyes were fixed on   37
Mrs. Turpin as if she had some very special reason for disliking her.

"This is wonderful weather, isn't it?" the girl's mother said.    38

"It's good weather for cotton if you can get the niggers    39
to pick it," Mrs. Turpin said, "but niggers don't want to pick
cotton any more. You can't get the white folks to pick it and
now you can't get the niggers—because they got to be right
up there with the white folks."

"They gonna *try* anyways," the white-trash woman said,    40
leaning forward.

"Do you have one of the cotton-picking machines?" the    41
pleasant lady asked.

"No," Mrs. Turpin said, "they leave half the cotton in the    42
field. We don't have much cotton anyway. If you want to
make it farming now, you have to have a little of everything.
We got a couple of acres of cotton and a few hogs and chickens and just enough white-face that Claud can look after them
himself."

"One thang I don't want," the white-trash woman said,    43
wiping her mouth with the back of her hand. "Hogs. Nasty
stinking things, a-gruntin and a-rootin all over the place."

Mrs. Turpin gave her the merest edge of her attention.    44
"Our hogs are not dirty and they don't stink," she said.
"They're cleaner than some children I've seen. Their feet
never touch the ground. We have a pig-parlor—that's where
you raise them on concrete," she explained to the pleasant
lady, "and Claud scoots them down with the hose every
afternoon and washes off the floor." Cleaner by far than that
child right there, she thought. Poor nasty little thing. He had
not moved except to put the thumb of his dirty hand into
his mouth.

The woman turned her face away from Mrs. Turpin. "I    45
know I wouldn't scoot down no hog with no hose," she said
to the wall.

You wouldn't have no hog to scoot down, Mrs. Turpin    46
said to herself.

"A-gruntin and a-rootin and a-groanin," the woman    47
muttered.

"We got a little of everything," Mrs. Turpin said to the    48
pleasant lady. "It's no use in having more than you can handle

yourself with help like it is. We found enough niggers to pick our cotton this year but Claud he has to go after them and take them home again in the evening. They can't walk that half a mile. No they can't. I tell you," she said and laughed merrily, "I sure am tired of buttering up niggers, but you got to love em if you want em to work for you. When they come in the morning, I run out and I say, 'Hi yawl this morning?' and when Claud drives them off to the field I just wave to beat the band and they just wave back." And she waved her hand rapidly to illustrate.

"Like you read out of the same book," the lady said, show-  49
ing she understood perfectly.

"Child, yes," Mrs. Turpin said. "And when they come in  50
from the field, I run out with a bucket of icewater. That's the way it's going to be from now on," she said. "You may as well face it."

"One thang I know," the white-trash woman said. "Two  51
thangs I ain't going to do: love no niggers or scoot down no hog with no hose." And she let out a bark of contempt.

The look that Mrs. Turpin and the pleasant lady exchanged  52
indicated they both understood that you had to *have* certain things before you could *know* certain things. But every time Mrs. Turpin exchanged a look with the lady, she was aware that the ugly girl's peculiar eyes were still on her, and she had trouble bringing her attention back to the conversation.

"When you got something," she said, "you got to look after  53
it." And when you ain't got a thing but breath and britches, she added to herself, you can afford to come to town every morning and just sit on the Court House coping and spit.

A grotesque revolving shadow passed across the curtain  54
behind her and was thrown palely on the opposite wall. Then a bicycle clattered down against the outside of the building. The door opened and a colored boy glided in with a tray from the drugstore. It had two large red and white paper cups on it with tops on them. He was a tall, very black boy in discolored white pants and a green nylon shirt. He was chewing gum slowly, as if to music. He set the tray down in the office opening next to the fern and stuck his head through to look

for the secretary. She was not in there. He rested his arms on the ledge and waited, his narrow bottom stuck out, swaying to the left and right. He raised a hand over his head and scratched the base of his skull.

"You see that button there, boy?" Mrs. Turpin said. "You   55
can punch that and she'll come. She's probably in the back somewhere."

"Is thas right?" the boy said agreeably, as if he had never   56
seen the button before. He leaned to the right and put his finger on it. "She sometime out," he said and twisted around to face his audience, his elbows behind him on the counter. The nurse appeared and he twisted back again. She handed him a dollar and he rooted in his pocket and made the change and counted it out to her. She gave him fifteen cents for a tip and he went out with the empty tray. The heavy door swung too slowly and closed at length with the sound of suction. For a moment, no one spoke.

"They ought to send all them niggers back to Africa," the   57
white-trash woman said. "That's wher they come from in the first place."

"Oh, I couldn't do without my good colored friends," the   58
pleasant lady said.

"There's a heap of things worse than a nigger," Mrs. Turpin   59
agreed. "It's all kinds of them just like it's all kinds of us."

"Yes, and it takes all kinds to make the world go round,"   60
the lady said in her musical voice.

As she said it, the raw-complexioned girl snapped her teeth   61
together. Her lower lip turned downward and inside out, revealing the pale pink inside of her mouth. After a second, it rolled back up. It was the ugliest face Mrs. Turpin had ever seen anyone make and for a moment she was certain that the girl had made it at her. She was looking at her as if she had known and disliked her all her life—all of Mrs. Turpin's life, it seemed too, not just all the girl's life. Why, girl, I don't even know you, Mrs. Turpin said silently.

She forced her attention back to the discussion. "It   62
wouldn't be practical to send them back to Africa," she said. "They wouldn't want to go. They got it too good here."

"Wouldn't be what they wanted—if I had anythang to do with it," the woman said. 63

"It wouldn't be a way in the world you could get all the niggers back over there," Mrs. Turpin said. "They'd be hiding out and lying down and turning sick on you and wailing and hollering and raring and pitching. It wouldn't be a way in the world to get them over there." 64

"They got over here," the trashy woman said. "Get back like they got over." 65

"It wasn't so many of them then," Mrs. Turpin explained. 66

The woman looked at Mrs. Turpin as if here was an idiot indeed but Mrs. Turpin was not bothered by the look, considering where it came from. 67

"Nooo," she said, "they're going to stay here where they can go to New York and marry white folks and improve their color. That's what they all want to do, every one of them, improve their color." 68

"You know what comes of that, don't you?" Claud asked. 69

"No, Claud, what?" Mrs. Turpin said. 70

Claud's eyes twinkled. "White-faced niggers," he said with never a smile. 71

Everybody in the office laughed except the white-trash and the ugly girl. The girl gripped the book in her lap with white fingers. The trashy woman looked around her from face to face as if she thought they were all idiots. The old woman in the feed sack dress continued to gaze expressionless across the floor at the high-top shoes of the man opposite her, the one who had been pretending to be asleep when the Turpins came in. He was laughing heartily, his hands still spread out on his knees. The child had fallen to the side and was lying now almost face down in the old woman's lap. 72

While they recovered from their laughter, the nasal chorus on the radio kept the room from silence. 73

> *You go to blank blank*
> *And I'll go to mine*
> *But we'll all blank along*
> *To-geth-ther,*

*And all along the blank*
*We'll hep each other out*
*Smile-ling in any kind of*
*Weath-ther!*

Mrs. Turpin didn't catch every word but she caught enough    74
to agree with the spirit of the song and it turned her thoughts
sober. To help anybody out that needed, it was her philosophy of life. She never spared herself when she found somebody in need, whether they were white or black, trash or
decent. And of all she had to be thankful for, she was most
thankful that this was so. If Jesus had said, "You can be
high society and have all the money you want and be thin
and svelte-like, but you can't be a good woman with it,"
she would have had to say, "Well don't make me that then.
Make me a good woman and it don't matter what else, how
fat or how ugly or how poor!" Her heart rose. He had not
made her a nigger or white-trash or ugly! He had made her
herself and given her a little of everything. Jesus, thank you!
she said. Thank you thank you thank you! Whenever she
counted her blessings she felt as buoyant as if she weighed
one hundred and twenty-five pounds instead of one hundred
and eighty.

"What's wrong with your little boy?" the pleasant lady    75
asked the white-trashy woman.

"He has a ulcer," the woman said proudly. "He ain't give    76
me a minute's peace since he was born. Him and her are just
alike," she said, nodding at the old woman, who was running
her leathery fingers through the child's pale hair. "Look like
I can't get nothing down them two but Co' Cola and candy."

That's all you try to get down em, Mrs. Turpin said to    77
herself. Too lazy to light the fire. There was nothing you
could tell her about people like them that she didn't know
already. And it was not just that they didn't have anything.
Because if you gave them everything, in two weeks, it would
all be broken or filthy or they would have chopped it up for
lightwood. She knew all this from her own experience. Help
them you must, but help them you couldn't.

All at once the ugly girl turned her lips inside out again. Her    78
eyes fixed like two drills on Mrs. Turpin. This time there was
no mistaking that there was something urgent behind them.

Girl, Mrs. Turpin exclaimed silently, I haven't done a thing    79
to you! The girl might be confusing her with somebody else.
There was no need to sit by and let herself be intimidated.
"You must be in college," she said boldly, looking directly at
the girl. "I see you reading a book there."

The girl continued to stare and pointedly did not answer.    80

Her mother blushed at this rudeness. "The lady asked you    81
a question, Mary Grace," she said under her breath.

"I have ears," Mary Grace said.    82

The poor mother blushed again. "Mary Grace goes to    83
Wellesley College," she explained. She twisted one of the buttons on her dress. "In Massachusetts," she added with a gri-
mace. "And in the summer she just keeps right on studying.
Just reads all the time, a real book worm. She's done real well
at Wellesley; she's taking English and Math and History and
Psychology and Social Studies," she rattled on, "and I think
it's too much. I think she ought to get out and have fun."

The girl looked as if she would like to hurl them all through    84
the plate glass window.

"Way up north," Mrs. Turpin murmured and thought,    85
well, it hasn't done much for her manners.

"I'd almost rather to have him sick," the white-trash    86
woman said, wrenching the attention back to herself. "He's so
mean when he ain't. Look like some children just take natural
to meanness. It's some gets bad when they get sick but he was
the opposite. Took sick and turned good. He don't give me
no trouble now. It's me waitin to see the doctor," she said.

If I was going to send anybody back to Africa, Mrs. Turpin    87
thought, it would be your kind, woman. "Yes, indeed," she
said aloud, but looking up at the ceiling, "it's a heap of things
worse than a nigger." And dirtier than a hog, she added to
herself.

"I think people with bad dispositions are more to be pitied    88
than anyone on earth," the pleasant lady said in a voice that
was decidedly thin.

"I thank the Lord he has blessed me with a good one," 89
Mrs. Turpin said. "The day has never dawned that I couldn't
find something to laugh at."

"Not since she married me anyways," Claud said with a 90
comical straight face.

Everybody laughed except the girl and the white-trash. 91

Mrs. Turpin's stomach shook. "He's such a caution," she 92
said, "that I can't help but laugh at him."

The girl made a loud ugly noise through her teeth. 93

Her mother's mouth grew thin and tight. "I think the 94
worst thing in the world," she said, "is an ungrateful person.
To have everything and not appreciate it. I know a girl," she
said, "who has parents who would give her anything, a little
brother who loves her dearly, who is getting a good education, who wears the best clothes, but who can never say a kind
word to anyone, who never smiles, who just criticizes and
complains all day long."

"Is she too old to paddle?" Claud asked. 95

The girl's face was almost purple. 96

"Yes," the lady said, "I'm afraid there's nothing to do but 97
leave her to her folly. Some day she'll wake up and it'll be
too late."

"It never hurt anyone to smile," Mrs. Turpin said. "It just 98
makes you feel better all over."

"Of course," the lady said sadly, "but there are just some 99
people you can't tell anything to. They can't take criticism."

"If it's one thing I am," Mrs. Turpin said with feeling, 100
"it's grateful. When I think who all I could have been besides
myself and what all I got, a little of everything, and a good
disposition besides, I just feel like shouting, 'Thank you, Jesus,
for making everything the way it is!' It could have been different!" For one thing, somebody else could have got Claud.
At the thought of this, she was flooded with gratitude and a
terrible pang of joy ran through her. "Oh thank you, Jesus,
Jesus, thank you!" she cried aloud.

The book struck her directly over her left eye. It struck 101
almost at the same instant that she realized the girl was about
to hurl it. Before she could utter a sound, the raw face came

crashing across the table toward her, howling. The girl's fingers sank like clamps into the soft flesh of her neck. She heard the mother cry out and Claud shout, "Whoa!" There was an instant when she was certain that she was about to be in an earthquake.

All at once her vision narrowed and she saw everything as if it were happening in a small room far away, or as if she were looking at it through the wrong end of a telescope. Claud's face crumpled and fell out of sight. The nurse ran in, then out, then in again. Then the gangling figure of the doctor rushed out of the inner door. Magazines flew this way and that as the table turned over. The girl fell with a thud and Mrs. Turpin's vision suddenly reversed itself and she saw everything large instead of small. The eyes of the white-trashy woman were staring hugely at the floor. There the girl, held down on one side by the nurse and on the other by her mother, was wrenching and turning in their grasp. The doctor was kneeling astride her, trying to hold her arm down. He managed after a second to sink a long needle into it. 102

Mrs. Turpin felt entirely hollow except for her heart which swung from side to side as if it were agitated in a great empty drum of flesh. 103

"Somebody that's not busy call for the ambulance," the doctor said in the off-hand voice young doctors adopt for terrible occasions. 104

Mrs. Turpin could not have moved a finger. The old man who had been sitting next to her skipped nimbly into the office and made the call, for the secretary still seemed to be gone. 105

"Claud!" Mrs. Turpin called. 106

He was not in his chair. She knew she must jump up and find him but she felt like some one trying to catch a train in a dream, when everything moves in slow motion and the faster you try to run the slower you go. 107

"Here I am," a suffocated voice, very unlike Claud's, said. 108

He was doubled up in the corner on the floor, pale as paper, holding his leg. She wanted to get up and go to him but she could not move. Instead, her gaze was drawn slowly 109 downward to the churning face on the floor, which she could see over the doctor's shoulder.

The girl's eyes stopped rolling and focused on her. They seemed a much lighter blue than before, as if a door that had been tightly closed behind them was now open to admit light and air. 110

Mrs. Turpin's head cleared and her power of motion returned. She leaned forward until she has looking directly into the fierce brilliant eyes. There was no doubt in her mind that the girl did know her, knew her in some intense and personal way, beyond time and place and condition. "What you got to say to me?" she asked hoarsely and held her breath, waiting, as for a revelation. 111

The girl raised her head. Her gaze locked with Mrs. Turpin's. "Go back to hell where you came from, you old wart hog," she whispered. Her voice was low but clear. Her eyes burned for a moment as if she saw with pleasure that her message had struck its target. 112

Mrs. Turpin sank back in her chair. 113

After a moment, the girl's eyes closed and she turned her head wearily to the side. 114

The doctor rose and handed the nurse the empty syringe. He leaned over and put both hands for a moment on the mother's shoulders, which were shaking. She was sitting on the floor, her lips pressed together, holding Mary Grace's hand in her lap. The girl's fingers were gripped like a baby's around her thumb. "Go on to the hospital," he said. "I'll call and make the arrangements." 115

"Now let's see that neck," he said in a jovial voice to Mrs. Turpin. He began to inspect her neck with his first two fingers. Two little moon-shaped lines like pink fish bones were indented over her windpipe. There was the beginning of an angry red swelling above her eye. His fingers passed over this also. 116

"Lea' me be," she said thickly and shook him off. "See about Claud. She kicked him." 117

"I'll see about him in a minute," he said and felt her pulse. He was a thin gray-haired man, given to pleasantries. "Go 118 home and have yourself a vacation the rest of the day," he said and patted her on the shoulder.

Quit your pattin me, Mrs. Turpin growled to herself.  119

"And put an ice pack over that eye," he said. Then he went  120
and squatted down beside Claud and looked at his leg. After a moment he pulled him up and Claud limped after him into the office.

Until the ambulance came, the only sounds in the room  121
were the tremulous moans of the girl's mother, who continued to sit on the floor. The white-trash woman did not take her eyes off the girl. Mrs. Turpin looked straight ahead at nothing. Presently, the ambulance drew up, a long dark shadow, behind the curtain. The attendants came in and set the stretcher down beside the girl and lifted her expertly onto it and carried her out. The nurse helped the mother gather up her things. The shadow of the ambulance moved silently away and the nurse came back in the office.

"That ther girl is going to be a lunatic, ain't she?" the  122
white-trash woman asked the nurse, but the nurse kept on to the back and never answered her.

"Yes, she's going to be a lunatic," the white-trash woman  123
said to the rest of them.

"Po' critter," the old woman murmured. The child's face  124
was still in her lap. His eyes looked idly out over her knees. He had not moved during the disturbance except to draw one leg up under him.

"I thank Gawd," the white-trash woman said fervently, "I  125
ain't a lunatic."

Claud came limping out and the Turpins went home.  126

As their pick-up truck turned into their own dirt road and  127
made the crest of the hill, Mrs. Turpin gripped the window ledge and looked out suspiciously. The land sloped gracefully down through a field dotted with lavender weeds and at the start of the rise their small yellow frame house, with its little flower beds spread out around it like a fancy apron, sat primly in its accustomed place between two giant hickory trees. She would not have been startled to see a burnt wound between two blackened chimneys.

Neither of them felt like eating so they put on their house  128
clothes and lowered the shade in the bedroom and lay down,
Claud with his leg on a pillow and herself with a damp washcloth over her eye. The instant she was flat on her back,
the image of a razor-backed hog with warts on its face and
horns coming out behind its ears snorted into her head. She
moaned, a low quiet moan.

"I am not," she said tearfully, "a wart hog. From hell."  129
But the denial had no force. The girl's eyes and her words,
even the tone of her voice, low but clear, directed only to
her, brooked no repudiation. She had been singled out for
the message, though there was trash in the room to whom
it might justly have been applied. The full force of this fact
struck her only now. There was a woman there who was
neglecting her own child but she had been overlooked. The
message had been given to Ruby Turpin, a respectable, hard-
working, church-going woman. The tears dried. Her eyes
began to burn instead with wrath.

She rose on her elbow and the washcloth fell into her hand.  130
Claud was lying on his back, snoring. She wanted to tell him
what the girl had said. At the same time, she did not wish to
put the image of herself as a wart hog from hell into his mind.

"Hey, Claud," she muttered and pushed his shoulder.  131

Claud opened one pale baby blue eye.  132

She looked into it warily. He did not think about any thing.  133
He just went his way.

"Wha, whasit?" he said and closed the eye again.  134

"Nothing," she said. "Does your leg pain you?"  135

"Hurts like hell," Claud said.  136

"It'll quit terreckly," she said and lay back down. In a  137
moment Claud was snoring again. For the rest of the afternoon, they lay there. Claud slept. She scowled at the ceiling.
Occasionally, she raised her fist and made a small stabbing
motion over her chest as if she was defending her innocence
to invisible guests who were like the comforters of Job, rea-
sonable-seeming but wrong.

About five-thirty Claud stirred. "Got to go after those nig-  138
gers," he sighed, not moving.

She was looking straight up as if there were unintelligible  139
handwriting on the ceiling. The protuberance over her eye
had turned a greenish-blue. "Listen here," she said.

"What?"  140

"Kiss me."  141

Claud leaned over and kissed her loudly on the mouth.  142
He pinched her side and their hands interlocked. Her expression of ferocious concentration did not change. Claud got
up, groaning and growling, and limped off. She continued
to study the ceiling.

She did not get up until she heard the pick-up truck com-  143
ing back with the Negroes. Then she rose and thrust her feet
in her brown oxfords, which she did not bother to lace, and
stumped out onto the back porch and got her red plastic
bucket. She emptied a tray of ice cubes into it and filled it half
full of water and went out into the back yard. Every afternoon
after Claud brought the hands in, one of the boys helped him
put out hay and the rest waited in the back of the truck until
he was ready to take them home. The truck was parked in the
shade under one of the hickory trees.

"Hi yawl this evening?" Mrs. Turpin asked grimly, appear-  144
ing with the bucket and the dipper. There were three women
and a boy in the truck.

"Us doin nicely," the oldest woman said. "Hi you doin?"  145
and her gaze stuck immediately on the dark lump on
Mrs. Turpin's forehead. "You done fell down, ain't you?"
she asked in a solicitous voice. The old woman was dark and
almost toothless. She had on an old felt hat of Claud's set
back on her head. The other two women were younger and
lighter and they both had new bright green sunhats. One of
them had hers on her head; the other had taken hers off and
the boy was grinning beneath it.

Mrs. Turpin set the bucket down on the floor of the truck.  146
"Yawl hep yourselves," she said. She looked around to make
sure Claud had gone. "No, I didn't fall down," she said, folding her arms. "It was something worse than that."

"Ain't nothing bad happen to you!" the old woman said.  147
She said it as if they all knew that Mrs. Turpin was protected

in some special way by Divine Providence. "You just had you a little fall."

"We were in town at the doctor's office for where the cow    148
kicked Mr. Turpin," Mrs. Turpin said in a flat tone that indicated they could leave off their foolishness. "And there was this girl there. A big fat girl with her face all broke out. I could look at that girl and tell she was peculiar but I couldn't tell how. And me and her mama was just talking and going along and all of a sudden WHAM! She throws this big book she was reading at me and . . ."

"Naw!" the old woman cried out.    149

"And then she jumps over the table and commences to    150
choke me."

"Naw!" they all exclaimed, "naw!"    151

"Hi come she do that?" the old woman asked. "What ail    152
her?"

Mrs. Turpin only glared in front of her.    153

"Somethin ail her," the old woman said.    154

"They carried her off in an ambulance," Mrs. Turpin con-    155
tinued, "but before she went she was rolling on the floor and they were trying to hold her down to give her a shot and she said something to me." She paused. "You know what she said to me?"

"What she say?" they asked.    156

"She said," Mrs. Turpin began, and stopped, her face    157
very dark and heavy. The sun was getting whiter and whiter, blanching the sky overhead so that the leaves of the hickory tree were black in the face of it. She could not bring forth the words. "Something real ugly," she muttered.

"She sho shouldn't said nothin ugly to you," the old    158
woman said. "You so sweet. You the sweetest lady I know."

"She pretty too," the one with the hat on said.    159

"And stout," the other one said. "I never knowed no    160
sweeter white lady."

"That's the truth befo' Jesus," the old woman said. "Amen!    161
You des as sweet and pretty as you can be."

Mrs. Turpin knew exactly how much Negro flattery was    162
worth and it added to her rage. "She said," she began again

and finished this time with a fierce rush of breath, "that I was an old wart hog from hell."

There was an astounded silence.                                                163

"Where she at?" the youngest woman cried in a piercing voice.                 164

"Lemme see her. I'll kill her!"                                               165

"I'll kill her with you!" the other one cried.                               166

"She b'long in the sylum," the old woman said emphatically. "You the sweetest white lady I know."   167

"She pretty too," the other two said. "Stout as she can be and sweet. Jesus satisfied with her!"   168

"Deed he is," the old woman declared.                                        169

Idiots! Mrs. Turpin growled to herself. You could never say anything intelligent to a nigger. You could talk at them but not with them. "Yawl ain't drunk your water," she said shortly. "Leave the bucket in the truck when you're finished with it. I got more to do than just stand around and pass the time of day," and she moved off and into the house.    170

She stood for a moment in the middle of the kitchen. The dark protuberance over her eye looked like a miniature tornado cloud which might any moment sweep across the horizon of her brow. Her lower lip protruded dangerously. She squared her massive shoulders. Then she marched into the front of the house and out the side door and started down the road to the pig parlor. She had the look of a woman going single-handed, weaponless, into battle.    171

The sun was a deep yellow now like a harvest moon and was riding westward very fast over the far tree line as if it meant to reach the hogs before she did. The road was rutted and she kicked several good-sized stones out of her path as she strode along. The pig parlor was on a little knoll at the end of a lane that ran off from the side of the barn. It was a square of concrete as large as a small room, with a board fence about four feet high around it. The concrete floor sloped slightly so that the hog wash could drain off into a trench where it was carried to the field for fertilizer. Claud was standing on the outside, on the edge of the concrete, hanging onto the top board, hosing down the floor    172 inside. The hose was connected to the faucet of a water trough nearby.

Mrs. Turpin climbed up beside him and glowered down 173 at the hogs inside. There were seven long-snouted bristly shoats in it—tan with liver-colored spots—and an old sow a few weeks off from farrowing. She was lying on her side grunting. The shoats were running about shaking themselves like idiot children, their little slit pig eyes searching the floor for anything left. She had read that pigs were the most intelligent animal. She doubted it. They were supposed to be smarter than dogs. There had even been a pig astronaut. He had performed his assignment perfectly but died of a heart attack afterward because they left him in his electric suit, sitting upright throughout his examination when naturally a hog should be on all fours.

A-gruntin and a-rootin and a-groanin. 174

"Gimme that hose," she said, yanking it away from Claud. 175 "Go on and carry them niggers home and then get off that leg."

"You look like you might have swallowed a mad dog," 176 Claud observed, but he got down and limped off. He paid no attention to her humors.

Until he was out of earshot, Mrs. Turpin stood on the side 177 of the pen, holding the hose and pointing the stream of water at the hind quarters of any shoat that looked as if it might try to lie down. When he had had time to get over the hill, she turned her head slightly and her wrathful eyes scanned the path. He was nowhere in sight. She turned back again and seemed to gather herself up. Her shoulders rose and she drew in her breath.

"What do you send me a message like that for?" she said in 178 a low fierce voice, barely above a whisper but with the force of a shout in its concentrated fury. "How am I a hog and me both? How am I saved and from hell too?" Her free fist was knotted and with the other she gripped the hose, blindly pointing the stream of water in and out of the eye of the old sow whose outraged squeal she did not hear.

The pig parlor commanded a view of the back pasture  179
where their twenty beef cows were gathered around the hay-
bales Claud and the boy had put out. The freshly cut pasture
sloped down to the highway. Across it was their cotton field
and beyond that a dark green dusty wood which they owned
as well. The sun was behind the wood, very red, looking over
the paling of trees like a farmer inspecting his own hogs.

"Why me?" she rumbled. "It's no trash around here, black  180
or white, that I haven't given to. And break my back to the
bone every day working. And do for the church."

She appeared to be the right size woman to command the  181
arena before her. "How am I a hog?" she demanded. "Exactly
how am I like them?" and she jabbed the stream of water at
the shoats. "There was plenty of trash there. It didn't have
to be me.

"If you like trash better, go get yourself some trash then,"  182
she railed. "You could have made me trash. Or a nigger. If
trash is what you wanted why didn't you make me trash?" She
shook her fist with the hose in it and a watery snake appeared
momentarily in the air. "I could quit working and take it easy
and be filthy," she growled. "Lounge about the sidewalks all
day drinking root beer. Dip snuff and spit in every puddle and
have it all over my face. I could be nasty.

"Or you could have made me a nigger. It's too late for me  183
to be a nigger," she said with deep sarcasm, "but I could act
like one. Lay down in the middle of the road and stop traffic.
Roll on the ground."

In the deepening light, everything was taking on a mysteri-  184
ous hue. The pasture was growing a peculiar glassy green and
the streak of highway had turned lavender. She braced herself
for a final assault and this time her voice rolled out over the
pasture. "Go on," she yelled, "call me a hog! Call me a hog
again. From hell. Call me a wart hog from hell. Put that bottom rail on top. There'll still be a top and bottom!"

A garbled echo returned to her.  185

A final surge of fury shook her and she roared, "Who do  186
you think you are?"

The color of everything, field and crimson sky, burned for    187
a moment with a transparent intensity. The question carried
over the pasture and across the highway and the cotton field
and returned to her clearly like an answer from beyond the
wood.

She opened her mouth but no sound came out of it.            188

A tiny truck, Claud's, appeared on the highway, heading       189
rapidly out of sight. Its gears scraped thinly. It looked like a
child's toy. At any moment, a bigger truck might smash into
it and scatter Claud's and the niggers' brains all over the road.

Mrs. Turpin stood there, her gaze fixed on the highway, all   190
her muscles rigid, until in five or six minutes the truck reappeared, returning. She waited until it had had time to turn
into their own road. Then like a monumental statue coming
to life, she bent her head slowly and gazed, as if through the
very heart of mystery, down into the pig parlor at the hogs.
They had settled all in one corner around the old sow who
was grunting softly. A red glow suffused them. They appeared
to pant with a secret life.

Until the sun slipped finally behind the tree line,          191
Mrs. Turpin remained there with her gaze bent to them as
if she were absorbing some abysmal life-giving knowledge.
At last she lifted her head. There was only a purple streak in
the sky, cutting through a field of crimson and leading, like
an extension of the highway, into the descending dusk. She
raised her hands from the side of the pen in a gesture hieratic
and profound. A visionary light settled in her eyes. She saw
the streak as a vast swinging bridge extending upward from
the earth through a field of living fire. Upon it a vast horde
of souls were rumbling toward heaven. There were whole
companies of white-trash, clean for the first time in their lives,
and bands of black niggers in white robes, and battalions of
freaks and lunatics shouting and clapping and leaping like
frogs. And bringing up the end of the procession was a tribe
of people whom she recognized at once as those who, like
herself and Claud, had always had a little of everything and the
God-given wit to use it right. She leaned forward to observe
them closer. They were marching behind the others with great

dignity, accountable as they had always been for good order and common sense and respectable behavior. They alone were on key. Yet she could see by their shocked and altered faces that even their virtues were being burned away. She lowered her hands and gripped the rail of the hog pen, her eyes small but fixed unblinkingly on what lay ahead. In a moment the vision faded but she remained where she was, immobile.

At length she got down and turned off the faucet and made 192 her slow way on the darkening path to the house. In the woods around her the invisible cricket choruses had struck up, but what she heard were the voices of the souls climbing upward into the starry field and shouting hallelujah.

## COMMENT ON "REVELATION"

Ruby Turpin, the central character in O'Connor's "Revelation," is obsessed with the classification process. At night she occupies herself "naming the classes of people": most "colored people" are on the bottom; "next to them— not above, just away from—are the white trash"; and so on. Mrs. Turpin puzzles about the exceptions to her system—the black dentist who owns property and the decent white folks who have lost their money—but for the most part, she is certain about her system and her place in it. In the doctor's waiting room, she sizes up the other patients, placing them in their appropriate classes. But her internal and external dialogue reveals the ironies and inconsistencies in her rigid system. Self-satisfied, pleased that Jesus is on her side, she is not prepared for the book on human development that is thrown at her or the events that follow—the transparent flattery of the black workers, her cleaning of the pig parlor, and, finally, her vision of the highway to heaven that reveals her real place in God's hierarchy.

# CHAPTER 5

# *Definition*

As a writer, both in and out of college, you're likely to spend a good deal of time writing definitions. In an astronomy class, you may be asked to explain what the Doppler effect is or what a white dwarf star is. In a literature class, you may be asked to define a sonnet and identify its different forms. If you become an engineer, you may write to define problems your company proposes to solve or to define a new product your company has developed. If you become a business executive, you may have to write a brochure to describe a new service your company offers or draft a letter that defines the company's policy on credit applications.

Writers use definitions to establish boundaries, show the essential nature of something, and explain the special qualities that identify a purpose, place, object, or concept and distinguish it from others similar to it. Writers often write extended definitions—definitions that go beyond the one-sentence or one-paragraph explanations that you find in a dictionary or encyclopedia—to expand on and examine the essential qualities of a policy, an event, a group, or a trend. Sometimes, an extended definition becomes an entire book. Some books are written to define the good life; others are written to define the ideal university or the best kind of government. In fact, many of the books on any current nonfiction best-seller list are primarily definitions. The essays in this chapter of *The River Reader* are all extended definitions.

## PURPOSE

When you write, you can use definitions in several ways. For instance, you can define to *point out the special nature* of something. You may want to show the special flavor of San Francisco that makes it different from other major cities in the world, or you may want to describe the unique features that make the Macintosh computer different from other personal computers.

You can also define to *explain*. In an essay about cross-country skiing, you might want to show your readers what the sport is like and point out why it's less hazardous and less expensive than downhill skiing but better exercise. You might also define to *entertain*—to describe the essence of what it means to be a "good old boy," for instance. Often, you define to *inform*; that is what you are doing in college papers when you write about West Virginia folk art or postmodern architecture. Often, you write to *establish a standard*, perhaps for a good exercise program, a workable environmental policy, or even the ideal pair of running shoes. Notice that when you define to set a standard, you may also be defining to *persuade*, to convince your reader to accept the ideal you describe. Many definitions are essentially arguments.

Sometimes, you may even write to *define yourself.* That is what you are doing when you write an autobiographical statement for a college admissions officer or a scholarship committee, or when you write a job application letter. You hope to give your readers the special information that will distinguish you from all other candidates. When that is your task, you'll profit by knowing the common strategies for defining and by recognizing how other writers have used them.

## AUDIENCE

When you're going to use definition in your writing, you can benefit by thinking ahead of time about what your readers expect from you. Why are they reading, and what questions will they want you to answer? You can't anticipate all their questions, but you should plan on responding to at least two kinds of queries.

First, your readers are likely to ask, "What distinguishes what you're writing about? What's typical or different about it? How do I know when I see one?" For example, if you were writing about the Olympic Games, your readers would perhaps want to know the difference between today's Olympic Games and the original games in ancient Greece. With a little research, you could tell them about several major differences.

Second, for more complex topics, you should expect that your readers will also ask, "What is the basic character or the essential nature of what you're writing about? What do you mean when you say 'alternative medicine,' 'Marxist theory,' or 'white-collar crime'?" Answering questions such as these is more difficult; but if you're going to use terms like these in an essay, you have an obligation to define them, using as many strategies as you need to clarify your terms. To define white-collar crime, for instance, you could specify that it is nonviolent, is likely to happen within businesses, and involves illegal manipulation of funds or privileged information. You should also strengthen your definition by giving examples with which your readers might be familiar.

## STRATEGIES

You can choose from several strategies for defining, using them singly or in combination. A favorite strategy we all use is *giving examples*, something we do naturally when we point to a special automobile we like or show a child a picture of a raccoon in a picture book. Writers use the same method when they describe a scene, create a visual image, or cite a specific instance of something.

Every author in this chapter uses an abundance of examples. Joseph Epstein, for one, uses a wealth of examples from literature, philosophy, and science to define the concept of boredom.

You can define by *analyzing qualities* to emphasize what specific traits distinguish the person or thing you're defining. When you use this strategy for people, you focus on certain qualities or behaviors that reveal that individual's personality and character. James Gleick uses this strategy to illustrate how people try to complete multiple tasks in smaller and smaller periods of time.

A similar strategy is *attributing characteristics.* Joseph Epstein uses this strategy when he describes emotional situations such as "ennui, apathy, depression, accidie, melancholia, *mal de vivre*" that are similar to but not quite the same as boredom.

Another strategy is *defining negatively.* In "A Word's Meaning Can Often Depend on Who Says It," Gloria Naylor explains how the black community has transformed a negative word into a complex word that signifies a variety of meanings.

Another way to define is by *using analogies.* James Gleick describes how a single computer serves multiple users as a way to explain the derivation of the word *multitasking.*

You can also define by *showing function.* Often, the most important feature about an object, agency, or institution is what it does. The element of function figures centrally in Toni Cade Bambara's story as Miss Moore tries to teach her students the meaning of the word *cost.*

## COMBINING STRATEGIES

Even when you're writing an essay that is primarily an exercise in definition, you may want to do as professional writers often do and bring in other strategies, perhaps narration or argument or process analysis. For instance, Joseph Epstein compares situational and existential boredom and then argues that we need an expanded definition.

Most of the writers in this chapter use definition with narration and description. So you can mix and mingle strategies even though one may dominate. As you read the essays in this chapter, and especially as you reread them, try to be conscious of the strategies the authors are using. You may find that you can incorporate some of them into your own writing.

## DEFINITION

### Points to Remember

1. Remember that you are obligated to define key terms that you use in your writing (such as *Marxism, alternative medicine,* or *nontraditional student*).
2. Understand your purpose in defining: to explain, to entertain, to persuade, to set boundaries, or to establish a standard.
3. Understand how writers construct an argument from a definition. For example, by defining the good life or good government, they argue for that kind of life or government.
4. Know the several ways of defining: giving examples, analyzing qualities, attributing characteristics, defining negatively, using analogies, and showing function.
5. Learn to use definition in combination with other strategies, as a basis on which to build an argument, or as supporting evidence.

*"Cute is whatever you can get away with."*

*In this quirky cartoon—which is also "cute"—Charles Barsotti challenges readers to think of how many different ways one can define the word cute. Brainstorm a list of similar slang terms. Then write an extended definition of one of those words, attempting to present as many definitions "as you can get away with."*

## Gloria Naylor: A Word's Meaning Can Often Depend on Who Says It

Gloria Naylor was born in 1950 in New York City and was educated at Brooklyn College and Yale University. For several years, she worked as a missionary for the Jehovah's Witnesses, working "for better world conditions." While teaching at several universities, such as George Washington and Princeton, Naylor published numerous stories and essays and interconnected novels: *The Women of Brewster Place* (1982), *Linden Hills* (1985), *Mamma Day* (1988), *Bailey's Café* (1992), *The Men of Brewster Place* (1998), and *1996* (2005). *The Women of Brewster Place*, which won the National Book Award for best first novel, was adapted as a television miniseries. Naylor is also the recipient of Guggenheim and National Endowment for the Arts fellowships for her novels and the New York Foundation for the Arts Fellowship for screenwriting. In "A Word's Meaning Can Often Depend on Who Says It," first published in the *New York Times* (1986), Naylor explains that the meaning of a word depends on social context and community consensus.

L ANGUAGE IS THE subject. It is the written form with which I've managed to keep the wolf away from the door and, in diaries, to keep my sanity. In spite of this, I consider the written word inferior to the spoken, and much of the frustration experienced by novelists is the awareness that whatever we manage to capture in even the most transcendent passages falls far short of the richness of life. Dialogue achieves its power in the dynamics of a fleeting moment of sight, sound, smell, and touch.

I'm not going to enter the debate here about whether it   2
is language that shapes reality or vice versa. That battle is
doomed to be waged whenever we seek intermittent reprieve
from the chicken and egg dispute. I will simply take the position that the spoken word, like the written word, amounts
to a nonsensical arrangement of sounds or letters without
a consensus that assigns "meaning." And building from the
meanings of what we hear, we order reality. Words themselves
are innocuous; it is the consensus that gives them true power.

---

*[T]he spoken word, like the written word,
amounts to a nonsensical arrangement of
sounds and letter without a consensus that
assigns meaning.*

---

I remember the first time I heard the word *nigger*. In my   3
third-grade class, our math tests were being passed down the
rows, and as I handed the papers to a little boy in back of me, I
remarked that once again he had received a much lower mark
than I did. He snatched his test from me and spit out that
word. Had he called me a nymphomaniac or a necrophiliac, I
couldn't have been more puzzled. I didn't know what a nigger was, but I knew that whatever it meant, it was something
he shouldn't have called me. This was verified when I raised
my hand, and in a loud voice repeated what he had said and
watched the teacher scold him for using a "bad" word. I was
later to go home and ask the inevitable question that every
black parent must face—"Mommy, what does *nigger* mean?"

And what exactly did it mean? Thinking back, I realize   4
that this could not have been the first time the word was
used in my presence. I was part of a large extended family
that had migrated from the rural South after World War II
and formed a close-knit network that gravitated around my
maternal grandparents. Their ground-floor apartment in one

of the buildings they owned in Harlem was a weekend mecca for my immediate family, along with countless aunts, uncles, and cousins who brought along assorted friends. It was a bustling and open house with assorted neighbors and tenants popping in and out to exchange bits of gossip, pick up an old quarrel, or referee the ongoing checkers game in which my grandmother cheated shamelessly. They were all there to let down their hair and put up their feet after a week of labor in the factories, laundries, and shipyards of New York.

Amid the clamor, which could reach deafening   5
proportions—two or three conversations going on simultaneously, punctuated by the sound of a baby's crying somewhere in the back rooms or out on the street—there was still a rigid set of rules about what was said and how. Older children were sent out of the living room when it was time to get into the juicy details about "you-know-who" up on the third floor who had gone and gotten herself "p-r-e-g-n-a-n-t!" But my parents, knowing that I could spell well beyond my years, always demanded that I follow the others out to play. Beyond sexual misconduct and death, everything else was considered harmless for our young ears. And so among the anecdotes of the triumphs and disappointments in the various workings of their lives, the word *nigger* was used in my presence, but it was set within contexts and inflections that caused it to register in my mind as something else.

In the singular, the word was always applied to a man who   6
had distinguished himself in some situation that brought their approval for his strength, intelligence, or drive:

"Did Johnny *really* do that?"                              7

"I'm telling you, that nigger pulled in $6,000 of over-   8
time last year. Said he got enough for a down payment on a house."

When used with a possessive adjective by a woman—"my   9
nigger"—it became a term of endearment for her husband or boyfriend. But it could be more than just a term applied to a man. In their mouths, it became the pure essence of - manhood—a disembodied force that channeled their past history of struggle and present survival against the odds into a

victorious statement of being: "Yeah, that old foreman found out quick enough—you don't mess with a nigger."

In the plural, it became a description of some group within the community that had overstepped the bounds of decency as my family defined it. Parents who neglected their children, a drunken couple who fought in public, people who simply refused to look for work, those with excessively dirty mouths or unkempt households were all "trifling niggers." This particular circle could forgive hard times, unemployment, the occasional bout of depression—they had gone through all of that themselves—but the unforgivable sin was a lack of self-respect.

A woman could never be a "nigger" in the singular, with its connotation of confirming worth. The noun *girl* was its closest equivalent in that sense, but only when used in direct address and regardless of the gender doing the addressing. *Girl* was a token of respect for a woman. The one-syllable word was drawn out to sound like three in recognition of the extra ounce of wit, nerve, or daring that the woman had shown in the situation under discussion.

"G-i-r-l, stop. You mean you said that to his face?"

But if the word was used in a third-person reference or shortened so that it almost snapped out of the mouth, it always involved some element of communal disapproval. And age became an important factor in these exchanges. It was only between individuals of the same generation, or from any older person to a younger (but never the other way around), that *girl* would be considered a compliment.

I don't agree with the argument that use of the word *nigger* at this social stratum of the black community was an internalization of racism. The dynamics were the exact opposite: The people in my grandmother's living room took a word that whites used to signify worthlessness or degradation and rendered it impotent. Gathering there together, they transformed *nigger* to signify the varied and complex human beings they knew themselves to be. If the word was to disappear totally from the mouths of even the most liberal of white society, no one in that room was naive enough to believe it would disappear from white minds. Meeting the word head-on, they proved it had absolutely nothing to do with the way they were determined to live their lives.

So there must have been dozens of times that *nigger*  15
was spoken in front of me before I reached the third grade. But I didn't "hear" it until it was said by a small pair of lips that had already learned it could be a way to humiliate me. That was the word I went home and asked my mother about. And since she knew that I had to grow up in America, she took me in her lap and explained.

## For Critical Thinking

### QUESTIONS ABOUT PURPOSE

1. Why does Naylor think that written language is inferior to spoken language?
2. How does she use the word *nigger* to support her assertion?

### QUESTIONS ABOUT AUDIENCE

1. What does Naylor assume about the racial identity of most of her readers?
2. What does she assume her readers think about the word *nigger*?

### QUESTIONS ABOUT STRATEGIES

1. How does Naylor illustrate the difference between the way the white community and the black community use the word *nigger*?
2. How does she explain why the word could never be applied to a woman?

*For Writing and Research*

1. *Analyze* how Naylor illustrates the various ways the black community uses the word *nigger*.
2. *Practice* by defining a word that has special, perhaps even an opposite, meaning when it is used in your social group.
3. *Argue* that the way a word is spoken—by particular people in a particular context—gives it its true meanings.
4. *Synthesize* the explanations of the way the black community uses the word *girl*. See paragraphs 11 through 13 in Naylor's essay. Then use this information to explain how the word is used among contemporary women, as in "You go, girl!"

James Gleick was born in 1954 in New York City and began his career as a copyeditor for the *New York Times*. He began writing articles on science for the *Times*, eventually publishing a series of widely acclaimed books, such as *Chaos: Making a New Science* (1987), *Year of Genius: The Life and Science of Richard Feynman* (1992), and *Faster: The Acceleration of Just About Everything* (1999). His more recent books include *What Just Happened: A Chronicle from the Information Frontier* (2002), *Isaac Newton* (2003), and *The Information: A History, a Theory, a Flood* (2011). In "Attention! Multitaskers," reprinted from *Faster: The Acceleration of Just About Everything*, Gleick defines the origin and significance of the word that describes the "simultaneous fragmentation and overloading of human attention."

T HE FINAL, FATAL flaw in the time-use pie chart is that 1 we are multitasking creatures. It is possible, after all, to tie shoes and watch television, to eat and read, and to shave and talk with the children. These days it is possible to drive, eat, listen to a book, and talk on the phone, all at once, if you dare. No segment of time—not a day, not a second—can really be a zero-sum game.

"Attention! Multitaskers," says an advertisement for an 2 AT&T wireless telephone service. "Demo all these exciting features"—namely E-mail, voice telephone, and pocket organizer. Pay attention if you can. We have always multitasked— inability to walk and chew gum is a time-honored cause for derision—but never so intensely or so self-consciously as now. If haste is the gas pedal, multitasking is overdrive. We are multitasking connoisseurs—experts in crowding, pressing, packing, and overlapping distinct activities in our all-too-finite moments. Some reports from the front lines:

---

*If haste is the gas pedal, multitasking is overdrive.*

---

David Feldman, in New York, schedules his tooth-flossing to coincide with his regular browsing of on-line discussion groups (the latest in food, the latest on Brian Wilson). He has learned to hit Page Down with his pinky. Mark Maxham of California admits to even more embarrassing arrangements of tasks. "I find myself doing strange little optimizations," he says, "like life is a set of computer code and I'm a compiler." Similarly, by the time, Michael Hartl heads for the bathroom in his California Institute of Technology digs each morning, he has already got his computer starting its progress through the Windows boot sequence, and then, as he runs to break-fast, he hits Control-Shift-D to dial into the campus computer network, and then he gets his Web browser started, down-loading graphics, so he can check the news while he eats. "I figure I save at least two or three minutes a day this way," he says. "Don't laugh." Then there's the subroutine he thinks of as "the mouthwash gambit," where he swigs a mouthful on one pass by the sink, swishes it around in his mouth as he gets his bicycle, and spits out as he heads back in the other direction, toward a class in general relativity.

The word *multitasking* came from computer scientists of the 1960s. They arranged to let a single computer serve multiple users on a network. When a computer multitasks, it usually just alternates tasks, but on the finest of timescales. It slices time and interleaves its tasks. Unless, that is, it has more than one processor running, in which case multitasking can be truly parallel processing. Either way, society grabbed the term as fast as it did *Type A*. We apply it to our own flesh-and-blood CPUs. Not only do we multitask, but, with computers as our guides, we multitask self-consciously.

Multitasking begins in the service of efficiency. Working at       5
a computer terminal in the London newsroom of Bloomberg News, Douglas McGill carried on a long telephone conversation with a colleague in New York. His moment of realization came when, still talking on the phone, he sent off an E-mail message to another colleague in Connecticut and immediately received her reply. "It squeezes more information than was previously squeezable into a given amount of time," he says. "I wonder if this contributes to that speeding-up sensation we all feel?" Clearly it does.

Is there any limit? A few people claim to be able to listen       6
to two different pieces of music at once. Many more learn to take advantage of the brain's apparent ability to process spoken and written text in separate channels. Mike Holderness, in London, watches television with closed captioning so that he can keep the sound off and listen to the unrelated music of his choice. Or he writes several letters at once—"in the sense that I have processes open and waiting." None of this is enough for a cerebral cortex conditioned to the pace of life on-line, he realizes:

> *Ten years ago, I was delighted and enthralled that I could get a telegram-like E-mail from Philadelphia to London in only fifteen minutes. Three years ago, I was delighted and enthralled that I could fetch an entire thesis from Texas to London in only five minutes. Now, I drum my fingers on the desk when a hundred-kilobyte file takes more than twenty seconds to arrive . . . damn, it's coming from New Zealand . . .*

It seems natural to recoil from this simultaneous frag-       7
mentation and overloading of human attention. How well can people really accomplish their multitasks? "It's hard to get around the forebrain bottleneck," said Earl Hunt, a

professor of psychology and computer science at the University of Washington. "Our brains function the same way the Cro-Magnon brains did, so technology isn't going to change that." But for many—humans, not computers—a sense of satisfaction and well-being comes with this saturation of parallel pathways in the brain. We divide ourselves into parts, perhaps, each receiving sensations, sending messages, or manipulating the environment in some way. We train ourselves as Samuel Renshaw would have trained us. Or, then again, we slice time just as a computer does, feeding each task a bit of our attention in turn. Perhaps the young have an advantage because of the cultural conditioning they received from early exposure to computers and fast entertainment media. Corporate managers think so. Marc Prensky, a Bankers Trust vice president, had to learn to overcome instinctive annoyance when a young subordinate began reading E-mail during a face-to-face conversation; the subordinate explained: "I'm still listening; I'm parallel processing." This whole generation of workers, Prensky decided, weaned on video games, operates at *twitch speed*—"your thumbs going a million miles a minute," and a good thing, if managers can take advantage of it.

At least one computer manufacturer, Gateway, applies multitasking to technical support. Customers call in for help, wait on hold, and then hear voices. "Hello," they are told. "You are on a conference call." William Slaughter, a lawyer calling from Philadelphia, slowly realizes that he has joined a tech-support group therapy session. He listens to Brian helping Vince. Next, Vince listens to Brian helping William. It's like a chess master playing a simultaneous exhibition, William thinks, though Brian seems a bit frazzled. Somehow the callers cope with their resentment at not being deemed worthy of Brian's undivided attention. Why should he sit daydreaming while they scurry to reboot? "Hello, Vicky," they hear him say. "You are on a conference call."

There is ample evidence that many of us choose this style of living. We're willing to pay for the privilege. An entire class of technologies is dedicated to the furthering of multitasking. Waterproof shower radios and, now, telephones. Car phones, of course. Objects as innocent-seeming as trays for magazines on exercise machines are tools for multitasking (and surely television sets are playing in the foreground, too). Picture-in-picture display on your television set. (Gregory Stevens, in Massachusetts: "PIP allows me to watch PBS/C-Span or the like, and keep the ball game on or an old movie. Of course, it is impossible for anyone else to enjoy this, with me changing the pictures and audio feed every few seconds. When the computer and the phone are available in a multiwindow form on the television, things are going to be very different.") Even without picture-in-picture, the remote control enables a time-slicing variation on the same theme. Marc Weidenbaum, in San Francisco, has a shorthand for describing an evening's activities to his girlfriend: "Got home. Ate some soup. Watched twenty or thirty shows." He means this more or less literally:

> *I'll watch two sitcoms and a* Star Trek: Voyager *episode and routinely check MTV (didn't they used to run music videos?) and CNN (didn't they used to run news?) in a single hour. And really not feel like I'm missing out on anything.*

Nothing could be more revealing of the transformation 10 of human sensibility over the past century than this widespread unwillingness to settle for soaking up, in single-task fashion, the dynamic flow of sound and picture coming from a television screen. Is any one channel, in itself, monotonous? Marshall McLuhan failed to predict this: the medium of television seemed *cool* and all-absorbing to him, so different from the experience available to us a generation later. For the McLuhan who announced that the medium was the message, television was a black-and-white, unitary stream. McLuhan did not surf with remote control. Sets were tiny and the resolution poor—"visually low in data," he wrote in 1964, "a ceaselessly forming contour of things limned by the scanning finger." People were seen mostly in close-up, perforce. Thus he asserted: "TV will not work as background. It engages you. You have to be *with* it."

No longer. Paradoxically, perhaps, as television has gained in 11 vividness and clarity, it has lost its command of our foreground. For some people, television has been bumped off its pedestal by the cool, fast, fluid, indigenously multitasking activity of browsing the Internet. Thus anyone—say, Steven Leibel of California—can counter McLuhan definitively (typing in one window while reading a World Wide Web page in another): "The Web and TV complement each other perfectly. TV doesn't require much attention from the viewer. It fits perfectly into the spaces created by downloading Web pages." If he really needs to concentrate, he turns down the sound momentarily. Not everyone bothers concentrating. Eight million American households report television sets and personal computers running, together in the same room, "often" or "always."

Not long ago, listening to the simpler audio stream of 12 broadcast radio was a single-task activity for most people. The radio reached into homes and grabbed listeners by the lapel. It could dominate their time and attention—for a few decades. "A child might sit," Robinson and Godbey recall sentimentally, "staring through the window at the darkening trees, hearing only the Lone Ranger's voice and the hooves of horses in the canyon." Now it is rare for a person to listen to the radio *and do nothing else.* Programmers structure radio's content with the knowledge that they can count on only a portion of the listener's attention, and only for intermittent intervals. And rarely with full attention. Much of the radio audience at any given moment has its senses locked up in a more demanding activity—probably driving. Or showering, or cooking, or jogging. Radio has become a secondary task in a multitasking world.

## For Critical Thinking

### QUESTIONS ABOUT PURPOSE

1. How does the title of Gleick's book, *Faster: The Acceleration of Just About Everything,* help explain the purpose of this essay?

2. What is he attempting to prove about the relationship between time and productivity?

---

### QUESTIONS ABOUT AUDIENCE

---

1. What assumptions does Gleick make about his readers' attitude toward the effective use of time?
2. How does he identify generational differences in his readers' attitude toward multitasking?

---

### QUESTIONS ABOUT STRATEGIES

---

1. How does Gleick explain the origin of the word *multitasking*?
2. How does he use the routines of people such as David Feldman, Mark Maxham, and Michael Hartl to illustrate the word?

## For Writing and Research

1. *Analyze* how Gleick uses television to help define *multitasking*.
2. *Practice* by describing a typical day when you have found yourself multitasking.
3. *Argue* that multitasking creates inefficiency rather than productivity.
4. *Synthesize:* Research the impact of emerging technologies such as computers, BlackBerry handheld devices, and iPhones. Then use this information to explain how multitasking has created a demand for these gadgets.

# Joseph Epstein: *Duh, Bor—ing*

Joseph Epstein was born in 1937 in Chicago and educated at the University of Chicago. For many years, he edited *American Scholar*, the quarterly journal of the national honor society Phi Beta Kappa, and is currently visiting lecturer in English at Northwestern University. His learned essays on American life and letters have appeared in magazines such as *Harper's, The New Yorker*, and *The New York Times Magazine*. In "Duh, Bor—ing," first published in *Commentary*, Epstein tries to define the elusive word *boredom*.

Somewhere I have read that boredom is the torment of hell that Dante forgot.

—Albert Speer, Spandau: The Secret Diaries

UNREQUITED LOVE, AS LORENZ HART instructed us, is a bore, but then so are a great many other things: old friends gone somewhat dotty from whom it is too late to disengage, the important social-science-based book of the month, 95 percent of the items on the evening news, discussions about the Internet, arguments against the existence of God, people who overestimate their charm, all talk about wine, *New York Times* editorials, lengthy lists (like this one), and, not least, oneself.

Some people claim never to have been bored. They lie. One cannot be human without at some time or other having known boredom. Even animals know boredom, we are told, though they are deprived of the ability to complain directly about it. Some of us are more afflicted with boredom than others. Psychologists make the distinction between ordinary and pathological boredom; the latter doesn't cause serious mental problems but is associated with them. Another distinction is that between situational boredom and existential boredom. Situational boredom is caused by the temporary tedium everyone at one time or another encounters: the dull sermon, the longueur-laden novel, the pompous gent extolling his prowess at the used-tire business. Existential boredom is thought to be the result of existence itself, caused by modern culture and therefore inescapable. Boredom even has some class standing and was once felt to be an aristocratic attribute. Ennui, it has been said, is the reigning emotion of the dandy.

When bored, time slows drastically, the world seems logy   3 and without promise, and reality itself can grow shadowy and vague. Truman Capote once described the novels of James Baldwin as "balls-achingly boring," which conveys something of the agony of boredom yet is inaccurate—not about Baldwin's novels, which are no stroll around the Louvre but about the effect of boredom itself. Boredom is never so clearly localized. The vagueness of boredom, its vaporousness and its torpor, is part of its mild but genuine torment.

> *[O]ne can tell a great deal about a person by what bores him.*

Boredom is often less pervasive in simpler cultures. One   4 hears little of boredom among the pygmies or the Trobriand Islanders, whose energies are taken up with the problems of mere existence. Ironically, it can be most pervasive where a great deal of stimulation is available. Boredom can also apparently be aided by overstimulation, or so we are all learning through the current generation of children, who, despite their vast arsenal of electronic toys, their many hours spent before screens of one kind or another, more often than any previous generation register cries of boredom. Rare is the contemporary parent or grandparent who has not heard these kids, when presented with a project for relief of their boredom—go outside, read a book—reply, with a heavy accent on each syllable, "Bor-ing."

My own experience of boredom has been intermittent, never chronic. As a boy of six or seven, I recall one day reporting to my mother that I was bored. A highly intelligent woman of even temperament, she calmly replied: "Really? May I suggest that you knock your head against the wall. It'll take your mind off your boredom." I never again told my mother that I was bored.

For true boredom, few things top life in a peacetime army. For the first eight weeks there, life consists of being screamed at while being put to tedious tasks: KP, guard duty, barracks cleanup, calisthenics, and endless drilling. After those first two months, the screaming lets up but the tedium of the tasks continues. In my case, these included marching off in helmet liner and fatigues to learn to touch-type to the strains of "The Colonel Bogey March" from *The Bridge Over the River Kwai*; later writing up cultural news (of which there wasn't any) at Fort Hood, Texas; in the evening, walking the streets of the nearby town of Kileen, where the entertainment on offer was a beer drunk, a hamburger, a tattoo, or an auto loan; and, later, typing up physical exams in an old bank building used as a recruiting station in downtown Little Rock, Arkansas. Was I bored? Yes, out of my gourd. But, then, so heavy is boredom in peacetime armies that, from the Roman Empire on, relief from it has often been a serious enticement on its own to war.

But, ah, the sweetness, the luxuriousness of boredom when the details of quotidian life threaten to plough one under through sheer aggravation, or real troubles (medical, familial, financial) are visited upon one, and supply, as Tacitus has it, "ample proof that the gods are indifferent to our tranquility but eager for our punishment." Except that most people cannot stand even gentle boredom for long.

"I have discovered that all evil comes from this," wrote   8
Pascal, "man's being unable to sit still in a room." Failing precisely this test, that of the ability to sit quietly alone in a room,
brought about *acedia*, a Greek word meaning "apathy," or
"indifference," among hermit monks in North Africa in the
fourth century c.e.

I come to this historical tidbit through reading *Boredom,*   9
*A Lively History* (Yale University Press, 224 pages) by Peter
Toohey, who teaches classics at Calgary University. His book
and *A Philosophy of Boredom* (Reaktion Books, 124 pages) by
Lars Svendsen are the two best contemporary works on the
subject. Noteworthy that men living, respectively, in western
Canada and Norway should be attracted to the subject of
boredom; obviously, their geography and occupations as aca-
demics qualify them eminently for the subject. A teacher, as I
myself discovered after three chalk-filled decades, is someone
who never says anything once—or, for that matter, never says
anything a mere 9 or 10 times.

The radical difference between Toohey and Svendsen is   10
that the former thinks boredom has its uses, while the latter
is confident that boredom is *the* major spiritual problem of
our day. "Is modern life," Svendsen asks, "first and foremost
an attempt to escape boredom?" He believes it is, and also
believes, I surmise, that this escape cannot be achieved. He
holds that boredom is not merely an individual but a social,
a cultural, finally a philosophical problem. He quotes Jean
Baudrillard, the French philosopher, saying that the traditional
philosophical problem used to be "why is there anything at all
rather than nothing?" but that today the real question is "why
is there just nothing, rather than something?" With Svendsen,
we arrive at the exposition of existential boredom.

Svendsen remarks on the difficulty of portraying boredom   11
in literature. (In *The Pale King*, the unfinished novel that
David Foster Wallace left at his desk after suicide at the age
of 46, Wallace set out to explore all the facets of boredom,
which, if reviewers are to be believed, he was, alas, unable
to bring off.) Toohey would not quite agree and includes
in the literature of boredom Ivan Goncharov's great novel

*Oblomov*, whose first 100 pages are about the inability of its title character to get out of bed and get dressed and do something, anything. But *Oblomov* is less about boredom than about sloth.

The difference is a reminder that boredom presents a semantic problem. One must discriminate and make distinctions when trying to define it. Ennui, apathy, depression, accidie, melancholia, and *mal de vivre*—these are all aspects of boredom, but they do not quite define it. Perhaps the most serious distinction that needs to be made is that between boredom and depression. Toohey is correct when he argues that chronic boredom can bring about agitation, anger, and depression but that boredom and depression are not the same. Boredom is chiefly an emotion of a secondary kind, like shame, guilt, envy, admiration, embarrassment, contempt, and others. Depression is a mental illness, and much more serious.

"Suicide," Toohey claims, "has no clear relationship with boredom," while it can have everything to do with depression. Perhaps. An exception is the actor George Sanders, who in 1972, at the age of 65, checked into a hotel near Barcelona and was found dead two days later, having taken five bottles of Nembutal. He left behind a suicide note that read:

Dear World, I am leaving because I am bored. I feel I have lived long enough. I am leaving you with your worries in this sweet cesspool. Good luck.

If boredom isn't easily defined—"a bestial and indefinable affliction," Dostoyevsky called it—it can be described. A "psychological Sahara," the Russian poet Joseph Brodsky called it. If one wants to experience it directly, I know no more efficient way than reading Martin Heidegger on the subject, specifically the sections on boredom in *The Fundamental Concepts of Metaphysics, World, Finitude, Solitude.* Boredom, for Heidegger, is valuable in that it rubs clear the slate of our mind and is, as Svendsen has it, "a privileged fundamental mood because it leads us directly into the very problem of time and being." Boredom, in this reading, readies the mind for profound vision. I could attempt to explain how, in Heidegger, this comes about, but your eyes, in reading it, would soon take on the glaze of a franchise donut. Besides, I don't believe it.

Neither does Toohey, who is excellent on drawing the line    16
of the existentialist tradition of boredom that runs from the acedia of the early monks through Heidegger and Jean-Paul Sartre to the present day. Toohey holds that existentialist boredom is neither an emotion nor a feeling but a concept, one "constructed from a union of boredom, chronic boredom, depression, a sense of superfluity, frustration, surfeit, disgust, indifference, apathy, and feelings of entrapment." As such, existential boredom has become a philosophical sickness, not part of the human condition at all, but available exclusively to intellectuals given to moodiness and dark views.

The most notable novel in the existentialist boredom tradi-    17
tion is Sartre's *Nausea* (1938), whose main character, Antoine Roquentin, lives in a condition of overpowering indifference that Sartre calls "contingency," in which the universe is uncaring and one's existence is without necessity. After reading the philosophers taken up with the problems of being and existence, I cheer myself up by recalling the anecdote about the student in one of his philosophy courses at CCNY who asked Morris Raphael Cohen to prove that he, the student, existed. "Ah," replied Cohen in his Yiddish-accented English, "who's eskin'?"

In France, boredom is given a philosophical tincture; in    18
England, an aristocratic one: Lord Byron, having seen and done it all, is the perfect type of the bored English aristocrat. George Santayana, travelling on a student fellowship from Harvard, made the discovery that the Germans had no conception of boredom whatsoever, which explains their tolerance for the *Ring* cycle and the novels of Hermann Broch, and for so many other lengthy productions in German high culture. In Italy, boredom can take on the coloration and tone of amusing decadence, an emotion perfectly embodied in several movies by Marcello Mastroianni.

Alberto Moravia's novel *Boredom* (1960) plays the subject    19
for darkish laughs. A man in his thirties, a failed painter with a

rich mother, hounded by boredom all his days, takes up with a young painter's model. He has regular and uncomplicated sex with her, but off the couch she bores him blue, until she begins cheating on him with another man, which arouses his interest in her. Preferring not to be interested, he concludes that his only solution is to marry her and give her a large number of children; Once she is his wife and he can insure her fidelity, he can lapse back into comfortable boredom. "In this lack of all roots and responsibilities," he thinks, "in this utter void created by boredom, marriage, for me, was something dead and meaningless, and in this way it would at least serve some purpose." To "divorce, Italian style" Moravia adds "marriage, Italian style," though in the novel the painter does not finally marry the young woman.

Moravia's novel is also a reminder that perhaps as many marriages fail out of boredom as out of anything else. "Of all the primary relations," Robert Nisbet writes in *Prejudices, A Philosophical Dictionary,* "marriage is probably the most fertile in its yield of boredom, to a wife perhaps more than to a husband if only because prior to recent times, her opportunities to forestall or relieve boredom were fewer." In Nisbet's view, the changing nature of marriage, from an institution with an economic foundation designed primarily for procreation to one that has become an almost "purely personal relationship," has rendered it all the more susceptible to the incursions of boredom. Nisbet speculates that, had God permitted Adam and Eve to remain in the Garden of Eden, their marriage, too, might have foundered on boredom.

Sameness and repetition are among the chief causes of boredom. If they haunt marriages, they are even more powerfully at work in the realm of vocation. Once work went beyond the artisanal state, where farmers and craftsman had a personal hand in their productions, once the assembly line and its white-collar equivalent, the large bureaucratic office, came into being, work, owing to its repetitious nature, became one of the chief sources of boredom in the modern world.

Views on boredom and work alter with changing economic conditions. For my father's generation, arriving at maturity with the onset of the Depression, the notion of "interesting" in connection with work didn't come into play. Making a good living did. Unless the work was utterly degrading, my father could not understand leaving one job for another at a lesser salary. How different from today when a friend in California recently told me that he thought he might cease hiring young college graduates for jobs in his financial firm. "Their minds aren't in it," he said. "They all want to write screenplays."

One can also tell a great deal about a person by what bores   23
him. Certainly this is so in my own case. After perhaps an hour of driving along the coast between Portland, Oregon, and Vancouver, British Columbia, encountering one dazzling landscape after another, I thought enough was enough; Mae West was wrong, you can get too much of a good thing; and I longed for the sight of a delicatessen stocked with febrile Jews.

Tolerance for boredom differs vastly from person to per-   24
son. Some might argue that a strong intolerance for boredom suggests, with its need for constant action, impressive ambition. Others longing to be always in play, have, as the old saying goes, ants in their pants, or, to use the good Yiddish word, *schplikes.*

No one longs to be bored, but, if I am a useful example,   25
as one grows older, one often finds oneself more patient with boredom. Pressureless, dull patches in life—bring them on. I recently read two very well-written but extremely boring novels by Barbara Pym—*A Glassful of Blessings* and *A Few Green Leaves.* She is a writer I much admire, and I found myself quietly amused by how little happens in these novels. *A Few Green Leaves* contains the following sentence: "'It is an art all too seldom met with,' Adam declared, 'the correct slicing of cucumber.'"

Toohey suggests that boredom is good for us. We should,   26
he feels, be less put off by it. For one thing, boredom can function as a warning sign, as angina warns of heart attack and gout of stroke, telling those who suffer unduly from it that they need to change their lives. For another, "boredom intensifies self-perception," by which I gather he means that

it allows time for introspection of a kind not available to those who live in a state of continuous agitation and excitation. Boredom can also in itself function as a stimulant; boredom with old arguments and ideas can, in this view, presumably lead to freshened thought and creativity.

In the last chapter of *Boredom, A Lively History*, Toohey 27 veers into a discussion of what brain science has to tell us about boredom. I almost wrote a "compulsory discussion," for with-it-ness now calls for checking in with what the neuroscientists have to say about your subject, whatever it might be. What they have to say is usually speculative, generally turns out to be based on studies of mice or chimps, and is never very persuasive. Boredom, neuroscientists believe, is thought to be experienced in the part of the brain called the "insula," where other secondary emotions are experienced, and which a neurologist named Arthur D. Craig calls the region of the brain that stands at "a crossroad of time and desire."

Having said this, one hasn't said much. Brain studies, crit- 28 ics of them argue, are still roughly at the stage that physiology was before William Harvey in the 17th century discovered the circulatory system. Boredom is after all part of consciousness, and about consciousness the neurologists still have much less to tell us than do the poets and the philosophers.

Boredom, like Parkinson's and Alzheimer's at a much 29 higher level of seriousness, is a disease with no known cure, but Professor Toohey feels the need to supply possible ameliorations, or palliatives, for it. Among these are aerobic exercise (good, some say, for the restoration of brain cells), music (Mozart, it has been discovered, calms agitated elephants in captivity), and social activity (along with crossword puzzles, a recipe for aging well from Toohey's Aunt Madge). Even Toohey has to admit that these sound "corny," which they do. Worse, they sound boring. He does not dwell on those more expensive and dangerous palliatives for boredom: alcoholism, drug addiction, adultery, divorce, skydiving, bungee-jumping, and psychotherapy.

Isaac Bashevis Singer once told an interviewer that the pur- 30 pose of art was to eliminate boredom, at least temporarily, for he held that boredom was the natural condition of men and women. Not artists alone but vast industries have long been at work to eliminate boredom permanently. Think of 24-hour-a-day cable television. Think of Steve Jobs, one of the current heroes of contemporary culture, who may be a genius, and just possibly an evil genius. With his ever more sophisticated iPhones and iPads, he is aiding people to distract themselves from boredom and allowing them to live nearly full- time in a world of games and information and communication with no time out for thought.

In 1989, Joseph Brodsky gave a commencement address [31] at Dartmouth College on the subject of boredom that has a higher truth quotient than any such address I have ever heard (or, for that matter, have myself given). Brodsky told the 1,100 Dartmouth graduates that, although they may have had some splendid samples of boredom supplied by their teachers, these would be as nothing compared with what awaits them in the years ahead. Neither originality nor inventiveness on their part will suffice to defeat the endless repetition that life will serve up to them, as it has served up to us all. Evading boredom, he pointed out, is a full-time job, entailing endless change—of jobs, geography, wives and lovers, and interests—and in the end a self-defeating one. Brodksy therefore advises: "When hit by boredom, go for it. Let yourself be crushed by it; submerge, hit bottom."

The lesson boredom teaches, according to Brodsky, is [32] that of one's own insignificance, an insignificance brought about by one's own finitude. We are all here a short while, and then—*poof!*—gone and, sooner or later, usually sooner, forgotten. Boredom "puts your existence into perspective, the net result of which is precision and humility." Brodsky advised the students to try "to stay passionate," for passion, whatever its object, is the closest thing to a remedy for boredom. But about one's insignificance boredom does not deceive. Brodsky, who served 18 months of hard labor in the Soviet Union and had to have known what true boredom is, closes by telling the students that "if you find this gloomy, you don't know what gloom is."

"Boredom," as Peter Toohey writes, "is a normal, useful, 33 and incredibly common part of human experience." Boredom is also part of the human condition, always has been, and, if we are lucky, always will be.

Live with it. 34

## For Critical Thinking

### QUESTIONS ABOUT PURPOSE

1. Why does Epstein says that "[i]f boredom isn't easily defined . . . it can be described"?
2. Why does he say that "one must discriminate and make distinctions when trying to define boredom"?

### QUESTIONS ABOUT AUDIENCE

1. How does he demonstrate that his readers who have said they have never been bored are lying?
2. How does his experience with boredom help him identify with his readers?

### QUESTIONS ABOUT STRATEGY

1. How does he use experiences in the army, with marriage, and at work to illustrate boredom?
2. How does he use the cures for boredom to illustrate further examples of boredom?

## For Writing and Research

1. *Analyze* the range of examples Epstein uses to help him define boredom.
2. *Practice* by describing an experience that you would characterize as truly boring.
3. *Argue* that creativity or inventiveness can or cannot defeat boredom.
4. *Synthesize* the various examples of the human condition that Epstein provides to describe or define chronic boredom.

# Toni Cade Bambara: *The Lesson*

Toni Cade Bambara (1939–1995) was born in New York City and educated at Queens College, the University of Florence, the Ecole de Mme. Etienne Decroux in Paris, and the City College of the City University of New York. Her work experience was extremely varied: a social investigator for the New York State Department of Welfare, a director of recreation in the psychiatry department of New York's Metropolitan Hospital, a visiting professor of Afro-American studies (Stephens College in Columbia, Missouri), a consultant on women's studies (Emory University in Atlanta), and a writer-in-residence at Spelman College in Atlanta. She contributed stories and essays to magazines as diverse as *Negro Digest, Prairie Schooner,* and *Redbook*. Her two collections of short stories, *Gorilla, My Love* (1972) and *The Sea Birds Are Still Alive: Collected Stories* (1977), deal with the emerging sense of self of black women. Her novels include *The Salt Eaters* (1980) and *Those Bones Are Not My Child* (1999). "The Lesson," reprinted from *Gorilla, My Love*, focuses on the experiences of several black children who learn how much things "cost."

BACK IN THE days when everyone was old and stupid or young and foolish and me and Sugar were the only ones just right, this lady moved on our block with nappy hair and proper speech and no makeup. And quite naturally we laughed at her, laughed the way we did at the junk man who went about his business like he was some big-time president and his sorry-ass horse his secretary. And we kinda hated her too, hated the way we did the winos who cluttered up our parks and pissed on our handball walls and stank up our hall-ways and stairs so you couldn't halfway play hide-and-seek without a goddamn gas mask. Miss Moore was her name. The only woman on the block with no first name. And she was black as hell, cept for her feet, which were fish-white and spooky. And she was always planning these boring-ass things for us to do, us being my cousin, mostly, who lived on the block cause we all moved North the same time and to the same apartment then spread out gradual to breathe. And our parents would yank our heads into some kinda shape and crisp up our clothes so we'd be presentable for travel with Miss Moore, who always looked like she was going to church, though she never did. Which is just one of the things the grownups talked about when they talked behind her back like a dog. But when she came calling with some sachet she'd sewed up or some gingerbread she'd made or some book, why then they'd all be too embarrassed to turn her down and we'd get handed over all spruced up. She'd been to college and said it was only right that she should take responsibility for the young ones' education, and she not even related by marriage or blood. So they'd go for it. Specially Aunt Gretchen. She was the main gofer in the family. You got some ole dumb shit foolishness you want somebody to go for, you send for Aunt Gretchen. She been screwed into the go-along for so long, it's a blood-deep natural thing with her. Which is how she got saddled with me and Sugar and Junior in the first place while our mothers were in a la-de-da apartment up the block having a good ole time.

So this one-day Miss Moore rounds us all up at the mailbox 2 and it's puredee hot and she's knockin herself out about arithmetic. And school suppose to let up in summer I heard, but she don't never let up. And the starch in my pinafore scratching the shit outta me and I'm really hating this nappy-head bitch and her goddamn college degree. I'd much rather go to the pool or to the show where it's cool. So me and Sugar leaning on the mailbox being surly, which is a Miss Moore word. And Flyboy checking out what everybody brought for lunch. And Fat Butt already wasting his peanut-butter-and-jelly

sandwich like the pig he is. And Junebug punching on Q. T.'s
arm for potato chips. And Rosie Giraffe shifting from one hip
to the other waiting for somebody to step on her foot or ask her
if she from Georgia so she can kick ass, preferably Mercedes'.
And Miss Moore asking us do we know what money is, like
we a bunch of retards. I mean real money, she say, like it's
only poker chips or monopoly papers we lay on the grocer.
So right away I'm tired of this and say so. And would much
rather snatch Sugar and go to the Sunset and terrorize the West
Indian kids and take their hair ribbons and their money too.
And Miss Moore files that remark away for next week's lesson
on brotherhood, I can tell. And finally I say we oughta get to
the subway cause it's cooler and besides we might meet some
cute boys. Sugar done swiped her mama's lipstick, so we ready.

So we heading down the street and she's boring us silly     3
about what things cost and what our parents make and how
much goes for rent and how money ain't divided up right in
this country. And then she gets to the part about we all poor
and live in the slums, which I don't feature. And I'm ready
to speak on that, but she steps out in the street and hails two
cabs just like that. Then she hustles half the crew in with her
and hands me a five-dollar bill and tells me to calculate 10
percent tip for the driver. And we're off. Me and Sugar and
Junebug and Flyboy hangin out the window and hollering
to everybody, putting lipstick on each other cause Flyboy a
faggot anyway, and making farts with our sweaty armpits. But
I'm mostly trying to figure how to spend this money. But
they all fascinated with the meter ticking and Junebug starts
laying bets as to how much it'll read when Flyboy can't hold
his breath no more. Then Sugar lays bets as to how much it'll
be when we get there. So I'm stuck. Don't nobody want to
go for my plan, which is to jump out at the next light and
run off to the first bar-b-que we can find. Then the driver tells
us to get the hell out cause we there already. And the meter
reads eighty-five cents. And I'm stalling to figure out the tip
and Sugar say give him a dime. And I decide he don't need
it bad as I do, so later for him. But then he tries to take off
with Junebug foot still in the door so we talk about his mama

something ferocious. Then we check out that we on Fifth Avenue and everybody dressed up in stockings. One lady in a fur coat, hot as it is. White folks crazy.

"This is the place," Miss Moore say, presenting it to us in  4 the voice she uses at the museum. "Let's look in the windows before we go in."

"Can we steal?" Sugar asks very serious like she's getting  5 the ground rules squared away before she plays. "I beg your pardon," say Miss Moore, and we fall out. So she leads us around the windows of the toy store and me and Sugar screamin, "This is mine, that's mine, I gotta have that, that was made for me, I was born for that," till Big Butt drowns us out.

"Hey, I'm goin to buy that there."  6

"That there? You don't even know what it is, stupid."  7

"I do so," he say punchin on Rosie Giraffe. "It's a  8 microscope."

"Whatcha gonna do with a microscope, fool?"  9

"Look at things."  10

"Like what, Ronald?" ask Miss Moore. And Big Butt ain't  11 got the first notion. So here go Miss Moore gabbing about the thousands of bacteria in a drop of water and the somethin-or-other in a speck of blood and the million and one living things in the air around us is invisible to the naked eye. And what she say that for? Junebug go to town on that "naked" and we rolling. Then Miss Moore ask what it cost. So we all jam into the window smudgin it up and the price tag say $300. So then she ask how long'd take for Big Butt and Junebug to save up their allowances. "Too long," I say. "Yeh," adds Sugar, "outgrown it by that time." And Miss Moore say no, you never outgrow learning instruments. "Why, even medical students and interns and," blah, blah, blah. And we ready to choke Big Butt for bringing it up in the first damn place.

"This here costs four hundred eighty dollars," say Rosie  12 Giraffe. So we pile up all over her to see what she pointing out. My eyes tell me it's a chunk of glass cracked with something heavy, and different-color inks dripped into the splits, then the whole thing put into a oven or something. But for $480 it don't make sense.

"That's a paperweight made of semi-precious stones fused    13
together under tremendous pressure," she explains slowly,
with her hands doing the mining and all the factory work.

"So what's a paperweight?" asks Rosie Giraffe.    14

"To weigh paper with, dumbbell," say Flyboy, the wise    15
man from the East.

"Not exactly," say Miss Moore, which is what she say when    16
you warm or way off too. "It's to weigh paper down so it
won't scatter and make your desk untidy." So right away me
and Sugar curtsy to each other and then to Mercedes who is
more the tidy type.

"We don't keep paper on top of the desk in my class," say    17
Junebug, figuring Miss Moore crazy or lyin one.

"At home, then," she say. "Don't you have a calendar and    18
a pencil case and a blotter and a letter-opener on your desk at
home where you do your homework?" And she know damn
well what our homes look like cause she nosys around in them
every chance she gets.

"I don't even have a desk," say Junebug. "Do we?"    19

"No. And I don't get no homework neither," says    20
Big Butt.

"And I don't even have a home," say Flyboy like he do at    21
school to keep the white folks off his back and sorry for him.
Send this poor kid to camp posters, is his specialty.

"I do," says Mercedes. "I have a box of stationery on my    22
desk and a picture of my cat. My godmother bought the stationery and the desk. There's a big rose on each sheet and the
envelopes smell like roses."

"Who wants to know about your smelly-ass stationery," say    23
Rosie Giraffe fore I can get my two cents in.

"It's important to have a work area all your own so    24
that . . ."

"Will you look at this sailboat, please," say Flyboy, cuttin    25
her off and pointing to the thing like it was his. So once again
we tumble all over each other to gaze at this magnificent
thing in the toy store which is just big enough to maybe sail
two kittens across the pond if you strap them to the posts
tight. We all start reciting the price tag like we in assembly.

"Handcrafted sailboat of fiberglass at one thousand one hundred ninety-five dollars."

"Unbelievable," I hear myself say and am really stunned. 26
I read it again for myself just in case the group recitation put me in a trance. Same thing. For some reason, this pisses me off. We look at Miss Moore and she lookin at us, waiting for I dunno what.

"Who'd pay all that when you can buy a sailboat set for 27
a quarter at Pop's, a tube of glue for a dime, and a ball of string for eight cents? It must have a motor and a whole lot else besides," I say. "My sailboat cost me about fifty cents."

"But will it take water?" say Mercedes with her smart ass. 28

"Took mine to Alley Pond Park once," say Flyboy. "String 29
broke. Lost it. Pity."

"Sailed mine in Central Park and it keeled over and sank. 30
Had to ask my father for another dollar."

"And you got the strap," laugh Big Butt. "The jerk didn't 31
even have a string on it. My old man wailed on his behind."

Little Q. T. was staring hard at the sailboat and you could 32
see he wanted it bad. But he too little and somebody'd just take it from him. So what the hell. "This boat for kids, Miss Moore?"

"Parents silly to buy something like that just to get all 33
broke up," say Rosie Giraffe.

"That much money it should last forever," I figure. 34

"My father'd buy it for me if I wanted it." 35

"Your father, my ass," say Rosie Giraffe getting a chance to 36
finally push Mercedes.

"Must be rich people shop here," say Q. T. 37

"You are a very bright boy," say Flyboy. "What was your 38
first clue?" And he rap him on the head with the back of his knuckles, since Q. T. the only one he could get away with. Though Q. T. liable to come up behind you years later and get his licks in when you half expect it.

"What I want to know is," I says to Miss Moore though I 39
never talk to her, I wouldn't give the bitch that satisfaction, "is how much a real boat costs? I figure a thousand'd get you a yacht any day."

"Why don't you check that out," she says, "and report    40
back to the group?" Which really pains my ass. If you gonna
mess up a perfectly good swim day least, you could do is
have some answers. "Let's go in," she say like she got something up her sleeve. Only she don't lead the way. So me and
Sugar turn the corner to where the entrance is, but when
we get there I kinda hang back. Not that I'm scared, what's
there to be afraid of, just a toy store. But I feel funny, shame.
But what I got to be shamed about? Got as much right to
go in as anybody. But somehow I can't seem to get hold of
the door, so I step away from Sugar to lead. But she hangs
back too. And I look at her and she looks at me and this is
ridiculous. I mean, damn, I have never ever been shy about
doing nothing or going nowhere. But then Mercedes steps
up and then Rosie Giraffe and Big Butt crowd in behind and
shove, and next thing we all stuffed into the doorway with
only Mercedes squeezing past us, smoothing out her jumper
and walking right down the aisle. Then the rest of us tumble
in like a glued-together jigsaw done all wrong. And people
looking at us. And it's like the time me and Sugar crashed
into the Catholic church on a dare. But once we got in there
and everything so hushed and holy and the candles and the
bowin and the handkerchiefs on all the drooping heads, I just
couldn't go through with the plan. Which was for me to run
up to the altar and do a tap dance while Sugar played the nose
flute and messed around in the holy water. And Sugar kept
giving me the elbow. Then later teased me so bad I tied her up
in the shower and turned it on and locked her in. And she'd
be there till this day if Aunt Gretchen hadn't finally figured I
was lying about the boarder takin a shower.

Same thing in the store. We all walking on tiptoe and hardly    41
touching the games and puzzles and things. And I watched
Miss Moore who is steady watching us like she waiting for a
sign. Like Mama Drewery watches the sky and sniffs the air
and takes note of just how much slant is in the bird formation.
Then me and Sugar bump smack into each other, so busy gazing at the toys, 'specially the sailboat. But we don't laugh and
go into our fat-lady bump-stomach routine. We just stare at

that price tag. Then Sugar run a finger over the whole boat.
And I'm jealous and want to hit her. Maybe not her, but I
sure want to punch somebody in the mouth.

"Watcha bring us here for, Miss Moore?"                        42

"You sound angry, Sylvia. Are you mad about something?"       43
Giving me one of them grins like she telling a grown-up joke
that never turns out to be funny. And she's looking very
closely at me like maybe she planning to do my portrait from
memory. I'm mad, but I won't give her that satisfaction. So I
slouch around the store being very bored and say, "Let's go."

Me and Sugar at the back of the train watching the tracks     44
whizzing by large then small then getting gobbled up in the
dark. I'm thinking about this tricky toy I saw in the store. A
clown that somersaults on a bar then does chin-ups just cause
you yank lightly at his leg. Cost $35. I could see me asking
my mother for a $35 birthday clown. "You wanna who that
costs what?" she'd say, cocking her head to the side to get a
better view of the hole in my head. Thirty-five dollars could
buy new bunk beds for Junior and Gretchen's boy. Thirty
five dollars and the whole household could go visit Grand-
daddy Nelson in the country. Thirty-five dollars would pay
for the rent and the piano bill too. Who are these people that
spend that much for performing clowns and $1000 for toy
sailboats? What kinda work they do and how they live and
how come we ain't in on it? Where we are is who we are, Miss
Moore always pointing out. But it don't necessarily have to
be that way, she always adds then waits for somebody to say
that poor people have to wake up and demand their share
of the pie and don't none of us know what kind of pie she
talking about in the first damn place. But she ain't so smart
cause I still got her four dollars from the taxi and she sure
ain't gettin it. Messin up my day with this shit. Sugar nudges
me in my pocket and winks.

Miss Moore lines us up in front of the mailbox where we      45
started from, seem like years ago, and I got a headache for
thinkin so hard. And we lean all over each other so we can
hold up under the draggy-ass lecture she always finishes us off
with at the end before we thank her for borin us to tears. But

she just looks at us like she reading tea leaves. Finally she say, "Well, what did you think of F.A.O. Schwarz?"

Rosie Giraffe mumbles, "White folks crazy."                    46

"I'd like to go there again when I get my birthday money,"      47
says Mercedes, and we shove her out the pack so she has to
lean on the mailbox by herself.

"I'd like a shower. Tiring day," say Flyboy.                    48

Then Sugar surprises me by saying, "You know, Miss             49
Moore, I don't think all of us here put together eat in a year
what that sailboat costs." And Miss Moore lights up like
somebody goosed her. "And?" she say, urging Sugar on. Only
I'm standin on her foot so she don't continue.

"Imagine for a minute what kind of society it is in which      50
some people can spend on a toy what it would cost to feed a
family of six or seven. What do you think?"

"I think," say Sugar pushing me off her feet like she never    51
done before, cause I whip her ass in a minute, "that this is
not much of a democracy if you ask me. Equal chance to
pursue happiness means an equal crack at the dough, don't
it?" Miss Moore is besides herself and I am disgusted with
Sugar's treachery. So I stand on her foot one more time to
see if she'll shove me. She shuts up, and Miss Moore looks at
me, sorrowfully I'm thinking. And somethin weird is going
on, I can feel it in my chest.

"Anybody else learn anything today?" looking dead at me.      52
I walk away and Sugar has to run to catch up and don't even
seem to notice when I shrug her arm off my shoulder.

"Well, we got four dollars anyway," she says.                 53

"Uh hunh."                                                     54

"We could go to Hascombs and get half a chocolate layer       55
and then go to the Sunset and still have plenty money for
potato chips and ice cream sodas."

"Uh hunh."                                                     56

"Race you to Hascombs," she say.                              57

We start down the block and she gets ahead which is O.K.      58
by me cause I'm going to the West End and then over to the
Drive to think this day through. She can run if she want to and
even run faster. But ain't nobody gonna beat me at nuthin.

## COMMENT ON "THE LESSON"

"The Lesson" is an excellent illustration of how narration and description are used in short fiction to create a definition of the word *cost*. Although the plot seems arranged in a simple chronology, the narrator, Sylvia, suggests that the events took place "Back in the days when everyone was old and stupid or young and foolish and me and Sugar were the only ones just right." Sylvia's tough talk is directed at an audience she presumes will understand why she sees Miss Moore and her activities as "boring-ass." But as Sylvia describes the various toys at F.A.O. Schwarz, she reveals that her point of view is defensive. She is stunned by what things cost, embarrassed by her ignorance, and confused by her anger and Sugar's treachery. She will not acknowledge publicly that she has learned Miss Moore's lesson about the inequities in society, but privately she concludes that "ain't nobody gonna beat me at nuthin."

# CHAPTER 6

# Cause and Effect

If you are like most people, you're just naturally curious: you look at the world around you and wonder why things happen. But you're also curious because you want some control over your life and over your environment, and you can't have that control unless you can understand **causes**. That's why so much writing is cause-and-effect writing, writing that seeks to explain the causes of change and new developments. In almost every profession, you will be asked to do writing that analyzes causes; that's why such writing has an important place in college composition courses.

You also want to understand **effects**. If A happens, will B be the effect? You want to try to predict the consequences of putting some plan into effect or look at some effect and explain what brought it about. Or you want to set a goal (the effect) and plan a strategy for reaching it. This kind of writing also prepares you for writing you're likely to do later in your career.

## PURPOSE

When you write cause-and-effect essays, you're likely to have one of three purposes. Sometimes, you want to *explain* why something happened or what might be likely to happen under certain circumstances. Daniel Goleman is writing that kind of essay in "Peak Performance: Why Records Fall" when he explains how new knowledge about training practices and about human mental capacities have led to athletic feats that seemed impossible only a few decades ago. At other times, you might write a cause-and-effect paper to *speculate* about an interesting topic—for instance, to speculate why a new computer game has become so popular or what the effects of a new kind of body suit will be for competitive swimmers.

Writers often use a cause-and-effect essay to *argue*, or prove a point. In "Comforting Thoughts," Calvin Trillin argues that a strange chain of causes and effects allows him to feel "much better."

## AUDIENCE

When you begin to analyze your audience for a cause-and-effect argument, it helps to think of them as jurors to whom you are going to present a case. You can make up a list of questions just as a lawyer would to help him or her formulate an argument. For example:

- How should I prepare my readers for my argument? What background information do they need?
- What kind of evidence are they likely to want? Factual, statistical, and anecdotal?
- How much do I have to explain? Will they have enough context to understand my points and make connections without my spelling them out?

Like a trial lawyer, you're trying to establish a chain of cause and effect. Perhaps you can't establish absolute proof, but you can show probability. The format for such arguments can be as follows:

- State your claim early, usually in the first paragraph.
- Show the connection you want to establish.
- Present your supporting evidence.
- Repeat your claim in your conclusion.

## STRATEGIES

Writers may choose among a number of strategies when they write about cause and effect. The simplest one is to describe an action or event and then show what its consequences were. People who write case studies in psychology or social work use this strategy. Trillin creates a humorous version of this strategy in "Comforting Thoughts" when he traces the consequences of his reading two scientific studies.

Another favorite strategy is to describe an event or circumstance that seems significant and then examine the probable reasons for it. Brent Staples does this when he speculates on why the white woman ran away from him.

Conversely, a writer sometimes begins a cause-and-effect essay by isolating an effect and then looking for plausible explanations of what caused it. Goleman follows this strategy when he tries to explain why there are so many peak performances in athletics. In writing this kind of essay, you must be careful to distinguish between the **direct** or **simple cause** and the **indirect** or **complex cause**. Calvin Trillin attempts to make such distinctions in "Comforting Thoughts" when he sorts through various studies that suggest ways to relieve stress.

Another way to approach cause-and-effect writing is to focus on two apparently related phenomena and speculate whether there may be a cause-and-effect connection between them. Such speculation is risky, and you must be prepared to back up your assertions with strong evidence. Nevertheless, this kind of hypothesizing can be fruitful and enlightening; it is essentially what Daniel Goleman is doing when he tries to account for "why records fall."

There are still other ways to write about cause and effect; the ones given here are by no means the only strategies writers use. To be effective and responsible, however, all strategies should meet the following criteria.

1. *Do not overstate your case.* When you write about complex situations, particularly those that involve people, you do best to say, "X will *probably* cause Y" or "A *seems* to be the effect of B," rather than insist that there must be a necessary and direct causal connection between two events. Many plausible cause-and-effect relationships are difficult to prove conclusively, and your readers will trust your analysis when you do not claim too much.

2. *Do not oversimplify cause-and-effect relationships.* Seldom does an important effect result from a simple and direct cause. For instance, if 15 percent fewer people died of heart attacks in 2016 than in 2015, a researcher should assume that many factors contributed to the decline—not one element. Furthermore, most happenings of any significance have more than one effect, and any cause and effect may be only one link in a long chain of causes and effects. For that reason, qualify your assertions with phrases such as "a major cause," "one result," and "an immediate effect."

3. *Do not mistake coincidence or simple sequence for a necessary cause-and-effect relationship.* The fact that the crime rate in a state rose the year after the legal drinking age was lowered to eighteen does not mean there is a direct connection between the two occurrences. If you jump to conclusions about cause and effect too quickly, you will be committing a fallacy known as *post hoc, ergo propter hoc* (Latin for "after this, therefore because of this").

These cautions do not, however, mean that you should refrain from drawing conclusions about cause and effect until you are absolutely certain of your conclusion. It is not always possible or wise to wait for complete certainty before analyzing what happened or forecasting what may happen. The best you can do is observe carefully and speculate intelligently.

## POINTS TO REMEMBER

1. Remember that, in human events, you can almost never prove direct, simple, cause-and-effect relationships. Qualify your claims.

2. Be careful not to oversimplify your cause-and-effect statements; be cautious about saying that a cause always produces a certain effect or that a remedy never succeeds.

3. Avoid confusing coincidence or simple sequence with cause and effect; because B follows A doesn't mean that A caused B.

4. Build your cause-and-effect argument as a trial lawyer would. Present as much evidence as you can, and argue for your hypothesis.

Bettmann Premium/Corbis

*This picture shows Rosa Parks sitting in a bus in Montgomery,
Alabama, after the Supreme Court ruled segregation illegal on
the city bus system on December 21, 1956. Parks was arrested on
December 1, 1955, for refusing to give up her seat in the front of
a bus in Montgomery. The man sitting behind Parks is Nicholas
C. Chriss, a reporter for United Press International. Research the
effects of Rosa Parks's refusal on the Civil Rights movement. Then
write an essay in which you present your findings. Or present a
similar event in which one person's act—or perhaps a refusal to
act—caused significant effects.*

Calvin Trillin was born in Kansas City, Missouri, in 1935 and educated at Yale University. He began his career by working as a reporter for *Time* magazine and then as a columnist for *The New Yorker*. In recent years, he has written a national newspaper column and staged a one-man show off-Broadway. His writing includes three novels, *Runestruck* (1977), *Floater* (1980), and *Tepper Isn't Going Out* (2001); books of poetry, including *Deadline Poet; or, My Life as a Doggerelist* (1994), and *Obliviously on He Sails: The Bush Administration in Rhyme* (2004); collections of reporting, including *U.S. Journal* (1971), *Killings* (1984), and *American Stories* (1991); a best-selling memoir, *Remembering Denny* (1993); numerous books of humor, such as *Family Man* (1998); and a portrait of his late wife, *About Alice* (2006). In "Comforting Thoughts," Trillin speculates on several procedures that are supposed to make him feel more comfortable.

F IRST I READ about a study in Meriden, Connecticut, which 1
indicated that talking to yourself is a perfectly legitimate way of getting comfort during a difficult time. Then I saw an item about research at Yale demonstrating that stress seems to be reduced in some people by exposing them to the aromas of certain desserts. Then I started talking to myself about desserts with aromas I find soothing. Then I felt a lot better. Isn't science grand?

I didn't feel perfect. One thing that was bothering me— 2
this is what I decided after I was asked by myself, "Well, what seems to be the trouble, guy?"—was that the ten most

popular methods of comforting yourself listed in the Meriden study didn't mention sniffing desserts, even though Yale, where all the sniffing research was going on, is only about twenty miles down the road. Does this mean that some of these scientists are so busy talking to themselves that they don't talk to each other? It got me so upset that I went to the back door of a baker in our neighborhood to sniff the aroma of chocolate chip cookies. I was talking to myself the whole time, of course.

## Isn't science grand?

"What the Yale people think," I said to myself, "is that a 3 person's soothed by the smell of, say, chocolate chip cookies because it brings back pleasant memories, like the memory of his mother baking chocolate chip cookies."

"What if his mother always burned the chocolate chip 4 cookies?" I replied.

"Are you talking about my mother?" 5

"Whose mother do you think I'm talking about?" I said. 6 "We're the only one here."

"Were those cookies burnt?" 7

"What do you think all that black stuff was?" 8

"I thought that was the chocolate chips." 9

"No, she always forgot the chocolate chips." 10

I wasn't finding the conversation very comforting at all. I 11 don't like to hear anyone make light of my mother's chocolate chip cookies, even me. I must have raised my voice, because the next thing I knew, the baker had come out to see what was going on.

Even though the Meriden study had shown that being with 12 someone else was the most comforting thing of all—it finished ahead of listening to music and even watching TV—I saw right away that being with the baker wasn't going to be much more comforting than talking to myself. He said, "What are you, some kind of nut case, or what?"

I told him that I was engaging in two therapies that had    13
been scientifically proven effective: sniffing chocolate chip cookies and talking to myself. He told me that I owed him two dollars and fifty cents. "For sniffing, we charge a buck and a quarter a dozen," he explained.

"How do you know I sniffed two dozen?" I asked.              14

"We got ways," he said.                                      15

I told him that according to the research done at Yale, cer-  16
tain odors caused the brain to produce alpha waves, which are associated with relaxation. I told him that in my case the odor of chocolate chip cookies—particularly slightly burnt chocolate chip cookies—was such an odor. I told him that he ought to be proud to confirm the scientific research done at one of the great universities of the English-speaking world. That alone, I told him, ought to be payment enough for whatever small part of the aroma of his chocolate chip cookies I had used up with my sniffing.

He thought about it for a moment. Then he said, "Take        17
a walk, buddy."

I was happy to. As it happens, going for a walk finished     18
tenth in the Meriden study, just behind recalling pleasant memories. Naturally, I talked to myself on the way.

"Maybe I can find someplace to smell what the Yale people     19
call 'spiced apple,'" I said to myself. "They found that the smell of spiced apple is so effective that with some people it can stop panic attacks."

"But I don't know what spiced apple smells like," I replied.  20
"Spiced with what?"

That was bothering me enough that my walk wasn't actu-       21
ally very soothing. I thought about bolstering it with some of the other activities on the list, but reading or watching TV seemed impractical. Prayer was also on the list, but praying for the aroma of spiced apple seemed frivolous.

I walked faster and faster. It occurred to me that I might    22
be getting a panic attack. Desperately I tried to recall some pleasant memories. I recalled the time before I knew about

the Meriden list, when I talked to myself only in private. I recalled the time before I knew about the Yale research and didn't have to worry about finding any spiced apple. Then I felt a lot better. I didn't feel perfect, but you can't always feel perfect.

## For Critical Thinking

### QUESTIONS ABOUT PURPOSE

1. What does Trillin's essay attempt to demonstrate about scientific studies?
2. How does he use his first paragraph to reveal that his purpose is to entertain?

### QUESTIONS ABOUT AUDIENCE

1. How does Trillin use dialogue—"talking to himself"—to engage his readers?
2. How does the baker's response (paragraph 17) anticipate the possible reaction of Trillin's readers to his speculations?

### QUESTIONS ABOUT STRATEGIES

1. How many of the "ten most popular methods for comforting yourself" does Trillin mention?
2. In paragraph 22, what causes Trillin to feel "a lot better"?

## For Writing and Research

1. *Analyze* the probable cause of Trillin's conclusion that you "can't always feel perfect."
2. *Practice* by describing a method you have developed for comforting yourself during times of stress.
3. *Argue* that the conclusions of a particular "pop scientific study" are based on faulty causal analysis.
4. *Synthesize:* Research scientific studies on one of the "ten most popular methods" Trillin mentions—such as walking. Then use this information to demonstrate that it can cause multiple positive effects.

## Daniel Goleman: *Peak Performance: Why Records Fall*

Daniel Goleman was born in 1946 in Stockton, California, and was educated at Amherst College and Harvard University. After working for several years as a professor of psychology, he began his career as an editor for *Psychology Today*. He has contributed more than fifty articles to psychology journals and has written a dozen books, including *The Meditative Mind* (1988); *The Creative Spirit* (1992); *Mind Body Medicine: How to Use Your Mind for Better Health* (1993); *Emotional Intelligence* (1995); *Working with Emotional Intelligence* (1998); *Social Intelligence* (2006); and *Ecological Intelligence* (2009). Goleman published a new management training series called "Leadership: A Master Class in 2012." In "Peak Performance: Why Records Fall," reprinted from a 1994 *New York Times* article, Goleman analyzes how dedication to practice contributes to peak performances.

THE OLD JOKE—How do you get to Carnegie Hall? 1 Practice, practice, practice—is getting a scientific spin. Researchers are finding an unexpected potency from deliberate practice in world-class competitions of all kinds, including chess matches, musical recitals, and sporting events.

Studies of chess masters, virtuoso musicians and star ath- 2 letes show that the relentless training routines of those at the top allow them to break through ordinary limits in memory and physiology, and so perform at levels that had been thought impossible.

World records have been falling inexorably over the last 3 century. For example, the marathon gold medalist's time in the 1896 Olympics Games was, by 1990, only about as good as the qualifying time for the Boston Marathon.

"Over the last century Olympics have become more and    4
more competitive, and so athletes steadily have had to put in more total lifetime hours of practice," said Dr. Michael Mahoney, a psychologist at the University of North Texas in Denton, who helps train the United States Olympic weight-lifting team. "These days you have to live your sport."

---

*Through their hours of practice, elite performers of all kinds master shortcuts that give them an edge.*

---

That total dedication is in contrast to the relatively leisurely    5
attitude taken at the turn of the century, when even world-class athletes would train arduously for only a few months before their competition.

"As competition got greater, training extended to a whole    6
season," said Dr. Anders Ericsson, a psychologist at Florida State University in Tallahassee who wrote an article on the role of deliberate practice for star performance recently in the journal *American Psychologist.* "Then it extended through the year, and then for several years. Now the elite performers start their training in childhood. There is a historical trend toward younger starting ages, which makes possible a greater and greater total number of hours of practice time."

To be sure, there are other factors at work: coaching    7
methods have become more sophisticated, equipment has improved and the pool of people competing has grown. But new studies are beginning to reveal the sheer power of training itself.

Perhaps the most surprising data show that extensive prac-    8
tice can break through barriers in mental capacities, particularly short-term memory. In short-term memory, information

is stored for the few seconds that it is used and then fades, as in hearing a phone number which one forgets as soon as it is dialed.

The standard view, repeated in almost every psychology   9 textbook, is that the ordinary limit on short-term memory is for seven or so bits of information—the length of a phone number. More than that typically cannot be retained in short-term memory with reliability unless the separate units are "chunked," as when the numbers in a telephone prefix are remembered as a single unit.

But, in a stunning demonstration of the power of sheer   10 practice to break barriers in the mind's ability to handle information, Dr. Ericsson and associates at Carnegie-Mellon University have taught college students to listen to a list of as many as 102 random digits and then recite it correctly. After 50 hours of practice with differing sets of random digits, four students were able to remember up to 20 digits after a single hearing. One student, a business major not especially talented in mathematics, was able to remember 102 digits. The feat took him more than 400 hours of practice.

The ability to increase memory in a particular domain is at the   11 heart of a wide range high-level performance, said Dr. Herbert Simon, professor of computer science and psychology at Carnegie-Mellon University and a Nobel laureate. Dr. Ericsson was part of a team studying expertise led by Dr. Simon.

"Every expert has acquired something like this mem-   12 ory ability" in his or her area of expertise, said Dr. Simon. "Memory is like an index; experts have approximately 50,000 chunks of familiar units of information they recognize. For a physician, many of those chunks are symptoms."

A similar memory training effect, Dr. Simon said, seems   13 to occur with many chess masters. The key skill chess players rehearse in practicing is, of course, selecting the best move. They do so by studying games between two chess masters and guessing the next move from their own study of the board as the game progresses.

Repeated practice results in a prodigious memory for   14 chess positions. The ability of some chess masters to play blindfolded, while simply told what moves their opponents make, has long been known; in the 1940s Adrian DeGroot, himself a Dutch grandmaster, showed that many chess masters are able to look at a chess board in midgame for as little as five seconds and then repeat the position of every piece on the board.

Later systematic studies by Dr. Simon's group showed that    15
the chess masters' memory feat was limited to boards used in actual games; they had no such memory for randomly placed pieces. "They would see a board and think, that reminds me of Spassky versus Lasker," said Dr. Simon.

This feat of memory was duplicated by a college student    16
who knew little about chess but was given 50 hours of training in remembering chess positions by Dr. Ericsson in a 1990 study.

Through their hours of practice, elite performers of all kinds    17
master shortcuts that give them an edge. Dr. Bruce Abernathy, a researcher at the University of Queensland in Australia, has found that the most experienced players in racquet sports like squash and tennis are able to predict where a serve will land by cues in the server's posture before the ball is hit.

A 1992 study of baseball greats like Hank Aaron and    18
Rod Carew by Thomas Hanson, then a graduate student at the University of Virginia in Charlottesville, found that the all-time best hitters typically started preparing for games by studying films of the pitchers they would face, to spot cues that would tip off what pitch was about to be thrown. Using such fleeting cues demands rehearsing so well that the response to them is automatic, cognitive scientists have found.

The maxim that practice makes perfect has been borne out    19
through research on the training of star athletes and artists. Dr. Anthony Kalinowski, a researcher at the University of Chicago, found that swimmers who achieved the level of national champion started their training at an average age of 10, while those who were good enough to make the United States Olympic teams started on average at 7. This is the same age difference found for national and international chess champions in a 1987 study.

Similarly, the best violinists of the 20th century, all with   20
international careers as soloists for more than 30 years, were
found to have begun practicing their instrument at an average age of 5, while violinists of only national prominence,
those affiliated with the top music academy in Berlin, started
at 8, Dr. Ericsson found in research reported last year in *The
Psychological Review*.

Because of limits on physical endurance and mental alert-   21
ness, world-class competitors—whether violinists or weight
lifters—typically seem to practice arduously no more than four
hours a day, Dr. Ericsson has found from studying a wide
variety of training regimens.

"When we train Olympic weight lifters, we find we often   22
have to throttle back the total time they work out," said
Dr. Mahoney. "Otherwise you find a tremendous drop in
mood, and a jump in irritability, fatigue and apathy."

Because their intense practice regimen puts them at risk for   23
burnout or strain injuries, most elite competitors also make
rest part of their training routine, sleeping a full eight hours
and often napping a half-hour a day, Dr. Ericsson found.

Effective practice focuses not just on the key skills involved   24
but also systematically stretches the person's limits. "You have
to tweak the system by pushing, allowing for more errors at
first as you increase your limits," said Dr. Ericsson. "You don't
get benefits from mechanical repetition, but by adjusting your
execution over and over to get closer to your goal."

Violin virtuosos illustrate the importance of starting early   25
in life. In his 1993 study, Dr. Ericsson found that by age 20
top-level violinists in music academies had practiced a lifetime
total of about 10,000 hours, while those who were slightly less
accomplished had practiced an average of about 7,500 hours.

A study of Chinese Olympic divers, done by Dr. John Shea   26
of Florida State University, found that some 11-year-old divers had spent as many hours in training as had 21-year-old
American divers. The Chinese divers started training at age 4.

"It can take 10 years of extensive practice to excel in any-   27
thing," said Dr. Simon. "Mozart was 4 when he started composing, but his world-class music started when he was about 17."

Total hours of practice may be more important than time   28
spent in competition, according to findings not yet published
by Dr. Neil Charness, a colleague of Dr. Ericsson at Florida
State University. Dr. Charness, comparing the rankings of
107 competitors in the 1993 Berlin City Tournament, found
that the more time they spent practicing alone, the higher
their ranking as chess players. But there was no relationship
between the chess players' rankings and the time they spent
playing others.

As has long been known, the extensive training of an elite   29
athlete molds the body to fit the demands of a given sport.
What has been less obvious is the extent of these changes.

"The sizes of hearts and lungs, joint flexibility and bone   30
strength all increase directly with hours of training," said
Dr. Ericsson. "The number of capillaries that supply blood to
trained muscles increases."

And the muscles themselves change, Dr. Ericsson said.   31
Until very recently, researchers believed that the percentage
of muscle fiber types was more than 90 percent determined
by heredity. Fast-twitch muscles, which allow short bursts
of intense effort, are crucial in sports like weight lifting and
sprinting, while slow-twitch muscles, richer in red blood cells,
are essential for endurance sports like marathons. "Muscle
fibers in those muscles can change from fast twitch to slow
twitch, as the sport demands," said Dr. Ericsson.

Longitudinal studies show that years of endurance training   32
at champion levels leads athletes' hearts to increase in size well
beyond the normal range for people their age.

Such physiological changes are magnified when training   33
occurs during childhood, puberty, and adolescence. Dr. Ericsson
thinks this may be one reason virtually all top athletes today
began serious practice as children or young adolescents, though
some events, like weight training, may be exceptions because
muscles need to fully form before intense lifting begins.

The most contentious claim made by Dr. Ericsson is that   34
practice alone, not natural talent, makes for a record-breaking
performance. "Innate capacities have very little to do with
becoming a champion," said his colleague, Dr. Charness.

"What's key is motivation and temperament, not a skill specific to performance. It's unlikely you can get just any child to apply themselves this rigorously for so long."

But many psychologists argue that the emphasis on practice 35 alone ignores the place of talent in superb performance. "You can't assume that random people who practice a lot will rise to the top," said Dr. Howard Gardner, a psychologist at Harvard University. Dr. Ericsson's theories "leave out the question of who selects themselves—or are selected—for intensive training," adding, "It also leaves out what we most value in star performance, like innovative genius in a chess player or emotional expressiveness in a concert musician."

Dr. Gardner said: "I taught piano for many years, and 36 there's an enormous difference between those who practice dutifully and get a little better every week, and those students who break away from the pack. There's plenty of room for innate talent to make a difference over and above practice time. Mozart was not like you and me."

## *For Critical Thinking*

### QUESTIONS ABOUT PURPOSE

1. What message do you think the experts quoted in this essay are giving to young people who want to excel in something? What do you see as the impact of that message?
2. What role do you think science plays in sports these days? What is your feeling about that role?

### QUESTIONS ABOUT AUDIENCE

1. What groups of readers do you see as people who would particularly benefit from learning about the research reported here? In what way would they benefit?
2. How would the value system of a reader—that is, the complex of things that the reader thinks is important—affect the way he or she responds to this essay?

## QUESTIONS ABOUT STRATEGIES

1. What is the impact of Goleman's pointing out that the marathon runner who won an Olympic gold medal a hundred years ago could barely qualify for the Boston Marathon today?
2. How does Goleman's use of diverse authorities strengthen his essay?

# For Writing and Research

1. *Analyze* the factors in a competitor's performance that Goleman fails to mention.
2. *Practice* by analyzing the effects that attempting to be a top performer have had on your friends and family.
3. *Argue* that talent rather than training explains "peak performances."
4. *Synthesize:* Research the lives of some top performers who started very young—for instance, violinist Midori, chess prodigy Bobby Fischer, or tennis player Jennifer Capriati. Then use this information to support Goldman's argument.

Brent Staples was born in Chester, Pennsylvania, in 1951 and was educated at Widener College and the University of Chicago. He worked for several years as a reporter for the *Chicago Sun-Times* before moving on to an editorial position with the *New York Times Sunday Book Review*. He currently serves as assistant editor of the "Metropolitan" section of *The New York Times*. He has contributed articles to journals such as the *New York Times Magazine* and *Harpers*. He has written an autobiography of his family and hometown, *Parallel Time: Growing Up Black and White* (1994). In "Black Men and Public Spaces," reprinted from *Ms.* magazine, Staples analyzes the effects of being perceived as dangerous.

MY FIRST VICTIM was a white woman, well dressed, probably in her early twenties. I came upon her late one evening on a deserted street in Hyde Park, a relatively affluent neighborhood in an otherwise mean, impoverished section of Chicago. As I swung onto the avenue behind her, there seemed to be a discreet, uninflammatory distance between us. Not so. She cast back a worried glance. To her, the youngish black man—a broad six feet two inches with a beard and billowing hair, both hands shoved into the pockets of a bulky military jacket—seemed menacingly close. After a few more quick glimpses, she picked up her pace and was soon running in earnest. Within seconds she disappeared into a cross street. 1

That was more than a decade ago. I was twenty-two years old, 2 a graduate student newly arrived at the University of Chicago. It was in the echo of that terrified woman's footfalls that I first began to know the unwieldy inheritance I'd come into—the ability to alter public space in ugly ways. It was clear that she thought herself the quarry of a mugger, a rapist, or worse. Suffering a bout of insomnia, however, I was stalking sleep, not defenseless wayfarers. As a softy who is scarcely able to take a knife to a raw chicken—let alone hold one to a person's throat—I was surprised, embarrassed, and dismayed all at once. Her flight made me feel like an accomplice in tyranny. It also made it clear that I was indistinguishable from the muggers who occasionally seeped into the area from the surrounding ghetto. That first encounter, and those that followed, signified that a vast, unnerving gulf lay between nighttime pedestrians—particularly women—and me. And soon I gathered that being perceived as dangerous is a hazard in itself. I only needed to turn a corner into a dicey situation, or crowd some frightened, armed person in a foyer somewhere, or make an errant move after being pulled over by a policeman. Where fear and weapons meet—and they often do in urban America—there is always the possibility of death.

*It was in the echo of that terrified woman's footfalls that I first began to know the unwieldy inheritance I'd come into—the ability to alter public space in ugly ways.*

In that first year, my first away from my hometown, I was 3
to become thoroughly familiar with the language of fear. At dark, shadowy intersections, I could cross in front of a car stopped at a traffic light and elicit the thunk, thunk, thunk of the driver—black, white, male, or female—hammering down the door locks. On less traveled streets after dark, I grew accustomed to but never comfortable with people crossing to the other side of the street rather than pass me. Then there were the standard unpleasantries with policemen, doormen, bouncers, cabdrivers, and others whose business it

is to screen out troublesome individuals before there is any nastiness. I moved to New York nearly two years ago, and I have remained an avid night walker. In central Manhattan, the near-constant crowd cover minimizes tense one-on-one street encounters. Elsewhere, in Soho, for example, where sidewalks are narrow and tightly spaced buildings shut out the sky—things can get very taut indeed.

After dark, on the warrenlike streets of Brooklyn where I   4
live, I often see women who fear the worst from me. They seem to have set their faces on neutral, and with their purse straps strung across their chests bandolier-style, they forge ahead as though bracing themselves against being tackled. I understand, of course, that the danger they perceive is not a hallucination. Women are particularly vulnerable to street violence, and young black men are drastically overrepresented among the perpetrators of that violence. Yet, these truths are no solace against the kind of alienation that comes of being ever the suspect, a fearsome entity with whom pedestrians avoid making eye contact.

It is not altogether clear to me how I reached the ripe old age   5
of twenty-two without being conscious of the lethality night-time pedestrians attributed to me. Perhaps it was because in Chester, Pennsylvania, the small, angry industrial town where I came of age in the 1960's, I was scarcely noticeable against the backdrop of gang warfare, street knifings, and murders. I grew up one of the good boys, had perhaps a half-dozen fist fights. In retrospect, my shyness of combat has clear sources.

As a boy, I saw countless tough guys locked away; I have   6
since buried several too. They were babies, really—a teenage cousin, a brother of twenty-two, a childhood friend in his mid-twenties—all gone down in episodes of bravado played out in the streets. I came to doubt the virtues of intimida-tion early on. I chose, perhaps unconsciously, to remain a shadow—timid, but a survivor.

The fearsomeness mistakenly attributed to me in public   7
places often has a perilous flavor. The most frightening of these confusions occurred in the late 1970's and early 1980's, when I worked as a journalist in Chicago. One day, rushing

into the office of a magazine I was writing for with a deadline story in hand, I was mistaken as a burglar. The office manager called security and, with an ad hoc posse, pursued me through the labyrinthine halls, nearly to my editor's door. I had no way of proving who I was. I could only move briskly toward the company of someone who knew me.

Another time I was on assignment for a local paper and  8 killing time before an interview. I entered a jewelry store on a city's affluent Near North Side. The proprietor excused herself and returned with an enormous red Doberman Pinscher straining at the end of a leash. She stood, the dog extended toward me, silent to my questions, her eyes bulging nearly out of her head. I took a cursory look around, nodded, and bade her goodnight.

Relatively speaking, however, I never fared as badly as  9 another black male journalist. He went to nearby Waukegan, Illinois, a couple of summers ago to work on a story about a murderer who was born there. Mistaking the reporter for the killer, police officers hauled him from his car at gunpoint and but for his press credentials, would probably have tried to book him. Such episodes are not uncommon. Black men trade tales like this all the time.

Over the years, I learned to smother the rage I felt at so often  10 being taken for a criminal. Not to do so would surely have led to madness. I now take precautions to make myself less threatening. I move about with care, particularly late in the evening. I give a wide berth to nervous people on subway platforms during the wee hours, particularly when I have exchanged business clothes for jeans. If I happen to be entering a building behind some people who appear skittish, I may walk by, letting them clear the lobby before I return, so as not to seem to be following them. I have been calm and extremely congenial on those rare occasions when I've been pulled over by the police.

And, on late-evening constitutionals, I employ what has  11 proved to be an excellent tension-reducing measure: I whistle melodies from Beethoven and Vivaldi and the more popular classical composers. Even steely New Yorkers hunching toward nighttime destinations seem to relax, and occasionally they even join in the tune. Virtually everybody seems to sense that a mugger wouldn't be warbling bright, sunny selections from Vivaldi's Four Seasons. It is my equivalent of the cowbell that hikers wear when they know they are in bear country.

## For Critical Thinking

### QUESTIONS ABOUT PURPOSE

1. What racial and sexual assumptions does Staples want to dispel?
2. What do you think Staples hopes his readers will learn from this article?

### QUESTIONS ABOUT AUDIENCE

1. What group of readers does Staples address most directly in this essay?
2. How does Staples anticipate that male and female readers will respond to his essay?

### QUESTIONS ABOUT STRATEGIES

1. What effect does Staples achieve with his first paragraph?
2. How does he use personal details to intensify the effects of his analysis?

## For Writing and Research

1. *Analyze* how Staples uses the language of crime to describe his experiences.
2. *Practice* by analyzing how your appearance caused the effect of mistaken identity.
3. *Argue* the case Staples presents from the woman's point of view. How does she demonstrate good judgment?
4. *Synthesize* the recent news stories that describe encounters between citizens, police officers, and young black men. Then analyze the solutions that have been proposed to avoid such unfortunate encounters.

Alice Adams (1926–1999) was born in Fredericksburg, Virginia, and educated at Radcliffe College. After twelve years of marriage, she began working at various office jobs while she mastered the skills of a writer. Adams published her first book of fiction, *Careless Love* (1966) at the age of forty. After that she published five widely acclaimed novels, *Families and Survivors* (1975), *Listening to Billie* (1978—the title refers to the legendary blues singer, Billie Holiday), *Rich Rewards* (1980), *Superior Women* (1984), and *Caroline's Daughters* (1991), as well as collections of short stories, *Beautiful Girl* (1979), *To See You Again (1982)*, and *The Stories of Alice Adams* (2003). The narrator of "Truth or Consequences," reprinted from *The Stories of Alice Adams,* tries to understand the consequences that resulted from her truthful answer in a childhood game.

THIS MORNING, when I read in a gossip column that a man named Carstairs Jones had married a famous former movie star, I was startled, thunderstruck, for I knew that he must certainly be the person whom I knew as a child, one extraordinary spring, as "Car Jones." He was a dangerous and disreputable boy, one of what were then called the "truck children," with whom I had a most curious, brief and frightening connection. Still, I noted that in a way I was pleased at such good fortune; I was "happy for him," so to speak, perhaps as a result of sheer distance, so many years. And before I could imagine Car as he might be now, Carstairs Jones, in Hollywood clothes, I suddenly saw, with the most terrific accuracy and bright sharpness of detail, the schoolyard of all those years ago, hard and bare, neglected. And I relived the fatal day, on the middle level of that schoolyard, when we were playing truth or consequences, and I said that I would rather kiss Car Jones than be eaten alive by ants.

Our school building then was three stories high, a formi-    2
dable brick square. In front a lawn had been attempted, some years back; graveled walks led up to the broad, forbidding entranceway, and behind the school were the playing fields, the playground. This area was on three levels: on the upper level, nearest the school, were the huge polished steel frames for the creaking swings, the big green splintery wooden see-saws, the rickety slides—all for the youngest children. On the middle level older girls played hopscotch, various games, or jumped rope—or just talked and giggled. And out on the lowest level, the field, the boys practiced football, or baseball, in the spring.

To one side of the school was a parking space, usually filled    3
with the bulging yellow trucks that brought children from out in the country in to town: truck children, country children. Sometimes they would go back to the trucks at lunchtime to eat their sandwiches, whatever; almost always there were sev-eral overgrown children, spilling out from the trucks. Or Car Jones, expelled from some class, for some new acts of rebel-liousness. That area was always littered with trash, wrappings from sandwiches, orange peel, Coke bottles.

Beyond the parking space was an empty lot, overgrown    4
with weeds, in the midst of which stood an abandoned trellis, perhaps once the support of wisteria; now wild honeysuckle almost covered it over.

The town was called Hilton, the seat of a distinguished uni-    5
versity, in the middle South. My widowed mother, Charlotte Ames, had moved there the previous fall (with me, Emily, her only child). I am still not sure why she chose Hilton; she never much liked it there, nor did she really like the brother-in-law, a professor, into whose proximity the move had placed us.

An interesting thing about Hilton, at that time, was that    6
there were three, and only three, distinct social classes. (Negroes could possibly make four, but they were so separate,

even from the poorest whites, as not to seem part of the social system at all; they were in effect invisible.) At the scale's top were professors and their families. Next were the townspeople, storekeepers, bankers, doctors and dentists, none of whom had the prestige nor the money they were later to acquire. Country people were the bottom group, families living out on the farms that surrounded the town, people who sent their children in to school on the yellow trucks.

The professors' children of course had a terrific advantage, academically, coming from houses full of books, from parental respect for learning; many of those kids read precociously and had large vocabularies. It was not so hard on most of the town children; many of their families shared qualities with the faculty people; they too had a lot of books around. But the truck children had a hard and very unfair time of it. Not only were many of their parents near-illiterates, but often the children were kept at home to help with chores, and sometimes, particularly during the coldest, wettest months of winter, weather prevented the trucks' passage over the slithery red clay roads of that countryside, that era. A child could miss out on a whole new skill, like long division, and fail tests, and be kept back. Consequently, many of the truck children were overage, oversized for the grades they were in.

In the seventh grade, when I was eleven, a year ahead of myself, having been tested for and skipped the sixth (attesting to the superiority of Northern schools, my mother thought, and probably she was right), dangerous Car Jones, in the same class, was fourteen, and taller than anyone.

There was some overlapping, or crossing, among those three social groups; there were hybrids, as it were. In fact, I was such a crossbreed myself: literally my mother and I were town people—my dead father had been a banker, but since his brother was a professor we too were considered faculty people. Also my mother had a lot of money, making us further élite. To me, being known as rich was just embarrassing, more freakish than advantageous, and I made my mother stop ordering my clothes from Best's; I wanted dresses from the local stores, like everyone else's.

Car Jones too was a hybrid child, although his case was less    10
visible than mine: his country family were distant cousins of
the prominent and prosperous dean of the medical school,
Dean Willoughby Jones. (They seem to have gone in for fancy
names, in all the branches of that family.) I don't think his
cousins spoke to him.

In any case, being richer and younger than the others in my    11
class made me socially very insecure, and I always approached
the playground with a sort of excited dread: would I be asked
to join in a game, and if it were dodge ball (the game I most
hated) would I be the first person hit with the ball, and thus
eliminated? Or, if the girls were just standing around and
talking, would I get all the jokes, and know which boys they
were talking about?

Then, one pale-blue balmy April day, some of the older    12
girls asked me if I wanted to play truth or consequences
with them. I wasn't sure how the game went, but anything
was better than dodge ball, and, as always, I was pleased at
being asked.

"It's easy," said Jean, a popular leader, with curly red hair;    13
her father was a dean of the law school. "You just answer the
questions we ask you, or you take the consequences."

I wasn't at all sure what consequences were, but I didn't    14
like to ask.

They began with simple questions. How old are you?    15
What's your middle name?

This led to more complicated (and crueler) ones.    16

"How much money does your mother have?"    17

"I don't know." I didn't, of course, and I doubt that she    18
did either, that poor vague lady, too young to be a widow,
too old for motherhood. "I think maybe a thousand dollars,"
I hazarded.

At this they all frowned, that group of older, wiser girls,    19
whether in disbelief or disappointment, I couldn't tell. They
moved a little away from me and whispered together.

It was close to the end of recess. Down on the playing field    20
below us one of the boys threw the baseball and someone
batted it out in a long arc, out to the farthest grassy edges

of the field, and several other boys ran to retrieve it. On the level above us, a rutted terrace up, the little children stood in line for turns on the slide, or pumped with furious small legs on the giant swings.

The girls came back to me. "Okay, Emily," said Jean. "Just  21 tell the truth. Would you rather be covered with honey and eaten alive by ants, in the hot Sahara Desert—or kiss Car Jones?"

Then, as now, I had a somewhat literal mind: I thought  22 of honey, and ants, and hot sand, and quite simply I said I'd rather kiss Car Jones.

*Well.* Pandemonium: Did you hear what she said? Emily  23 would kiss Car Jones! *Car Jones.* The truth—Emily would like to kiss Car Jones! Oh, Emily, if your mother only knew! Emily is going to kiss Car Jones! Emily said she would! Oh, Emily!

The boys, just then coming up from the baseball field,  24 cast bored and pitying looks at the sources of so much noise; they had always known girls were silly. But Harry McGinnis, a glowing, golden boy, looked over at us and laughed aloud. I had been watching Harry timidly for months; that day I thought his laugh was friendly.

Recess being over, we all went back into the schoolroom,  25 and continued with the civics lesson. I caught a few ambiguous smiles in my direction, which left me both embarrassed and confused.

That afternoon, as I walked home from school, two of the  26 girls who passed me on their bikes called back to me, "Car Jones!" and in an automatic but for me new way I squealed out, "Oh no!" They laughed, and repeated, from their distance, "Car Jones!"

The next day I continued to be teased. Somehow the boys  27 had got wind of what I had said, and they joined in with remarks about Yankee girls being fast, how you couldn't tell about quiet girls, that sort of wit. Some of the teasing sounded mean; I felt that Jean, for example, was really out to discomfit me, but most of it was high-spirited friendliness. I was suddenly discovered, as though hitherto I had been invisible. And I continued to respond with that exaggerated, phony squeal of embarrassment that seemed to go over so well. Harry McGinnis addressed me as Emily Jones, and the others took that up. (I wonder if Harry had ever seen me before.)

Curiously, in all this new excitement, the person I thought    28 of least was the source of it all: Car Jones. Or, rather, when I saw the actual Car, hulking over the water fountain or lounging near the steps of a truck, I did not consciously connect him with what felt like social success, new popularity. (I didn't know about consequences.)

Therefore, when the first note from Car appeared on my    29 desk, it felt like blackmail, although the message was innocent, was even kind. "You mustn't mind that they tease you. You are the prettiest one of the girls. C. Jones." I easily recognized his handwriting, those recklessly forward-slanting strokes, from the day when he had had to write on the blackboard, "I will not disturb the other children during Music." Twenty-five times. The note was real, all right.

Helplessly I turned around to stare at the back of the room,    30 where the tallest boys sprawled in their too small desks. Truck children, all of them, bored and uncomfortable. There was Car, the tallest of all, the most bored, the least contained. Our eyes met, and even at that distance I saw that his were not black, as I had thought, but a dark slate blue; stormy eyes, even when, as he rarely did, Car smiled. I turned away quickly, and I managed to forget him for a while.

Having never witnessed a Southern spring before, I was    31 astounded by its bursting opulence, that soft fullness of petal and bloom, everywhere the profusion of flowering shrubs and trees, the riotous flower beds. Walking home from school, I was enchanted with the yards of the stately houses (homes of professors) that I passed, the lush lawns, the rows of brilliant iris, the flowering quince and dogwood trees, crepe myrtle, wisteria vines. I would squint my eyes to see the tiniest palegreen leaves against the sky.

My mother didn't like the spring. It gave her hay fever, and    32 she spent most of her time languidly indoors, behind heavily lined, drawn draperies. "I'm simply too old for such exuberance," she said.

"Happy" is perhaps not the word to describe my own state     33
of mind, but I was tremendously excited, continuously. The
season seemed to me so extraordinary in itself, the colors,
the enchanting smells, and it coincided with my own altered
awareness of myself: I could command attention, I was pretty
(Car Jones was the first person ever to say that I was, after
my mother's long-ago murmurings to a late-arriving baby).

Now everyone knew my name, and called it out as I walked     34
onto the playground. Last fall, as an envious, unknown new
girl, I had heard other names, other greetings and teasing-
insulting nicknames, "Hey, Red," Harry McGinnis used to
shout, in the direction of popular Jean.

The next note from Car Jones said, "I'll bet you hate it     35
down here. This is a cruddy town, but don't let it bother
you. Your hair is beautiful. I hope you never cut it. C. Jones."

This scared me a little: the night before I had been argu-   36
ing with my mother on just that point, my hair, which was
long and straight. Why couldn't I cut and curl it, like the
other girls? How had Car Jones known what I wanted to do? I
forced myself not to look at him; I pretended that there was no
Car Jones; it was just a name that certain people had made up.

I felt—I was sure—that Car Jones was an "abnormal" per-      37
son. (I'm afraid "different" would have been the word I used,
back then.) He represented forces that were dark and strange,
whereas I myself had just come out into the light. I had joined
the world of the normal. (My "normality" later included three
marriages to increasingly "rich and prominent" men; my
current husband is a surgeon. Three children, and as many
abortions. I hate the symmetry, but there you are. I haven't
counted lovers. It comes to a normal life, for a woman of my
age.) For years, at the time of our coming to Hilton, I had felt
a little strange, isolated by my father's death, my older-than-
most-parents mother, by money. By being younger than other
children, and new in town. I could clearly afford nothing to
do with Car, and at the same time my literal mind acknowledged a certain obligation.

Therefore, when a note came from Car telling me to meet      38
him on a Saturday morning in the vacant lot next to the

school, it didn't occur to me that I didn't have to go. I made excuses to my mother, and to some of the girls who were getting together for Cokes at someone's house. I'd be a little late, I told the girls. I had to do an errand for my mother.

It was one of the palest, softest, loveliest days of that spring. 39 In the vacant, lot weeds bloomed like the rarest of flowers; as I walked toward the abandoned trellis I felt myself to be a sort of princess, on her way to grant an audience to a courtier.

Car, lounging just inside the trellis, immediately brought 40 me up short. "You're several minutes late," he said, and I noticed that his teeth were stained (from tobacco?) and his hands were dirty: couldn't he have washed his hands, to come and meet me? He asked, "Just who do you think you are, the Queen of Sheba?"

I am not sure what I had imagined would happen between 41 us, but this was wrong; I was not prepared for surliness, this scolding. Weakly I said that I was sorry I was late.

Car did not acknowledge my apology; he just stared at me, 42 stormily, with what looked like infinite scorn.

Why had he insisted that I come to meet him? And now 43 that I was here, was I less than pretty, seen close up?

A difficult minute passed, and then I moved a little away. 44 I managed to say that I had to go; I had to meet some girls, I said.

At that Car reached and grasped my arm. "No, first we 45 have to do it."

Do it? I was scared. 46

"You know what you said, as good as I do. You said kiss Car Jones, now didn't you?" I began to cry.

Car reached for my hair and pulled me toward him; he 47 bent down to my face and for an instant our mouths were mashed together. (Christ, my first kiss!) Then, so suddenly that I almost fell backward, Car let go of me. With a last look of pure rage he was out of the trellis and striding across the field, toward town, away from the school.

For a few minutes I stayed there in the trellis; I was no 48 longer crying (that had been for Car's benefit, I now think) but melodramatically I wondered if Car might come back and do something else to me—beat me up, maybe. Then a stronger fear took over: someone might find out, might have seen us, even. At that I got out of the trellis fast, out of the vacant lot. (I was learning conformity fast, practicing up for the rest of my life.)

I think, really, that my most serious problem was my utter       49
puzzlement: what did it mean, that kiss? Car was mad, no doubt about that, but did he really hate me? In that case, why a kiss? (Much later in life I once was raped, by someone to whom I was married, but I still think that counts; in any case, I didn't know what he meant either.)

Not sure what else to do, and still in the grip of a monu-       50
mental confusion, I went over to the school building, which was open on Saturdays for something called Story Hours, for little children. I went into the front entrance and up to the library where, to the surprise of the librarian, who may have thought me retarded, I listened for several hours to tales of the Dutch Twins, and Peter and Polly in Scotland. Actually it was very soothing, that long pasteurized drone, hard even to think about Car while listening to pap like that.

When I got home I found my mother for some reason in       51
a livelier, more talkative mood than usual. She told me that a boy had called while I was out, three times. Even before my heart had time to drop—to think that it might be Car, she babbled on, "Terribly polite. Really, these *bien élevé* Southern boys." (No, not Car.) "Harry something. He said he'd call again. But, darling, where were you, all this time?"

I was beginning to murmur about the library, homework,       52
when the phone rang. I answered, and it was Harry McGinnis, asking me to go to the movies with him the following Saturday afternoon. I said of course, I'd love to, and I giggled in a silly new way. But my giggle was one of relief; I was saved, I was normal, after all. I belonged in the world of light of lightheartedness. Car Jones had not really touched me.

I spent the next day, Sunday, in alternating states of agita-       53
tion and anticipation.

On Monday, on my way to school, I felt afraid of seeing       54
Car, at the same time that I was both excited and shy at the

prospect of Harry McGinnis—a combination of emotions that was almost too much for me, that dazzling, golden first of May, and that I have not dealt with too successfully in later life.

Harry paid even less attention to me than he had before; it was a while before I realized that he was conspicuously not looking in my direction, not teasing me, and that in itself was a form of attention, as well as being soothing to my shyness. 55

I realized too, after a furtive scanning of the back row, that Car Jones was *not at school* that day. Relief flooded through my blood like oxygen, like spring air. 56

Absences among the truck children were so unremarkable, and due to so many possible causes, that any explanation at all for his was plausible. Of course, it occurred to me, among other imaginings, that he had stayed home out of shame for what he did to me. Maybe he had run away to sea, had joined the Navy or the Marines? Coldheartedly, I hoped so. In any case, there was no way for me to ask. 57

Later that week the truth about Car Jones did come out— at first as a drifting rumor, then confirmed, and much more remarkable than joining the Navy: Car Jones had gone to the principal's office, a week or so back, and had demanded to be tested for entrance (immediate) into high school, a request so unprecedented (usually only pushy academic parents would ask for such a change) and so dumbfounding that it was acceded to. Car took the test and was put into the sopho-more high-school class, on the other side of town, where he by age and size—and intellect, as things turned out; he tested high—most rightfully belonged. 58

I went to a lot of Saturday movies with Harry McGinnis, where we clammily held hands, and for the rest of that spring, and into summer, I was teased about Harry. No one seemed to remember having teased me about Car Jones. 59

Considering the size of Hilton at that time, it seems sur-prising that I almost never saw Car again, but I did not, except for a couple of tiny glimpses, during the summer that I was still going to the movies with Harry. On both those occasions, seen from across the street, or on the other side of 60 a dim movie house, Car was with an older girl, a high-school girl, with curled hair, and lipstick, all that. I was sure that his hands and teeth were clean.

By the time I had entered high school, along with all those 61 others who were by now my familiar friends, Car was a freshman in the local university, and his family had moved into town. Then his name again was bruited about among us, but this time as an underground rumor: Car Jones was reputed to have "gone all the way"—to have "done it" with a pretty and most popular senior in our high school. (It must be remembered that this was more unusual among the young then than now.) The general (whispered) theory was that Car's status as a college boy had won the girl; traditionally, in Hilton, the senior high-school girls began to date the freshmen in the university, as many and as often as possible. But this was not necessarily true; maybe the girl was simply drawn to Car, his height and his shoulders, his stormy eyes. Or maybe they didn't do it after all.

The next thing I heard about Car, who was by then an 62 authentic town person, a graduate student in the university, was that he had written a play which was to be produced by the campus dramatic society. (Maybe that is how he finally met his movie star, as a playwright? The column didn't say.) I think I read this item in the local paper, probably in a clipping forwarded to me by my mother; her letters were always thick with clippings, thin with messages of a personal nature.

My next news of Car came from my uncle, the French 63 professor, a violent, enthusiastic partisan in university affairs, especially in their more traditional aspects. In scandalized tones, one family Thanksgiving, he recounted to me and my mother, that a certain young man, a graduate student in English, named Carstairs Jones, had been offered a special sort of membership in D.K.E., his own beloved fraternity, and "Jones had *turned it down*." My mother and I laughed later and privately over this; we were united in thinking my uncle a fool, and I am sure that I added, Well, good for him. But I did not, at that time, reconsider the whole story of Car Jones, that most unregenerate and wicked of the truck children.

But now, with this fresh news of Carstairs Jones, and his wife    64
the movie star, it occurs to me that we two, who at a certain time and place were truly misfits, although quite differently— we both have made it: what could be more American dreamy, more normal, than marriage to a lovely movie star? Or, in my case, marriage to the successful surgeon?

And now maybe I can reconstruct a little of that time;    65
specifically, can try to see how it really was for Car, back then. Maybe I can even understand that kiss.

Let us suppose that he lived in a somewhat better than    66
usual farmhouse; later events make this plausible—his family's move to town, his years at the university. Also, I wish him well. I will give him a dignified white house with a broad front porch, set back among pines and oaks, in the red clay countryside. The stability and size of his house, then, would have set Car apart from his neighbors, the other farm families, other truck children. Perhaps his parents too were somewhat "different," but my imagination fails at them; I can easily imagine and clearly see the house, but not its population. Brothers? sisters? Probably, but I don't know.

Car would go to school, coming out of his house at the    67
honk of the stained and bulging, ugly yellow bus, which was crowded with his supposed peers, toward whom he felt both contempt and an irritation close to rage. Arrived at school, as one of the truck children, he would be greeted with a total lack of interest; he might as well have been invisible, or been black, *unless* he misbehaved in an outright, conspicuous way. And so he did: Car yawned noisily during history class, he hummed during study hall and after recess he dawdled around the playground and came in late. And for these and other assaults on the school's decorum he was punished in one way or another, and then, when all else failed to curb his ways, he would be *held back*, forced to repeat an already insufferably boring year of school.

One fall there was a minor novelty in school: a new girl    68
(me), a Yankee, who didn't look much like the other girls,

with long straight hair, instead of curled, and Yankee clothes, wool skirts and sweaters, instead of flowery cotton dresses worn all year round. A funny accent, a Yankee name: Emily Ames. I imagine that Car registered those facts about me, and possibly the additional information that I was almost as invisible as he, but without much interest.

Until the day of truth or consequences. I don't think Car 69 was around on the playground while the game was going on; one of the girls would have seen him, and squealed out, "Oooh, there's Car, there *he is!*" I rather believe that some skinny little kid, an unnoticed truck child, overheard it all, and then ran over to where Car was lounging in one of the school buses, maybe peeling an orange and throwing the peel, in spirals, out the window. "Say, Car, that little Yankee girl, she says she'd like to kiss you."

"Aw, go on." 70

He is still not very interested; the little Yankee girl is as dumb as the others are.

And then he hears me being teased, everywhere, and teased 71 with his name. "Emily would kiss Car Jones—Emily Jones!" Did he feel the slightest pleasure at such notoriety? I think he must have; a man who would marry a movie star must have at least a small taste for publicity. Well, at that point he began to write me those notes: "You are the prettiest one of the girls" (which I was not). I think he was casting us both in ill-fitting roles, me as the prettiest, defenseless girl, and himself as my defender.

He must have soon seen that it wasn't working out that 72 way. I didn't need a defender, I didn't need him. I was having a wonderful time, at his expense, if you think about it, and I am pretty sure Car did think about it.

Interestingly, at the same time he had his perception of 73 my triviality, Car must have got his remarkable inspiration in regard to his own life: there was a way out of those miserably boring classes, the insufferable children who surrounded him. He would demand a test, he would leave this place for the high school.

Our trellis meeting must have occurred after Car had taken 74 the test and had known that he did well. When he kissed me he was doing his last "bad" thing in that school, was kissing it off, so to speak. He was also insuring that I, at least, would remember him; he counted on its being my first kiss. And he may have thought that I was even sillier than I was, and that I would tell, so that what had happened would get around the school, waves of scandal in his wake.

For some reason, I would also imagine that Car is one of those persons who never look back; once kissed, I was readily dismissed from his mind, and probably for good. He could concentrate on high school, new status, new friends. Just as, now married to his movie star, he does not ever think of having been a truck child, one of the deprived, the disappointed. In his mind there are no ugly groaning trucks, no hopeless littered playground, no squat menacing school building. 75

But of course I could be quite wrong about Car Jones. He could be another sort of person altogether; he could be as haunted as I am by everything that ever happened in his life. 76

## COMMENT ON "TRUTH OR CONSEQUENCES"

"Truth or Consequences" is an excellent illustration of how a simple act can cause all sorts of effects. The catalyst for the story is the narrator's reading in a gossip column about Car Jones's marriage to a famous former movie star. His name sparks a memory, and the narrator (Emily) tries to reconstruct the events that occurred during her school years. The story is paced at two speeds: the opening is slow as Emily describes the various social divisions on the playground; the action speeds up once Emily says she would rather kiss Car Jones than be eaten by ants. The plot reaches its climax when Car Jones calls Emily's bluff and asks her to meet him by the trellis near the school. The story concludes as Emily (older and wiser) continues to wonder about the "truth" and "consequences" of this brief encounter.

# CHAPTER 7

# *Persuasion and Argument*

Readers encounter persuasion and argument every day as writers try to persuade them to spend money, take action, support a cause, accept an opinion, or consider an idea. The starting point for persuasion and argument is an assertion, a statement of belief or a claim that the writer undertakes to explain and support. At one extreme, both the statement and the support may be highly emotional, depending heavily on biased language and strong appeals to feelings and instincts; this kind of writing is classified as **persuasion**. At the other extreme, the assertion and support may be strictly rational, depending on logical explanations and appeals to intelligence; this kind of writing is classified as **argument**. Advertising and political writing cluster toward the persuasion end of the continuum, whereas scientific writing and grant proposals cluster toward the argument end.

Seldom, however, does persuasive writing appeal only to emotions, and seldom does argument rely entirely on reason. Rather, when people write to convince, they appeal to both emotions and intelligence, but they vary the balance of emotion and reason according to their audience and purpose.

Writing that is primarily rational is not necessarily better than writing that is  primarily emotional. Some occasions call for appeals to pride and patriotism, for vivid metaphors that reach the senses, and for strong language that arouses the passions. This kind of writing is called **ceremonial discourse**. The audience already knows and probably agrees with what the writer (or speaker) is going to say and expects not intellectual stimulation but emotional satisfaction and inspiration. Inaugural speeches, graduation addresses, and political speeches usually fit into this emotional category and are often successful precisely because they are emotional.

Most arguments, however, must be fairly rational if they are to convince critical readers, and those readers are justified in expecting writers to support a major assertion with evidence and logic. Generally speaking, people who write effective arguments do what a good trial lawyer does: they present a case persuasively but give strong reasons to support their assertions. In the final analysis, the quality of any argument must be judged not by some absolute standard of rationality, but by how well it has accomplished its intended purpose with its intended audience.

## PURPOSE

Although you may think of disagreement when you hear the word *argument*, not all people who write arguments are trying to win a dispute. Instead, they may want to persuade people to *support a cause* or *make a commitment*. Political leaders and ministers frequently write for these purposes. Writers may also argue to get people to *take action* or to try to *change a situation*. Editorial writers, reformers, and political activists often have these purposes in mind.

Sometimes, writers persuade in order to *change behavior* or *attitudes*. Someone advocating a new approach to child rearing would have such a purpose, as would a person arguing against racial or sexual prejudice. Other writers argue to *refute a theory*. For example, feminist writers continually seek to disprove the belief that women are less talented and creative than men. Writers also use persuasive strategies to *arouse sympathies, to stimulate concern, to win agreement,* and *to provoke anger.* They may incorporate several of these purposes into one piece of writing.

## AUDIENCE

More than any other kind of writing, persuasion, and argument require you to think about your audience. To choose effective rhetorical strategies, you must have a clear sense of who may read your writing, what kinds of attitudes and biases those persons will bring to the reading, and what readers expect to get from an essay. Making such analysis of an audience may be difficult, and sometimes you have to work by instinct rather than by information. Usually, however, you can assume that readers will fit into one of the following classes:

1. *Readers who already agree with your ideas and are reading mainly for reinforcement or encouragement.* These readers do not expect a tightly reasoned and carefully structured argument; rather, they want to see their position stated with vigor and conviction.
2. *Readers who are interested in and are inclined to agree with the issue you are discussing but want to know more.* Although they are interested in evidence that will help them make a decision, they do not expect a completely rational argument and will not object if you use slanted language or emotional examples to strengthen a point.
3. *Readers who are neutral on an issue and want explanations and arguments based on evidence and logical reasoning before they make up their minds.* For these readers, you must make a carefully developed and factual argument, although you can also reinforce facts with opinions.
4. *Readers who are skeptical about an issue and will not take a stand until they hear both sides of an argument explained in complete detail.* They expect you to provide appropriate data and documentation and provide the impression that you are knowledgeable, capable, and balanced.

*Collecting Evidence*

To construct an argument you need to collect one or more of the following kinds of evidence: *facts*, *judgments*, and *testimony*.

**Facts** are a valuable ally in building an argument because they cannot be debated. It is a fact that the stock market crashed on October 29, 1929. It is a fact that on September 11, 2001, terrorists crashed two airplanes into the twin towers of the World Trade Center, killing nearly 3,000 people. But not all facts are so clear-cut, and some statements that look like facts may not be facts. A stock analyst who announces a company's projected earnings for the next five years is making an estimate, not a statement of fact.

**Judgments** are conclusions inferred from facts. Unlike opinions, judgments lend credibility to an argument because they result from careful reasoning. A doctor considering a patient's symptoms reaches a tentative diagnosis of either tuberculosis or a tumor. If the laboratory test eliminates tuberculosis, then the patient probably has a tumor that is either malignant or benign, a question that can be settled by surgery and further testing.

**Testimony** affirms or asserts facts. A person who has had direct experience (an *eyewitness*) or who has developed expertise in a subject (an *expert witness*) can provide testimony based on facts, judgment, or both. An eyewitness is asked to report facts, as when an observer reports seeing a man drown in a strong current. An expert witness is asked to study facts and render a judgment, as when a coroner reports that an autopsy has shown that the victim did not drown but died of a heart attack.

Both kinds of testimony can constitute powerful evidence. Eyewitness testimony provides authenticity. Expert testimony provides authority. Each has its limitations, however. An eyewitness is not always trustworthy; eyewitness testimony can be distorted by faulty observation or biased opinion. An expert witness is not infallible or always unbiased; expert testimony, though often difficult for the nonexpert to challenge, can be disputed by other experts employing a different method of investigation. Each type of testimony can be abused. An eyewitness account of an event may be convincing, but it should not be used to draw parallels to unrelated events. And an expert's credentials in one field, whatever eminence they convey, do not automatically carry over to other fields.

The best way to evaluate evidence in an argument is to determine whether it is *pertinent, verifiable,* and *reliable*. A stock analyst who uses the success of the polio vaccine as a reason for investing in a drug company researching a vaccine for the common cold is not presenting evidence that is *pertinent* to the argument. A historian who claims that Amelia Earhart's flying ability was impaired by Alzheimer's disease is using an argument that is not *verifiable*. And an attorney who builds a case on the eyewitness testimony of a person who has been arrested several times for public intoxication is not using the most *reliable* evidence.

## Arranging Evidence

After you have collected your evidence, you need to determine how to *arrange* it. Because every argument creates its own problems and possibilities, no one method of arrangement will always work best. Sometimes, you may have to combine methods to make your case. To make an informed decision, you need to consider how you might adapt your evidence to one of the four common strategies: **induction, deduction, claims and warrants**, and **accommodation**.

Induction    Often called the ***scientific method,*** *induction* begins by presenting specific evidence and then moves to a general conclusion. This arrangement reflects the history of your investigation. You begin your research with a question you want to answer. You then collect a cross section of evidence until a pattern emerges, and you arrange your individual pieces of evidence in a way that helps your readers see the pattern you have discovered. You need not list all the false leads or blind alleys you encountered along the way unless they changed your perspective or confirmed your judgment. At this point, you make what scientists call an ***inductive leap:*** you determine that although you have not collected every example, you have examined enough to risk proposing a probable conclusion.

For example:

*Research question:* Why is our company losing so many valuable data processors to other companies?

*Evidence:*

1. Most data processors are women who have preschool children. (Provide facts.)
2. A nearby day-care center used by employees has closed because it lost federal funding. (Provide facts.)
3. Other day-care centers in the area are inconvenient and understaffed. (Provide testimony.)
4. Other companies provide on-site day care for children of employees. (Provide facts.)
5. On-site day care is beneficial to the emotional well-being of both preschool children and their mothers because of the possibility of contact during the workday.

*Conclusion:* Therefore, our company needs to provide on-site day care to retain valuable employees.

Deduction   Usually identified with classical reasoning, *deduction* begins with a general statement or ***major premise*** that when restricted by a ***minor premise*** leads to a specific conclusion. Unlike induction, which in theory makes an assertion only in its conclusion, deduction does make initial assertions (based on evidence) from which a conclusion is derived. This strategy is called a *three-step **syllogism:***

> Major premise: Retention of data processors who have preschool children is promoted by on-site day care.
> Minor premise: Our company wants to retain data processors who have preschool children.

<u>Conclusion</u>: Our company should establish on-site day-care centers.

To gain your audience's acceptance of your major and minor premises, you must support each assertion with specific evidence. Demonstrate that retaining data processors who have preschool children is promoted by on-site day-care centers and that "our company" wants to retain computer operators who have preschool children. If your readers accept your premises, then they are logically committed to accepting your conclusion.

*Claims and Warrants*   Often called the ***Toulmin argument*** after Stephen Toulmin, the legal philosopher who analyzed the process and defined its terminology, *claims and warrants*, argues from a general principle to a specific example, but it presents a more complex arrangement than a syllogism.

You begin by asserting a ***claim*** (or a general assertion about the argument you intend to make), then provide evidence to support your claim. The statement that links the claim to the evidence is called a ***warrant***. In some arguments, the warrant is implied; in others, you need to state it directly. Additional parts of the claims and warrants strategy include *support* to strengthen your argument, *qualifiers* to modify or limit your claim, and *reservations* to point out instances in which your claim may not apply.

For example:
*Claim:* Retention of data processors who have preschool children is promoted by on-site day-care centers.

*Evidence:*

1. Many of our data processors have preschool children.
2. These employees have difficulties arranging and paying for day-care services.
3. Mothers are more effective employees when they don't have to worry about their children.

*Warrant:* Our company should establish on-site day-care centers.

*Support:*

1. Competitors who provide on-site day care for their employees have a high retention rate.
2. Data processors at such companies have a lower absentee rate.
3. The cost of training new data processors is expensive.

*Qualification:* Some of our data processors do not have pre-school children.

*Reservation:* Because our company wants to retain a qualified workforce, we don't want to add expenses to the workplace that will penalize data processors who do not have children.

Claims and warrants is an effective arrangement because, like induction, it enables you to present evidence systematically; and, like induction, the inclusion of qualifiers and reservations suggests that you are considering your evidence objectively. But, like deduction, claims and warrants enables you to provide a clear and cogent link (warrant) between your general assertion (claim) and the data you have collected (evidence).

Accommodation   Sometimes called *nonthreatening argument*, *accommodation* arranges evidence so that all parties believe that their position has received a fair hearing. Induction reveals how a chain of evidence leads to a conclusion. Deduction demonstrates why certain premises demand a single conclusion. Although both procedures work effectively in specific situations, they occasionally defeat your purpose. Readers may feel trapped by the relentless march of your argument; though unable to refute your logic, they are still unwilling to listen to reason. Accommodation takes your audience's hesitations into account. Instead of trying to win the argument, you try to improve communication and increase understanding.

To employ this strategy, begin by composing an objective description of the controversy:

> *Women data processors who have preschool children are leaving the company.*

Then draft a complete and accurate statement of the contending positions, supplying evidence that makes each position credible:

*Corporation board:* We need a qualified workforce, but we are not in business to provide social services. (Provide evidence.)

*Fellow workers (single, male, etc.):* We understand their problem, but providing an on-site day-care center is giving expensive, preferential treatment to a small segment of the workforce. (Provide evidence.)

*Competitors:* We need better data processors if we are going to compete, and we will provide what is necessary to hire them. (Provide evidence.)

Next, show where and why you and the various parties agree:

> *The corporation should not be in the day-care business; women data processors have the right to market their skills in a competitive market.*

Then present your own argument explaining where it differs from other positions and why it deserves serious consideration:

> *We have invested a large amount of money in training our workforce; child care is an appropriate investment in view of the long-term contribution these people will make to the corporation.*

Finally, present a proposal that might resolve the issue in a way that recognizes the interests of all concerned:

> *The corporation might help to fund the nearby day-care center that was previously supported by government money.*

## Monitoring the Appeals

In developing an argument, you must keep track of how you are using the three basic appeals of argument: the *emotional appeal*, the *ethical appeal*, and the *logical appeal*. These three appeals are rarely separate; they all weave in and out of virtually every argument. But to control their effects to your advantage, you must know when and why you are using them.

*The Emotional Appeal*    Readers feel as well as think, and to be thoroughly convinced, they must be emotionally as well as intellectually engaged by your argument. Some people think that the *emotional appeal* is suspect because it relies on the feelings, instincts, and opinions of readers. They connect it to the devious manipulations of advertising or politics. The emotional appeal is often used to stampede an audience into thoughtless action, but such abuses do not negate its value. The emotional appeal should never replace more rational appeal, but it can be an effective strategy for convincing your readers that they need to pay attention to your argument.

The greatest strength of the emotional appeal is also its greatest weakness. Dramatic examples, presented in concrete images and connotative language, personalize a problem and produce powerful emotions. Some examples produce predictable emotions: an abandoned puppy or a lonely old woman evokes pity; a senseless accident or recurring incompetence evokes anger; a smiling face or a heroic deed evokes delight. Some examples, however, produce unpredictable results, and their dramatic presentation often works against your purpose. It would be difficult to predict, for instance, how your readers would respond to the plight of an undocumented immigrant working mother's need for health insurance. Some might pity her; others might disdain her illegal status and her desire for federal funding from taxpaying citizens. Because controversial issues attract a range of passions, use the emotional appeal with care.

All the writers in this chapter use emotional appeals, but those who rely on it most heavily are Taylor Branch's argument against the corruption in college sports and Peter Cohan argument to eliminate the humanities.

*The Ethical Appeal* The character (or *ethos*) of the writer—not the writer's morality—is the basis of the *ethical appeal*. It suggests that the writer is someone to be trusted, a claim that emerges from a demonstration of competence as an authority on the subject under discussion. Readers trust a writer who has established a reputation for informed, reasonable, and reliable writing about controversial subjects.

You can use the ethical appeal in your argument either by citing authorities who have conducted thorough investigations of your subject or by following the example of authorities in your competent treatment of evidence. There are two potential dangers with the ethical appeal. First, you cannot win the trust of your readers by citing as an authority in one field someone who is best known to be an authority in another field. Second, you cannot convince your readers that you are knowledgeable if you present your argument exclusively in personal terms. Your own experience may allow you to assemble detailed and powerful evidence. But to establish your ethical appeal, you need to balance such evidence with the experience of other authorities.

All the writers in this chapter rely on their ethical appeal, but it works most effectively for writers such as Taylor Branch, who has established himself as an authority on civil rights, and William Deresiewicz, who has established himself as a teacher at an esteemed liberal arts college.

*The Logical Appeal* The rational strategies used to develop an argument constitute a *logical appeal*. Some people think that the forceful use of logic makes an argument absolutely true. But controversies contain many truths, no one of which can be graded simply true or false. By using the logical appeal, you acknowledge that arguments are conducted in a world of probability, not certainty. By offering a series of reasonable observations and conclusions, you establish the most reliable case.

The logical appeal is widely used and accepted in argument. Establishing the relationships that bind your evidence to your assertion engages your readers' reasoning power, and an appeal to their intelligence and common sense is likely to win their assent. But the logical appeal is not infallible. Its limit is in acknowledging limits: How much evidence is enough? There is no simple answer to this question. For example, the amount of evidence required to convince fellow workers that your company should provide on-site day care may not be sufficient to persuade the company's board of directors. On the other hand, too much evidence, however methodically analyzed, may win the argument but lose your audience. Without emotional or ethical appeal, your "reasonable" presentation may be put aside in favor of more urgent issues. Accurate and cogent reasoning is the basis for any sound argument, but the logical appeal, like the emotional and ethical appeals, must be monitored carefully to accomplish your purpose.

The essays in this chapter use a variety of evidence. Taylor Branch relies on historical evidence to explain the recent scandals in college sports; Seth Davis cites the same evidence but interprets it from a different set of assumptions. Peter Cohan creates an intriguing argument depending on financial outcomes; William Deresiewicz creates a different argument by focusing on a different outcome—a good life rather than a good job.

## PERSUASION AND ARGUMENT

### Points to Remember

1. To argue well, you have to know your audience and your purpose. Do you understand your audience's interests, their backgrounds, and what questions they might have? Do you know what you want to accomplish with this particular group of readers? It's useful to write out the answers to both of these questions before you start.

2. Understand the three principal kinds of persuasive appeals.
   - *Appeal to reason.* Emphasizes logic, evidence, authority, cause and effect, precedent, and comparison and analogy.
   - *Appeal to emotion.* Emphasizes feelings, the senses, personal biases, connotative language, and images and metaphor.
   - *Appeal from integrity and character.* Emphasizes the writer's (ethos)—competence, experience, and reputation.

   The most persuasive writers usually combine elements from all three kinds of appeals.

3. Construct your arguments as a lawyer would construct a case to present to a jury: state your claim and back it up with evidence and reason, but, when appropriate, also use metaphor and connotation.

4. Always assume that your audience is intelligent, if perhaps uninformed about some particulars. Be respectful; avoid a superior tone.

5. Argue responsibly.
   - Don't overstate your claim.
   - Don't oversimplify complex issues.
   - Support your claims with specific details and evidence.

*This photo suggests that there are two roads—one to health care and one to reform. The photo also suggests that there is an argument about which road should be taken to achieve reform in health care. Research the current debate about health care and then write a persuasive essay about the best way health care can be reformed.*

# A DEBATE ABOUT COLLEGE SPORTS

## Taylor Branch: *The Shame of College Sports*

Taylor Branch was born in 1947 in Atlanta, Georgia, and educated at the University of North Carolina–Chapel Hill and Princeton University. He has worked as a journalist for *Washington Monthly*, *Harper's*, and *Esquire*. He covers a wide range of subjects, including the memoirs of basketball star Bill Russell, as well as the Pulitzer Prize–winning "Martin Luther King Trilogy": *Parting the Waters: America in the King Years, 1954–1963* (1988); *Pillar of Fire: America in the King Years, 1963–1968* (1997); and *At Canaan's Edge: America in the King Years, 1965–1968* (2006). In 2009, he completed another ambitious project, *The Clinton Tapes: Wrestling History with the President* (2009). "The Shame of College Sports" is excerpted from a longer article that appeared in *The Atlantic* magazine, which was expanded into an e-book, *The Cartel: Inside the Rise and Imminent Fall of the NCAA* (2011), in which Branch argues that money is ruining college sports.

"I'M NOT HIDING," Sonny Vaccaro told a closed hearing at the Willard Hotel in Washington, D.C., in 2001. "We want to put our materials on the bodies of your athletes, and the best way to do that is buy your school. Or buy your coach." 1

Vaccaro's audience, the members of the Knight Commission on Intercollegiate Athletics, bristled. These were eminent reformers—among them the president of the National Collegiate Athletic Association, two former heads of the U.S. Olympic Committee, and several university presidents and 2

297

chancellors. The Knight Foundation, a nonprofit that takes an interest in college athletics as part of its concern with civic life, had tasked them with saving college sports from runaway commercialism as embodied by the likes of Vaccaro, who, since signing his pioneering shoe contract with Michael Jordan in 1984, had built sponsorship empires successively at Nike, Adidas, and Reebok. Not all the members could hide their scorn for the "sneaker pimp" of schoolyard hustle, who boasted of writing checks for millions to everybody in higher education.

"Why," asked Bryce Jordan, the president emeritus of   3 Penn State, "should a university be an advertising medium for your industry?"

---

*The United States is the only country in the world that hosts big-time sports at institutions of higher learning."*

---

Vaccaro did not blink. "They shouldn't, sir," he replied.   4 "You sold your souls, and you're going to continue selling them. You can be very moral and righteous in asking me that question, sir," Vaccaro added with irrepressible good cheer, "but there's not one of you in this room that's going to turn down any of our money. You're going to take it. I can only offer it."

William Friday, a former president of North Carolina's uni-   5 versity system, still winces at the memory. "Boy, the silence that fell in that room," he recalled recently. "I never will forget it." Friday, who founded and co-chaired two of the three Knight Foundation sports initiatives over the past 20 years, called Vaccaro "the worst of all" the witnesses ever to come before the panel.

But what Vaccaro said in 2001 was true then, and it's true   6 now: corporations offer money so they can profit from the glory of college athletes, and the universities grab it. In 2010, despite the faltering economy, a single college athletic league, the football-crazed Southeastern Conference (SEC), became the first to crack the billion-dollar barrier in athletic receipts. The Big Ten pursued closely at $905 million. That money comes from a combination of ticket sales, concession sales, merchandise, licensing fees, and other sources—but the great bulk of it comes from television contracts.

Educators are in thrall to their athletic departments because  7 of these television riches and because they respect the political furies that can burst from a locker room. "There's fear," Friday told me when I visited him on the University of North Carolina campus in Chapel Hill last fall. As we spoke, two giant construction cranes towered nearby over the university's Kenan Stadium, working on the latest $77 million renovation. (The University of Michigan spent almost four times that much to expand its Big House.) Friday insisted that for the networks, paying huge sums to universities was a bargain. "We do every little thing for them," he said. "We furnish the theater, the actors, the lights, the music, and the audience for a drama measured neatly in time slots. They bring the camera and turn it on." Friday, a weathered idealist at 91, laments the control universities have ceded in pursuit of this money. If television wants to broadcast football from here on a Thursday night, he said, "we shut down the university at 3 o'clock to accommodate the crowds." He longed for a campus identity more centered in an academic mission.

The United States is the only country in the world that  8 hosts big-time sports at institutions of higher learning. This should not, in and of itself, be controversial. College athletics are rooted in the classical ideal of *Mens sana in corpore sano*— a sound mind in a sound body—and who would argue with that? College sports are deeply inscribed in the culture of our nation. Half a million young men and women play competitive intercollegiate sports each year. Millions of spectators flock into football stadiums each Saturday in the fall, and tens of millions more watch on television. The March Madness basketball tournament each spring has become a major national event, with upward of 80 million watching it on television and talking about the games around the office water cooler. ESPN has spawned ESPNU, a channel dedicated to college sports, and Fox Sports and other cable outlets are developing channels exclusively to cover sports from specific regions or divisions.

With so many people paying for tickets and watching on ⁹ television, college sports has become Very Big Business. According to various reports, the football teams at Texas, Florida, Georgia, Michigan, and Penn State—to name just a few big-revenue football schools—each earn between $40 million and $80 million in profits a year, even after paying coaches multimillion-dollar salaries. When you combine so much money with such high, almost tribal, stakes—football boosters are famously rabid in their zeal to have their alma mater win—corruption is likely to follow.

Scandal after scandal has rocked college sports. In 2010, ¹⁰ the NCAA sanctioned the University of Southern California after determining that star running back Reggie Bush and his family had received "improper benefits" while he played for the Trojans. (Among other charges, Bush and members of his family were alleged to have received free airfare and limousine rides, a car, and a rent-free home in San Diego, from sports agents who wanted Bush as a client.) The Bowl Championship Series stripped USC of its 2004 national title, and Bush returned the Heisman Trophy he had won in 2005. Last fall, as Auburn University football stormed its way to an undefeated season and a national championship, the team's star quarterback, Cam Newton, was dogged by allegations that his father had used a recruiter to solicit up to $180,000 from Mississippi State in exchange for his son's matriculation there after junior college in 2010. Jim Tressel, the highly successful head football coach of the Ohio State Buckeyes, resigned last spring after the NCAA alleged he had feigned ignorance of rules violations by players on his team. At least 28 players over the course of the previous nine seasons, according to *Sports Illustrated*, had traded autographs, jerseys, and other team memorabilia in exchange for tattoos or cash at a tattoo parlor in Columbus, in violation of NCAA rules. Late this summer, Yahoo Sports reported that the NCAA was investigating allegations that a University of

Miami booster had given millions of dollars in illicit cash and services to more than 70 Hurricanes football players over eight years.

The list of scandals goes on. With each revelation, there is much wringing of hands. Critics scold schools for breaking faith with their educational mission, and for failing to enforce the sanctity of "amateurism." Sportswriters denounce the NCAA for both tyranny and impotence in its quest to "clean up" college sports. Observers on all sides express jumbled emotions about youth and innocence, venting against professional mores or greedy amateurs. 11

For all the outrage, the real scandal is not that students are getting illegally paid or recruited, it's that two of the noble principles on which the NCAA justifies its existence— "amateurism" and the "student-athlete"—are cynical hoaxes, legalistic confections propagated by the universities so they can exploit the skills and fame of young athletes. The tragedy at the heart of college sports is not that some college athletes are getting paid but that more of them are not. 12

Don Curtis, a UNC trustee, told me that impoverished football players cannot afford movie tickets or bus fare home. Curtis is a rarity among those in higher education today, in that he dares to violate the signal taboo: "I think we should pay these guys something." 13

Fans and educators alike recoil from this proposal as though from original sin. Amateurism is the whole point, they say. Paid athletes would destroy the integrity and appeal of college sports. Many former college athletes object that money would have spoiled the sanctity of the bond they enjoyed with their teammates. I, too, once shuddered instinctively at the notion of paid college athletes. 14

But after an inquiry that took me into locker rooms and ivory towers across the country, I have come to believe that sentiment blinds us to what's before our eyes. Big-time college sports are fully commercialized. Billions of dollars flow through them each year. The NCAA makes money, and enables universities and corporations to make money, from the unpaid labor of young athletes. 15

Slavery analogies should be used carefully. College athletes   16
are not slaves. Yet to survey the scene—corporations and universities enriching themselves on the backs of uncompensated
young men, whose status as "student-athletes" deprives them
of the right to due process guaranteed by the Constitution—is
to catch an unmistakable whiff of the plantation. Perhaps a
more apt metaphor is colonialism: college sports, as overseen
by the NCAA, is a system imposed by well-meaning paternal-
ists and rationalized with hoary sentiments about caring for
the well-being of the colonized. But it is, nonetheless, unjust.
The NCAA, in its zealous defense of bogus principles, sometimes destroys the dreams of innocent young athletes.

The NCAA today is in many ways a classic cartel. Efforts to   17
reform it—most notably by the three Knight Commissions
over the course of 20 years—have, while making changes
around the edges, been largely fruitless. The time has come
for a major overhaul. And whether the powers that be like it
or not, big changes are coming. Threats loom on multiple
fronts: in Congress, the courts, breakaway athletic confer-
ences, student rebellion, and public disgust. Swaddled in
gauzy clichés, the NCAA presides over a vast, teetering glory.

## For Critical Thinking

### QUESTIONS ABOUT PURPOSE

1. How does Branch demonstrate that "college sports are deeply
   inscribed in the culture of our nation"?
2. How does he demonstrate that college sports are fully
   commercialized?

### QUESTIONS ABOUT AUDIENCE

1. What assumptions does Branch make about the millions of spectators who watch college sports?
2. How does he use the Knight Commission to illustrate that his
   readers are conflicted?

## QUESTIONS ABOUT STRATEGIES

1. How does Branch illustrate that "educators are in thrall to their athletic departments"?
2. How does he use the examples of Reggie Bush and Cam Newton to make his case?

## *For Writing and Research*

1. *Analyze* the way Branch presents the response of those in charge to "scandal after scandal."
2. *Practice* by writing an essay about how an athlete you know at your school is compensated.
3. *Argue* that college sports is/is not a form of colonialism.
4. *Synthesize* the evidence that has been collected at Northwestern University to support the argument that college athletes can be unionized.

## Seth Davis: *Should College Athletes Be Paid? Why, They Already Are*

Seth Davis was born in 1970 in New Haven, Connecticut, and educated at Duke University. Davis has worked as a sports writer for *Sports Illustrated* and a television broadcaster for shows such as "At the Half" and *The NFL Today*. His books include a memoir, *Equinunk, Tell Your Story: My Return to Summer Camp* (2002) and two books about basketball, *When March Went Mad: The Game That Transformed Basketball* (2009) and *Wooden: A Coach's Life* (2014). In "Should College Athletes Be Paid? Why, They Already Are," reprinted from *Sports Illustrated*, Davis responds to the many details in Branch's argument.

A LENGTHY ARTICLE in an esteemed national publication criticizes the hypocrisies of college athletics. The author details a multitude of scandals involving seedy recruiting, nefarious boosters and academic fraud. The narrative winds to a damning conclusion: "[T]hanks to the influence of the colleges, there is growing up a class of students tainted with commercialism."

You might think I'm referring to the essay by Taylor Branch that was published last week in *The Atlantic* under the headline "The Shame of College Sports." But I'm not. I'm actually referring to an article that appeared in the June 1905 edition of *McClure's*, a prestigious monthly academic journal. The two-part series, authored by a former Harvard football player named Henry Beach Needham, makes a compelling case that the enterprise of amateur athletics is doomed. In *The Atlantic*, Branch also writes that "scandal after scandal has rocked college sports," but while that phrase implies this is a recent trend, Needham shows us that it actually extends back more than a century.

I mention this as a counterweight to the prevailing conventional wisdom—namely, that the publication of Branch's article is a landmark event that has skewered the NCAA's bogus amateurism model for good. The piece has certainly spurred much discussion. A post on *The New Yorker's* website deemed it a "watershed." Jeff MacGregor of ESPN.com suggested "a kind of cultural critical mass has finally been reached." Frank Deford called it "the most important article ever written about college sports." From NPR to MSNBC to *Business Insider* to every sport outlet in between, the story has been hailed as a slam-dunk, once-and-for-all indictment of the NCAA.

---

*Branch derides college athletics as "Very Big Business," but the truth is, it's actually a "Very Lousy Business."*

---

To be sure, Branch's article represents a brilliant piece of reporting, which is not surprising considering he won a Pulitzer Prize for his three-volume series on the American civil rights movement. Branch lays out in fascinating detail the structural and legal history of the NCAA that has led us to this point. However, when it comes to analysis, fairness and context, Branch's work leaves much to be desired. If there is a reasonable counter-argument to be made, Branch ignores it. If there is a fact that contradicts his conclusions, he omits it.

Indeed, the entire article is based on a faulty premise, which is introduced right away in the sub-headline: "[S]tudent-athletes generate billions of dollars for universities and private companies while earning nothing for themselves." This is indisputably untrue. Student-athletes earn free tuition, which over the course of four years can exceed $200,000. They are also provided with housing, textbooks, food, and academic tutoring. When they travel to road games, they are given per diems for meals. They also get coaching, training, game experience, and media exposure they "earn" in their respective crafts. Despite all that, Branch asserts that "[t]he tragedy at the heart of college sports is not that some college athletes are getting paid but that more of them are not."

If Branch or anyone else wants to argue that college ath-  6
letes should be paid more, let them have at it. But to claim that college athletes earn "nothing?" Pure fiction.

So then: Should college athletes be paid more? As the sub-  7
ject of Branch's most recent bestseller, Bill Clinton, might say, it depends on what the definition of "paid" is. There is a significant and growing gap between the value of a scholarship and what a student-athlete genuinely needs. This is what is referred to as the "cost of attendance" issue. Many people in college sports, from NCAA president Mark Emmert on down, have argued that the scholarship model needs to be updated so this gap can be closed. Part of the challenge is that the gap exists for every athlete in every sport, so the fix must be applied broadly—and expensively. Yes, I'll believe it when I see it, but at least the discourse on this front is moving in the right direction.

However, when Branch and so many others talk about  8
college athletes getting "paid," they are not talking about merely the cost of attendance. They're talking about giving athletes what they're "worth." It's a convincing argument when cast alongside the mind-boggling dollars that are pouring in. Branch points out the SEC recently surpassed the $1 billion mark for football receipts. The Big Ten is close behind at $905 million. He reminds us that the football programs at Texas, Florida, Georgia, Michigan and Penn State earn between $40 million and $80 million each year in profits. The NCAA received $771 million from CBS and Turner to broadcast last year's basketball tournament, a sum that Branch asserts was "built on the backs of amateurs—unpaid labor. The whole edifice depends on the players' willingness to perform what is effectively volunteer work."

So we learn a lot in this article about how much the  9
schools are making. We learn almost nothing, however, about what they're spending. Branch virtually ignores the basic

profit-and-loss structure of college sports. For example, did you know that out of 332 schools currently competing in the NCAA's Division I, fewer than a dozen have athletic departments that are operating in the black? And that of the 120 programs that comprise the Football Bowl Subdivision, just 14 are profitable? That means some 88 percent of the top football programs lose money for their universities—and that doesn't even include the reams of cash the schools are spending on the so-called nonrevenue sports. Those are some basic, salient facts, but you won't find them anywhere in Branch's 15,000-word opus.

We might want to believe that the reason schools lose so 10 much money is because of the runaway spending on coaches salaries, new facilities and frivolous items like private jets. Those are indeed reckless expenditures; Myles Brand, the late NCAA president, frequently railed against them. They don't, however, begin to account for just how expensive it is to operate an athletic program. Branch derides college athletics as "Very Big Business," but the truth is, it's actually a "Very Lousy Business."

People who say that college athletes should be paid as pro- 11 fessionals like to invoke the principles of the free market. That's the framework advanced by an entity called the National College Players Association, which recently issued a study that put some dollar figures on this question. The NCPA says those numbers demonstrate what the players would be worth "if allowed access to the fair market like the pros."

Left unsaid is the fact that the players do have access to 12 the fair market. If they want to be compensated for their abilities, they can simply turn professional. Yes, the NFL and NBA have draft age minimums, but those rules were put in place by the leagues, not the NCAA. Does that not fall under the rubric of the "fair market"? Since the NFL won't accept a player who is not yet three years removed from his senior year in high school, the "fair market value" for a freshman or sophomore in college is actually zero. Yet, the NCAA is still "compensating" those players with a free education and other expenses, even if they are among the

98 percent who will never make a dime playing football. If anything, most of these guys are overpaid.

The NCPA found that, at the highest end, the fair mar- 13 ket value for a football player at the University of Texas is $513,922. Setting aside that this number does not account for the money the university is spending on the athlete (for starters, out-of-state tuition at the school runs north of $45,000 per year), I can't help but wonder what's "fair" about the market the NCPA describes. Clearly, the starting quarterback generates much more revenue for Texas than does the third-string safety. Would the NCPA argue those two players should be paid the same? There's nothing fair about that.

If we're going to say that players be paid according to their 14 value, then we should pay them less if their team doesn't make a bowl game. That's only fair. Or maybe the school should enter into individual contracts mandating that in return for access to its training program, practice facilities, game experiences, and television exposure, the players should pay the school a percentage of their future earnings. If the players don't like the deal, they can sign somewhere else. Hey, it's just business, right?

These are just the first small steps down a long and slippery 15 slope. That's why Ben Cohen's assertion last week in *The Wall Street Journal* that the case for paying salaries to college athletes was "gaining momentum" is so wrong. The only place this idea is gaining momentum is in the media. There is no movement—none—within the actual governing structure of the NCAA to professionalize college athletes. It's not just that it would ruin the amateurism ideal. It's that from a business standpoint, it makes no sense.

The other arguments in favor of paying athletes also do 16 not hold up. Some people claim it would serve as a deterrent against the temptation to accept largesse from agents. This insults our intelligence. Does anyone really think that if the schools give athletes another three thousand bucks a year that those kids are going to turn away a fist full of Benjamins proffered by an agent? On what planet?

Then there's the idea, promulgated by Jay Bilas among 17
others, that athletes should have limitless opportunity to
pursue ancillary marketing deals. This works much better in
theory than it would in practice. Do we really want a bidding
war between Under Armour and Nike to determine whether
a recruit attends Maryland or Oregon? Do we want Nick
Saban going into a kid's living room and saying, "I know
Bob Stoops has a car dealership who will pay you $50,000,
but I can line you up with a furniture store that will give you
$75,000?"

To be sure, there are a lot of legitimate questions about 18
whether many of the NCAA's policies are in line with laws
governing trade and copyrights. This terrain is in Taylor
Branch's wheelhouse, and his article is at its best when he
dissects the various cases that are currently making their way
through the courts. The most interesting one is the class
action suit being spearheaded by former UCLA basketball
player Ed O'Bannon, who claims the NCAA is violating
licensing law by continuing to make money off his likeness
without compensating him. I'm not a lawyer, but it seems
to me O'Bannon has a reasonable argument, and I certainly
have no problem with anyone suing the NCAA to address
such grievances. But when someone like Branch charac-
terizes these issues as part of a larger civil rights struggle,
he loses me. And I suspect he loses a lot of other open-
minded people who agree with him that the system that
needs fixing.

We need look no further than the current conference 19
expansion madness to understand that many of the presidents who are running college sports are feckless, greedy
hypocrites. It's also apparent that the NCAA's enforcement
process has gone off the rails. Still, in the final analysis, it's not
the NCAA's responsibility to stop schools and athletes from
cheating. It's the responsibility of those schools and athletes
not to cheat. Any system is only as good as the people who
are in it. You can make all the reforms you want, but at the
end of the day, where there's money, there's corruption. It's
a problem as old as time.

We spend way too much energy worrying about how the     20
system affects a very small number of elite athletes, young
men who are going to be multimillionaires as soon as they
leave campus. Thus, it was disappointing to see Branch fall
back on the argument that these select young men are being
exploited. As the father of three children under the age of
eight, I can only pray that someone "exploits" my sons someday by giving them tuition, room and board at one of America's finest universities. Branch also relies on some surprisingly
lazy reporting. He reveals without a dollop of skepticism that
a basketball team (he doesn't say which one) decided it would
not play in the NCAA championship game (he doesn't say
which year) out of protest. Thankfully, Armageddon was
averted when said team lost in the semifinal (Branch doesn't
say to whom or explain why the players couldn't have boy-
cotted the semifinal). Given that this fantastic scenario has
been peddled for decades without ever materializing, it is
remarkable that a reporter of Branch's stature would accept
the account at whole cloth.

In the end, the greatest flaw of Branch's article is his fail-     21
ure to address the question of why schools operate athletics
programs despite having to incur such financial losses. Could
it be that maybe—just maybe—they really do believe there is
educational value in competing? That they think sports is a
worthy investment because it gives tens of thousands of young
people the opportunity to learn discipline, teamwork and time
management alongside calculus and English lit? Could it be
that the schools really do want to enrich the lives of their "student-athletes" regardless of whether they are turning a profit?

As I read through Branch's essay, I kept waiting for him     22
to acknowledge that the student-athlete gets something of
value from all of this. I finally found it in the last paragraph,
when Branch quotes a member of the Knight Commission as
referring to the "free education" a student-athlete receives.
For Branch, this is the final straw. It is, he writes, "worse than
self-serving. It echoes masters who once claimed that heavenly
salvation would outweigh earthly injustice to slaves."

Giving someone a free college education is akin to enslave- 23
ment? If that's the great watershed idea of our time, then we
are living in a very dry world indeed.

## For Critical Thinking

### QUESTIONS ABOUT PURPOSE

1. How does Davis position his argument in relation to Branch's
   argument?
2. What is the "pure fiction" that Davis sees in Branch's argument?

### QUESTIONS ABOUT AUDIENCE

1. How does Davis identify with his readers by pointing out the
   "salient facts" Branch fails to present in his argument?
2. How does his discussion of "fair-market value" help him connect with his audience?

### QUESTIONS ABOUT STRATEGIES

1. How does Davis use Henry Beach Needham's article to
   demonstrate that the argument about college sports and money
   is over one hundred years old?
2. How does Davis use the "current conference expansion madness" to support his case?

## For Writing and Research

1. *Analyze* the way Davis "punches" and "counterpunches" with
   the facts in Branch's argument.
2. *Practice* by analyzing the athletic budget at your school. For
   example, you might focus on how much money your college
   athletic team made or lost by going to a bowl game.
3. *Argue* that your school should/should not operate an athletics
   program.
4. *Synthesize* the two arguments with the facts in Henry Beach
   Needham's article in *McClure's* magazine (June 1905).

# A DEBATE ABOUT THE LIBERAL ARTS

## Peter Cohan: *To Boost Post-College Prospects, Cut Humanities Departments*

Peter Cohan earned degrees in art history and electrical engineering from Swarthmore College, computer science from MIT, and finance from the Wharton School. He worked at Index Systems and the Monitor Company before starting Peter S. Cohan and Associates, a management consulting and venture capital firm. He has taught business strategy at Stanford, MIT, the University of Hong Kong, and Babson College. Cohan is a frequent commentator on economics and technology on *Good Morning America* and *Wall Street Week*. He writes the "Start-Up Economy" columns for *Forbes* magazine and a weekly column for *Entrepreneur*. His books include *Net Profit* (2001), *You Can't Order Change* (2009), and *Hungry Start-up Strategy* (2012). In "To Boost Post-College Prospects, Cut Humanities Departments," Cohan argues that academic departments that cannot guarantee a direct pipeline to a job should be cut.

H ALF OF FRESHLY minted college graduates are unemployed or underemployed. And they're saddled with a portion of the U.S.'s $1 trillion in student loan debt to pay record high tuitions. To fix this problem, the answer is simple enough: cut out the departments offering majors that make students unemployable. 1

The waste produced by the mismatch between the educational system and the demand for labor is astonishingly high. The Labor Department reports that "about 1.5 million, or 2

53.6%, of bachelor's degree-holders under the age of 25 last year were jobless or underemployed, the highest share in at least 11 years."

Young people are far more likely to be employed in jobs    3
that do not require college education than in jobs that do demand it. 100,000 of them work as "waiters, waitresses, bartenders and food-service helpers" while only 90,000 have jobs as "engineers, physicists, chemists, and mathematicians," according to the Labor Department.

---

*Those who still wanted to study zoology, anthropology, philosophy, art history, and humanities could read the books during their Starbucks barista work breaks.*

---

And in the white collar world, there are more jobs at the    4
low- end than the higher end. For example, 163,000 young people worked as receptionists or payroll clerks while only 100,000 were computer professionals.

Not surprisingly, some majors generate higher rates of    5
under-employment than others. Those with majors "in zoology, anthropology, philosophy, art history, and humanities" don't stand much of a chance of getting jobs requiring a college degree. However, those with "nursing, teaching, accounting, or computer science degrees" were among the most likely to find jobs that required those degrees, according to the Labor Department.

While I would be in favor of conducting more research on    6
this, the solution could be as simple as eliminating the departments that offer majors that employers do not value. Sure, there may be art history majors who do get jobs in their field. Moreover, in some parts of the world, humanities majors have a shot at finding employment in their field. So there, it may make sense for colleges to have departments.

Having said that, for students, lenders, and parents it    7
makes no sense to send a child to college to study humanities

if they do not have a chance at getting a job that uses the skills they've developed. If colleges cut those humanities departments, their costs would drop because they could stop paying teachers and administrators in those departments and slash the related overhead.

Those students could skip college and go right to their jobs   8
as waiters and receptionists. They would be better off because they would not incur the crushing debt loads that they would never be able to pay back. Or their parents could hold onto the money they would have spent on tuition and save it for their retirement. Moreover, lenders would lower the rate of student loan defaults.

Meanwhile, by retaining only those majors for which   9
employers would pay, the colleges could operate with lower costs and pass those lower costs on to students in the form of reduced tuition payments. Those lower costs to students would mean less borrowing—thus boosting the odds that the students would be able to generate a positive net worth more quickly.

I can hear the howls of protest now. So let's consider the   10
arguments from the professors in the departments that my proposal would eliminate. They would argue that the purpose of an education is not to create cogs in the corporate wheel but to create well-rounded citizens who can contribute to society.

Moreover, they would claim that their departments offer   11
unique perspectives without which society would be poorer. And they would cite a student or two from their department who had gone on to an exemplary career.

No doubt this argument would have significant sway within   12
many corridors. However, I would ask colleges to consider a dictum preached by Harvard University—*every tub on its own bottom (ETOB)* (http://harvardmagazine.com/2004/05/harvard-a-to-z.html). I don't know if this concept is actually practiced there—but it means to me that every department should be economically self-sustaining.

To that end, I would suggest that every university develop   13
an income statement for each of its academic departments. The income statement would reflect revenue in the form of tuition from enrolled students, government grants, and

donations from alumni of those departments. That income statement would also include expenses for the people and facilities that deliver the department's programs.

Departments that are profitable and likely to remain so would stick around. Those that are not and would not, get cut. 14

The beauty of this idea is that it would make students better off by saving them from making an investment in a college experience that would not pay off. And for those who could benefit from college, they would pay less tuition than they do now and thus would end up taking on less debt. Their return on investment in college would rise. 15

Those who still wanted to study zoology, anthropology, philosophy, art history, and humanities could read the books during their Starbucks barista work breaks. Or, in the ETOB spirit, perhaps all the humanities departments could be spun off from the universities and consolidated regionally to achieve greater efficiencies. 16

One thing is clear—academia's effort to preserve its special exemption from the laws of economics is becoming too burdensome for many students, parents, and lenders to bear. 17

## For Critical Thinking

### QUESTIONS ABOUT PURPOSE

1. How does Cohan propose to solve the student loan debt problem?
2. Why does he argue that it makes no sense to study the humanities?

### QUESTIONS ABOUT AUDIENCE

1. How does Cohan's discussion of potential employment connect with his readers?
2. How does he anticipate the arguments of the faculty in the departments he proposes to cut?

## QUESTIONS ABOUT STRATEGIES

1. How does Cohan's statistics from the Labor Department lend credibility to his argument?
2. How does his suggestion that "every university develop an income statement for each of its departments" support his argument?

## *For Writing and Research*

1. *Analyze* how Cohan organizes his criticism against the humanities.
2. *Practice* by preparing an "income statement" for your academic department.
3. *Argue* that taking courses in the humanities helps you build the skills that you need to find a good job.
4. *Synthesize* the information presented by George D. Kuh in *High Impact Education Practices: What They Are, Who Has Access to Them and Why They Matter* (Washington: American Colleges and Universities, 2008). Then argue that such practices are essential to a good education.

William Deresiewicz was born in 1964 in Englewood, New Jersey, and educated at Columbia University. He worked for the *Financial Times*, the *Nation*, the *New Republic*, and the *American Scholar*. He is best known for two books, *Jane Austin and the Romantic Poets* (2004) and *A Jane Austin Education: How Six Novels Taught Me About Love, Friendship and Things That Really Matter* (2011). As a member of Yale's admissions committee, Deresiewicz saw firsthand how students were being forced to shift their focus away from the humanities to "practical subjects," losing in the process their ability to think independently. In "What is College For?" excerpted from *Excellent Sheep: The Miseducation of the American Elite and the Way to a Meaningful Life* (2014), Deresiewicz argues that "the first thing college is for is to teach you to think."

"RETURN ON INVESTMENT": that's the phrase you often 1 hear today when people talk about college. How much money will you get out of doing it, in other words, relative to the amount that you have to put in. What no one seems to ask is what the "return" that college is supposed to give you is. Is it just about earning more money? Is the only purpose of an education to enable you to get a job? What, in short, is college for?

We talk, in the overheated conversation we've been hav- 2 ing about higher education lately, about soaring tuition, rising student debt, and the daunting labor market for new graduates. We talk about the future of the university: budget squeezes, distance learning, massive open online courses, and whether college in its present form is even necessary. We talk about national competitiveness, the twenty-first-century labor force, technology and engineering, and the outlook for our future prosperity. But we never talk about the premises that underlie this conversation, as if what makes for a happy life and a good society were simply self-evident, and as if in either case the exclusive answer were more money.

Of course money matters: jobs matter, financial security     3 matters, and national prosperity matters. The question is, are they the only things that matter? Life is more than a job; jobs are more than a paycheck; and a country is more than its wealth. Education is more than the acquisition of marketable skills, and you are more than your ability to contribute to your employer's bottom line or the nation's GDP, no matter what the rhetoric of politicians or executives would have you think. To ask what college is for is to ask what life is for, what society is for—what people are for.

---

*An undergraduate experience devoted*
*exclusively to career preparation is four years*
*largely wasted.*

---

Do students ever hear this? What they hear is a constant     4 drumbeat, in the public discourse, that seeks to march them in the opposite direction. When policy makers talk about higher education, from the president all the way down, they talk exclusively in terms of math and science. Journalists and pundits—some of whom were humanities majors and none of whom are nurses or engineers—never tire of lecturing the young about the necessity of thinking prudently when choosing a course of study, the naïveté of wanting to learn things just because you're curious about them. "Top Ten Majors" means the most employable, not the most interesting. "Top Ten Fields" means average income, not job satisfaction. "What are you going to do with that?" the inevitable sneering question goes. "Liberal arts" has become a put-down, and "English major" a punch line.

I'm not sure what the practicality police are so concerned       5
about. It's not as if our students were clamoring to get into classes on Milton or Kant. The dreaded English major is now the choice of all of 3 percent. Business, at 21 percent, accounts for more than half again as many majors as all of the arts and humanities combined. In 1971, 73 percent of incoming freshmen said that it is essential or very important to "develop a meaningful philosophy of life," 37 percent to be "very well-off financially" (not well-off, note, but *very* well-off). By 2011, the numbers were almost reversed, 47 percent and 80 percent, respectively. For well over thirty years, we've been loudly announcing that happiness is money, with a side order of fame. No wonder students have come to believe that college is all about getting a job.

You need to get a job, but you also need to get a life.       6
What's the return on investment of college? What's the return on investment of having children, spending time with friends, listening to music, reading a book? The things that are most worth doing are worth doing for their own sake. Anyone who tells you that the sole purpose of education is the acquisition of negotiable skills is attempting to reduce you to a productive employee at work, a gullible consumer in the market, and a docile subject of the state. What's at stake, when we ask what college is for, is nothing less than our ability to remain fully human.

The first thing that college is for is to teach you to think.       7
That's a cliché, but it does actually mean something, and a great deal more than what is usually intended. It doesn't simply mean developing the mental skills particular to individual disciplines—how to solve an equation or construct a study or analyze a text—or even acquiring the ability to work across the disciplines. It means developing the habit of skepticism and the capacity to put it into practice. It means learning not to take things for granted, so you can reach your own conclusions.

Before you can learn, you have to unlearn. You don't    8
arrive in college a blank slate; you arrive having already been
inscribed with all the ways of thinking and feeling that the
world has been instilling in you from the moment you were
born: the myths, the narratives, the pieties, the assumptions,
the values, and the sacred words. Your soul, in the words
of Allan Bloom, is a mirror of what is around you. I always
noticed, as a teacher of freshmen, that my students could be
counted on to produce an opinion about any given subject
the moment that I brought it up. It was not that they had
necessarily considered the matter before. It was that their
minds were like a chemical bath of conventional attitudes that
would instantly precipitate out of solution and coat whatever
object you introduced. (I've also noticed the phenomenon is
not confined to eighteen-year-olds.)

Society is a conspiracy to keep itself from the truth. We    9
pass our lives submerged in propaganda: advertising messages; political rhetoric; the journalistic affirmation of the
status quo; the platitudes of popular culture; the axioms of
party, sect, and class; the bromides we exchange every day
on Facebook; the comforting lies our parents tell us and the
sociable ones our friends do; and the steady stream of false-
hoods that we each tell ourselves all the time, to stave off
the threat of self-knowledge. Plato called this *doxa*, opinion,
and it is as powerful a force among progressives as among
conservatives, in Massachusetts as in Mississippi, for atheists
as for fundamentalists. The first purpose of a real education
(a "liberal arts" education) is to liberate us from *doxa* by
teaching us to recognize it, to question it, and to think our
way around it.

In *Teacher*, Mark Edmundson describes the man who    10
played this role for him when he was seventeen and thereby
saved him from the life of thoughtless labor that appeared
to be his fate. His teacher's methods were the same as those
of Socrates, the teacher of Plato himself: he echoed your
opinions back to you or forced you to articulate them for
yourself. By dragging them into the light, asking you to
defend them or just acknowledge having them, he began to

break them down, to expose them to the operations of the critical intelligence—and thus to develop that intelligence in the first place. The point was not to replace his students' opinions with his own. The point was to bring his charges into the unfamiliar, uncomfortable, and endlessly fertile condition of doubt. He was teaching them not what to think but how.

Why college? College, after all, as those who like to denigrate it often say, is "not the real world." But that is precisely its strength. College is an opportunity to stand outside the world for a few years, between the orthodoxy of your family and the exigencies of career, and contemplate things from a distance. It offers students "the precious chance," as Andrew Delbanco has put it, "to think and reflect before life engulfs them." You can start to learn to think in high school, as Edmundson did—you're certainly old enough by then— but your parents are still breathing down your neck, and your teachers are still teaching to the test, in one respect or another. College should be different: an interval of freedom at the start of adulthood, a pause before it all begins. Is this a privilege that most young people in the world can only dream of? Absolutely. But you won't absolve yourself by throwing it away. Better, at least, to get some good from it.

College also offers you professors. Yes, it is theoretically possible to learn how to think on your own, but the chances are not good. Professors can let in some air, show you approaches that wouldn't have occurred to you and put you on to things you wouldn't have encountered by yourself. Autodidacts tend to be cranks, obtuse, and self-enclosed. A professor's most important role is to make you think with rigor: precisely, patiently, responsibly, remorselessly, and not only about your "deepest ingrained presuppositions," as my own mentor, Karl Kroeber, once wrote, but also about your "most exhilarating new insights, most of which turn out to be fallacious." You want some people in your life whose job it is to tell you when you're wrong.

College also gives you peers with whom to question and debate the ideas you encounter in the classroom. "Late-night bull sessions" is another one of those phrases people like to throw at the college experience, a way of shaming students out of their intellectual appetites. But the classroom and the dorm room are two ends of the same stick. The first puts ideas into your head; the second makes them part of your soul. The first requires stringency; the second offers freedom. The first is normative; the second is subversive. "Most of what I learned at Yale," writes Lewis Lapham, "I learned in what I now remember as one long, wayward conversation in the only all-night restaurant on Chapel Street. The topics under discussion—God, man, existence, Alfred Prufrock's peach—were borrowed from the same anthology of large abstraction that supplied the texts for English 10 or Philosophy 116." The classroom is the grain of sand; it's up to you to make the pearl.

College is not the only chance to learn to think. It is not    14 the first; it is not the last; but it is the best. One thing is certain: if you haven't started by the time you finish your BA, there's little likelihood you'll do it later. That is why an undergraduate experience devoted exclusively to career preparation is four years largely wasted. The purpose of college is to enable you to live more alertly, more responsibly, more freely: more fully. I was talking with a couple of seniors during a visit to Bryn Mawr. One of them said, "The question I leave Bryn Mawr with is how to put my feminist ideals into practice as I go forward." I liked "ideals," but I loved the first part. A real education sends you into the world bearing questions, not resumes.

## *For Critical Thinking*

---
### QUESTIONS ABOUT PURPOSE
---

1. How does Deresiewicz answer the question, "Is the only purpose of an education to enable you to get a job?"
2. Why does he think it is necessary to unlearn before you can learn?

## QUESTIONS ABOUT AUDIENCE

1. Why does he address what his readers are likely to be hearing about marketable skills?
2. What are they likely to be hearing from the "practicality police"?

## QUESTIONS ABOUT STRATEGIES

1. How does Deresiewicz use the example of Socrates to demonstrate a liberal education?
2. How does he characterize the importance of teachers and peers?

## *For Writing and Research*

1. *Analyze* how Deresiewicz demonstrates that "[l]ife is more than a job."
2. *Practice* by making the case for the Top Ten Majors that—for you—have been the most interesting.
3. *Argue* that the purpose of a real education is to liberate us from opinion.
4. *Synthesize* the information in Cohan's and Deresiewicz's arguments. Where do they agree about the purpose of a college education? Where do they appear to be in rigid disagreement? Would they advise you to take the same courses? What kind of experiences do they think you should have outside of the classroom?

# Kurt Vonnegut Jr.: *Harrison Bergeron*

Kurt Vonnegut Jr. (1922–2007) was born in Indi-
anapolis, Indiana, and attended Cornell University, where he studied biochemistry before being
drafted into the infantry in World War II. Vonnegut was captured by the Germans at the Battle of
the Bulge and sent to Dresden, where he worked in
the underground meat locker of a slaughterhouse.
He miraculously survived the Allied firebombing
of Dresden and, following the war, returned to the
United States to study anthropology at the University of Chicago and to work for a local news
bureau. In 1947, Vonnegut accepted a position
writing publicity for the General Electric Research
Laboratory in Schenectady, New York, but left the
company in 1950 to work on his own writing. His
first three novels—*Player Piano* (1952), a satire on
the tyrannies of corporate automation; *The Sirens
of Titan* (1959), a science-fiction comedy on the
themes of free will and determination; and *Cat's
Cradle* (1963), a science fantasy on the amorality
of atomic scientists—established Vonnegut's reputation as a writer who could blend humor with
serious insights into the human experience. His
most successful novel, *Slaughterhouse-Five, or the
Children's Crusade* (1969), is based on his wartime
experiences in Dresden. His other works include
*God Bless You, Mr. Rosewater* (1966), *Breakfast of
Champions* (1973), *Jailbird* (1979), *Palm Sunday*
(1981), *Galápagos* (1985), *Hocus Pocus* (1990),
and *Timequake* (1997). His best-known short
stories are collected in *Canary in the Cat House*
(1961) and *Welcome to the Monkey House* (1968).
"Harrison Bergeron," reprinted from the latter collection, is the story of the apparatus that a future
society must create to make everyone equal.

T HE YEAR WAS 2081, and everybody was finally equal. They weren't only equal before God and the law. They were equal every which way. Nobody was smarter than anybody else. Nobody was better looking than anybody else. Nobody was stronger or quicker than anybody else. All this equality was due to the 211th, 212th, and 213th Amendments to the Constitution, and to the unceasing vigilance of agents of the United States Handicapper General.

Some things about living still weren't quite right, though. April, for instance, still drove people crazy by not being springtime. And it was in that clammy month that the H-G men took George and Hazel Bergeron's fourteen-year-old son, Harrison, away.

It was tragic, all right, but George and Hazel couldn't think about it very hard. Hazel had a perfectly average intelligence, which meant she couldn't think about anything except in short bursts. And George, while his intelligence was way above normal, had a little mental handicap radio in his ear. He was required by law to wear it at all times. It was tuned to a government transmitter. Every twenty seconds or so, the transmitter would send out some sharp noise to keep people like George from taking unfair advantage of their brains.

George and Hazel were watching television. There were tears on Hazel's cheeks, but she'd forgotten for the moment what they were about.

On the television screen were ballerinas.

A buzzer sounded in George's head. His thoughts fled in panic, like bandits from a burglar alarm.

"That was a real pretty dance, that dance they just did," said Hazel.

"Huh?" said George.

"That dance—it was nice," said Hazel.

"Yup," said George. He tried to think a little about the ballerinas. They weren't really very good—no better than anybody else would have been, anyway. They were burdened with sashweights and bags of birdshot, and their faces were masked, so that no one, seeing a free and graceful gesture or a pretty face, would feel like something the cat drug in. George was toying with the vague notion that maybe dancers shouldn't be handicapped. But he didn't get very far with it before another noise in his car radio scattered his thoughts.

George winced. So did two of the eight ballerinas.    11

Hazel saw him wince. Having no mental handicap herself,    12
she had to ask George what the latest sound had been.

"Sounded like somebody hitting a milk bottle with a ball    13
peen hammer," said George.

"I'd think it would be real interesting, hearing all the dif-    14
ferent sounds," said Hazel, a little envious. "All the things
they think up."

"Um," said George.    15

"Only, if I was Handicapper General, you know what I    16
would do?" said Hazel. Hazel, as a matter of fact, bore a
strong resemblance to the Handicapper General, a woman
named Diana Moon Glampers. "If I was Diana Moon Glampers," said Hazel, "I'd have chimes on Sunday—just chimes.
Kind of in honor of religion."

"I could think, if it was just chimes," said George.    17

"Well—maybe make 'em real loud," said Hazel. "I think    18
I'd make a good Handicapper General."

"Good as anybody else," said George.    19

"Who knows better'n I do what normal is?" said Hazel.    20

"Right," said George. He began to think glimmeringly    21
about his abnormal son who was now in jail, about Harrison,
but a twenty-one-gun salute in his head stopped that.

"Boy!" said Hazel, "that was a doozy, wasn't it?"    22

It was such a doozy that George was white and trembling,    23
and tears stood on the rims of his red eyes. Two of the eight
ballerinas had collapsed on the studio floor, were holding
their temples.

"All of a sudden you look so tired," said Hazel. "Why    24
don't you stretch out on the sofa, so's you can rest your handicap bag on the pillows, honeybunch." She was referring to
the forty-seven pounds of birdshot in a canvas bag, which was
padlocked around George's neck. "Go on and rest the bag

for a little while," she said. "I don't care if you're not equal
to me for a while."

George weighed the bag with his hands. "I don't mind it," 25
he said. "I don't notice it any more. It's just a part of me."

"You been so tired lately—kind of wore out," said Hazel. 26
"If there was just some way we could make a little hole in the
bottom of the bag, and just take out a few of them lead balls.
Just a few."

"Two years in prison and two thousand dollars fine for 27
every ball I took out," said George. "I don't call that a
-bargain."

"If you could just take a few out when you came home 28
from work," said Hazel. "I mean—you don't compete with
anybody around here. You just set around."

"If I tried to get away with it," said George, "then other 29
people'd get away with it—and pretty soon we'd be right back
to the dark ages again, with everybody competing against
everybody else. You wouldn't like that, would you?"

"I'd hate it," said Hazel. 30

"There you are," said George. "The minute people start 31
cheating on laws, what do you think happens to society?"

If Hazel hadn't been able to come up with an answer to 32
this question, George couldn't have supplied one. A siren was
going off in his head.

"Reckon it'd fall all apart," said Hazel. 33

"What would?" said George blankly. 34

"Society," said Hazel uncertainly. "Wasn't that what you 35
just said?"

"Who knows?" said George. 36

The television program was suddenly interrupted for a 37
news bulletin. It wasn't clear at first as to what the bulletin
was about, since the announcer, like all announcers, had a
serious speech impediment. For about half a minute, and in a
state of high excitement, the announcer tried to say, "Ladies
and gentlemen—"

He finally gave up, handed the bulletin to a ballerina to 38
read.

"That's all right—" Hazel said to the announcer, "he tried. 39
That's the big thing. He tried to do the best he could with
what God gave him. He should get a nice raise for trying so
hard."

"Ladies and gentlemen—" said the ballerina, reading 40
the bulletin. She must have been extraordinarily beautiful,
because the mask she wore was hideous. And it was easy to
see that she was the strongest and most graceful of all the
dancers, for her handicap bags were as big as those worn by
two-hundred-pound men.

And she had to apologize at once for her voice, which was 41
a very unfair voice for a woman to use. Her voice was a warm,
luminous, timeless melody. "Excuse me—" she said, and she
began again, making her voice absolutely uncompetitive.

"Harrison Bergeron, age fourteen," she said in a grackle 42
squawk, "has just escaped from jail, where he was held on
suspicion of plotting to overthrow the government. He is a
genius and an athlete, is under-handicapped, and should be
regarded as extremely dangerous."

A police photograph of Harrison Bergeron was flashed on 43
the screen upside down, then sideways, upside down again,
then right side up. The picture showed the full length of Harrison against a background calibrated in feet and inches. He
was exactly seven feet tall.

The rest of Harrison's appearance was Halloween and 44
hardware. Nobody had ever borne heavier handicaps. He had
outgrown hindrances faster than the H-G men could think
them up. Instead of a little ear radio for a mental handicap,
he wore a tremendous pair of earphones, and spectacles with
thick wavy lenses. The spectacles were intended to make him
not only half blind but also to give him whanging headaches
besides.

Scrap metal was hung all over him. Ordinarily, there was a 45
certain symmetry, a military neatness to the handicaps issued
to strong people, but Harrison looked like a walking junkyard.
In the race of life, Harrison carried three hundred pounds.

And to offset his good looks, the H-G men required that 46
he wear at all times a red rubber ball for a nose, keep his

eyebrows shaved off, and cover his even white teeth with black caps at snaggle-tooth random.

"If you see this boy," said the ballerina, "do not—I repeat, 47 do not—try to reason with him."

There was the shriek of a door being torn from its hinges. 48

Screams and barking cries of consternation came from the 49 television set. The photograph of Harrison Bergeron on the screen jumped again and again, as though dancing to the tune of an earthquake.

George Bergeron correctly identified the earthquake, and 50 well he might have—for many was the time his own home had danced to the same crashing tune. "My God—" said George, "that must be Harrison!"

The realization was blasted from his mind instantly by the 51 sound of an automobile collision in his head.

When George could open his eyes again, the photograph 52 of Harrison was gone. A living, breathing Harrison filled the screen.

Clanking, clownish, and huge, Harrison stood in the center 53 of the studio. The knob of the uprooted studio door was still in his hand. Ballerinas, technicians, musicians, and announcers cowered on their knees before him, expecting to die.

"I am the Emperor!" cried Harrison. "Do you hear? I am 54 the Emperor! Everybody must do what I say at once!" He stamped his foot and the studio shook.

"Even as I stand here—" he bellowed, "crippled, hobbled, 55 sickened—I am a greater ruler than any man who ever lived! Now watch me become what I *can* become!"

Harrison tore the straps of his handicap harness like wet 56 tissue paper, tore straps guaranteed to support five thousand pounds.

Harrison's scrap-iron handicaps crashed to the floor. 57

Harrison thrust his thumbs under the bars of the padlock 58 that secured his head harness. The bar snapped like celery. Harrison smashed his headphones and spectacles against the wall.

He flung away his rubber-ball nose, revealed a man that 59 would have awed Thor, the god of thunder.

"I shall now select my Empress!" he said, looking down on    60
the cowering people. "Let the first woman who dares rise to
her feet claim her mate and her throne!"

A moment passed, and then a ballerina arose, swaying like    61
a willow.

Harrison plucked the mental handicap from her ear,    62
snapped off her physical handicaps with marvelous delicacy.
Last of all, he removed her mask.

She was blindingly beautiful.    63

"Now—" said Harrison, taking her hand, "shall we show    64
the people the meaning of the word dance? Music!" he
commanded.

The musicians scrambled back into their chairs, and Har-    65
rison stripped them of their handicaps, too. "Play your best,"
he told them, "and I'll make you barons and dukes and earls."

The music began. It was normal at first—cheap, silly, false.    66
But Harrison snatched two musicians from their chairs, waved
them like batons as he sang the music as he wanted it played.
He slammed them back into their chairs.

The music began again and was much improved.    67

Harrison and his Empress merely listened to the music for a    68
while—listened gravely, as though synchronizing their heart-
beats with it.

They shifted their weights to their toes.    69

Harrison placed his big hands on the girl's tiny waist, let-    70
ting her sense the weightlessness that would soon be hers.

And then, in an explosion of joy and grace, into the air    71
they sprang!

Not only were the laws of the land abandoned, but the law    72
of gravity and the laws of motion as well.

They reeled, whirled, swiveled, flounced, capered, gam-    73
boled, and spun.

They leaped like deer on the moon.    74

The studio ceiling was thirty feet high, but each leap    75
brought the dancers nearer to it.

It became their obvious intention to kiss the ceiling.    76

They kissed it.    77

And then, neutralizing gravity with love and pure will, they   78
remained suspended in air inches below the ceiling, and they
kissed each other for a long, long time.

It was then that Diana Moon Glampers, the Handicapper   79
General, came into the studio with a double-barreled ten-
gauge shotgun. She fired twice, and the Emperor and the
Empress were dead before they hit the floor.

Diana Moon Glampers loaded the gun again. She aimed   80
it at the musicians and told them they had ten seconds to get
their handicaps back on.

It was then that the Bergerons' television tube burned out.   81

Hazel turned to comment about the blackout to George.   82
But George had gone out into the kitchen for a can of beer.

George came back in with the beer, paused while a handi-   83
cap signal shook him up. And then he sat down again. "You
been crying?" he said to Hazel.

"Yup," she said.   84

"What about?" he said.   85

"I forgot," she said. "Something real sad on television."   86

"What was it?" he said.   87

"It's all kind of mixed up in my mind," said Hazel.   88

"Forget sad things," said George.   89

"I always do," said Hazel.   90

"That's my girl," said George. He winced. There was the   91
sound of a riveting gun in his head.

"Gee—I could tell that one was a doozy," said Hazel.   92

"You can say that again," said George.   93

"Gee—" said Hazel, "I could tell that one was a doozy."   94

## COMMENT ON "HARRISON BERGERON"

Known for his offbeat and sometimes bizarre vision of reality, Vonnegut has created in "Harrison Bergeron" a science-fiction story full of black humor and grotesque details. The society he creates in the story is reminiscent of the society pictured in Orwell's *1984*, totally controlled by a government that invades and interferes in every facet of its citizens' lives. In a travesty of the famous declaration that "All men are created equal," the government has set out to legislate equality. Vonnegut portrays the results of such legislation in macabre images of people forced to carry weighted bags to reduce their strength, wear grotesque masks to conceal their beauty, and suffer implants in their brain to disrupt their thinking. When a fourteen-year-old boy, Harrison Bergeron, shows signs of excellence, he is first arrested and then ruthlessly destroyed when he throws off his restraints and literally rises to the top.

Underneath the farce, Vonnegut has created a tragic picture of a culture so obsessed with equality that people must be leveled by decree. Mediocrity reigns; any sign of excellence or superiority threatens law and order and must be suppressed immediately. Ultimately, of course, such a society will perish because it will kill its talent and stagnate.

Vonnegut wrote this story in 1961, after the repressive Stalinist regime that wiped out thousands of leaders and intellectuals in Russia; it precedes by a few years the disastrous era of Mao's Red Guards in China, when hundreds of thousands of intellectuals and artists were killed or imprisoned in the name of equality. Is Vonnegut commenting on the leveling tendencies of these totalitarian societies? Or does he see such excesses reflected in our own society? No one knows, but it's the genius of artists to prod us to think about such concerns.

# CHAPTER 8

# *Resources for Writing: Food: A Casebook*

As you have worked your way through this book, you have discovered that you already possess many resources for reading and writing. You read essays on a wide variety of themes. You encountered new and complicated information shaped by unusual and unsettling assertions. But you discovered experiences and feelings that you recognize—the challenge of learning, the ordeal of disappointment, and the cost of achievement. As you examined these essays, you realized that you had something to say about your reading, something to contribute to the themes explored by the writers.

Your work with this book has also enabled you to identify and practice strategies that at each stage of the writing process helped you transform your ideas about a theme into writing. In the beginning, these strategies give rise to certain questions you might ask to explain any topic. (See "Selecting Your Strategy," pages 20 to 25.)

Suppose you want to write an essay on the theme of green technology. You might begin by asking what kinds of green technology are currently available to save energy and protect the environment. You might continue asking questions: What historical forces have created the need for green technology (cause and effect)? How do scientists recommend that our culture convert to green technology (process analysis)? How do they distinguish between the way we currently use energy and the way we would use energy if we were to convert to green technology (comparison and contrast)? How can we convince advocates of traditional technology to convert to green technology (persuasion and argument)? Such questions work like the different lenses you attach to your camera: each lens gives you a different perspective on a subject, a variation on a theme.

If your initial questions enable you to envision your theme from a different perspective, then answering one of these questions encourages you to develop your theme according to a purpose associated with one of the common patterns of organization. For instance, if you decide to write about why you traded your gas guzzler for a hybrid, your choice of purpose seems obvious: to answer the question "Why did it happen?" You would write a cause-and-effect essay. In drafting the essay, however, you may discover questions that you had not anticipated: What caused carmakers to develop hybrid cars? What other types of energy-saving vehicles are currently available? What are the limitations of hybrid cars? How are hybrid cars similar to or different from electric cars?

Responding to these new questions forces you to decide whether your new information develops or distorts your draft. The history of why carmakers decided to develop hybrids may help your readers see a context for your analysis. On the other hand, such information may confuse them, distracting them from your original purpose—to explain why you decided to trade for a hybrid.

As you struggle with your new themes, you may decide that your original purpose no longer drives your writing. You may decide to change your purpose and write a comparison-and-contrast essay. Instead of explaining why you traded for a hybrid, you might decide to use your personal experience, together with some reading, to write a more technical essay explaining how hybrid cars compare with electric cars.

This book has helped you make such decisions by showing how the common patterns of organization evoke different purposes, audiences, and strategies. In this thematic unit, you will have the opportunity to make decisions about a little anthology of writing on the theme of *Food*.

Before reading these selections, take an initial inventory:

- *What kind of direct experiences have you had with food?*
  What are the most important memories you have of food?
  What problems did you encounter with food?
  How did you overcome these problems?
- *What kind of indirect experiences have you had with food?*
  What have you observed about food in other families and cultures?
  What kind of stories have you read about food in newspapers or literature?
  What have you learned by watching stories about food on television or in film?
- *What do you know—or suspect you could learn—about the history and significance of food in our culture?*
  What are the foods that define the traditional cuisines in our culture?
  How have the different ideas about food defined our history?
  How have the revolutions in technology changed the way food is preserved and prepared?
  Why are we so fascinated by stories about charismatic cooks and delightful meals?

Thinking about such questions will remind you of the extensive resources you bring to the theme of *Food*. It is a subject that touches all our lives in some way. And it affects our behavior in countless other ways—what we do with our time, with whom we associate, how we spend our money, what skills we wish to acquire, and what we think of ourselves and our culture.

After you have made a preliminary inventory of your knowledge of and attitudes toward food, read the writings in this chapter. You will notice that each selection asks you to think about food from a different perspective.

1. *What happened? (Narration and Description)* Teresa Lust recounts her mother's dilemma about preparing the Thanksgiving meal.
2. *How do you do it? How is it done? (Process Analysis)* Laurie Colwin analyzes the process of frying a chicken.
3. *How is it similar to or different from something else? (Comparison and Contrast)* Suzanne Britt Jordan compares and contrasts overweight and thin people.
4. *What kind of subdivisions does it contain? (Division and Classification)* Alexander Theroux classifies the many delicious subcategories of candy.
5. *How would you characterize it? (Definition)* Michael Pollan tries to establish the boundaries that separate real food from foodlike products.
6. *How did it happen? (Cause and Effect)* Eric Schlosser analyzes the reasons why McDonald's french fries have such a distinctive taste.
7. *How do you prove it? (Persuasion and Argument)* Peter Singer and Laura Fraser present opposing arguments about vegetarianism.

This collection also includes a *photo essay* that presents various "visual texts"—images and photographs—that evoke questions about the way we *see* food. Each visual text is also followed by a writing assignment that asks you to interpret the significance of what you are looking at.

The collection ends with Andre Dubus's story, "The Fat Girl," an engaging story about how the consumption of food complicates and creates character.

As you examine these selections, keep track of how your reading and seeing expand the theme of food—provoking memories, adding information, and suggesting questions you had not considered when you made your initial inventory about food. Because this information will give you new ways to think about your original questions, you will want to explore your thinking in writing.

## Teresa Lust: *The Same Old Stuffing*

Teresa Lust was born in 1964 in the state of Washington and educated at Washington State University and Dartmouth College. She learned to cook in her mother's kitchen, but took up the job as a profession when she cooked in various restaurants in Washington State, California, and New England. Her first book, *Pass the Polenta* (1998) is part memoir, part cookbook, and part exploration into the origins of favorite dishes. In "The Same Old Stuffing," excerpted from that book, Lust traces her mother's attempt to balance traditions at the Thanksgiving meal.

B EFORE YOU SET OUT to revamp your Thanksgiving meal, it pays to consider all the repercussions. Just because the editors of the glossy food magazines have grown weary of the same old turkey and fixings, and even though they are absolutely giddy with excitement over the smoked quail, the spicy black bean stuffing, and the sun-dried tomato and arugula gratin they have in store for this year's feast, it does not mean that everyone will welcome innovation at the Thanksgiving table. Quite the contrary. All some people really want is the tried and true. Some people have grown quite fond of their annual mix of turkey and trimmings, each and every dish, and they do not consider it an onerous task to repeat the meal from one year to the next. They gain comfort from the familiarity and the ritual of it all; any tampering with the menu, no matter how minor or well intentioned, only serves to make them feel shortchanged.

This fact my mother discovered to her dismay when she 2 tried out a little something at our own Thanksgiving meal. For years before anyone realized it had become a tradition, she roasted our holiday turkey with two types of stuffing inside it. She filled the bird's main cavity with my paternal grandmother's sage-and-onion dressing. This quintessential American farmhouse preparation was a genuine family heirloom, as Nana had learned to make it at her own mother's side. And for the bird's neck cavity, my mom fixed what you could call an Italian-American hybrid stuffing. Although this filling was not authentically Italian, it was a recipe from my mother's family, and it bespoke her immigrant heritage with its classic Mediterranean combination of sausage, spinach, raisins and nuts.

*[T]ime-honored traditions get their start*
*while you are not looking, it seems.*

Then one autumn as the holiday loomed near, my mom 3 found herself contemplating our annual Thanksgiving spread. She saw it suddenly in a new and somewhat bothersome light. What had seemed a skillful act of diplomacy all these years, this bringing together of two family traditions inside one bird, why, it now smacked to her of excess. How the fact had escaped her for so long, she did not know, for she did not go for over-indulgence when it came to family meals. My mother was accommodating, don't misunderstand me. She was a mom who once finished up a marathon session of Dr. Seuss books with a breakfast of green eggs and ham at the behest of her four daughters. Still, she made us eat our peas, and she said things like, "The day your papa starts raising cows that don't come with livers is the day I'll quit serving liver and onions for dinner. Now eat up." Yes, she knew where to draw the line.

What suddenly struck my mother as disturbing was not a 4 matter of gluttony or expense or grams of fat, but of balance. What with the mashed potatoes, the baked yams, the penny rolls, and two types of stuffing, there was altogether too much starch on the plate. Starch, starch, starch. The redundancy of it became an offense that the English teacher in her could no longer abide. Of an instant, the solution became clear: two stuffings were one stuffing too many. One of them would have to go.

So she said to my father, "Jim, which stuffing do you prefer ₅ at Thanksgiving?"

He replied, "My mother's sage-and-onion dressing, of ₆ course. It's the stuffing of my youth. It's the heart of the Thanksgiving meal. By God, it's a national tradition, that stuffing, and I can't even imagine the holiday without it."

This was not the response my mother had in mind. Nana's ₇ sage-and-onion dressing had been her candidate for dismissal, because naturally, she preferred her family's stuffing, the one with the Italian touch of sausage, spinach, and raisins. She saw my father's point, though. We celebrated the holiday with his side of the family, and she had them to bear in mind. The children would be too preoccupied with the mashed potatoes to care a whit one way or the other about the stuffing, but her in-laws would feel deprived, no doubt, if Nana's dish didn't grace the table. And she had to admit that the sage-and-onion version was more in keeping with the all-American spirit of the holiday. It was more faithful, she assumed, to history. Good heavens, even schoolchildren knew that sage-and-onion dressing appeared on the Pilgrims' rough-hewn banquet table, right alongside the spit-roasted wild turkey, the hearth-braised sweet potatoes, the cranberry sauce, and the pumpkin pie.

I must admit I envisioned such a meal, just as I pictured ₈ Miles Standish brandishing a kitchen knife and gallantly carving the turkey roast while he gazed deep into the limpid eyes of Priscilla Mullens. But there is no record of stuffing—sage-and-onion or otherwise—bedecking the table at the Pilgrims' first thanksgiving, which it turns out was not a somber meal, but a frolicsome affair of hunting, games, and wine which lasted three days. For that matter, there isn't even any specific mention of turkeys having been served, though one colonist wrote of an abundance of fowl at the event, and most scholars feel safe in assuming this bounty included a few turkeys. All anyone knows for certain is that the Mayflower folks cooked up five deer, oysters, cod, eel, corn bread, goose, watercress, leeks, berries, and plums. Pumpkins made an appearance, too, but no one bothered to record just how they were cooked. They certainly were not baked in a pie crust, though, for the wheat crop had failed and the ship's supply of flour had long since run out.

The traditional meal as we know it dates back not to the    9
solemn, high-collared Pilgrims, nor even to Colonial times, but to home cooks of the nineteenth century. Not until this era did the idea of an annual day of Thanksgiving first take hold. The driving force behind the holiday was New Englander Sarah Josepha Hale (whose legacy also includes the nursery rhyme "Mary Had a Little Lamb"). As editor of the popular magazine *Godey's Lady's Book*, she promoted the holiday for nearly twenty years within the periodical's pages. She wrote letters annually to the state governors and to the president, and one by one the states gradually took up the idea. Finally, Abraham Lincoln, desperate for any means to promote unity in the war-ravaged country, declared the first national Thanksgiving in 1863.

And what did the mistress of the house serve up at this    10
new holiday meal? Her standard company fare for autumn, of course: roast turkey with cranberry sauce, scalloped and mashed potatoes, candied sweet potatoes, braised turnips, creamed onions, cranberry sauce, mince pie, pumpkin pie— the menu has endured remarkably unchanged. And yes, it was standard procedure then to roast the turkey with a stuffing.

The actual practice of filling up a bird's cavity dates back to    11
antiquity; the space made a handy cooking vessel for families who all too often owned only one pot. Recipes have varied over the millennia. The cookbook attributed to the Roman gastronome Apicius gives a formula that includes ground meat, chopped brains, couscous, pine nuts, lovage, and ginger; other than the brains, it sounds like something right out of a trendy contemporary cookbook. English cooks during the Middle Ages favored heavily spiced and honeyed productions based on pieces of offal that today would make our rarefied stomachs churn. Nineteenth-century American cooks

went on stuffing birds, no matter how many pots and pans they had on hand in the kitchen, and recipes much like Nana's sage-and-onion dressing were a beloved part of many an early Thanksgiving repast.

No less dear, though, or popular, or traditional, were a number of other variations. Homemakers in the corn-growing south who went to stuff a turkey favored cornbread in their recipes. Along the eastern seaboard, they tucked in dozens of nectar-sweet shucked oysters, while across the country as far north as the chestnut tree once grew, they featured loads of tender chestnuts in their fillings. And many cooks treasured recipes that called for ground meat, dried fruits, autumn greens, and shelled nuts—the very products of the fall harvest upon which my mother's family recipe was based, so she need not have dismissed her version as unconventional so hastily.

The genteel ladies of the last century would have viewed my mother's dilemma not as a surplus of starch at the meal, but as a paucity of meats. They were impassioned carnivores, these American predecessors of ours, and one meager turkey would have seemed woefully inadequate at a meal showcasing the prodigious bounty of the land. Pull out the stops, Darlene, I can all but hear them tell her. Along with the requisite turkey, they decorated their tables with a chicken pie, a joint of beef, a roast goose, if the budget would allow. Certainly these additional viands would serve to put my mother's menu back in kilter.

I'm sure, too, that at least one of these women would have felt bound by duty to draw my mother aside and whisper that she really ought to call her preparation *dressing* and not *stuffing*. The word "stuffing" has been in use for centuries. Sir Thomas Elyot's *Dictionary* of 1538 uses it as a synonym for "forcemeat," defined as "that wherewith any foule is crammed." Sir Thomas obviously wasn't much of a cook, or he would have known that cramming a fowl isn't such a great idea, for the filling expands during the roasting, and it can burst out at the seams if it is packed too tightly. At any rate, all this stuffing and forcing and cramming proved simply too much for the delicate sensibilities of the Victorian age, and the more discreet term "dressing" came into fashion. Today, schoolmarmish cookbooks often wag a finger and insist that when it is on the inside of the bird it is stuffing, and when it is baked in a separate dish, it's dressing. In reality, this does not play out. If Grandma calls her dish stuffing, then stuffing it is, regardless of its location inside or alongside the bird. Same goes for Aunt Pearl's dressing, no matter where she puts it.

Had my mother sought the counsel of Mrs. Sarah Josepha   15 Hale or her contemporaries, then, she might have spared herself some anxiety. For although she had resolved herself to her decision, the idea of forgoing her family recipe did not rest easy with her. The days wore on and she grew positively disgruntled. Then one brisk, gray morning with two weeks yet to go before Thanksgiving, she found herself pushing her cart down the butcher's aisle at the supermarket when inspiration struck. Who ever said holiday recipes were for holidays, and holidays only? Who? She need not go without her annual dose of her family's stuffing after all. So she hoisted a fresh turkey into the cart, made a few other spur-of-the-moment additions to her shopping list, and went home and set to work.

She pulled her big frying pan out of the cupboard, set it   16 over a low flame on the stove-top, melted half a stick of butter in it, then crumbled in three-quarters of a pound of bulk pork sausage. After the meat began to brown, she stirred in a diced onion, a couple of cloves of pressed garlic, a few stalks of cut-up celery, and a cup or so of sliced button mushrooms. These she let simmer gently until the onions were translucent. She added a large container of the chopped garden spinach she had blanched and frozen last spring, heated it through, then scraped the contents of the pan into a large ceramic bowl. When the mixture cooled to room temperature she sliced a stale loaf of French bread into cubes—enough to make about four cups— then added the bread to the bowl along with a couple of ample handfuls of raisins, sliced almonds, and freshly grated Parmesan cheese—a good half cup of each. She seasoned the stuffing with salt, black pepper, and generous pinches of oregano and rosemary, then drizzled in a glass of white wine. Using her hands, she combined all the ingredients thoroughly, then put a finger to her tongue. A pinch more salt and that would do it. Finally, she spooned the stuffing into the bird, trussed it up, and put it in the oven to roast for the rest of the afternoon.

Incidentally, my mother is quite an accomplished seam- 17 stress. She could sew bound buttonholes on a turkey if she wanted to. But she agrees with me that trussing need not be the intricate knit-one-purl-two operation that many cookbooks describe. Such elaborate needlework lingers from the days of the kitchen hearth-fire, when trussing was done to keep the drumsticks and wings from dangling in the flames as the bird turned on a spit. It now functions as a stuffy, old guard test of a cook's dexterity—yes, but can she truss a turkey? By the turn of this century, the massive iron kitchen range had become a standard feature in the American home, and oven roasting rendered unnecessary all the knotting and stitching and battening down. Trussing now primarily serves to keep the stuffing in place, and to give the bird a demure appearance, its ankles politely crossed, when it arrives at the table. Folding back the wings and tying the drumsticks together with kitchen twine usually make for ample treatment.

As my mom put the neck and giblets into a stock-pot on 18 the stove for gravy, she decided a side dish of mashed potatoes would be just the accompaniment to round out the meal. Then she discovered she had a few sweet potatoes in the bin under the kitchen sink, and she thought, now wouldn't those be nice, too, roasted with a little butter, ginger, and brown sugar? And when she remembered the tiny boiling onions that had been rolling around in the refrigerator's bottom drawer, she decided she might as well bake them up au gratin with some bread crumbs and cream.

The turkey spittered and spattered away in the oven, filling 19 every nook in the house with its buttery, winter-holiday scent, and the next thing my mom knew, she was rolling out the crust for a pumpkin pie. My father arrived home from work, draped his overcoat across the banister, and walked into the kitchen just in time to see her plopping the cranberry sauce out of the can. She placed it on the table in a sterling silver dish, its ridged imprints still intact and its jellied body quivering gloriously—God bless those folks at Ocean Spray, they were always a part of our turkey dinners, too. She turned to my father and said, "Dinner's almost ready."

My mom watched as her family gathered around the table    20
and enjoyed a complete turkey feast on that evening in early November. After the meal, my father stretched back in his chair and folded his hands behind his head. He'd always thought it a shame, he said, a needless deprivation, that Americans ate roast turkey only once a year at Thanksgiving. This fine dinner just proved his point. What a treat, yes, what a treat. But the family's pleasure that night was merely an added perk for my mother, as she had prepared the meal for herself, only for herself, and she was feeling deeply satisfied.

When the official holiday finally arrived, my mother made    21
good on her vow and let Nana's sage-and-onion dressing preside at the evening meal. Out came the frying pan, and she started to sauté two chopped onions and four thinly sliced stalks of celery, including the leaves, in a stick of butter. After a moment's thought, she added two plump cloves of minced garlic to the simmering pan. She couldn't resist. She knew Nana thought her a bit heavy-handed in the garlic department, but so what, it was her kitchen.

When the vegetables were limp and fragrant, she pulled the    22
pan from the heat and set it aside to cool. She put the mixture into a bowl along with eight cups of firm, stale bread cubes, a generous spoonful of dried sage, a healthy handful of chopped fresh parsley, some salt and pepper, and a pinch of nutmeg. She gave these ingredients a light mixing, drizzled in enough broth to make the filling hold together when she squeezed a handful of it between her fingers—three-quarters of a cup, maybe a bit more—then tossed the dressing together again lightly before she spooned it into the Thanksgiving bird.

That evening Nana arrived with her sweet pickles and    23
her three pies—apple, pumpkin, mincemeat. Cousins poured into the house toting covered casserole dishes, an uncle walked through the door, then an aunt. We soon sat down around two tables to dine, our plates heaped to the angle of

repose. Amid the clanking of cutlery and the giggling and guffawing, and the festive bustle, my father paused. His fork pierced a juicy slice of dark thigh meat and his knife was poised in midstroke. He looked down intently and his eyes circled clockwise, studying the contents of his plate. He craned his neck and took an inventory of the platters and bowls laid out on the buffet counter across the room. "Darlene," he said, "this is some spread we have here, don't get me wrong. But you know what's missing is that other stuffing you make. The one we had the other day with the cornucopia of raisins and nuts and such."

My mom nearly dropped her fork. "But you told me you preferred your mother's dressing." 24

He looked back down at the turkey and trimmings before him. "Well, yes, but that doesn't mean I don't prefer yours, too. It just doesn't seem like a proper Thanksgiving without that second stuffing on the table. Don't you agree?" 25

What he meant, of course, was that my mom's dish had to turn up missing before he understood just what a part of the celebration it had become. So the year the turkey had only one stuffing was the year that both recipes became permanent fixtures on my mother's Thanksgiving menu. When time-honored traditions get their start while you're not looking, it seems, they need not concern themselves with balance, or daily nutritional requirements, or even historical accuracy. For such rituals rise up out of memories, and memories are not subject to hard facts. They are not interested in making room for change. 26

## For Critical Thinking

### QUESTIONS ABOUT PURPOSE

1. What does Lust want to demonstrate about "time-honored" traditions?
2. How does she use her mother's concern about balance to shape her narrative?

## QUESTIONS ABOUT AUDIENCE

1. How does Lust use the prospect of "innovations" in the Thanksgiving meal to connect with her readers?
2. How does she speculate on the way other audiences might have viewed "my mother's dilemma"?

## QUESTIONS ABOUT STRATEGIES

1. How does Lust record the way her mother attempts to solve the problem of which stuffing to use during the Thanksgiving holidays?
2. How does she use historical information to explain the traditions of Thanksgiving?

## For Writing and Research

1. *Analyze* how Lust embeds other writing strategies—for example, process analysis—in her narrative.
2. *Practice* by telling a story about how one of your favorite dishes became a tradition.
3. *Argue* for an innovation to the traditional Thanksgiving meal.
4. *Synthesize* the information about how agricultural products in a given geographical region revise the traditions of a special meal.

## Laurie Colwin: *How to Fry Chicken*

Laurie Colwin (1944–1992) was born in New York City and educated at Barnard College and Columbia School of General Studies. Her love of food became evident when she cooked for protesting classmates during the 1968 demonstrations against her school. She worked as a food columnist for *Gourmet* magazine. Her writing about food is collected in *Home Cooking: A Writer in the Kitchen* (1988) and *More Home Cooking: A Writer Returns to the Kitchen* (1993). She also wrote three collections of short stories: *Passion and Affect* (1974), *The Lone Pilgrim* (1981), and *Another Marvelous Thing* (1988). Her novels include *Happy All the Time* (1978) and *Family Business* (1982). In "How to Fry Chicken," taken from *Home Cooking: A Writer in the Kitchen*, Colwin describes "the right way" to fry chicken.

A S EVERYONE KNOWS, there is only one way to fry chicken 1 correctly. Unfortunately, most people think their method is best, but most people are wrong. Mine is the only right way, and on this subject I feel almost evangelical.

It is not that I am a bug on method—I am fastidious about 2 results. Fried chicken must have a crisp, deep (but not too deep) crust. It must be completely cooked, yet juicy and tender. These requirements sound minimal, but achieving them requires technique. I have been frying chicken according to the correct method for about ten years, and I realize that this skill improves over time. The last batch fried was far, far better than the first. The lady who taught my sister and me, a black woman who cooked for us in Philadelphia, was of course the apotheosis: no one will ever be fit to touch the top of her chicken fryer.

I have had all kinds of nasty fried chicken served to me, 3 usually with great flourish: crisp little baby shoes or hockey pucks turned out by electric frying machines with names such as Little Fry Guy. Beautifully golden morsels completely raw on the inside. Chicken that has been fried and put into the fridge, giving the crust the texture of a wet paper towel.

I have also had described to me Viennese fried chicken, 4 which involves egg and bread crumbs and is put in the oven after frying and drizzled with butter. It sounds very nice, but it is *not* fried chicken.

---

*To fry chicken that makes people want to stand up and sing "The Star-Spangled Banner," the following facts of life must be taken seriously.*

---

To fry chicken that makes people want to stand up and sing 5 "The Star-Spangled Banner," the following facts of life must be taken seriously.

- Fried chicken should be served warm. It should never be eaten straight from the fryer—it needs time to cool down and set. Likewise, fried chicken must never see the inside of a refrigerator because this turns the crisp into something awful and cottony.
- Contrary to popular belief, fried chicken should not be deep-fried.
- Anyone who says you merely shake up the chicken in a bag with flour is fooling himself. (More on this later.)
- Fried chicken must be made in a chicken fryer—a steep-sided frying pan with a domed top.
- It must never be breaded or coated with anything except flour (which can be spiced with salt, pepper, and paprika). No egg, no crumbs, no crushed Rice Krispies.

Now that the basics have been stated, the preparation is the next 6 step. The chicken pieces should be roughly the same size—this means that the breast is cut into quarters. The breast is the hardest to cook just right as it tends to get dry. People who don't quarter the breast usually end up with either a large, underdone half, or they overcompensate and fry it until it resembles beef jerky.

The chicken should be put in a dish and covered with a 7 little water or milk. This will help to keep the flour on. Let the chicken stand at room temperature. It is not a good thing to put cold raw chicken into hot oil.

Meanwhile, the flour should be put into a deep, wide bowl, 8 with salt, pepper and paprika added to taste. I myself adore paprika and feel it gives the chicken a smoky taste and a beautiful color.

To coat the chicken, lay a few pieces at a time in the bowl 9 and pack the flour on as if you were a child making sand pies. Any excess flour should be packed between the layers. It is important to make sure that every inch of chicken has a nice thick cover. Now heat the oil and let the chicken sit.

And now to the frying. There are people who say, and 10 probably correctly, that chicken should be fried in lard and Crisco, but I am not one of these people. Fried food is bad enough for you. I feel it should not be made worse. The lady who taught me swore by Wesson oil, and I swear by it, too, with the addition of about one-fourth part of light sesame oil. This gives a wonderful taste and is worth the added expense. It also helps to realize that both oils are polyunsaturated in case one cannot fry without guilt.

The oil should come up to just under the halfway mark of 11 your chicken fryer. Heat it slowly until a piece of bread on a skewer fries as soon as you dip it. If it does, you are ready to start.

Carefully slip into the oil as many pieces as will fit. The 12 rule is to crowd a little. Turn down the heat at once and *cover*. The idea of covering frying chicken makes many people squeal, but it is the only correct method. It gets the chicken cooked through. Remember that the chicken must be just done—juicy and crisp. About six minutes or so per side—and you must turn it once—is probably about right, although dark meat takes a little longer. A sharp fork makes a good tester.

When the chicken just slips off the fork, it is done inside. 13 Take the cover off, turn up the heat, and fry it to the color of Colonial pine stain—a dark honey color. Set it on a platter and put it in the oven. If your oven is gas, there is no need for any more warmth than that provided by the pilot light. If electric, turn it up a little in advance and then turn it off. You have now made perfect fried chicken.

And you have suffered. There are many disagreeable things 14 about frying chicken. No matter how careful you are, flour gets all over everything and the oil splatters far beyond the stove. It is impossible to fry chicken without burning yourself at least once. For about twenty-four hours your house smells of fried chicken. This is nice only during dinner and then begins to pall. Waking up to the smell of cooking fat is not wonderful.

Furthermore, frying chicken is just about the most boring 15 thing you can do. You can't read while you do it. Music is drowned out by constant sizzling. Finally, as you fry you are consumed with the realization that fried food is terrible for you, even if you serve it only four times a year.

But the rewards are many, and when you appear with your 16 platter your family and friends greet you with cries of happiness. Soon your table is full of ecstatic eaters, including, if you are lucky, some delirious Europeans—the British are especially impressed by fried chicken. As the cook you get to take the pieces you like best. As for me, I snag the backs, those most neglected and delectable bits, and I do it without a trace of remorse. After all, I did the cooking.

Not only have you mastered a true American folk tradition, 17 but you know that next time will be even better.

## For Critical Thinking

### QUESTIONS ABOUT PURPOSE

1. Why does Colwin declare that she feels almost "evangelical" about her way to fry chicken?
2. How does she present "the results" as proof of her method?

## QUESTIONS ABOUT AUDIENCE

1. How does Colwin use her first paragraph to connect with her readers?
2. How does she address the people with whom she disagrees?

## QUESTIONS ABOUT STRATEGIES

1. How does Colwin analyze the "basic facts of life"?
2. What are the disadvantages and rewards of cooking chicken her way?

## *For Writing and Research*

1. *Analyze* the tone of Colwin's process analysis.
2. *Practice* by describing the rules you follow (or require someone else to follow) to prepare a special dish.
3. *Argue* that fried chicken is (or is not) a true American folk tradition.
4. *Synthesize:* Research and test various recipes for fried chicken. Then write an essay in which you compare and contrast the distinctive qualities of each recipe, arguing in the last analysis for one unique way to fry chicken.

## Suzanne Britt Jordan:
## *That Lean and Hungry Look*

Suzanne Britt Jordan was born in Winston-Salem, North Carolina, and educated at Salem College and Washington University. Her poetry has appeared in many literary magazines, and her essays have been published in *Newsweek*, the *Boston Globe*, the *New York Times*, and *Newsday*. Her books include *Show and Tell* (1982), *Skinny People Are Dull and Crunchy Like Carrots* (1982), *A Writer's Rhetoric* (1988), and *Images: A Centennial Journey* (1991). In "That Lean and Hungry Look," which originally appeared in *Newsweek*, Jordan compares and contrasts the characteristics of those people who are forever watching their weight and those who know the true value of a hot-fudge sundae.

CAESAR WAS RIGHT. Thin people need watching. I've been watching them for most of my adult life, and I don't like what I see. When these narrow fellows spring at me, I quiver to my toes. Thin people come in all personalities, most of them menacing. You've got your "together" thin person, your mechanical thin person, your condescending thin person, your tsk-tsk thin person, your efficiency-expert thin person. All of them are dangerous.

In the first place, thin people aren't fun. They don't know how to goof off, at least in the best, fat sense of the word. They've always got to be adoing. Give them a coffee break, and they'll jog around the block. Supply them with a quiet evening at home, and they'll fix the screen door and lick S&H green stamps. They say things like "there aren't enough hours in the day." Fat people never say that. Fat people think the day is too damn long already.

Thin people make me tired. They've got speedy little   3
metabolisms that cause them to bustle briskly. They're forever rubbing their bony hands together and eyeing new problems to "tackle". I like to surround myself with sluggish, inert, easygoing fat people, the kind who believe that if you clean it up today, it'll just get dirty again tomorrow.

---

### Fat people will take you in.

---

Some people say the business about the jolly fat person is   4
a myth, that all of us chubbies are neurotic, sick, sad people. I disagree. Fat people may not be chortling all day long, but they're a hell of a lot *nicer* than the wizened and shriveled. Thin people turn surly, mean and hard at a young age because they never learn the value of a hot-fudge sundae for easing tension. Thin people don't like gooey soft things because they themselves are neither gooey nor soft. They are crunchy and dull, like carrots. They go straight to the heart of the matter while fat people let things stay all blurry and hazy and vague, the way things actually are. Thin people want to face the truth. Fat people know that there is no truth. One of my thin friends is always staring at complex, unsolvable problems and saying, "The key thing is . . ." Fat people never say things like that. They know there isn't any such thing as the key thing about anything.

Thin people believe in logic. Fat people see all sides. The   5
sides fat people see are rounded blobs, usually gray, always nebulous, and truly not worth worrying about. But the thin person persists, "If you consume more calories than you burn," says one of my thin friends, "you will gain weight. It's that simple." Fat people always grin when they hear statements like that. They know better.

Fat people realize that life is illogical and unfair. They know   6
very well that God is not in his heaven and all is not right with

the world. If God was up there, fat people could have two doughnuts and a big orange drink anytime they wanted it.

Thin people have a long list of logical things they are always 7 spouting off to me. They hold up one finger at a time as they reel off these things, so I won't lose track. They speak slowly as if to a young child. The list is long and full of holes. It contains tidbits like "get a grip on yourself," "cigarettes kill," "cholesterol clogs," "fit as a fiddle," "ducks in a row," "organize," and "sound fiscal management." Phrases like that.

They think these 2000-point plans lead to happiness. Fat 8 people know happiness is elusive at best and even if they could get the kind thin people talk about, they wouldn't want it. Wisely, fat people see that such programs are too dull, too hard, too off the mark. They are never better than a whole cheesecake.

Fat people know all about the mystery of life. They are 9 the ones acquainted with the night, with luck, with fate, with playing it by the ear. One thin person I know once suggested that we arrange all the parts of a jigsaw puzzle into groups according to size, shape and color. He figured this would cut the time needed to complete the puzzle by at least 50 percent. I said I wouldn't do it. One, I like to muddle through. Two, what good would it do to finish early? Three, the jigsaw puzzle isn't the important thing. The important thing is the fun of four people (one thin person included) sitting around a card table, working a jigsaw puzzle. My thin friend had no use for my list. Instead of joining us, he went outside and mulched the boxwoods. The three remaining fat people finished the puzzle and made chocolate double-fudged brownies to celebrate.

The main problem with thin people is they oppress. Their 10 good intentions, bony torsos, tight ships, neat corners, cerebral machinations, and pat solutions loom like dark clouds over the loose, comfortable, spread-out, soft world of the fat. Long after fat people have removed their coats and shoes and put their feet up on the coffee table, thin people are still sitting on the edge of the sofa, looking neat as a pin, discussing rutabagas. Fat people are heavily into fits of laughter, slapping their thighs, and whooping it up, while thin people are still politely waiting for the punch line.

Thin people are downers. They like math and morality and    11
reasoned evaluation of the limitations of human beings. They
have their skinny little acts together. They expound, prog-
nose, probe, and prick.

Fat people are convivial. They will like you even if you're    12
irregular and have acne. They will come up with a good reason why you never wrote the great American novel. They
will cry in your beer with you. They will put your name in
the pot. They will let you off the hook. Fat people will gab,
giggle, guffaw, gallumph, gyrate, and gossip. They are generous, giving and gallant. They are gluttonous and goodly and
great. What you want when you're down is soft and jiggly,
not muscled and stable. Fat people know this. Fat people have
plenty of room. Fat people will take you in.

## For Critical Thinking

### QUESTIONS ABOUT PURPOSE

1. Why does Jordan think thin people are dull and dangerous?
2. What are the positive characteristics she identifies with
   fat people?

### QUESTIONS ABOUT AUDIENCE

1. How does Jordan's use of the pronoun "us" identify her readers
   as fat or who like "fat people"?
2. What assumptions does she make about her "thin" readers?

### QUESTIONS ABOUT STRATEGIES

1. How does Jordan use the alternating pattern to clarify the distinctions between thin and fat people?
2. How does she use the example of the jigsaw puzzle to illustrate
   the differences between thin and fat people?

## For Writing and Research

1. *Analyze* the way Jordan combines both alternating and then divided strategies to clarify her comparison.
2. *Practice* by comparing and contrasting two other personality types, such as neat and sloppy people.
3. *Argue* that there are true psychological, social, and health benefits to being thin.
4. *Synthesize:* Research the primary dangers of obesity. Then use your findings to argue for the value of a balanced approach to food consumption.

## Alexander Theroux: *The Candy Man*

Alexander Theroux was born in 1939 in Medford, Massachusetts, and educated at St. Francis College and the University of Virginia. The "somewhat eccentric" member of a literary family, Theroux once entered a Trappist monastery, observing two years of silence. He writes for such magazines as *Esquire, The New Yorker,* and *Harper's.* His longer writing includes three novel—*Three Wogs* (1972), *Darconville's Cat* (1981), and *An Adultery* (1987),—several collections of essays, and *Enigma of Al Capp* (1999) and *Laura Warholic: or, The Sexual Intellectual* (2007). In "The Candy Man," Theroux uses his "good taste" to classify various types of candy.

I BELIEVE THERE are few things that show as much variety—that there is so much of—as American candy. The national profusion of mints and munch, pops and drops, creamfills, cracknels, and chocolate crunch recapitulates the good and plenty of the Higher Who.

Candy has its connoisseurs and critics both. To some, for instance, it's a subject of endless fascination—those for whom a root-beer lozenge can taste like a glass of Shakespeare's "brown October" and for whom little pilgrims made of maple sugar can look like Thracian gold—and to others, of course, it's merely a wilderness of abominations. You can sample one piece with a glossoepiglottic gurgle of joy or chew down another empty as shade, thin as fraud.

In a matter where tastes touch to such extremes one is  3
compelled to seek through survey what in the inquiry might
yield, if not conclusions sociologically diagnostic, then at least
a simple truth or two. Which are the best candies? Which are
the worst? And why? A sense of fun can feed on queer candy,
and there will be no end of argument, needless to say. But,
essentially, it's all in the *taste*.

---

*It's with candy . . . that we say hello, goodbye,
and I'm sorry.*

---

The trash candies—a little lobby, all by itself, of the American  4
Dental Association—we can dismiss right away: candy cigarettes, peanut brittle, peppermint lentils, Life Savers (white
only), Necco Wafers (black especially), Christmas candy in
general, gumballs, and above all that glaucous excuse for tuck
called ribbon candy, which little kids, for some reason, pounce
on like a duck on a June bug. I would put in this category all
rock candy, general Woolworthiana, and all those little nerks,
cupcake sparkles, and decorative sugars like silver buckshot
that, though inedible, are actually eaten by the young and
indiscriminate, whose teeth turn eerie almost on contact.

In the category of the most abominable tasting, the win-  5
ner— on both an aesthetic and a gustatory level—must surely
be the inscribed Valentine candy heart ("Be Mine," "Hot
Stuff," "Love Ya," etc.). In high competition, no doubt, are
bubble-gum cigars, candy corn, marshmallow chicks (bunnies,
pumpkins, etc.), Wacky Wafers (eight absurd-tasting coins in
as many flavors), Blow Pops—an owl's pellet of gum inside a
choco-pop!—Canada Mints, which taste like petrified Egyptian
lime, and, last but not least, those unmasticable beige near-
candy peanuts that, insipid as rubber erasers, not only have no
bite—the things just give up—but elicit an indescribable anti-
taste that is best put somewhere between stale marshmallow
and dry wall. Every one of these candies, sweating right now in
a glass case at your corner store, is to my mind proof positive
of original sin. They can be available, I suggest, only for having

become favorites of certain indiscriminate fatties at the Food and Drug Administration who must buy them by the bag. But a bat could see they couldn't be a chum of ours if they chuckled.

Now, there are certain special geniuses who can distinguish  6 candies, like wine, by rare deduction: district, commune, vineyard, growth. They know all the wrappers, can tell twinkle from tartness in an instant, and often from sniffing nothing more than the empty cardboard sled of a good candy bar can summon up the scent of the far Moluccas. It is an art, or a skill at least *tending* to art. I won't boast the ability, but allow me, if you will, to be a professor of the fact of it. The connoisseur, let it be said, has no special advantage. Candy can be found everywhere: the airport lounge, the drugstore, the military PX, the student union, the movie house, the company vending machine—old slugs, staler than natron, bonking down into a tray—but the *locus classicus*, of course, is the corner store.

The old-fashioned candy store, located on a corner in the  7 American consciousness, is almost obsolete. Its proprietor is always named Sam; for some reason he's always Jewish. Wearing a hat and an apron, he shuffles around on spongy shoes, still tweezers down products from the top shelf with one of those antique metal grapplers, and always keeps the lights off. He has the temperament of a black mamba and makes his best customers, little kids with faces like midway balloons, show him their nickels before they order. But he keeps the fullest glass case of penny candy in the city—spiced baby gums, malted-milk balls, fruit slices, candy fish, aniseed balls, candy pebbles, jelly beans, raspberry stars, bull's-eyes, boiled sweets, the lot. The hit's pretty basic. You point, he scoops a dollop into a little white bag, weighs it, subtracts two, and then asks, "Wot else?"

A bright rack nearby holds the bars, brickbats, brand  8 names. Your habit's never fixed when you care about candy. You tend to look for new bars, recent mints, old issues. The log genre, you know, is relatively successful: Bolsters, Butter-fingers, Clark Bars, Baby Ruths, O. Henrys, and the Zagnut with its sweet razor blades. Although they've dwindled in size, like the dollar that buys fewer and fewer of them, all have a lushness of weight and good nap and nacre, a chewiness, a thewiness, with tastes in suitable *contre coup* to the bite. You pity their distant cousins, the airy and unmemorable Kit-Kats, Choco'lites, Caravels, and Paydays, Johnny-come-latelies with shallow souls and Rice Krispie hearts that taste like budgie food. A submember of American candy, the peanut group, is strong—crunch is often the kiss in a candy romance—and you might favorably settle on several: Snickers, Go Aheads, Mr. Goodbars, Reese's Peanut Butter Cups (of negligible crunch, however), the Crispy, the Crunch, the Munch—a nice trilogy of onomatopoeia—and even the friendly little Creeper, a peanut-butter-filled tortoise great for the one-bite dispatch: Pleep!

Vices, naturally, coexist with virtues. The coconut category, 9 for instance—Mounds, Almond Joys, Waleecos, and their ilk—is toothsome, but can often be tasted in flakes at the folds and rim of your mouth days later. The licorice group, Nibs, Licorice Rolls, Twizzlers, Switzer Twists, and various whips and shoelaces, often smoky to congestion, usually leave a nice smack in the aftertaste. The jawbreaker may last a long time, yes—but who wants it to? Tootsie Pop Drops, Charms, Punch, Starburst Fruit Chews (sic!), base-born products of base beds, are harder than affliction and better used for checker pieces or musket flints or supports to justify a listing bureau.

There are certain candies, however—counter, original, 10 spare, strange—that are gems in both the bite and the taste, not the usual grim marriage of magnesium stearate to lactic acid, but rare confections at democratic prices. Like lesser breeds raising pluperfect cain with the teeth, these are somehow always forgiven, any such list must include: Mary Janes, Tootsie Rolls, Sky Bars, Squirrels, Mint Juleps, the wondrous B-B Bats (a hobbit-sized banana taffy pop still to be had for 3¢), and other unforgettable knops and knurls like turtles, chocolate bark, peanut clusters, burnt peanuts, and those genius-inspired pink pillows with the peanut-butter surprise inside for which we're all so grateful. There's an *intelligence* here that's difficult to explain, a sincerity at the essence of each, where solid line plays against stipple and a truth

function is solved always to one's understanding and always—
*O altitudo!*—to one's taste.

Candy is sold over the counter, won in raffles, awarded    11
on quiz shows, flogged door to door, shipped wholesale in
boxes, thrown out at ethnic festivals, and incessantly hawked
on television commercials by magic merrymen—clownish
pied-pipers in cap-and-bells—who inspirit thousands of kids
to come hopping and hurling after them, singing all the way
to Cavityville. Why do we eat it? Who gets us started eating it?
What sexual or social or semantic preferences are indicated by
which pieces? The human palate—tempted perhaps by Nature
*herself* in things like slippery elm, spruce gum, sassafras, and
various berries—craves sweetness almost everywhere, so much
so, in fact, that the flavor of candy commonly denominates
American breath-fresheners, throat discs, mouthwash, lipstick, fluoride treatments, toothpaste, cough syrup, breakfast
cereals, and even dental floss, fruit salts, and glazes. It's with
candy—whether boxed, bottled, or bowed—that we say hello,
goodbye, and I'm sorry. There are regional issues, candies
that seem at home only in one place and weirdly forbidden
in others (you don't eat it at the ballpark, for instance, but
on the way there), and of course seasonal candies: Christmas
tiffin, Valentine's Day assortments, Thanksgiving mixes, and
the diverse quiddities of Easter: spongy chicks, milk-chocolate
rabbits, and those monstrositous roc-like eggs twilled with
piping on the outside and filled with a huge blob of neosac-
charine galvaslab! Tastes change, develop, grow fixed. Your
aunt likes mints. Old ladies prefer jars of crystallized ginger.
Rednecks wolf Bolsters, trollops suck lollipops, college girls
opt for berries-in-tins. Truck drivers love to click Gobstoppers
around the teeth, pubescents crave sticky sweets, the viler the
better, and of course great fat teenage boys, their complex-
ions aflame with pimples and acne, aren't fussy and can gorge
down a couple of dollars' worth of Milky Ways, $100,000
Bars, and forty-eleven liquid cherries at one go!

The novelty factor can't be discounted. The wrapper often    12
memorizes a candy for you, so capitalism, with its Hollywood
brain, has devised for us candies in a hundred shapes and

shocks—no, I'm not thinking of the comparatively simple Bit-O-Honey, golden lugs on waxed paper, or Little Nips, wax tonic bottles filled with disgustingly sweet liquid, or even the Pez, those little units that, upon being thumbed, dispense one of the most evil-tasting cacochymicals on earth. Buttons-on-paper—a trash candy—is arguably redeemed by inventiveness of vehicle. But here I'm talking about packaging *curiosa*—the real hype! Flying Saucers, for example, a little plasticene capsule with candy twinkles inside! Big Fake Candy Pens, a goofy fountain pen cartridged with tiny pills that taste like canvatex! Razzles ("First It's a Candy, Then It's a Gum")! Bottle Caps ("The Soda Pop Candy")! Candy Rings, a rosary of cement-tasting beads strung to make up a fake watch, the dial of which can be eaten as a final emetic. Rock Candy on a String, blurbed on the box as effective for throat irritation: "Shakespeare in *Henry IV* mentions its therapeutic value." You believe it, right?

And then there's the pop group: Astro Pops, an umbrella-shaped sugar candy on a stick; Whistle Pops ("The Lollipop with the Built-in Whistle"); and Ring Pops, cherry- or watermelon-flavored gems on a plastic stick—you suck the jewel. So popular are the fizzing Zotz, the trifling Pixie Stix with its powdered sugar to be lapped out of a straw, the Lik-M-Aid Fun Dip, another do-it-yourself stick-licker, and the explosion candies like Space Dust, Volcano Rocks, and Pop Rocks that candy-store merchants have to keep behind the counter to prevent them from getting nobbled. Still, these pale next to the experience of eating just plain old jimmies (or sprinkles or chocolate shot, depending on where you live), which although generally reserved for, and ancillary to, ice cream, can be deliciously munched by the fistful for a real reward. With jimmies, we enter a new category all its own. M&M's, for example: you don't eat them, you mump them. [13]

Other mumping candies might be sugar babies, hostia almonds, bridge mixes, burnt peanuts, and pectin jelly beans. (Jelloids in general lend themselves well to the mump.) I don't think Goobers and Raisinets—dull separately—are worth anything unless both are poured into the pocket, [14]

commingled, and mumped by the handful at the movies.
(The clicking sound they make is surely one of the few pleasures left in life.) This is a family that can also include Pom
Poms, Junior Mints, Milk Duds, Boston Baked Beans, Sixlets
("Candy-coated chocolate-flavored candies"—a nice flourish,
that), and the disappointingly banal Jujubes—which reminds
me. There are certain candies, Jujubes for instance, that one
is just too embarrassed to name out loud (forcing one to
point through the candy case and simply grunt), and num-
bered among these must certainly be Nonpareils, Jujyfruits,
Horehound Drops, and Goldenberg's Peanut Chews. You
know what I mean. "Give me a *mrmrglpxph* bar." And you
point. Interesting, right?

Interesting. The very word is like a bell that tolls me back to     15
more trenchant observations. Take the Sugar Daddy—it curls
up like an elf-shoe after a manly bite and upon being sucked
could actually be used for flypaper. (The same might be said
for the gummier but more exquisite Bonomo's Turkish Taffy.)
The Heath bar—interesting again—a knobby little placket
that can be drawn down half-clenched teeth with a slucking
sound for an instant chocolate rush, whereupon you're left
with a lovely ingot of toffee as a sweet surprise. The flac-
cid Charleston Chew, warm, paradoxically becomes a proud
phallus when cold. (Isn't there a metaphysics in the making
here?) Who, until now, has ever given these candies the kind
of credit they deserve?

I have my complaints, however, and many of them cross     16
categories. M&M's, for instance, click beautifully but never
perspire—it's like eating bits of chrysoprase or sea shingle, you
know? Tic Tacs, as well: brittle as gravel and brainless. And
while Good 'n' Plenty's are worthy enough mumpers, that
little worm of licorice inside somehow puts me off. There is,
further, a tactile aspect in candy to be considered. Milk Duds
are too nobby and ungeometrical, Junior Mints too relentlessly exact, whereas Reese's Peanut Butter Cups, with their
deep-dish delicacy, fascinate me specifically for the strict rib-
bing around the sides. And then color. The inside of the vapid
Three Musketeers bar is the color of wormwood. White bark?

Leprosy. Penuche? Death. And then of Hot Tamales, Atom Bombs, cinnamon hearts, and red hots?—swift, slow, sweet, sour, a dazzle, dim, okay, but personally I think it a matter of breviary that *heat* should have nothing at all to do with candy.

And then Chunkies—tragically, too big for one bite, too    17 little for two. Tootsie Pops are always twiddling off the stick. The damnable tab never works on Hershey Kisses, and it takes a month and two days to open one; even the famous Hershey bar, maddeningly overscored, can never be opened without breaking the bar, and prying is always required to open the ridiculously overglued outer wrapper. (The one with almonds—why?—always slides right out!) And then there are those candies that always promise more than they ever give— the Marathon bar for length, cotton candy for beauty: neither tastes as good as it looks, as no kipper ever tastes as good as it smells, disappointment leads to resentment, and biases form. Jujyfruits—a viscous disaster that is harder than the magnificent British wine-gum (the single greatest candy on earth)—stick in the teeth like tar and have ruined more movies for me than Burt Reynolds, which is frankly going some. And finally Chuckles, father of those respectively descending little clones—spearmint leaves, orange slices, and gum drops—always taste better if dipped in ice water before eating, a want that otherwise keeps sending you to a water fountain for hausts that never seem to end.

You may reasonably charge me, in conclusion, with an    18 insensibility for mistreating a particular kind of candy that you, for one reason or another, cherish, or bear me ill will for passing over another without paying it due acknowledgment. But here it's clearly a question of taste, with reasoning generally subjective. Who, after all, can really explain how tastes develop? Where preferences begin? That they exist is sufficient, and fact, I suppose, becomes its own significance. Which leads me to believe that what Dr. Johnson said of Roman Catholics might less stupidly be said of candies: "In every thing in which they differ from us, they are wrong."

## For Critical Thinking

### QUESTIONS ABOUT PURPOSE

1. Is Theroux's purpose to describe the various types of candy or to argue that some types are better than others?
2. How does his assertion that "essentially, it's all in the *taste*" determine the purpose of his essay?

### QUESTIONS ABOUT AUDIENCE

1. Does Theroux assume that his readers are connoisseurs or critics of candy?
2. What is his purpose in addressing his readers in the last paragraph of his essay?

### QUESTIONS ABOUT STRATEGIES

1. How many subcategories—trash, gem, seasonal, tactile, color—does Theroux use to illustrate his assertion that "few things . . . show as much variety . . . as American candy"?
2. How does he use the word *mumping* to identify a special subcategory of candy?

## For Writing and Research

1. *Analyze* the way Theroux's elaborate style appeals to his reader's taste.
2. *Practice* by classifying different kinds of cereal or beverage.
3. *Argue* that the craving for sweetness is biologically or environmentally determined.
4. *Synthesize* the information about candy from the American Dental Association and the Food and Drug Administration. Then argue that candy is a valuable or valueless food product.

## Michael Pollan: *Eat Food: Food Defined*

Michael Pollan was born in 1955 in New York
City, and educated at Bennington College and
Columbia University. He has taught writing
at the University of Pittsburgh, the University
of Wisconsin, and the University of California
at Berkeley. He has written numerous articles
and books, including four *New York Times* best
sellers: *The Botany of Desire: A Plant's-Eye View
of the World* (2001), *The Omnivore's Dilemma: A
Natural History of Four Meals* (2006), *In Defense
of Food: An Eater's Manifesto* (2008), and *Food
Rules: An Eater's Manual* (2010). In "Eat Food:
Food Defined," taken from *In Defense of Food: An
Eater's Manifesto*, Pollan works to define just what
should count as food.

THE FIRST TIME I heard the advice to "just eat food" it was   1
in a speech by Joan Gussow, and it completely baffled
me. Of course you should eat food—what else is there to eat?
But Gussow, who grows much of her own food on a flood-
prone finger of land jutting into the Hudson River, refuses
to dignify most of the products for sale in the supermarket
with that title. "In the thirty-four years I've been in the field
of nutrition," she said in the same speech, "I have watched
real food disappear from large areas of the supermarket and
from much of the rest of the eating world." Taking food's
place on the shelves has been an unending stream of foodlike
substitutes, some seventeen thousand new ones every year—
"products constructed largely around commerce and hope,
supported by frighteningly little actual knowledge." Ordinary

food is still out there, however, still being grown and even occasionally sold in the supermarket, and this ordinary food is what we should eat.

But given our current state of confusion and given the thousands of products calling themselves food, this is more easily said than done. So consider these related rules of thumb. Each proposes a different sort of map to the contemporary food landscape, but all should take you to more or less the same place. 2

DON'T EAT ANYTHING YOUR GREAT GRAND- 3
MOTHER WOULDN'T RECOGNIZE AS FOOD. Why your great grandmother? Because at this point your mother and possibly even your grandmother is as confused as the rest of us; to be safe we need to go back at least a couple generations, to a time before the advent of most modern foods. So depending on your age (and your grandmother), you may need to go back to your great or even great-great grandmother. Some nutritionists recommend going back even further. John Yudkin, a British nutritionist whose early alarms about the dangers of refined carbohydrates were overlooked in the 1960s and 1970s, once advised, "Just don't eat anything your Neolithic ancestors wouldn't have recognized and you'll be ok."

What would shopping this way mean in the supermarket? 4
Well imagine your great grandmother at your side as you roll down the aisles. You're standing together in front of the dairy case. She picks up a package of Go-Gurt Portable Yogurt tubes—and has no idea what this could possibly be. Is it a food or a toothpaste? And how, exactly, do you introduce it into your body? You could tell her it's just yogurt in a squirtable form, yet if she read the ingredients label she would have every reason to doubt that that was in fact the case. Sure, there's some yogurt in there,  but there are also a dozen other things that aren't remotely yogurtlike, ingredients she would probably fail to recognize as foods of any kind, including high-fructose corn syrup, modified corn starch, kosher gelatin, carrageenan, tricalcium phosphate, natural and artificial flavors, vitamins, and so forth. (And there's a whole other list of ingredients for the "berry bubblegum bash" flavoring,

containing everything but berries or bubblegum.) How did yogurt, which in your great grandmother's day consisted of simply milk inoculated with a bacterial culture, ever get to be so complicated? Is a product like Go-Gurt Portable Yogurt still a whole food? A food of any kind? Or is it just a food product?

There are in fact hundreds of foodish products in the supermarket that your ancestors simply wouldn't recognize as food: breakfast cereal bars transacted by bright white veins representing, but in reality having nothing to do with milk; "protein waters" and "non-dairy creamer"; cheeselike food-stuffs equally innocent of any bovine contribution; cakelike cylinders (with creamlike fillings) called Twinkles that never grow stale. *Don't eat anything incapable of rotting* is another personal policy you might consider adopting. 5

---

### *"More fattening, less nutritious!"*

---

There are many reasons to avoid eating such complicated food products beyond the various chemical additives and corn and soy derivatives they contain. One of the problems with products of food science is that, as Joan Gussow has pointed out, they lie to your body; their artificial colors and flavors and synthetic sweeteners and novel fats confound the senses we rely on to assess new foods and prepare our bodies to deal with them. Foods that lie leave us with little choice but eat by numbers, consulting labels rather than our senses. 6

It's true that foods have long been processed in order to preserve them, as when we pickle or ferment or smoke, but industrial processing aims to do much more than extend shelf life. Today foods are processed in ways specifically designed to sell us more food by pushing our evolutionary buttons—our inborn preferences for sweetness and fat and salt. These qualities are difficult to find in nature but cheap and easy for the food scientist to deploy, with the result that processing induces us to consume much more of these ecological rarities 7 than is good for us. "Tastes great, less filling!" could be the motto for most processed foods, which are far more energy dense than most whole foods: They contain much less water, fiber, and micronutrients, and generally much more sugar and fat, making them at the same time, to coin a marketing slogan, "More fattening, less nutritious!"

The great grandma rule will help keep many of these prod- 8 ucts out of your cart. But not all of them. Because thanks to the FDA's willingness, post-1973, to let food makers freely alter the identity of "traditional foods that everyone knows" without having to call them imitations, your great grand- mother could easily be fooled into thinking that that loaf of bread or wedge of cheese is in fact a loaf of bread or a wedge of cheese. This is why we need slightly more detailed personal policy to capture these imitation foods; to wit.

AVOID FOOD PRODUCTS CONTAINING INGRE- 9 DIENTS THAT ARE A) UNFAMILIAR, B) UNPRO- NOUNCEABLE, C) MORE THAN FIVE IN NUMBER, OR THAT INCLUDE D) HIGH-FRUCTOSE CORN SYRUP. None of these characteristics, not even the last one, is necessarily harmful in and of itself, but all of them are reli- able markers for foods that have been highly processed to the point where they may no longer be what they purport to be. They have crossed over from foods to food products.

Consider a loaf of bread, one of the "traditional foods that 10 everyone knows" specifically singled out for protection in the 1938 imitation rule. As your grandmother could tell you, bread is traditionally made using a remarkably small num- ber of familiar ingredients: flour, yeast, water, and a pinch of salt will do it. But industrial bread—even industrial whole- grain bread—has become a far more complicated product of modern food science (not to mention commerce and hope). Here's the complete ingredients list for Sara Lee's Soft & Smooth Whole Grain White Bread. (Wait a minute—isn't "Whole Grain White Bread" a contradiction in terms? Evi- dently not any more.)

Enriched bleached flour [wheat flour, malted barley flour, 11 niacin, iron thiamine mononitrate (vitamin $B_1$), riboflavin (vitamin B$_2$), folic acid], water, whole grains [whole wheat flour, brown rice flour (rice flour, rice bran)], high-fructose corn syrup [hello], whey, wheat gluten, yeast, cellulose. Contains 2 percent or less of each of the following: honey, calcium sulfate, vegetable oil (soybean and/or cottonseed oils), salt, butter (cream, salt), dough conditioners (may contain one or more of the following; mono- and diglycerides, ethoxylated mono- and diglycerides, ascorbic acid, enzymes, azodicarbonamide), guar gum, calcium propionate (preservative), distilled vinegar, yeast nutrients (monocalcium phosphate, calcium sulfate, ammonium sulfate), corn starch, natural flavor, betacarontene (color), vitamin D$_3$, soy lecithin, soy flour.

There are many things you could say about this intricate    12
loaf of "bread," but note first that even if it managed to slip by your great grandmother (because it is a loaf of bread, or at least is called one and strongly resembles one), the product fails every test proposed under rule number two: It's got unfamiliar ingredients (monoglycerides I've heard of before, but ethoxylated monoglycerides?); unpronounceable ingredients (try "azodicarbonamide"); it exceeds the maximum of five ingredients (by roughly thirty-six); and it contains high-fructose corn syrup. Sorry, Sara Lee, but your Soft & Smooth Whole Grain White Bread is not food and if not for the indulgence of the FDA could not even be labeled "bread."

Sara Lee's Soft & Smooth Whole Grain White Bread could    13
serve as a monument to the age of nutritionism. It embodies the latest nutritional wisdom from science and government (which in its most recent food pyramid recommends that at least half our consumption of grain come from whole grains) but leavens that wisdom with the commercial recognition that American eaters (and American children in particular) have come to prefer their wheat highly refined—which is to say, cottonly soft, snowy white, and exceptionally sweet on the tongue. In its marketing materials, Sara Lee treats this clash of interests as some sort of Gordian knot—it speaks in terms of an ambitious quest to build a "no compromise" loaf—which only the most sophisticated food science could possibly cut.

And so it has, with the invention of whole-grain white bread. 14
Because the small percentage of whole grains in the bread would
render it that much less sweet than, say, all-white Wonder
Bread—which scarcely waits to be chewed before transforming itself into glucose—the food scientists have added high-
fructose corn syrup and honey to make up the difference; to
overcome the problematic heft and toothsomeness of a real
whole-grain bread, they've deployed "dough conditioner,"
including guar gum and the aforementioned azodicarbonamide, to simulate the texture of supermarket white bread. By
incorporating certain varieties of albino wheat, they've managed to maintain that deathly appealing Wonder Bread pallor.

Who would have thought Wonder Bread would ever 15
become an ideal of aesthetic and gustatory perfection to
which bakers would actually aspire—Sara Lee's Mona Lisa?

Very often food science's efforts to make traditional foods 16
more nutritious make them much more complicated, but not
necessarily any better for you. To make dairy products low
fat, it's not enough to remove the fat. You then have to go
to great lengths to preserve the body or creamy texture by
working in all kinds of food additives. In the case of low-fat
or skim milk, that usually means adding powdered milk. But
powdered milk contains oxidized cholesterol, which scientists
believe is much worse for your arteries than ordinary cholesterol, so food makers sometimes compensate by adding
antioxidants, further complicating what had been a simple
one-ingredient whole food. Also, removing the fat makes it
that much harder for your body to absorb the fat-soluble vitamins that are one of the reasons to drink milk in the first place.

All this heroic and occasionally counterproductive food 17
science has been undertaken in the name of our health—so
that Sara Lee can add to its plastic wrapper the magic words
"good source of whole grain" or a food company can bally-
hoo the even more magic words "low fat." Which brings us to
a related food policy that may at first sound counterproductive to a health-conscious eater:

AVOID FOOD PRODUCTS THAT MAKE HEALTH 18
CLAIMS. For a food product to make health claims on its

package it must first have a package, so right off the bat it's more likely to be a processed than a whole food. Generally speaking, it is only the big food companies that have the wherewithal to secure FDA-approved health claims for their products and then trumpet them to the world. Recently, however, some of the tonier fruits and nuts have begun boasting about their health-enhancing properties, and there will surely be more as each crop council scrounges together the money to commission its own scientific study. Because all plants contain antioxidants, all these studies are guaranteed to find something on which to base a health-oriented marketing campaign.

19    But for the most part it is the products of food science that make the boldest health claims, and these are often founded on incomplete and often erroneous science—the dubious fruits of nutritionism. Don't forget that trans-fat-rich margarine, one of the first industrial foods to claim it was healthier than the traditional food it replaced, turned out to give people heart attacks. Since that debacle, the FDA, under tremendous pressure from industry, has made it only easier for food companies to make increasingly doubtful health claims, such as the one Frito-Lay now puts on some of its chips—that eating them is somehow good for your heart. If you bother to read the health claims closely (as food marketers make sure consumers seldom do), you will find that there is often considerably less to them than meets the eye.

20    Consider a recent "qualified" health claim approved by the FDA for (don't laugh) corn oil. ("Qualified" is a whole new category of health claim, introduced in 2002 at the behest of industry.) Corn oil, you may recall, is particularly high in the omega-6 fatty acids we're already consuming far too many of.

21    Very limited and preliminary scientific evidence suggests that eating about one tablespoon (16 grams) of corn oil daily may reduce the risk of heart disease due to the unsaturated fat content in corn oil.

22    The tablespoon is a particularly rich touch, conjuring images of moms administering medicine, or perhaps cod-liver oil, to their children. But what the FDA gives with one hand,

it takes away with the other. Here's the small-print "qualification" of this already notably diffident health claim:

[The] FDA concludes that there is little scientific evidence   23
supporting this claim.

And then to make matters still more perplexing:               24

To achieve this possible health benefit, corn oil is to replace  25
a similar amount of saturated fat and not increase the total
number of calories you eat in a day.

This little masterpiece of pseudoscientific bureaucratese    26
was extracted from the FDA by the manufacturer of Mazola
corn oil. It would appear that "qualified" is an official FDA
euphemism for "all but meaningless." Though someone
might have let the consumer in on this game: The FDA's
own research indicates that consumers have no idea what to
make of qualified health claims (how would they?), and its
rules allow companies to promote the claims pretty much any
way they want—they can use really big type for the claim, for
example, and then print the disclaimers in teeny-tiny type.
No doubt we can look forward to a qualified health claim
for high-fructose corn syrup, a tablespoon of which probably does contribute to your health—as long as it replaces a
comparable amount of, say, poison in your diet and doesn't
increase the total number of calories you eat in a day.

When corn oil and chips and sugary breakfast cereals can all  27
boast being good for your heart, health claims have become
hopelessly corrupt. The American Heart Association currently
bestows (for a fee) its heart-healthy seal of approval on Lucky
Charms, Cocoa Puffs, and Trix cereals, Yoo-hoo lite chocolate drink, and Healthy Choice's Premium Caramel Swirl Ice
Cream Sandwich—this at a time when scientists are coming
to recognize that dietary sugar probably plays a more important role in heart disease than dietary fat. Meanwhile, the
genuinely heart-healthy whole foods in the produce section,
lacking the financial and political clout of the packaged goods
a few sales aisles over, are mute. But don't take the silence
of the yams as a sign that they have nothing valuable to say
about health.

## For Critical Thinking

### QUESTIONS ABOUT PURPOSE

1. What is Pollan's purpose in trying to distinguish between real food and foodlike substitutes?
2. How do his "rules of thumb" help him define real food?

### QUESTIONS ABOUT AUDIENCE

1. How does Pollan's rule about "your grandmother" help him identify his audience?
2. How does his rule about "unpronounceable ingredients" help him connect with his readers?

### QUESTIONS ABOUT STRATEGIES

1. How does Pollan use the example of a loaf of bread to illustrate the difference between real food and foodlike products?
2. How does his warnings about health claims clarify his definition?

## For Writing and Research

1. *Analyze* the way Pollan uses the strategy of defining negatively to establish his definition of real food.
2. *Practice:* "Shake the hand that feeds you." Use this adage to compare the taste of the food you purchased at a farmer's market with the same "food" purchased at a supermarket.
3. *Argue* that a simple change in government policy—such as restricting the number of words that can be used in food labeling—will eliminate fraudulent health claims.
4. *Synthesize:* Research the ingredients in a processed food you like to eat. Then explain what such ingredients add or subtract from the value of the food.

## Eric Schlosser:
### *Why McDonald's Fries Taste So Good*

Eric Schlosser was born in 1959 in New York City and educated at Princeton University and Oxford University. He works as an investigative reporter for *Atlantic Monthly*. His books include *Fast Food Nation: The Dark Side of the All-American Meal* (2001), *Reefer Madness: Sex, Drugs, and Cheap Labor in the American Black Market* (2003), and *Command and Control: Nuclear Weapons, the Damascus Accident, and the Illusion of Safety* (2013). His disclosure in *Fast Food Nation* that McDonald's fries taste so good because, until 1990, they were fried in "beef tallow" caused Hindus to destroy McDonald's restaurants in India and vegetarians to file a class action suit against McDonald's in America.

T HE FRENCH FRY WAS "almost sacrosanct for me," Ray Kroc, one of the founders of McDonald's, wrote in his autobiography, "its preparation a ritual to be followed religiously." During the chain's early years french fries were made from scratch every day. Russet Burbank potatoes were peeled, cut into shoestrings, and fried in McDonald's kitchens. As the chain expanded nationwide, in the mid-1960s, it sought to cut labor costs, reduce the number of suppliers, and ensure that its fries tasted the same at every restaurant. McDonald's began switching to frozen french fries in 1966—and few customers noticed the difference. Nevertheless, the change had a profound effect on the nation's agriculture and diet. A familiar food had been transformed into a highly processed industrial commodity. McDonald's fries now come from huge manufacturing plants that can peel, slice, cook, and freeze two million pounds of potatoes a day. The rapid expansion of McDonald's and the popularity of its low-cost, mass-produced fries changed the way Americans eat. In 1960, Americans consumed an average of about eighty-one pounds of fresh potatoes and four pounds of frozen french fries. In 2000, they consumed an average of about fifty pounds of fresh potatoes and thirty pounds of frozen fries. Today, McDonald's is the largest buyer of potatoes in the United States.

*The rise and fall of corporate empires—of soft-drink companies, snack-food companies, and fast-food chains—is often determined by how their products taste.*

The taste of McDonald's french fries played a crucial role    2
in the chain's success—fries are much more profitable than hamburgers—and was long praised by customers, competitors, and even food critics. James Beard loved McDonald's fries. Their distinctive taste does not stem from the kind of potatoes that McDonald's buys, the technology that processes them, or the restaurant equipment that fries them: other chains use Russet Burbanks, buy their french fries from the same large processing companies, and have similar fryers in their restaurant kitchens. The taste of a french fry is largely determined by the cooking oil. For decades McDonald's cooked its french fries in a mixture of about seven percent cottonseed oil and 93 percent beef tallow. The mixture gave the fries their unique flavor—and more saturated beef fat per ounce than a McDonald's hamburger.

In 1990, amid a barrage of criticism over the amount of    3
cholesterol in its fries, McDonald's switched to pure vegetable oil. This presented the company with a challenge: how to make fries that subtly taste like beef without cooking them in beef tallow. A look at the ingredients in McDonald's french fries suggests how the problem was solved. Toward the end of

the list is a seemingly innocuous yet oddly mysterious phrase: "natural flavor." That ingredient helps to explain not only why the fries taste so good but also why most fast food—indeed, most of the food Americans eat today—tastes the way it does.

Open your refrigerator, your freezer, your kitchen cup-   4 boards, and look at the labels on your food. You'll find "natural flavor" or "artificial flavor" in just about every list of ingredients. The similarities between these two broad categories are far more significant than the differences. Both are man-made additives that give most processed food most of its taste. People usually buy a food item the first time because of its packaging or appearance. Taste usually determines whether they buy it again. About 90 percent of the money that Americans now spend on food goes to buy processed food. The canning, freezing, and dehydrating techniques used in processing destroy most of food's flavor—and so a vast industry has arisen in the United States to make processed food palatable. Without this flavor industry today's fast food would not exist. The names of the leading American fast-food chains and their best-selling menu items have become embedded in our popular culture and famous worldwide. But few people can name the companies that manufacture fast food's taste.

The flavor industry is highly secretive. Its leading companies   5 will not divulge the precise formulas of flavor compounds or the identities of clients. The secrecy is deemed essential for protecting the reputations of beloved brands. The fast-food chains, understandably, would like the public to believe that the flavors of the food they sell somehow originate in their restaurant kitchens, not in distant factories run by other firms. A McDonald's french fry is one of countless foods whose flavor is just a component in a complex manufacturing process. The look and the taste of what we eat now are frequently deceiving—by design.

## THE FLAVOR CORRIDOR

The New Jersey Turnpike runs through the heart of the fla-   6 vor industry, an industrial corridor dotted with refineries and chemical plants. International Flavors & Fragrances (IFF), the

world's largest flavor company, has a manufacturing facility off
Exit 8A in Dayton, New Jersey; Givaudan, the world's second-
largest flavor company, has a plant in East Hanover. Haarmann
& Reimer, the largest German flavor company, has a plant in
Teterboro, as does Takasago, the largest Japanese flavor company.
Flavor Dynamics has a plant in South Plainfield; Frutarom is in
North Bergen; Elan Chemical is in Newark. Dozens of com-
panies manufacture flavors in the corridor between Teaneck
and South Brunswick. Altogether the area produces about two
thirds of the flavor additives sold in the United States.

The IFF plant in Dayton is a huge pale-blue building     7
with a modern office complex attached to the front. It sits
in an industrial park, not far from a BASF plastics factory,
a Jolly French Toast factory, and a plant that manufactures
Liz Claiborne cosmetics. Dozens of tractor-trailers were
parked at the IFF loading dock the afternoon I visited, and
a thin cloud of steam floated from a roof vent. Before entering the plant, I signed a nondisclosure form, promising not
to reveal the brand names of foods that contain IFF flavors.
The place reminded me of Willy Wonka's chocolate factory.
Wonderful smells drifted through the hallways, men and
women in neat white lab coats cheerfully went about their
work, and hundreds of little glass bottles sat on laboratory
tables and shelves. The bottles contained powerful but fragile flavor chemicals, shielded from light by brown glass and
round white caps shut tight. The long chemical names on the
little white labels were as mystifying to me as medieval Latin.
These odd-sounding things would be mixed and poured and
turned into new substances, like magic potions.

I was not invited into the manufacturing areas of the IFF     8
plant, where, it was thought, I might discover trade secrets.
Instead I toured various laboratories and pilot kitchens, where
the flavors of well-established brands are tested or adjusted,
and where whole new flavors are created. IFF's snack-and-
savory lab is responsible for the flavors of potato chips, corn
chips, breads, crackers, breakfast cereals, and pet food. The
confectionery lab devises flavors for ice cream, cookies, candies, toothpastes, mouthwashes, and antacids. Everywhere

I looked, I saw famous, widely advertised products sitting on laboratory desks and tables. The beverage lab was full of brightly colored liquids in clear bottles. It comes up with flavors for popular soft drinks, sports drinks, bottled teas, and wine coolers, for all-natural juice drinks, organic soy drinks, beers, and malt liquors. In one pilot kitchen I saw a dapper food technologist, a middle-aged man with an elegant tie beneath his crisp lab coat, carefully preparing a batch of cookies with white frosting and pink-and-white sprinkles. In another pilot kitchen I saw a pizza oven, a grill, a milk-shake machine, and a french fryer identical to those I'd seen at innumerable fast-food restaurants.

In addition to being the world's largest flavor company,   9 IFF manufactures the smells of six of the ten best-selling fine perfumes in the United States, including Estée Lauder's Beautiful, Clinique's Happy, Lancôme's Trésor, and Calvin Klein's Eternity. It also makes the smells of household products such as deodorant, dishwashing detergent, bath soap, shampoo, furniture polish, and floor wax. All these aromas are made through essentially the same process: the manipulation of volatile chemicals. The basic science behind the scent of your shaving cream is the same as that governing the flavor of your TV dinner.

## "NATURAL" AND "ARTIFICIAL"

Scientists now believe that human beings acquired the sense   10 of taste as a way to avoid being poisoned. Edible plants generally taste sweet, harmful ones bitter. The taste buds on our tongues can detect the presence of half a dozen or so basic tastes, including sweet, sour, bitter, salty, astringent, and umami, a taste discovered by Japanese researchers—a rich and full sense of deliciousness triggered by amino acids in foods such as meat, shellfish, mushrooms, potatoes, and seaweed. Taste buds offer a limited means of detection, however, compared with the human olfactory system, which can perceive thousands of different chemical aromas. Indeed, "flavor" is primarily the smell of gases being released by the chemicals you've just put in your mouth. The aroma of a food can be responsible for as much as 90 percent of its taste.

The act of drinking, sucking, or chewing a substance 11 releases its volatile gases. They flow out of your mouth and up your nostrils, or up the passageway in the back of your mouth, to a thin layer of nerve cells called the olfactory epithelium, located at the base of your nose, right between your eyes. Your brain combines the complex smell signals from your olfactory epithelium with the simple taste signals from your tongue, assigns a flavor to what's in your mouth, and decides if it's something you want to eat.

A person's food preferences, like his or her personality, are 12 formed during the first few years of life, through a process of socialization. Babies innately prefer sweet tastes and reject bitter ones; toddlers can learn to enjoy hot and spicy food, bland health food, or fast food, depending on what the people around them eat. The human sense of smell is still not fully understood. It is greatly affected by psychological factors and expectations. The mind focuses intently on some of the aromas that surround us and filters out the overwhelming majority. People can grow accustomed to bad smells or good smells; they stop noticing what once seemed overpowering. Aroma and memory are somehow inextricably linked. A smell can suddenly evoke a long-forgotten moment. The flavors of childhood foods seem to leave an indelible mark, and adults often return to them, without always knowing why. These "comfort foods" become a source of pleasure and reassurance—a fact that fast-food chains use to their advantage. Childhood memories of Happy Meals, which come with french fries, can translate into frequent adult visits to McDonald's. On average, Americans now eat about, four servings of french fries every week.

The human craving for flavor has been a largely unac- 13 knowledged and unexamined force in history. For millennia royal empires have been built, unexplored lands traversed, and great religions and philosophies forever changed by the spice trade. In 1492 Christopher Columbus set sail to find seasoning. Today the influence of flavor in the world marketplace is no less decisive. The rise and fall of corporate empires—of soft-drink companies, snack-food companies, and fast-food chains—is often determined by how their products taste.

The flavor industry emerged in the mid-nineteenth cen- 14 tury, as processed foods began to be manufactured on a large scale. Recognizing the need for flavor additives, early food processors turned to perfume companies that had long experience working with essential oils and volatile aromas. The great perfume houses of England, France, and the Netherlands produced many of the first flavor compounds. In the early part of the twentieth century Germany took the technological lead in flavor production, owing to its powerful chemical industry. Legend has it that a German scientist discovered methyl anthranilate, one of the first artificial flavors, by accident while mixing chemicals in his laboratory. Suddenly the lab was filled with the sweet smell of grapes. Methyl anthranilate later became the chief flavor compound in grape Kool-Aid. After World War II much of the perfume industry shifted from Europe to the United States, settling in New York City near the garment district and the fashion houses. The flavor industry came with it, later moving to New Jersey for greater plant capacity. Man-made flavor additives were used mostly in baked goods, candies, and sodas until the 1950s, when sales of processed food began to soar. The invention of gas chromatographs and mass spectrometers—machines capable of detecting volatile gases at low levels—vastly increased the number of flavors that could be synthesized. By the mid-1960s flavor companies were churning out compounds to supply the taste of Pop Tarts, Bac-Os, Tab, Tang, Filet-O-Fish sandwiches, and literally thousands of other new foods.

The American flavor industry now has annual revenues of 15 about $1.4 billion. Approximately 10,000 new processed-food products are introduced every year in the United States. Almost all of them require flavor additives. And about nine out of ten of these products fail. The latest flavor innovations and corporate realignments are heralded in publications such as *Chemical Market Reporter*, *Food Chemical News*, *Food Engineering*, and *Food Product Design*. The progress of IFF has mirrored that of the flavor industry as a whole. IFF was formed in 1958, through the merger of two small companies. Its annual revenues have grown almost fifteenfold since the early 1970s, and it currently has manufacturing facilities in twenty countries.

Today's sophisticated spectrometers, gas chromatographs, 16 and headspace-vapor analyzers provide a detailed map of a food's flavor components, detecting chemical aromas present in amounts as low as one part per billion. The human nose, how-ever, is even more sensitive. A nose can detect aromas present in quantities of a few parts per trillion—an amount equivalent to about 0.000000000003 percent. Complex aromas, such as those of coffee and roasted meat, are composed of volatile gases from nearly a thousand different chemicals. The smell of a strawberry arises from the interaction of about 350 chemicals that are present in minute amounts. The quality that people seek most of all in a food—flavor—is usually present in a quan-tity too infinitesimal to be measured in traditional culinary terms such as ounces or teaspoons. The chemical that provides the dominant flavor of bell pepper can be tasted in amounts as low as 0.02 parts per billion; one drop is sufficient to add flavor to five average-size swimming pools. The flavor additive usually comes next to last in a processed food's list of ingredients and often costs less than its packaging. Soft drinks contain a larger proportion of flavor additives than most products. The flavor in a twelve-ounce can of Coke costs about half a cent.

The color additives in processed foods are usually present 17 in even smaller amounts than the flavor compounds. Many of New Jersey's flavor companies also manufacture these color additives, which are used to make processed foods look fresh and appealing. Food coloring serves many of the same decorative purposes as lipstick, eye shadow, mascara—and is often made from the same pigments. Titanium dioxide, for example, has proved to be an especially versatile mineral. It gives many processed candies, frostings, and icings their bright white color; it is a common ingredient in women's cosmetics; and it is the pigment used in many white oil paints and house paints. At Burger King, Wendy's, and McDonald's coloring agents have been added to many of the soft drinks, salad dressings, cookies, condiments, chicken dishes, and sandwich buns.

Studies have found that the color of a food can greatly 18 affect how its taste is perceived. Brightly colored foods frequently seem to taste better than bland-looking foods, even when the flavor compounds are identical. Foods that somehow look off-color often seem to have off tastes. For thousands of years human beings have relied on visual cues to help determine what is edible. The color of fruit suggests whether it is ripe, the color of meat whether it is rancid. Flavor researchers sometimes use colored lights to modify the influence of visual cues during taste tests. During one experiment in the early 1970s people were served an oddly tinted meal of steak and french fries that appeared normal beneath colored lights. Everyone thought the meal tasted fine until the lighting was changed. Once it became apparent that the steak was actually blue and the fries were green, some people became ill.

The federal Food and Drug Administration (FDA) does not 19 require companies to disclose the ingredients of their color or flavor additives so long as all the chemicals in them are considered by the agency to be GRAS ("generally recognized as safe"). This enables companies to maintain the secrecy of their formulas. It also hides the fact that flavor compounds often contain more ingredients than the foods to which they give taste. The phrase "artificial strawberry flavor" gives little hint of the chemical wizardry and manufacturing skill that can make a highly processed food taste like strawberries.

A typical artificial strawberry flavor, like the kind found 20 in a Burger King strawberry milk shake, contains the following ingredients: amyl acetate, amyl butyrate, amyl valerate, anethol, anisyl formate, benzyl acetate, benzyl isobutyrate, butyric acid, cinnamyl isobutyrate, cinnamyl valerate, cognac essential oil, diacetyl, dipropyl ketone, ethyl acetate, ethyl amyl ketone, ethyl butyrate, ethyl cinnamate, ethyl heptanoate, ethyl heptylate, ethyl lactate, ethyl methylphenylglycidate, ethyl nitrate, ethyl propionate, ethyl valerate, heliotropin, hydroxyphenyl-2-butanone (10 percent solution in alcohol), α-ionone, isobutyl anthranilate, isobutyl butyrate, lemon essential oil, maltol, 4-methylacetophenone, methyl anthranilate, methyl benzoate, methyl cinnamate, methyl heptine carbonate, methyl naphthyl ketone, methyl salicylate, mint essential oil, neroli essential oil, nerolin, neryl isobutyrate, orris butter, phenethyl alcohol, rose, rum ether, γ-undecalactone, vanillin, and solvent.

Although flavors usually arise from a mixture of many different volatile chemicals, often a single compound supplies the dominant aroma. Smelled alone, that chemical provides an unmistakable sense of the food. Ethyl-2-methyl butyrate, for example, smells just like an apple. Many of today's highly processed foods offer a blank palette: whatever chemicals are added to them will give them specific tastes. Adding methyl-2-pyridyl ketone makes something taste like popcorn. Adding ethyl-3-hydroxy butanoate makes it taste like marshmallow. The possibilities are now almost limitless. Without affecting appearance or nutritional value, processed foods could be made with aroma chemicals such as hexanal (the smell of freshly cut grass) or 3-methyl butanoic acid (the smell of body odor). [21]

The 1960s were the heyday of artificial flavors in the United States. The synthetic versions of flavor compounds were not subtle, but they did not have to be, given the nature of most processed food. For the past twenty years food processors have tried hard to use only "natural flavors" in their products. According to the FDA, these must be derived entirely from natural sources—from herbs, spices, fruits, vegetables, beef, chicken, yeast, bark, roots, and so forth. Consumers prefer to see natural flavors on a label, out of a belief that they are more healthful. Distinctions between artificial and natural flavors can be arbitrary and somewhat absurd, based more on how the flavor has been made than on what it actually contains. [22]

"A natural flavor," says Terry Acree, a professor of food science at Cornell University, "is a flavor that's been derived with an out-of-date technology." Natural flavors and artificial flavors sometimes contain exactly the same chemicals, produced through different methods. Amyl acetate, for example, provides the dominant note of banana flavor. When it is [23] distilled from bananas with a solvent, amyl acetate is a natural flavor. When it is produced by mixing vinegar with amyl alcohol and adding sulfuric acid as a catalyst, amyl acetate is an artificial flavor. Either way it smells and tastes the same. "Natural flavor" is now listed among the ingredients of everything from Health Valley Blueberry Granola Bars to Taco Bell Hot Taco Sauce.

A natural flavor is not necessarily more healthful or purer    24 than an artificial one. When almond flavor—benzaldehyde—is derived from natural sources, such as peach and apricot pits, it contains traces of hydrogen cyanide, a deadly poison. Benzaldehyde derived by mixing oil of clove and amyl acetate does not contain any cyanide. Nevertheless, it is legally considered an artificial flavor and sells at a much lower price. Natural and artificial flavors are now manufactured at the same chemical plants, places that few people would associate with Mother Nature.

## A TRAINED NOSE AND A POETIC SENSIBILITY

The small and elite group of scientists who create most of the    25 flavor in most of the food now consumed in the United States are called "flavorists." They draw on a number of disciplines in their work: biology, psychology, physiology, and organic chemistry. A flavorist is a chemist with a trained nose and a poetic sensibility. Flavors are created by blending scores of different chemicals in tiny amounts—a process governed by scientific principles but demanding a fair amount of art. In an age when delicate aromas and microwave ovens do not easily co-exist, the job of the flavorist is to conjure illusions about processed food and, in the words of one flavor company's literature, to ensure "consumer likeability." The flavorists with whom I spoke were discreet, in keeping with the dictates of their trade. They were also charming, cosmopolitan, and ironic. They not only enjoyed fine wine but could identify the chemicals that give each grape its unique aroma. One flavorist compared his work to composing music. A well-made flavor compound will have a "top note" that is often followed by a "dry-down" and a "leveling-off," with different chemicals responsible for each stage. The taste of a food can be radically altered by minute changes in the flavoring combination. "A little odor goes a long way," one flavorist told me.

In order to give a processed food a taste that consumers 26 will find appealing, a flavorist must always consider the food's "mouthfeel"—the unique combination of textures and chemical interactions that affect how the flavor is perceived. Mouthfeel can be adjusted through the use of various fats, gums, starches, emulsifiers, and stabilizers. The aroma chemicals in a food can be precisely analyzed, but the elements that make up mouthfeel are much harder to measure. How does one quantify a pretzel's hardness, a french fry's crispness? Food technologists are now conducting basic research in rheology, the branch of physics that examines the flow and deformation of materials. A number of companies sell sophisticated devices that attempt to measure mouthfeel. The TA.XT2i Texture Analyzer, produced by the Texture Technologies Corporation, of Scarsdale, New York, performs calculations based on data derived from as many as 250 separate probes. It is essentially a mechanical mouth. It gauges the most-important rheological properties of a food—bounce, creep, breaking point, density, crunchiness, chewiness, gumminess, lumpiness, rubberiness, springiness, slipperiness, smoothness, softness, wetness, juiciness, spreadability, springback, and tackiness.

Some of the most important advances in flavor manufactur- 27 ing are now occurring in the field of biotechnology. Complex flavors are being made using enzyme reactions, fermentation, and fungal and tissue cultures. All the flavors created by these methods—including the ones being synthesized by fungi— are considered natural flavors by the FDA. The new enzyme-based processes are responsible for extremely true-to-life dairy flavors. One company now offers not just butter flavor but also fresh creamy butter, cheesy butter, milky butter, savory melted butter, and super-concentrated butter flavor, in liquid or powder form. The development of new fermentation techniques, along with new techniques for heating mixtures of sugar and amino acids, have led to the creation of much more realistic meat flavors.

The McDonald's Corporation most likely drew on these    28
advances when it eliminated beef tallow from its french fries.
The company will not reveal the exact origin of the natural
flavor added to its fries. In response to inquiries from *Vegetarian Journal*, however, McDonald's did acknowledge that its
fries derive some of their characteristic flavor from "an animal
source." Beef is the probable source, although other meats
cannot be ruled out. In France, for example, fries are sometimes cooked in duck fat or horse tallow.

Other popular fast foods derive their flavor from unex-    29
pected ingredients. McDonald's Chicken McNuggets contain beef extracts, as does Wendy's Grilled Chicken Sandwich.
Burger King's BK Broiler Chicken Breast Patty contains "natural smoke flavor." A firm called Red Arrow Products special-
izes in smoke flavor, which is added to barbecue sauces, snack
foods, and processed meats. Red Arrow manufactures natural
smoke flavor by charring sawdust and capturing the aroma
chemicals released into the air. The smoke is captured in water
and then bottled, so that other companies can sell food that
seems to have been cooked over a fire.

The Vegetarian Legal Action Network recently petitioned    30
the FDA to issue new labeling requirements for foods that
contain natural flavors. The group wants food processors to
list the basic origins of their flavors on their labels. At the
moment vegetarians often have no way of knowing whether a
flavor additive contains beef, pork, poultry, or shellfish. One of
the most widely used color additives—whose presence is often
hidden by the phrase "color added"—violates a number of
religious dietary restrictions, may cause allergic reactions
in susceptible people, and comes from an unusual source.
Cochineal extract (also known as carmine or carminic acid) is
made from the desiccated bodies of female *Dactylopius coccus
Costa*, a small insect harvested mainly in Peru and the Canary
Islands. The bug feeds on red cactus berries, and color from
the berries accumulates in the females and their unhatched
larvae. The insects are collected, dried, and ground into a
pigment. It takes about 70,000 of them to produce a pound
of carmine, which is used to make processed foods look pink,

red, or purple. Dannon strawberry yogurt gets its color from carmine, and so do many frozen fruit bars, candies, and fruit fillings, and Ocean Spray pink-grapefruit juice drink.

In a meeting room at IFF, Brian Grainger let me sample some of the company's flavors. It was an unusual taste test—there was no food to taste. Grainger is a senior flavorist at IFF, a soft-spoken chemist with graying hair, an English accent, and a fondness for understatement. He could easily be mistaken for a British diplomat or the owner of a West End brasserie with two Michelin stars. Like many in the flavor industry, he has an Old World, old-fashioned sensibility. When I suggested that IFF's policy of secrecy and discretion was out of step with our mass-marketing, brand-conscious, self-promoting age, and that the company should put its own logo on the countless products that bear its flavors, instead of allowing other companies to enjoy the consumer loyalty and affection inspired by those flavors, Grainger politely disagreed, assuring me that such a thing would never be done. In the absence of public credit or acclaim, the small and secretive fraternity of flavor chemists praise one another's work. By analyzing the flavor formula of a product, Grainger can often tell which of his counterparts at a rival firm devised it. Whenever he walks down a supermarket aisle, he takes a quiet pleasure in seeing the well-known foods that contain his flavors. 31

Grainger had brought a dozen small glass bottles from the lab. After he opened each bottle, I dipped a fragrance-testing filter into it—a long white strip of paper designed to absorb aroma chemicals without producing off notes. Before placing each strip of paper in front of my nose, I closed my eyes. Then I inhaled deeply, and one food after another was conjured from the glass bottles. I smelled fresh cherries, black olives, sautéed onions, and shrimp. Grainger's most remarkable creation took me by surprise. After closing my eyes, I suddenly smelled a grilled hamburger. The aroma was uncanny, almost miraculous—as if someone in the room were flipping burgers on a hot grill. But when I opened my eyes, I saw just a narrow strip of white paper and a flavorist with a grin. 32

## For Critical Thinking

### QUESTIONS ABOUT PURPOSE

1. What does Schlosser want to demonstrate about the effect of McDonald's transforming a familiar food into an industrial commodity?
2. How does his description of the flavor industry support his analysis?

### QUESTIONS ABOUT AUDIENCE

1. How does Schlosser's description of his tour of International Flavors and Fragrances establish his credibility with his audience?
2. How does his invitation to "Open your refrigerator, your freezer, your kitchen cupboards and look at the labels on your food" help him connect with his readers?

### QUESTIONS ABOUT STRATEGIES

1. How does Schlosser's analysis of "the human craving for flavor" support his argument?
2. How does his description of "natural" and "artificial" flavors explain how McDonald's eliminated beef tallow from its french fries?

## For Writing and Research

1. *Analyze* the way Schlosser explains various scientific processes to determine flavor and taste.
2. *Practice* by writing an essay about the way you formed a taste for a particular food.
3. *Argue* that the Food and Drug Administration needs to develop a more sophisticated set of regulations to control the practices Schlosser describes.
4. *Synthesize:* Research some of the latest flavor innovations heralded in *Chemical Market Reporter; Food Chemical News; Food Engineering;* and *Food Product Design.* Then speculate about how one of these flavors might add to the taste of one of your favorite foods.

Peter Singer was born in 1946 in Melbourne, Australia, and educated at University of Melbourne and Oxford University. He is widely known for his writing about animal equality, most notably in *Animal Liberation* (1975). He has lectured at universities around the world, such as Harvard, Stanford, Yale, and Oxford. He is currently a Laureate Professor at the Centre for Applied Philosophy and Public Ethics at the University of Melbourne, and Professor of Bioethics at Princeton University. His books include *Practical Ethics* (1979), *The Expanding Circle: Ethics and Sociobiology* (1981), *How Are We to Live?* (1994), and *The Life You Can Save: Acting Now to End World Poverty* (2009). In "Equality for Animals," excerpted from *Practical Ethics*, Singer argues against eating meat as part of a larger argument in favor of equality for animals.

## ANIMALS AS FOOD

For most people in modern, urbanized societies, the principal   1
form of contact with nonhuman animals is at meal times. The use of animals for food is probably the oldest and the most widespread form of animal use. There is also a sense in which it is the most basic form of animal use, the foundation stone of an ethic that sees animals as things for us to use to meet our needs and interests.

If animals count in their own right, our use of animals for   2
food becomes questionable. Inuit living a traditional lifestyle in the far north where they must eat animals or starve can

reasonably claim that their interest in surviving overrides that of the animals they kill. Most of us cannot defend our diet in this way. People living in industrialized societies can easily obtain an adequate diet without the use of animal flesh. Meat is not necessary for good health or longevity. Indeed, humans can live healthy lives without eating any animal products at all, although a vegan diet requires greater care, especially for young children, and a B12 vitamin supplement should be taken. Nor is animal production in industrialized societies an efficient way of producing food, because most of the animals consumed have been fattened on grains and other foods that we could have eaten directly. When we feed these grains to animals, only about one-quarter—and in some cases, as little as one-tenth—of the nutritional value remains as meat for human consumption. So, with the exception of animals raised entirely on grazing land unsuitable for crops, animals are eaten neither for health nor to increase our food supply. Their flesh is a luxury, consumed because people like its taste. (The livestock industry also contributes more to global warming than the entire transport sector.)

---

*The case against using animals for food is at its strongest when animals are made to lead miserable lives so that their flesh can be made available to humans at the lowest possible cost.*

---

In considering the ethics of the use of animal products for human food in industrialized societies, we are considering a situation in which a relatively minor human interest must be balanced against the lives and welfare of the animals involved. The principle of equal consideration of interests does not allow major interests to be sacrificed for minor interests. 3

The case against using animals for food is at its strongest when animals are made to lead miserable lives so that their flesh can be made available to humans at the lowest possible 4 cost. Modern forms of intensive farming apply science and technology to the attitude that animals are objects for us to use. Competition in the marketplace forces meat producers to copy rivals who are prepared to cut costs by giving animals more miserable lives. In buying the meat, eggs, or milk produced in these ways, we tolerate methods of meat production that confine sentient animals in cramped, unsuitable conditions for the entire duration of their lives. They are treated like machines that convert fodder into flesh, and any innovation that results in a higher "conversion ratio" is liable to be adopted. As one authority on the subject has said, "cruelty is acknowledged only when profitability ceases." To avoid speciesism, we must stop these practices. Our custom is all the support that factory farmers need. The decision to cease giving them that support may be difficult, but it is less difficult than it would have been for a white Southerner to go against the values of his community and free his slaves. If we do not change our dietary habits, how can we censure those slave holders who would not change their own way of living?

These arguments apply to animals reared in factory farms— which means that we should not eat chicken, pork, or veal unless we know that the meat we are eating was not produced by factory farm methods. The same is true of beef that has come from cattle kept in crowded feedlots (as most beef does in the United States). Eggs come from hens kept in small wire cages, too small even to allow them to stretch their wings, unless the eggs are specifically sold as "cage-free" or "free-range." (At the time of writing, Switzerland has banned the battery cage, and the European Union is in the process of phasing it out. In the United States, California voted in 2008 to ban it, and that ban will come into effect in 2015. A law passed in Michigan in 2009 requires battery cages to be phased out over ten years.) Dairy products also often come from cows confined to a barn, unable to go out to pasture. Moreover, to continue to give milk, dairy cows have to be made pregnant every year, and their calf then taken away from them shortly after birth, so we can have the milk. This causes distress to both the cow and the calf.

Concern about the suffering of animals in factory farms 6
does not take us all the way to a vegan diet, because it is possible to buy animal products from animals allowed to graze
outside. (When animal products are labeled "organic," this
should mean that the animals have access to the outdoors,
but the interpretation of this rule is sometimes loose.) The
lives of free-ranging animals are undoubtedly better than
those of animals reared in factory farms. It is still doubtful if
using them for food is compatible with equal consideration
of interests. One problem is, of course, that using them for
food involves killing them (even laying hens and dairy cows
are killed when their productivity starts to drop, which is far
short of their natural life span). . . . Apart from killing them,
there are also many other things done to animals in order to
bring them cheaply to our dinner table. Castration, the separation of mother and young, the breaking up of herds, brand-
ing, transporting, slaughterhouse handling, and finally the
moment of slaughter itself—all of these are likely to involve
suffering and do not take the animals' interests into account.
Perhaps animals can be reared on a small scale without suffering in these ways. Some farmers take pride in producing
"humanely raised" animal products, but the standards of what
is regarded as "humane" vary widely. Any shift toward more
humane treatment of animals is welcome, but it seems unlikely
that these methods could produce the vast quantity of animal products now consumed by our large urban populations.
At the very least, we would have to considerably reduce the
amount of meat, eggs, and dairy products that we consume. In
any case, the important question is not whether animal products *could* be produced without suffering, but whether those
we are considering buying *were* produced without suffering.
Unless we can be confident that they were, the principle of
equal consideration of interests implies that their production
wrongly sacrificed important interests of the animals to satisfy less important interests of our own. To buy the results
of this process of production is to support it and encourage
producers to continue to do it. Because those of us living in
developed societies have a wide range of food choices and do

not need to eat these products, encouraging the continuation of a cruel system of producing animal products is wrong.

For those of us living in cities where it is difficult to know 7 how the animals we might eat have lived and died, this conclusion brings us very close to a vegan way of life. . . .

## ANIMALS EAT EACH OTHER, SO WHY SHOULDN'T WE EAT THEM?

This might be called the Benjamin Franklin Objection because 8 Franklin recounts in his *Autobiography* that he was for a time a vegetarian, but his abstinence from animal flesh came to an end when he was watching some friends prepare to fry a fish they had just caught. When the fish was cut open, it was found to have a smaller fish in its stomach. "Well," Franklin said to himself, "if you eat one another, I don't see why we may not eat you," and he proceeded to do so.

Franklin was at least honest. In telling this story, he con- 9 fesses that he convinced himself of the validity of the objection only after the fish was already in the frying pan and smelling "admirably well"; and he remarks that one of the advantages of being a "reasonable creature" is that one can find a reason for whatever one wants to do. The replies that can be made to this objection are so obvious that Franklin's acceptance of it does testify more to his hunger on that occasion than to his powers of reason. For a start, most animals who kill for food would not be able to survive if they did not, whereas we have no need to eat animal flesh. Next, it is odd that humans, who normally think of the behavior of animals as "beastly" should, when it suits them, use an argument that implies that we ought to look to animals for moral guidance. The most decisive point, however, is that nonhuman animals are not capable of considering the alternatives open to them or of reflecting on the ethics of their diet. Hence, it is impossible to hold the animals responsible for what they do or to judge that because of their killing they "deserve" to be treated in a similar way. Those who read these lines, on the other hand, must consider the justifiability of their dietary habits. You cannot evade responsibility by imitating beings who are incapable of making this choice.

Sometimes people draw a slightly different conclusion from the fact that animals eat each other. This suggests, they think, not that animals deserve to be eaten, but rather that there is a natural law according to which the stronger prey on the weaker, a kind of Darwinian "survival of the fittest" in which by eating animals we are merely playing our part. 10

This interpretation of the objection makes two basic mistakes, one of fact and the other of reasoning. The factual mistake lies in the assumption that our own consumption of animals is part of some natural evolutionary process. This might be true of those who still hunt for food, but it has nothing to do with the mass production of domestic animals in factory farms. 11

Suppose that we did hunt for our food, though, and this was part of some natural evolutionary process. There would still be an error of reasoning in the assumption that because this process is natural it is right. It is, no doubt, "natural" for women to produce an infant every year or two from puberty to menopause, but this does not mean that it is wrong to interfere with this process. We need to understand nature and develop the best theories we can to explain why things are as they are, because only in that way can we work out what the consequences of our actions are likely to be; but it would be a serious mistake to assume that natural ways of doing things are incapable of improvements. . . . 12

## For Critical Thinking

### QUESTIONS ABOUT PURPOSE

1. How does Singer demonstrate that animal flesh is a luxury?
2. How does he make the case against the cruel system of producing animal products?

## QUESTIONS ABOUT AUDIENCE

1. How does Singer's use of the words *our* and *us* help him to identify with his readers?
2. How does his description of factory farms, feed lots, and battery cages evoke his readers' sympathy for his argument?

## QUESTIONS ABOUT STRATEGIES

1. How does Singer challenge Benjamin Franklin's Objection?
2. How does he use the "principle of equal consideration of interests" to make his case against using animals for food?

## For Writing and Research

1. *Analyze* how Singer uses logic to challenge the claims of those people who choose to eat animals at their dinner table.
2. *Practice* by writing about your visit to a place where animals are raised or slaughtered.
3. *Argue* that the livestock industry does or does not contribute to global warming.
4. *Synthesize:* Research the technological innovations that result in a higher "conversion ratio"—a technique that converts cheap fodder into expensive flesh.

# Essay on Food

PHOTO 1 BALANCED DIET

My Plate. On June 2, 2011, First Lady Michelle Obama and USDA Secretary Tom Vilsack released the federal government's new food icon, MyPlate, to serve as a reminder to help consumers make healthier food choices. Examine your own daily diet to determine the degree to which you conform to the balanced meal portrayed in this icon. Then write an essay explaining the reasons for your success or failure in conforming to this healthy plate.

PHOTO 2 FRUIT

Paul Cezanne (1839–1906) painted this still life, *Apples and Oranges*, toward the end of his life. Research the historical tradition of the still life genre and why art historians argue that Cezanne brought new life to this genre. Then write an essay in which you explain how the sumptuous beauty of this painting lured you into eating more fruit.

PHOTO 3 VEGETABLES

The United Nations defines migrant workers as any people working outside their home country. America depends on a migrant workforce to harvest a large portion of its food supply. Research the job descriptions, the living conditions, and the wages of this unskilled workforce that picks our vegetables. Then write an analysis of how this knowledge influences your shopping habits when you arrive in the produce section of your supermarket.

## PHOTO 4 GRAINS

The harvesting combine was invented in the United States in 1834. Early combines were drawn by mules, but after World War II, many farms began to use tractors. Compare the way this photo presents harvesting grains with Photo 3 that presents migrant workers harvesting vegetables. Then write an essay in which you praise or criticize the way machines have changed the work of the farmer.

PHOTO 5 PROTEIN

Most people select some form of meat when they think about adding protein to their diet. And when they select meat to prepare at home or to order off a restaurant menu, most people prefer steak. As this menu from a steak house illustrates, steaks can come from different parts of the cow, and can be cooked to different temperatures. Write an essay on "confessions of a steak eater" in which you document your history selecting, grilling, and eating America's favorite meat.

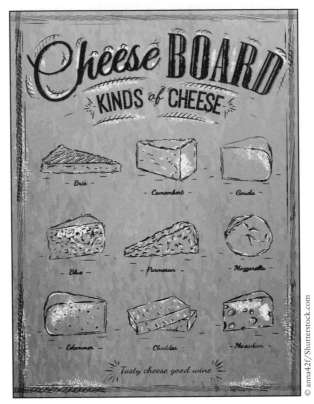

## PHOTO 6 DAIRY

All dairy products come from milk, but the most complex product is cheese because it comes in so many tastes, textures, and colors. Cheeses are often served on a board that, at formal meals, is passed with the fruit or salad course—which may come first, or, in many European countries, last. The British Cheese Board, a government agency, claims that there are more than 700 distinct cheeses in the United Kingdom. Write an essay on one of the many fascinating topics related to cheese—from the history of cheese making to the development of processed cheese—that you can find on websites such as Cheese.com.

© 1000 Words/Shutterstock.com

## PHOTO 7 SUPERMARKET

This photograph illustrates the long aisles, the high shelves stacked with product, and the absence of a grocery clerk you encounter at the typical supermarket. The hands on the cart suggest there is a shopper present, but she is faceless. Write an essay analyzing the psychological effect of shopping for your food in such a store.

## PHOTO 8 FARMER'S MARKET

This photograph illustrates a completely different kind of shopping experience. The handsome clerk—perhaps the farmer—is showing his prospective customer samples of locally grown food. Her shopping basket suggests that she sees shopping for food at this farmer's market as an intimate transaction. Write an essay comparing the advantages and disadvantages of shopping at a farmer's market. If you have never shopped at a farmer's market, check out the experience before you write your essay.

Laura Fraser:
*Why I Stopped Being a Vegetarian*

Laura Fraser was born in 1961 in Denver, Colorado, and educated at Wesleyan University. She has taught writing at the University of California, Berkeley School of Journalism. Her writing, mostly about food, has appeared in *Vogue, Mother Jones, Gourmet, Bon Appétit,* and the *New York Times.* Her books include *The Animal Rights Handbook: Everyday Ways to Save Lives* (1990), *Losing It: America's Obsession with Weight and the Industry That Feeds It* (1997), and a memoir, *An Italian Affair* (2001). In "Why I Stopped Being a Vegetarian," originally published in Salon.com, Fraser enumerates the many reasons why she became and then, after fifteen years, gave up being a vegetarian.

U NTIL A FEW MONTHS AGO, I had been a vegetarian for 1 15 years. Like most people who call themselves vegetarians (somewhere between 4 and 10 percent of us, depending on the definition; only 1 percent of Americans are vegans, eating no animal products at all), I wasn't strict about it. I ate dairy products and eggs, as well as fish. That made me a pesco-ovo-lacto-vegetarian, which isn't a category you can choose for special meals on airlines.

About a year ago, in Italy, it dawned on me that a little pan- 2 cetta was really good in pasta, too. After failing to convince myself that pancetta was a vegetable, I became a pesco-ovo-lacto-pancetta-vegetarian, with a "Don't Ask, Don't Tell" policy about chicken broth. It was a slippery slope from there.

Nevertheless, for most of those 15 years, hardly a piece of   3
animal flesh crossed my lips. Over the course of that time,
many people asked me why I became a vegetarian. I came up
with vague answers: my health, the environment, the imprac-
ticality and heartlessness of killing animals for food when we
can survive perfectly well on soy burgers. It was political, it
was emotional and it made me special, not to mention slightly
morally superior to all those bloodthirsty carnivores out there.

---

*But who was I kidding? If I were hungry
enough, I'd kill a cow in a heartbeat. I'd
practically kill a cow for a great pair of shoes.*

---

The truth is, I became a vegetarian in college for two rea-   4
sons. One was that meat was more expensive than lentils, and
I was broke, or broke enough to choose to spend my limited
budget on other classes of ingestibles. The other was that
I was not a lesbian.

This is not to say that all lesbians are carnivores; in fact,   5
there's probably a higher percentage of vegetarians among
lesbians than most other groups. But there was a fair amount
of political pressure to be something in those days. Since, as a
privileged white girl from suburban Denver, I couldn't really
identify with any oppressed minority group, I was faced with
becoming a lesbian in order to prove my political mettle. I
had to decide between meat and men, and for better or worse,
I became a vegetarian.

The identity stuck, even though the political imperative   6
for my label faded. It wasn't an identity that ever really fit:
My friends thought it odd that such an otherwise hedonistic
woman should have that one ascetic streak. It was against my
nature, they said. But by then, I'd started to believe the other
arguments about vegetarianism.

First was health. There's a lot of evidence that vegetarians   7
live longer, have lower cholesterol levels and are thinner than

meat-eaters. This is somewhat hard to believe, since for the first few years of not eating meat, I was basically a cheese-tarian. Try leafing through some of those vegetarian recipe books from the early '80s: You added three cups of grated cheddar to everything but the granola. Then vegetarianism went through that mathematical phase where you had to fig-ure out which proteins you had to combine with which in order to get a complete protein. Since many nutritionists will tell you people don't need that much protein anyway, I gave up, going for days and days without so much as contemplat-ing beans or tofu.

For whatever haphazard combination of proteins I ate, 8 being a vegetarian did seem to have a stunning effect on my cholesterol level. This, of course, could be genetic. But when I had a very involved physical exam once at the Cooper Insti-tute for Aerobic Fitness in Dallas, my total cholesterol level was a super-low 135, and my ratio of HDL (good) choles-terol to LDL (evil) was so impressive that the doctor drawled, "Even if you had heart disease, you would be reversing it." This good news, far from reassuring me that I could well afford a few barbecued ribs now and then, spurred me on in my vegetarianism, mainly because my cholesterol numbers effectively inoculated me against the doctor's advice that I also needed to lose 15 pounds.

"Why?" I asked. "Don't you lose weight to lower your 9 cholesterol?"

He couldn't argue with that. Whether or not vegetarians 10 are leaner than carnivores, in my case I was happy to more than make up the calories with carbohydrates, which, perhaps not coincidentally, I always craved.

After the health rationale came the animal rights one. Like 11 most vegetarians, I cracked Peter Singer's philosophical trea-tise on animal rights, and bought his utilitarian line that if you don't have to kill animals, and it potentially causes suf-fering, you shouldn't do it. (Singer, now at Princeton, has recently come under attack for saying that if a human being's incapacitated life causes more suffering than good, it is OK to kill him.)

It's hard to know where to stop with utilitarianism. Do I    12
need a cashmere sweater more than those little shorn goats
need to be warm themselves? Do animals really suffer if they
have happy, frolicking lives before a quick and painless end?
Won't free-range do?

My animal rights philosophy had a lot of holes from the    13
start. First of all, I excluded fish from the animal kingdom—
not only because fish taste delicious grilled with a little butter and garlic, but also because they make it a lot easier to
be a vegetarian when you go out to restaurants. Now that's
utilitarian. Besides, as soon as you start spending your time
fretting about the arguments that crowd the inner pens of animal rights philosophy—do fish think?—then you know you're
experiencing a real protein deficiency.

I rationalized the fish thing by telling myself I would eat    14
anything I would kill myself. I had been fly-fishing with my
dad and figured a few seconds of flopping around was out-
weighed by the merits of trout almondine. (Notice that I, not
the fish, was doing the figuring.) But who was I kidding? If I
were hungry enough, I'd kill a cow in a heartbeat. I'd practically kill a cow just for a great pair of shoes.

Which brings me to the leather exception. As long as other    15
people are eating cow, I decided, I might as well recycle the
by-products and diminish the harm by wearing leather jackets
and shoes. When everyone stopped eating meat, I'd stop buying leather jackets and shoes. In the meantime, better stock up.

Then there's the environmental rationale. There is no    16
doubt, as Frances Moore Lappe first pointed out in her 1971
book *Food First*, that there is a huge loss of protein resources
going from grain to meat, and that some animals, especially
cattle and Americans, use up piggish amounts of water, grain
and crop land.

But the problem really isn't meat, but too much meat—    17
over-grazing, over-fishing and over-consumption. If Americans just ate less meat—like driving cars less often—the
problem could be alleviated without giving up meat entirely.
That approach has worked for centuries, and continues to
work in Europe.

All my deep vegetarian questioning was silenced one day ₁₈ when a friend ordered roasted rosemary chicken for two. I thought I'd try "just a bite," and then I was ripping into it like a starving hyena. Roasted chicken, I realized, is wonderful. Meat is good.

From a culinary point of view, that's obvious. Consider ₁₉ that most vegetarians live in America and England, places tourists do not visit for the food. You don't find vegetarians in France, and rarely in Italy. Enough said.

As for health, if nutritionists are always telling you to "lis- ₂₀ ten to your body," mine was definitely shouting for more meat. One roasted bird unleashed 15 years' worth of cravings. All of a sudden I felt like I had a bass note playing in my body to balance out all those soprano carbohydrates. Forget about winning the low-cholesterol Olympics. For the first time in a long time, I felt satisfied.

As a vegetarian, not only had I denied myself something ₂₁ I truly enjoyed, I had been anti-social. How many times had I made a hostess uncomfortable by refusing the main course at a dinner party, lamely saying I'd "eat around it"? How often did my vegetarianism cause other people to go to extra trouble to make something special for me to eat, and why did it never occur to me that that was selfish? How about the time, in a small town in Italy, when the chef had presented me with a plate of very special local sausage, since I was the American guest—and I had refused it, to the mortification of my Italian friends? Or when a then-boyfriend, standing in the meat section of the grocery store, forlornly told a friend, "If only I had a girlfriend who ate meat"? If eating is a socially conscious act, you have to be conscious of the society of your fellow homo sapiens along with the animals. And we humans, as it happens, are omnivores.

## For Critical Thinking

### QUESTIONS ABOUT PURPOSE

1. How does Fraser create situational excuses to avoid complete devotion to vegetarianism?
2. How does her realization that she is being selfish support her argument?

### QUESTIONS ABOUT AUDIENCE

1. How does Fraser's presentation of her visit to the doctor help her connect with her readers?
2. What assumptions about her readers does she make when she presents the European approach to eating?

### QUESTIONS ABOUT STRATEGIES

1. How does Fraser present her two initial reasons for becoming a vegetarian?
2. How does she present her more serious reasons?

## For Writing and Research

1. *Analyze* the terms Fraser creates to replace strict vegetarianism.
2. *Practice* by writing a narrative about your attempts to avoid or assert your special dietary preferences.
3. *Argue* that genetics rather than diet is the real cause of your low (or high) cholesterol.
4. *Synthesize:* Research several diet regimens, paying particular attention to the advice about meat and too-much meat. Then write an essay synthesizing this advice into a simple set of rules.

*Story*

## Andre Dubus: *The Fat Girl*

Andre Dubus (1936–1999) was born in Lake Charles, Louisiana, and received his undergraduate degree at McNeese State College. Upon graduation, he was commissioned as a lieutenant in the Marine Corps, rising to the rank of captain when he left the service in 1964 to pursue graduate work in creative writing at the University of Iowa. In 1977, he accepted a professorship at Bradford College where he taught modern fiction and creative writing. He published his short stories in journals such as *Sewanee Review, Carlton Miscellany,* and *North American Review.* His first novel, *The Lieutenant* (1967), based on his military experience, received excellent reviews, as did his novella and his collections of stories, including *Separate Flights* (1975), *Finding a Girl in America* (1980), and *Dancing After Hours* (1996). "The Fat Girl," reprinted from *Adultery and Other Choices* (1977), tells the story of a woman struggling with the difficulties of equating self-identity with the numbers on a scale.

HER NAME WAS LOUISE. Once when she was sixteen, a boy     1
kissed her at a barbecue; he was drunk and he jammed his tongue into her mouth and ran his hands up and down her hips. Her father kissed her often. He was thin and kind and she could see in his eyes when he looked at her the lights of love and pity.

It started when Louise was nine. You must start watching     2
what you eat, her mother would say. I can see you have my metabolism. Louise also had her mother's pale blond hair.

Her mother was slim and pretty, carried herself erectly, and ate very little. The two of them would eat bare lunches, while her older brother ate sandwiches and potato chips, and then her mother would sit smoking while Louise eyed the bread box, the pantry, the refrigerator. Wasn't that good, her mother would say. In five years you'll be in high school and if you're fat the boys won't like you; they won't ask you out. Boys were as far away as five years, and she would go to her room and wait for nearly an hour until she knew her mother was no longer thinking of her, then she would creep into the kitchen and, listening to her mother talking on the phone, or her footsteps upstairs, she would open the bread box, the pantry, the jar of peanut butter. She would put the sandwich under her shirt and go outside or to the bathroom to eat it.

Her father was a lawyer and made a lot of money and came    3
home looking pale and happy. Martinis put color back in his face, and at dinner he talked to his wife and two children. Oh give her a potato, he would say to Louise's mother. She's a growing girl. Her mother's voice then became tense: If she has a potato she shouldn't have dessert. She should have both, her father would say, and he would reach over and touch Louise's cheek, or hand, or arm.

In high school she had two girlfriends and at night and    4
on weekends they rode in a car or went to movies. In movies she was fascinated by fat actresses. She wondered why they were fat. She knew why she was fat: she was fat because she was Louise. Because God had made her that way. Because she wasn't like her friends Joan and Marjorie, who drank milkshakes after school and were all bones and tight skin. But what about those actresses, with their talents, with their broad and profound faces? Did they eat as heedlessly as Bishop Humphries and his wife who sometimes came to dinner and, as Louise's mother said, gorged between amenities? Or did they try to lose weight, did they go about hungry and angry and thinking of food? She thought of them eating lean meats and salads with friends, and then going home and building strange large sandwiches with French bread. But mostly she believed they did not go through these failures; they were

fat because they chose to be. And she was certain of something else too: she could see it in their faces: they did not eat secretly. Which she did: her creeping to the kitchen when she was nine became, in high school, a ritual of deceit and pleasure. She was a furtive eater of sweets. Even her two friends did not know her secret.

Joan was thin, gangling, and flat-chested; she was attractive 5 enough and all she needed was someone to take a second look at her face, but the school was large and there were pretty girls in every classroom and walking all the corridors, so no one ever needed to take a second look at Joan. Marjorie was thin too, an intense, heavy-smoking girl with brittle laughter. She was very intelligent, and with boys she was shy because she knew she made them uncomfortable, and because she was smarter than they were and so could not understand or could not believe the levels they lived on. She was to have a nervous breakdown before earning her Ph.D. in philosophy at the University of California, where she met and married a physicist and discovered within herself an untrammelled passion: she made love with her husband on the couch, the carpet, in the bathtub, and on the washing machine. By that time much had happened to her and she never thought of Louise. Joan would finally stop growing and begin moving with grace and confidence. In college she would have two lovers and then several more during the six years she spent in Boston before marrying a middle-aged editor who had two sons in their early teens, who drank too much, who was tenderly, boyishly grateful for her love, and whose wife had been killed while rock-climbing in New Hampshire with her lover. She would not think of Louise either, except in an earlier time, when lovers were still new to her and she was ecstatically surprised each time one of them loved her and, sometimes at night, lying in a man's arms, she would tell how in high school no one dated her, she had been thin and plain (she would still believe that: that she had been plain; it had never been true) and so had been forced into the weekend and night-time company of a neurotic smart girl and a shy fat girl. She would say this with self-pity exaggerated by Scotch and her need to be more deeply loved by the man who held her.

She never eats, Joan and Marjorie said of Louise. They    6
ate lunch with her at school, watched her refusing potatoes,
ravioli, fried fish. Sometimes she got through the cafeteria
line with only a salad. That is how they would remember
her: a girl whose hapless body was destined to be fat. No one
saw the sandwiches she made and took to her room when
she came home from school. No one saw the store of Milky
Ways, Butterfingers, Almond Joys, and Hersheys far back on
her closet shelf, behind the stuffed animals of her childhood.
She was not a hypocrite. When she was out of the house she
truly believed she was dieting; she forgot about the candy,
as a man speaking into his office dictaphone may forget the
lewd photographs hidden in an old shoe in his closet. At other
times, away from home, she thought of the waiting candy
with near lust. One night driving home from a movie, Marjorie said: "You're lucky you don't smoke; it's *incredible* what I
go through to hide it from my parents." Louise turned to her
with a smile which was elusive and mysterious; she yearned
to be home in bed, eating chocolate in the dark. She did not
need to smoke; she already had a vice that was insular and
destructive.

She brought it with her to college. She thought she would    7
leave it behind. A move from one place to another, a new
room without the haunted closet shelf, would do for her what
she could not do for herself. She packed her large dresses and
went. For two weeks she was busy with registration, with
shyness, with classes; then she began to feel at home. Her
room was no longer like a motel. Its walls had stopped watching her, she felt they were her friends, and she gave them
her secret. Away from her mother, she did not have to be as
elaborate; she kept the candy in her drawer now.

The school was in Massachusetts, a girls' school. When she    8
chose it, when she and her father and mother talked about it
in the evenings, everyone so carefully avoided the word *boys*
that sometimes the conversations seemed to be about nothing
but boys. There are no boys there, the neuter words said; you
will not have to contend with that. In her father's eyes were
pity and encouragement; in her mother's was disappointment,

and her voice was crisp. They spoke of courses, of small classes where Louise would get more attention. She imagined herself in those small classes; she saw herself as a teacher would see her, as the other girls would; she would get no attention.

The girls at the school were from wealthy families, but  9 most of them wore the uniform of another class: blue jeans and work shirts, and many wore overalls. Louise bought some overalls, washed them until the dark blue faded, and wore them to classes. In the cafeteria she ate as she had in high school, not to lose weight nor even to sustain her lie, but because eating lightly in public had become as habitual as good manners. Everyone had to take gym, and in the locker room with the other girls, and wearing shorts on the volleyball and badminton courts, she hated her body. She liked her body most when she was unaware of it: in bed at night, as sleep gently took her out of her day, out of herself. And she liked parts of her body. She liked her brown eyes and sometimes looked at them in the mirror: they were not shallow eyes, she thought; they were indeed windows of a tender soul, a good heart. She liked her lips and nose, and her chin, finely shaped between her wide and sagging cheeks. Most of all she liked her long pale blond hair, she liked washing and drying it and lying naked on her bed, smelling of shampoo, and feeling the soft hair at her neck and shoulders and back.

Her friend at college was Carrie, who was thin and wore  10 thick glasses and often at night she cried in Louise's room. She did not know why she was crying. She was crying, she said, because she was unhappy. She could say no more. Louise said she was unhappy too, and Carrie moved in with her. One night Carrie talked for hours, sadly and bitterly, about her parents and what they did to each other. When she finished she hugged Louise and they went to bed. Then in the dark Carrie spoke across the room: "Louise? I just wanted to tell you. One night last week I woke up and smelled chocolate. You were eating chocolate, in your bed. I wish you'd eat it in front of me, Louise, whenever you feel like it."

Stiffened in her bed, Louise could think of nothing to say.  11 In the silence she was afraid Carrie would think she was asleep and would tell her again in the morning or tomorrow night. Finally she said okay. Then after a moment she told Carrie if she ever wanted any she could feel free to help herself; the candy was in the top drawer. Then she said thank you.

They were roommates for four years and in the summers   12 they exchanged letters. Each fall they greeted with embraces, laughter, tears, and moved into their old room, which had been stripped and cleansed of them for the summer. Neither girl enjoyed summer. Carrie did not like being at home because her parents did not love each other. Louise lived in a small city in Louisiana. She did not like summer because she had lost touch with Joan and Marjorie; they saw each other, but it was not the same. She liked being with her father but with no one else. The flicker of disappointment in her mother's eyes at the airport was a vanguard of the army of relatives and acquaintances who awaited her: they would see her on the streets, in stores, at the country club, in her home, and in theirs; in the first moments of greeting, their eyes would tell her she was still fat Louise, who had been fat as long as they could remember, who had gone to college and returned as fat as ever. Then their eyes dismissed her, and she longed for school and Carrie, and she wrote letters to her friend. But that saddened her too. It wasn't simply that Carrie was her only friend, and when they finished college they might never see each other again. It was that her existence in the world was so divided; it had begun when she was a child creeping to the kitchen; now that division was much sharper, and her friendship with Carrie seemed disproportionate and perilous. The world she was destined to live in had nothing to do with the intimate nights in their room at school.

In the summer before their senior year, Carrie fell in love.   13 She wrote to Louise about him, but she did not write much, and this hurt Louise more than if Carrie had shown the joy her writing tried to conceal. That fall they returned to their room; they were still close and warm, Carrie still needed Louise's ears and heart at night as she spoke of her parents and her recurring malaise whose source the two friends never discovered. But on most weekends Carrie left, and caught a

bus to Boston where her boyfriend studied music. During
the week she often spoke hesitantly of sex; she was not sure
if she liked it. But Louise, eating candy and listening, did not
know whether Carrie was telling the truth or whether, as in
her letters of the past summer, Carrie was keeping from her
those delights she may never experience.

Then one Sunday night when Carrie had just returned from   14
Boston and was unpacking her overnight bag, she looked at
Louise and said: "I was thinking about you. On the bus coming home tonight." Looking at Carrie's concerned, determined
face, Louise prepared herself for humiliation. "I was thinking
about when we graduate. What you're going to do. What's
to become of you. I want you to be loved the way I love you.
Louise, if I help you, *really* help you, will you go on a diet?"

Louise entered a period of her life she would remember   15
always, the way some people remember having endured poverty. Her diet did not begin the next day. Carrie told her to
eat on Monday as though it were the last day of her life. So
for the first time since grammar school Louise went into a
school cafeteria and ate everything she wanted. At breakfast
and lunch and dinner she glanced around the table to see if
the other girls noticed the food on her tray. They did not. She
felt there was a lesson in this, but it lay beyond her grasp. That
night in their room she ate the four remaining candy bars.
During the day Carrie rented a small refrigerator, bought an
electric skillet, an electric broiler, and bathroom scales.

On Tuesday morning Louise stood on the scales, and   16
Carrie wrote in her notebook: *October 14: 184 lbs.* Then she
made Louise a cup of black coffee and scrambled one egg and
sat with her while she ate. When Carrie went to the dining
room for breakfast, Louise walked about the campus for thirty
minutes. That was part of the plan. The campus was pretty, on
its lawns grew at least one of every tree native to New England, and in the warm morning sun Louise felt a new hope. At
noon they met in their room, and Carrie broiled her a piece of
hamburger and served it with lettuce. Then while Carrie ate
in the dining room Louise walked again. She was weak with
hunger and she felt queasy. During her afternoon classes she

was nervous and tense, and she chewed her pencil and tapped her heels on the floor and tightened her calves. When she returned to her room late that afternoon, she was so glad to see Carrie that she embraced her; she had felt she could not bear another minute of hunger, but now with Carrie she knew she could make it at least through tonight. Then she would sleep and face tomorrow when it came. Carrie broiled her a steak and served it with lettuce. Louise studied while Carrie ate dinner, then they went for a walk.

That was her ritual and her diet for the rest of the year, Carrie alternating fish and chicken breasts with the steaks for dinner, and every day was nearly as bad as the first. In the evenings she was irritable. In all her life she had never been afflicted by ill temper and she looked upon it now as a demon which, along with hunger, was taking possession of her soul. Often she spoke sharply to Carrie. One night during their after-dinner walk Carrie talked sadly of night, of how darkness made her more aware of herself, and at night she did not know why she was in college, why she studied, why she was walking the earth with other people. They were standing on a wooden foot bridge, looking down at a dark pond. Carrie kept talking; perhaps soon she would cry. Suddenly Louise said: "I'm sick of lettuce. I never want to see a piece of lettuce for the rest of my life. I hate it. We shouldn't even buy it, it's immoral."   17

Carrie was quiet. Louise glanced at her, and the pain and irritation in Carrie's face soothed her. Then she was ashamed. Before she could say she was sorry, Carrie turned to her and said gently: "I know. I know how terrible it is."   18

Carrie did all the shopping, telling Louise she knew how hard it was to go into a supermarket when you were hungry. And Louise was always hungry. She drank diet soft drinks and started smoking Carrie's cigarettes, learned to enjoy inhaling, thought of cancer and emphysema but they were as far away as those boys her mother had talked about when she was nine. By Thanksgiving she was smoking over a pack a day and her weight in Carrie's notebook was one hundred and sixty-two pounds. Carrie was afraid if Louise went home at   19

Thanksgiving she would lapse from the diet, so Louise spent the vacation with Carrie, in Philadelphia. Carrie wrote her family about the diet, and told Louise that she had. On the phone to Philadelphia, Louise said: "I feel like a bedwetter. When I was a little girl I had a friend who used to come spend the night and Mother would put a rubber sheet on the bed and we all pretended there wasn't a rubber sheet and that she hadn't wet the bed. Even me, and I slept with her." At Thanksgiving dinner she lowered her eyes as Carrie's father put two slices of white meat on her plate and passed it to her over the bowls of steaming food.

When she went home at Christmas she weighed a hundred and fifty-five pounds; at the airport her mother marveled. Her father laughed and hugged her and said: "But now there's less of you to love." He was troubled by her smoking but only mentioned it once; he told her she was beautiful and, as always, his eyes bathed her with love. During the long vacation her mother cooked for her as Carrie had, and Louise returned to school weighing a hundred and forty-six pounds. 20

Flying north on the plane she warmly recalled the surprised and congratulatory eyes of her relatives and acquaintances. She had not seen Joan or Marjorie. She thought of returning home in May, weighing the hundred and fifteen pounds which Carrie had in October set as their goal. Looking toward the stoic days ahead, she felt strong. She thought of those hungry days of fall and early winter (and now: she was hungry now: with almost a frown, almost a brusque shake of the head, she refused peanuts from the stewardess): those first weeks of the diet when she was the pawn of an irascibility which still, conditioned to her ritual as she was, could at any moment take command of her. She thought of the nights of trying to sleep while her stomach growled. She thought of her addiction to cigarettes. She thought of the people at school: not one teacher, not one girl, had spoken to her about her loss of weight, not even about her absence from meals. And without warning her spirit collapsed. She did not feel strong, she did not feel she was committed to and within reach of achieving a valuable goal. She felt that somehow she had lost 21 more than pounds of fat; that some time during her dieting she had lost herself too. She tried to remember what it had felt like to be Louise before she had started living on meat and fish, as an unhappy adult may look sadly in the memory of childhood for lost virtues and hopes. She looked down at the earth far below, and it seemed to her that her soul, like her body aboard the plane, was in some rootless flight. She neither knew its destination nor where it had departed from; it was on some passage she could not even define.

During the next few weeks she lost weight more slowly    22
and once for eight days Carrie's daily recording stayed at a hundred and thirty-six. Louise woke in the morning thinking of one hundred and thirty-six and then she stood on the scales and they echoed her. She became obsessed with that number, and there wasn't a day when she didn't say it aloud, and through the days and nights the number stayed in her mind, and if a teacher had spoken those digits in a classroom she would have opened her mouth to speak. What if that's me, she said to Carrie. I mean what if a hundred and thirty-six is my real weight and I just can't lose anymore. Walking hand-in-hand with her despair was a longing for this to be true, and that longing angered her and wearied her, and every day she was gloomy. On the ninth day she weighed a hundred and thirty-five and a half pounds. She was not relieved; she thought bitterly of the months ahead, the shedding of the last twenty and a half pounds.

On Easter Sunday, which she spent at Carrie's, she weighed    23
one hundred and twenty pounds, and she ate one slice of glazed pineapple with her ham and lettuce. She did not enjoy it: she felt she was being friendly with a recalcitrant enemy who had once tried to destroy her. Carrie's parents were laudative. She liked them and she wished they would touch sometimes, and look at each other when they spoke. She guessed they would divorce when Carrie left home, and she vowed that her own marriage would be one of affection and tenderness. She could think about that now: marriage. At school she had read in a Boston paper that this summer the cicadas would come out of their seventeen-year hibernation on Cape Cod, for a

month they would mate and then die, leaving their young to burrow into the ground where they would stay for seventeen years. That's me, she had said to Carrie. Only my hibernation lasted twenty-one years.

Often her mother asked in letters and on the phone about 24 the diet, but Louise answered vaguely. When she flew home in late May she weighed a hundred and thirteen pounds, and at the airport her mother cried and hugged her and said again and again: You're so *beautiful*. Her father blushed and bought her a martini. For days her relatives and acquaintances congratulated her, and the applause in their eyes lasted the entire summer, and she loved their eyes, and swam in the country club pool, the first time she had done this since she was a child.

She lived at home and ate the way her mother did and every 25 morning she weighed herself on the scales in her bathroom. Her mother liked to take her shopping and buy her dresses and they put her old ones in the Goodwill box at the shopping center; Louise thought of them existing on the body of a poor woman whose cheap meals kept her fat. Louise's mother had a photographer come to the house, and Louise posed on the couch and standing beneath a live oak and sitting in a wicker lawn chair next to an azalea bush. The new clothes and the photographer made her feel she was going to another country or becoming a citizen of a new one. In the fall she took a job of no consequence, to give herself something to do.

Also in the fall a young lawyer joined her father's firm, 26 he came one night to dinner, and they started seeing each other. He was the first man outside her family to kiss her since the barbecue when she was sixteen. Louise celebrated Thanksgiving not with rice dressing and candied sweet potatoes and mince meat and pumpkin pies, but by giving Richard her virginity which she realized, at the very last moment of its existence, she had embarked on giving him over thirteen months ago, on that Tuesday in October when Carrie had made her a cup of black coffee and scrambled one egg. She wrote this to Carrie, who replied happily by return mail. She also, through glance and smile and innuendo, tried to tell her mother too. But finally she controlled that impulse, because

Richard felt guilty about making love with the daughter of his partner and friend. In the spring they married. The wedding was a large one, in the Episcopal church, and Carrie flew from Boston to be maid of honor. Her parents had recently separated and she was living with the musician and was still victim of her unpredictable malaise. It overcame her on the night before the wedding, so Louise was up with her until past three and woke next morning from a sleep so heavy that she did not want to leave it.

Richard was a lean, tall, energetic man with the metabolism   27 of a pencil sharpener. Louise fed him everything he wanted. He liked Italian food and she got recipes from her mother and watched him eating spaghetti with the sauce she had only tasted, and ravioli and lasagna, while she ate antipasto with her chianti. He made a lot of money and borrowed more and they bought a house whose lawn sloped down to the shore of a lake; they had a wharf and a boathouse, and Richard bought a boat and they took friends waterskiing. Richard bought her a car and they spent his vacations in Mexico, Canada, the Bahamas, and in the fifth year of their marriage they went to Europe and, according to their plan, she conceived a child in Paris. On the plane back, as she looked out the window and beyond the sparkling sea and saw her country, she felt that it was waiting for her, as her home by the lake was, and her parents, and her good friends who rode in the boat and waterskied; she thought of the accumulated warmth and pelf of her marriage, and how by slimming her body she had bought into the pleasures of the nation. She felt cunning, and she smiled to herself, and took Richard's hand.

But these moments of triumph were sparse. On most days   28 she went about her routine of leisure with a sense of certainty about herself that came merely from not thinking. But there were times, with her friends, or with Richard, or alone in the house, when she was suddenly assaulted by the feeling that she had taken the wrong train and arrived at a place where no one knew her, and where she ought not to be. Often, in bed with Richard, she talked of being fat: "I was the one who started the friendship with Carrie, I chose her, I started the conversations. When I understood that she was my friend I understood something else: I had chosen her for the same reason I'd chosen Joan and Marjorie. They were all thin. I was always thinking about what people saw when they looked at me and I didn't want them to see two fat girls. When I was alone I didn't mind being fat but then I'd have to leave the house again and then I didn't want to look like me. But at home I didn't mind except when I was getting dressed to go out of the house and when Mother looked at me. But I stopped looking at her when she looked at me. And in college I felt good with Carrie; there weren't any boys and I didn't have any other friends and so when I wasn't with Carrie I thought about her and I tried to ignore the other people around me, I tried to make them not exist. A lot of the time I could do that. It was strange, and I felt like a spy."

If Richard was bored by her repetition he pretended not to be. But she knew the story meant very little to him. She could have been telling him of a childhood illness, or wearing braces, or a broken heart at sixteen. He could not see her as she was when she was fat. She felt as though she were trying to tell a foreign lover about her life in the United States, and if only she could command the language he would know and love all of her and she would feel complete. Some of the acquaintances of her childhood were her friends now, and even they did not seem to remember her when she was fat. 29

Now her body was growing again, and when she put on a maternity dress for the first time she shivered with fear. Richard did not smoke and he asked her, in a voice just short of demand, to stop during her pregnancy. She did. She ate carrots and celery instead of smoking, and at cocktail parties she tried to eat nothing, but after her first drink she ate nuts and cheese and crackers and dips. Always at these parties Richard had talked with his friends and she had rarely spoken to him until they drove home. But now when he noticed her at the hors d'oeuvres table he crossed the room and, smiling, led her back to his group. His smile and his hand on her arm told her he was doing his clumsy, husbandly best to help her through a time of female mystery. 30

She was gaining weight but she told herself it was only ₃₁ the baby, and would leave with its birth. But at other times she knew quite clearly that she was losing the discipline she had fought so hard to gain during her last year with Carrie. She was hungry now as she had been in college, and she ate between meals and after dinner and tried to eat only carrots and celery, but she grew to hate them, and her desire for sweets was as vicious as it had been long ago. At home she ate bread and jam and when she shopped for groceries she bought a candy bar and ate it driving home and put the wrapper in her purse and then in the garbage can under the sink. Her cheeks had filled out, there was loose flesh under her chin, her arms and legs were plump, and her mother was concerned. So was Richard. One night when she brought pie and milk to the living room where they were watching television, he said: "You already had a piece. At dinner."

She did not look at him. ₃₂

"You're gaining weight. It's not all water, either. It's fat. ₃₃ It'll be summertime. You'll want to get into your bathing suit."

The pie was cherry. She looked at it as her fork cut through ₃₄ it; she speared the piece and rubbed it in the red juice on the plate before lifting it to her mouth.

"You never used to eat pie," he said. "I just think you ₃₅ ought to watch it a bit. It's going to be tough on you this summer."

In her seventh month, with a delight reminiscent of climb- ₃₆ ing the stairs to Richard's apartment before they were married, she returned to her world of secret gratification. She began hiding candy in her underwear drawer. She ate it during the day and at night while Richard slept, and at breakfast she was distracted, waiting for him to leave.

She gave birth to a son, brought him home, and nursed ₃₇ both him and her appetites. During this time of celibacy she enjoyed her body through her son's mouth; while he suckled she stroked his small head and back. She was hiding candy but she did not conceal her other indulgences: she was smoking

again but still she ate between meals, and at dinner she ate
what Richard did, and coldly he watched her, he grew petu-
lant, and when the date marking the end of their celibacy
came they let it pass. Often in the afternoons her mother
visited and scolded her and Louise sat looking at the baby
and said nothing until finally, to end it, she promised to diet.
When her mother and father came for dinners, her father
kissed her and held the baby and her mother said nothing
about Louise's body, and her voice was tense. Returning from
work in the evenings Richard looked at a soiled plate and glass
on the table beside her chair as if detecting traces of infidelity,
and at every dinner they fought.

"Look at you," he said. "Lasagna, for God's sake. When      38
are you going to start? It's not simply that you haven't lost
any weight. You're gaining. I can see it. I can feel it when you
get in bed. Pretty soon you'll weigh more than I do and I'll
be sleeping on a trampoline."

"You never touch me anymore."                                39

"I don't want to touch you. Why should I? Have you         40
*looked* at yourself?"

"You're cruel," she said. "I never knew how cruel you      41
were."

She ate, watching him. He did not look at her. Glaring at   42
his plate, he worked with fork and knife like a hurried man at
a lunch counter.

"I bet you didn't either," she said.                         43

That night when he was asleep she took a Milky Way to      44
the bathroom. For a while she stood eating in the dark, then
she turned on the light. Chewing, she looked at herself in
the mirror; she looked at her eyes and hair. Then she stood
on the scales and looking at the numbers between her feet,
one hundred and sixty-two, she remembered when she had
weighed a hundred and thirty-six pounds for eight days. Her
memory of those eight days was fond and amusing, as though
she were recalling an Easter egg hunt when she was six. She
stepped off the scales and pushed them under the lavatory and
did not stand on them again.

It was summer and she bought loose dresses and when   45
Richard took friends out on the boat she did not wear a bathing suit or shorts; her friends gave her mischievous glances,
and Richard did not look at her. She stopped riding on the
boat. She told them she wanted to stay with the baby, and
she sat inside holding him until she heard the boat leave the
wharf. Then she took him to the front lawn and walked with
him in the shade of the trees and talked to him about the
blue jays and mockingbirds and cardinals she saw on their
branches. Sometimes she stopped and watched the boat out
on the lake and the friend skiing behind it.

Every day Richard quarreled, and because his rage went no   46
further than her weight and shape, she felt excluded from it,
and she remained calm within layers of flesh and spirit, and
watched his frustration, his impotence. He truly believed they
were arguing about her weight. She knew better: she knew
that beneath the argument lay the question of who Richard
was. She thought of him smiling at the wheel of his boat, and
long ago courting his slender girl, the daughter of his partner and friend. She thought of Carrie telling her of smelling
chocolate in the dark and, after that, watching her eat it night
after night. She smiled at Richard, teasing his anger.

He is angry now. He stands in the center of the living room,   47
raging at her, and he wakes the baby. Beneath Richard's voice
she hears the soft crying, feels it in her heart, and quietly she
rises from her chair and goes upstairs to the child's room and
takes him from the crib. She brings him to the living room
and sits holding him in her lap, pressing him gently against
the folds of fat at her waist. Now Richard is pleading with her.
Louise thinks tenderly of Carrie broiling meat and fish in their
room, and walking with her in the evenings. She wonders if
Carrie still has the malaise. Perhaps she will come for a visit.
In Louise's arms now the boy sleeps.

"I'll help you," Richard says. "I'll eat the same things   48
you eat."

But his face does not approach the compassion and deter-   49
mination and love she had seen in Carrie's during what she

now recognizes as the worst year of her life. She can remember nothing about that year except hunger, and the meals in her room. She is hungry now. When she puts the boy to bed she will get a candy bar from her room. She will eat it here, in front of Richard. This room will be hers soon. She considers the possibilities: all these rooms and the lawn where she can do whatever she wishes. She knows he will leave soon. It has been in his eyes all summer. She stands, using one hand to pull herself out of the chair. She carries the boy to his crib, feels him against her large breasts, feels that his sleeping body touches her soul. With a surge of vindication and relief she holds him. Then she kisses his forehead and places him in the crib. She goes to the bedroom and in the dark takes a bar of candy from her drawer. Slowly she descends the stairs. She knows Richard is waiting but she feels his departure so happily that, when she enters the living room, unwrapping the candy, she is surprised to see him standing there.

## COMMENT ON "THE FAT GIRL"

Louise's life is shaped by her need for love and her obsession with food. When she can't find love, she eats. When she eats, she loses the chance for love. At least that's what her mother tells her—"if you are fat the boys won't like you." In her public life, she does the best she can—eating very little at the school cafeteria. But in private, she gives in to the "ritual of deceit and pleasure"—consuming the food she hides in her "haunted" closet.

When she goes away to a girl's college, where she does not have to worry about the judgement of her mother or boys, she no longer needs to hide her stash of candy. But her roommate, Carrie, in an act of affection helps her go on a diet. As she loses weight, Louise sees the return of affection in her mother's eyes. But as she loses pounds, she wonders if she is losing her "self." Still slim, she returns home and attracts the attention of Richard, a young lawyer in her father's firm. They marry and begin acquiring the trappings of wealth. Louise tries to tell Richard that it wasn't always this way. But he seems unable to understand her "fat story."

Once Louise becomes pregnant, she begins gaining weight. All the old rituals return as does the criticism. She and Richard argue constantly about her weight, prompting Louise to wonder if she will lose Richard and what "Louise" he loved in the first place.

# Rhetorical Glossary

**abstract terms** Terms that refer to qualities or characteristics we can conceive of mentally but cannot see, touch, or hear—for example, *bravery, laziness, perseverance*. Writers often illustrate such terms with examples to help readers grasp their significance. See also *concrete terms*.

**accommodation** Sometimes called "nonthreatening argument." The arrangement of evidence in such a way that all parties believe their position has received a fair hearing.

**active reading** A manner of reading in which one reads intently and consciously, simultaneously reading for meaning and being aware of one's responses to content and style. An active reader often reads with a pencil, underlining important phrases or sentences and writing notes in the margin.

**allusion** A reference to a person, event, or story familiar to the reader and that will enrich the writer's meaning because it draws on shared knowledge with the reader.

**analogy** A comparison between two things or concepts that share certain characteristics although in most ways they are not similar.

**analysis** The process that divides something into its parts to understand the whole more clearly.

**annotate** To make notes or comments about a piece of writing.

**appeals** Strategies used in persuasion and argument. Although most arguments combine different kinds of appeals, many rely on one dominant appeal to make a compelling case.

**emotional appeal** A strategy that appeals to feelings, relying heavily on figurative language and provocative imagery to persuade readers.

**ethical appeal** A strategy that appeals to the character (or *ethos*) of the writer, relying on the writer's reputation and competence to persuade readers.

**logical appeal** A strategy that appeals to reason, relying on factual evidence, expert testimony, and logic to persuade readers.

**argument** A piece of writing or an oral presentation in which an author or speaker seeks to persuade an audience to accept a proposition or an opinion by giving reasons and evidence. An argument does not necessarily involve controversy or anger; often it is simply a statement that presents a claim or a particular point of view.

**assumption** Something taken for granted, presumed to be true without need for further explanation or proof. Writers usually make the assumption that their readers have certain knowledge and experiences that they can count on as they present their arguments.

**audience** The readers for whom a piece of writing is intended. That audience may be close or distant, a small group or a large number, popular or specialized. Professional writers nearly always tailor their writing toward a particular audience about whom they know a good deal—for example, the readers of the *New York Times* or *Parade*—and they adapt their vocabulary and style to suit that audience.

**audience analysis** Questions that help identify the writer's audience: (1) Who am I writing for? (2) What do they expect of me? (3) What knowledge do

**421**

they already have? (4) What kind of evidence and strategies are they most likely to respond to?

**brainstorming** A way of generating ideas and material for writing by thinking about a topic intently and jotting down random thoughts as they occur to you without regard to whether they seem immediately useful and relevant.

**cause and effect** A mode of writing that explains or persuades by analyzing cause-and-effect relationships.

**central pattern** The dominant mode of exposition in an essay. Most writers use more than one expository pattern when they construct an essay.

**ceremonial discourse** An argument, usually presented orally on special occasions, that appeals to the audience's pride, loyalty, and compassion.

**claims and warrants** Often called the Toulmin argument after Stephen Toulmin, the legal philosopher who analyzed and defined its terminology. A method of arranging evidence in an argument that begins by asserting a *claim* (or general assertion), then presents evidence to support that claim, and provides a *warrant* (or justification) that links the claim to the evidence.

**classification and division** A method of organizing an explanation or argument by dividing a topic into distinct parts or classes and discussing the characteristics of those classes.

**comparison and contrast** A popular and convenient way of organizing an essay or article to highlight important ways in which two things or processes can be similar yet different.

**concept** A broad intellectual notion that captures the essential nature of an idea, system, or process—for example, the concept of affirmative action or the concept of intellectual property.

**conclusion** The final paragraph or section of an essay that brings the argument or explanation to appropriate closure and leaves the reader feeling that the author has dealt with all the issues or questions he or she has raised.

**concrete terms** Terms that refer to something specific and tangible that can be perceived through the senses—for example, *rocky, sizzling, bright yellow*. See also *abstract terms*.

**connotation** The added psychological and emotional associations that certain words and phrases carry in addition to their simple meaning. For instance, words like *liberty* and *individualism* carry heavily positive connotations in our culture; they may carry negative connotations in a culture that puts great value on tradition and discipline.

**critical reading** Questioning and analyzing content while reading in order to judge the truth, merit, and general quality of an essay or article. A critical reader might ask, What is the source of the author's information? What evidence does he cite in support of his claim? or, What organization or special interest might she be affiliated with?

**deduction** Usually identified with classical reasoning, or the *syllogism*. A method of arranging evidence that begins with a *major premise*, is restricted by a *minor premise*, and ends with a *conclusion*.

**definition** A type of essay that identifies and gives the qualities of a person, object, institution, pattern of behavior, or political theory in a way that highlights its special characteristics.

**denotation** The specific, exact meaning of a word, independent of its emotional associations.

**description** A kind of factual writing that aims to help the reader visualize and grasp the essential nature of an object, an action, a scene, or a person by giving details that reveal the special characteristics of that person or scene.

**diction** The selection of words to form a desired effect. To achieve this effect, writers consider words from various levels of usage—*popular, learned, colloquial,* and *slang*—and vary words that have appropriate *denotations* and *connotations.*

**discovery draft** The first draft of an essay. In a discovery draft, writers expect to discover something new about their purpose, audience, and strategies.

**division and classification** See *classification and division.*

**documentation** A system used for giving readers information about where the writer found the sources he or she used in an academic or research paper or a technical report. Writers document their sources by inserting footnotes, endnotes, or in-text citations so a reader who wants to know more about the topic can easily find the article or book the author is citing or track down other related articles by the same author. The most common system writers use for documentation in academic papers in writing classes is Modern Language Association (MLA) style.

**draft** A preliminary version of a piece of writing that enables the author to get started and develop an idea as he or she writes. Authors often write and revise several drafts before they are satisfied with a piece of writing.

**editing** Small-scale changes in a piece of writing that is close to being complete. Editing may involve changing some word choices, checking for correct spelling and punctuation, eliminating repetition, rearranging sentences or paragraphs, and generally polishing a manuscript into final form before submitting it to an instructor or editor.

**essay** An article or short nonfiction composition that focuses on a specific topic or theme. An essay is generally analytical, speculative, or interpretive. Thus a news story would not be an essay, but an opinion piece could be.

**evidence** Specific kinds of information that support the claims of an argument. The most common forms of evidence are:

**facts** Specific, detailed evidence—often reported in numbers—that is difficult to refute.

**judgments** Conclusions that are inferred from facts. Judgments lend credibility to an argument because they result from careful reasoning.

**testimony** Statements that affirm or assert facts. *Eyewitness testimony* enables a person who has had direct experience with an event to report what he or she saw. *Expert witness testimony* enables a recognized authority on a subject to present facts and judgments.

**example** A specific incident, object, or anecdote used to illustrate and support a claim or expand on an assertion or generalization. Skillful writers know that readers expect and need examples to clarify a statement, develop a thesis sentence, or support an opening assertion.

**figurative language** Language that uses vivid and sometimes fanciful comparisons to enliven and enrich prose. Such language often takes the form of metaphors that explain an unfamiliar thing or process by comparing it to a familiar thing.

**focus** As a verb, to concentrate or emphasize; as a noun, the point of concentration or emphasis. Skillful writers know how to focus their writing on a single central idea or point; they have learned to "write more about less," to narrow their topic down to one that they can explore fully and enrich with details.

**free-writing** A way to generate ideas for an essay or article by writing down whatever comes to mind about a topic, without concern for organization or style. In free-writing, work quickly to capture ideas. Don't stop to consider whether a phrase or sentence is pertinent or useful—just get it down. After you accumulate a substantial amount of material, you can comb through it to find a starting point for your first draft.

**generalization** A broad statement that makes a general claim or an assertion without giving specific details or supporting evidence. Writers often begin an essay with a generalization and then use the next sentences and paragraphs to give details and information that expand on and support the generalization.

**headnote** A short introductory note before a piece of writing. For example, before each essay in *The River Reader* is a headnote about its author. Its purpose is to give you enough information about the author's age, cultural heritage, and education to put him or her in some cultural context and to give you a few other pertinent facts, such as what else he has written or where she has published other articles.

**hypothesis** A statement, created during *planning*, of a possible or working purpose for your writing.

**image** In writing, an impression or visual effect created by an author through the skillful use of language that appeals to the senses of sight and sound.

**logic** An intellectual system or process that uses reason and evidence to arrive at conclusions. Often writers not only construct a logical framework for their arguments, setting up cause-and-effect relationships or establishing a chain of reasoning, but also embellish the logic with some figurative and emotional language.

**metaphor** See *figurative language*.

**mode** A style or pattern of writing or discourse that has certain features that characterize it and make it distinctive. The essays in *The River Reader* are classified according to their mode: narration and description, process analysis, division and classification, definition, cause and effect, persuasion and argument, and so on. Often a writer combines two or three modes in an essay or article but emphasizes one dominant mode.

**narration** A mode of nonfiction writing that develops an idea or makes a point by telling a story or anecdote. The major strategy for fiction.

**pace** The rate at which an essay or article moves. Writers can create different paces through word choice, sentence length, and the selection of verbs.

**paraphrase** A passage that briefly restates in the writer's own words the content of a passage written by someone else, in such a way that it retains the original meaning.

**persuasion** The process of using language to get readers to accept opinions, beliefs, or points of view. The essays in the Persuasion and Argument chapter of *The River Reader* are the most strongly persuasive, but in an important sense, most essays tend to be persuasive.

**plagiarism** Using someone else's words or ideas without giving proper credit to the original author. Having another person write something that you turn in for credit—for instance, a term paper taken from the Internet or a commercial source—also constitutes plagiarism and can bring serious consequences.

**planning** The first stage in the writing purpose. A series of strategies designed to find and formulate information in writing. See *brainstorming* and *free-writing*.

**plot** The chain of events that develops a story, enabling a writer to put characters into a set of circumstances, describe their behavior, and show the consequences that ensue.

**point of view** The angle or perspective from which a story or account is told. An account in which the narrator uses "I" and gives an account of an event as it appeared to him or her is called *first-person* point of view. When the narrator recounts an incident as a detached but fully informed observer, he or she is using the *third-person omniscient* point of view.

**purpose** The goal of an author in a piece of writing. An author may wish to inform, to persuade, to explain, to support an assertion, or to entertain. Sometimes an author combines two or more of these purposes, but usually the author has a primary goal, one that should be evident to the reader.

**quotation** A passage that gives the actual words a speaker or writer has used in an article, book, speech, or conversation. Authors often use quotations to support their arguments. Such passages must always appear in quotation marks in academic papers or, indeed, in any writing done by a responsible author. Writers who fail to give proper credit for a quotation risk losing the respect of their readers or, in college, getting disciplined for plagiarism. You'll find the proper format for citing quotations in Chapter 9, "Using and Documenting Sources."

**refute** To counteract an argument or seek to disprove a claim or proposition.

**response** A reader's reaction to what he or she reads. Readers can respond in different ways—analytically, critically, emotionally, or approvingly—but in nearly every case, that response will come from their own experiences and background: what they know, where they grew up, what kind of culture they lived in, and so on. Readers look at an essay through the lens shaped by their own lives, and that lens affects what they see.

**revising** Making substantial changes in a written draft, changes that may involve narrowing the topic, adding or deleting material, rearranging sections, or rewriting the introduction or conclusion. Don't look at revising as a process of correcting a draft; rather, you develop your essay by the process of revising and often can clarify and strengthen your ideas by the process. Many writers revise an essay through three or four drafts.

**strategy** The means or tactic a writer uses to achieve his or her purpose. In the essays in *The River Reader*, authors use various strategies: narration and description, comparison and contrast, process analysis, cause and effect, and so on.

**summary** A passage that condenses the ideas and content of a long passage in a few sentences or paragraphs; a summary should be objective and accurate.

**synthesis** An essay that requires writers to incorporate sources, including images, to support an argument. Synthesis essays require the writer to synthesize or integrate these varied sources, particularly to evaluate, cite, and utilize the source material effectively. These researched synthesis essays help writers formulate informed arguments, as well as remind them that they must consider various interpretations to analyze, reflect on, and write about a given topic.

**testimony** Evidence offered in support of a claim or assertion. The term suggests factual statements given by experts or taken from sources such as historical or government records or from statistical data. Eyewitness accounts are frequently used as testimony.

**thesis sentence** A comprehensive sentence, usually coming in the first paragraph or so of an essay, that summarizes and previews the main idea the author is going to develop in the essay.

**tone** The emotional attitude toward their topic that authors convey in their writing. They create tone through the choices they make of words— particularly verbs—of sentence and paragraph length, of styles—formal or informal—and with the kinds of images and figurative language they use.

**visual texts** Texts that provide a pictorial method for displaying information. These representational graphics can add visual interest to your subject, illustrate complicated ideas with shapes and images, and provide powerful and dramatic evidence to support your purpose.

**works cited** The list of references and sources that appears at the end of an academic paper or report that uses Modern Language Association (MLA) style; this list gives enough information about those sources to enable readers to evaluate them or use them for further research.

**writing process** The steps used in creating a piece of writing. Although there is no single writing process that works for every writer or every writing task, writing specialists have found certain patterns when they analyze how most writers seem to work. They agree that productive writers tend to work through a series of steps in the process of creating an essay or article.

*Stage 1: Planning.* The process of discovering one's topic and generating material. Typical activities are reading and researching, brainstorming, free-writing, talking with fellow writers, and making rough preliminary outlines.

*Stage 2: Drafting.* Writing a first version of the paper that puts down ideas in some organized form. Many writers continue to generate ideas as they write and often write two or three drafts before they complete one they think is fairly satisfactory.

*Stage 3: Revising and rewriting.* Reviewing the completed first draft and making substantial changes, perhaps by narrowing the focus, reorganizing, adding and deleting material, or writing a new introduction or conclusion.

*Stage 4: Editing, polishing, and proofreading.* Making minor word changes, polishing style, and checking for spelling and typographical errors.

**writing situation** The context in which a piece of writing is created. Every piece of writing, from business memos to inaugural speeches, is created within some context. Its components are (1) the writer, (2) the topic, (3) the purpose, (4) the audience, and (5) the strategy. To figure out what your writing situation is for any particular assignment, ask yourself,

- What is my persona or role in this situation?
- What do I want to say?

- What is my purpose?
- Whom am I writing to or for?
- What strategy, or organization pattern, clarifies my purpose?

By working out an answer to each of these questions before you begin to write, you'll have a good start on turning out a focused and effective product.

# Credits

# Subject Index

# Name/Title Index